As provocative as he may have been, 'Sh[...] millions of Muslims worldwide. In their [...] white man and prompted the most pow[...] hugely misunderstood and marginalised by most Christian theologians, [...] had a voice.
– Shafiq Morton, *Muslim Views*, South Africa

Deedat had a firm belief in the magic of words, not just because he was aware of his skill in debating, but because he was a man who understood that Islam had won hearts over the centuries through the peaceful strength of its spoken word and not through the hoofs of its horses. Unshackled by the traditional, elitist language of Islamic academia and untainted by the jihadist rhetoric of radical ideologues, Deedat adopted the simple and peaceful approach of the medieval Muslim traders who spread Islam through their character and their intellectual acumen.
– Bashir Goth, *Khaleej Times*, Somalia

Ahmed Deedat's contribution to Islam in South Africa can never be ignored, nor denied. His role in defending Islam from malicious and hostile propagandists needs to be accorded due respect and honour. Now!
– Iqbal Jassat, *Muslim Review Network*

Shaikh Ahmed Deedat's distinguished leadership in the field of da'wa, and his bold initiatives in reaching out to other faith-based communities, left an indelible mark on the sphere of global interfaith dialogue. His books and pamphlets, the result of five decades of work, offer a wealth of knowledge. Against the backdrop of the unprecedented and profound sociopolitical and financial challenges occurring across the globe, it is particularly necessary that we build strong and enduring bridges between communities and nations based on universal principles of truth, justice and morality. This was indeed one of the driving forces behind Shaikh Deedat's passion and zeal for engagement with members of other faith groups.
– Dr Ahmad Mohammed Ali, *President: Islamic Development Bank*, Saudi Arabia

# AHMED DEEDAT

## THE MAN AND HIS MISSION

GOOLAM VAHED

Published by the Islamic Propagation Centre International (IPCI)
PO Box 2439, Durban 4000, South Africa
www.ipci.co.za

First published 2013
Second edition 2014

ISBN: 978-0-6205-3897-8 (soft cover)
ISBN: 978-0-6205-3909-8 (PDF)
ISBN: 978-0-6205-3910-4 (eBook)

© 2014 IPCI

The views expressed in this publication are those of the author. In quoting from this publication, readers are requested to attribute the source of the information to the author. All rights reserved. No part of this publication may be reproduced, stored in a retrieval system, or transmitted in any form or by any means without the prior permission, in writing, from the publisher or as expressly permitted by law.

Designed and typeset by Jenny Young
Printed by Halal Trades, New Delhi
+91 9810103786

Distributed by IPCI
Copies are available from IPCI,
4th Floor, 124 Denis Hurley Street (formerly Queen Street),
Durban 4001, South Africa.
Tel: +27 31 306 0026/7
Email: info@ipcisa.com

Trustees: Haroon Kalla (Chairman), Yusuf Ally, Ahmed Saeed Moola, Dr Mahomed Khan, Ebrahim Jadwat, Ahmed Shaikh, Anwar Ballim, Akhtar Thokan, Tahir Sitoto, Dr Prof Kholeka Constance Moloi, Dr Yusuf Osman

# CONTENTS

FOREWORD ................................................................................................ IV

1. INTRODUCTION: THE ARGUMENTATIVE MUSLIM ............................ 1
2. THE INDELIBLE THUMBPRINT ............................................................ 17
3. FROM ADAMS MISSION TO AHMED'S MISSION ............................... 29
4. THE BEGGAR'S PREDICTION ............................................................... 37
5. PAKKA MUSALMAN ............................................................................ 49
6. DISCOVERING DA'WAH ...................................................................... 57
7. THE ISLAMIC PROPAGATION CENTRE AND ITS FOUNDERS ........... 65
8. IS THE BIBLE GOD'S WORD? .............................................................. 81
9. 'REVILE NOT LEST YE BE REVILED' ..................................................... 91
10. CAPE OF STORMS ............................................................................... 101
11. AS-SALAAM: A BRIDGE TOO FAR ...................................................... 115
12. CREATING CHANGE ............................................................................ 131
13. CONTROVERSIES AND DIVERSIONS .................................................. 143
14. PALESTINE ........................................................................................... 149
15. GOING GLOBAL ................................................................................... 157
16. THE KING FAISAL INTERNATIONAL PRIZE ........................................ 169
17. THE SWAGGER OF DEEDAT ............................................................... 175
18. 'FAISAL LAUREATE' ............................................................................. 187
19. RUSH-DIE? .......................................................................................... 201
20. FOR PROPHET OR PROFIT? ................................................................ 207
21. THE BEST OF TIMES, THE WORST OF TIMES: THE 1980s AND 1990s ... 217
22. ISLAM AND HINDUISM: SOWING THE SEEDS OF DIVISION ............ 227
23. THE COMBAT KIT ............................................................................... 235
24. OTHER PERSUASIONS ........................................................................ 243
25. ON GOD'S WAVELENGTH? ................................................................ 253

# FOREWORD

Shaikh Ahmed Deedat's most popular book, *Choice*, aptly represents the way he lived his life. He chose to study biblical texts and mastered the various narratives and interpretations. His quest led him to discover the idiosyncrasies and inaccuracies that had crept into the New Testament through human intervention. Horrified by such distortions, he realised that the New Testament – no matter what version – could not be considered a direct revelation from Allah, subhanahu wa ta'ala (glory to Him the Exalted), to his noble Prophet, Jesus, peace be upon him.

While this journey of discovery greatly distressed Shaikh Deedat, he decided to use his knowledge to effectively rebut attacks by Christian missionaries on Islam and the Islamic way of life. Realising that many Muslims were on the defensive because they had little or no knowledge of what the New Testament contained, Shaikh Deedat adopted the motto that the best form of defence is attack. An example of his creativity was the slogan, 'Read the Last Testament – Al Qur'an'.

Shaikh Deedat went on to pioneer this approach at a global level. He is a great role model for Muslims and he achieved recognition worldwide. Never afraid to speak his mind, his style was confident, clear, concise and perhaps controversial at times. His leadership style gave other Muslims the confidence to say what they believed in. In the 1960s and 1970s, when Shaikh Deedat emerged as a well-known public figure, the Muslim psyche was completely demoralised by so-called Christian colonialists. The defeats that Muslims had suffered at the hands of western colonialism resulted in the complete dismantling of the Caliphate and the dismemberment of the Muslim Ummah. Secular elites completed the task of colonising the Muslim mind, by showcasing the 'liberation' of our lands as progress when, in fact, this ushered in the neo-colonialist era – the ill effects of which continue affect millions of people worldwide.

Regrettably, the decline in scholarship among Muslims meant that, for years, most did not have the confidence to defend their faith. They had even less ability to showcase Islam's socio-economic system as a viable alternative to the exploitative and oppressive western model. Instead, most Muslim states adopted the secular western model, the primary purpose of which was the advancement of the west's imperialist agenda. In this context, most Muslims did not feel competent or confident to challenge the onslaught of Christian missionary propaganda that worked hand-in-glove with the colonial project. Shaikh Deedat saw this as a major problem. He took on the challenge by confronting Christian missionaries and began to undermine their assault on Islam and Muslims. Instead of waiting for them to attack, he chose to take the battle to the missionaries. His pro-active approach captured the hearts and minds of the confused and battered Muslim community.

Our purpose in sharing the story of Shaikh Deedat's life and work with a wider readership is to assess and explain his mission, which we believe has often been misconstrued and misunderstood. We also present his example to show Muslims how to withstand the west's cultural, religious, intellectual, and social onslaught against Islam. Shaikh Deedat did not resort to violence even though Muslims were made to feel inferior and powerless in the face of colonial domination. Instead, he used intellectual arguments, participated in open debates, tried to reason with Christian missionaries, and exposed their spurious arguments. There is an important lesson in this for all Muslims. Shaikh Deedat also built an international organisation, Islamic Propagation Centre International (IPCI), to encourage Muslims to join him on this path.

At the IPCI, we have come to recognise that the Muslim psyche today is very different from the one that Shaikh Deedat encountered during his lifetime. The renewal of Islamic consciousness evident in events in the Middle East and North Africa since 2010 has revealed that Muslims are increasingly confident, self-assured and able to take on the world on their own terms. This mindset is very much in tune with the view that Islam now holds the moral high ground that the west has lost. In fact, the west never really held that ground; it simply fell to the west by default while Muslims were largely absent from the scene. The self-confident Muslim of today can present Islamic solutions to the civilisational challenges gripping the world, not only in the present but well into the future.

Essentially Islam is beginning to offer an alternative to the collapsing western capitalist model. Islamic interest-free banking and free-market policies are being closely studied as alternatives to western capitalism. The bankrupt system of controlling Muslim countries via proxies and imposed governments is coming to an end. This will transform our socio-political and economic landscape in radical ways.

The challenge for organisations involved in da'wah work today is not so much to debate the merits of a particular religion. The key to da'wah is to invite the larger community to look at the pristine principles of Islam as a solution for many of the ills that afflict societies today. Da'wah organisations should act as facilitators to bring communities closer to Islam so that they can view its beauty from close quarters. In addition to the wealth of writings that we inherited from Shaikh Deedat, the IPCI has completely repositioned its work to build bridges with other communities, and to encourage people to see Islam through a lens other than that offered by western media.

We thank all our invaluable employees, friends and trustees for assisting us in steering IPCI so that is has not only survived all the challenges it faced but, Alhamdulillah, continues to thrive.

We pray that Allah grant us success in all our endeavours.

**Haroon Kalla**
Chairman, IPCI

Board of Trustees: Yusuf Ally, Ahmed Saeed Moola, Dr Mahomed Khan, Ebrahim Jadwat, Ahmed Shaikh, Anwar Ballim, Akhtar Thokan, Tahir Sitoto, Dr Prof Kholeka Constance Moloi, Dr Yusuf Osman

# Photographs

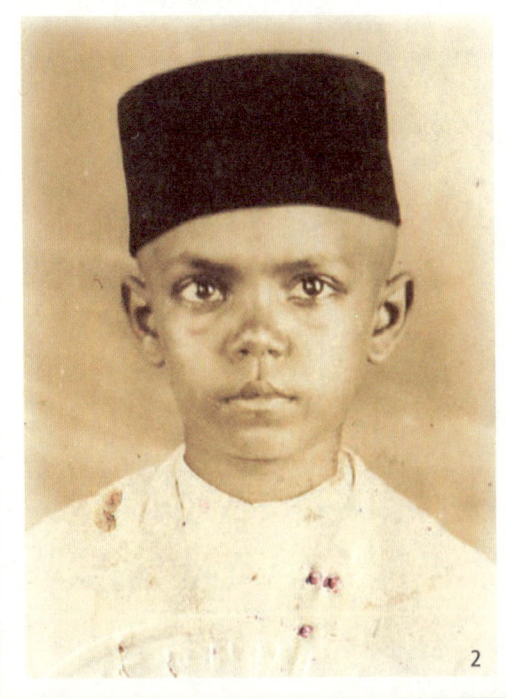

## EARLIEST DAYS

1. The house in the village of Tadkeshwar, India, in which Ahmed Deedat was born.

2. Deedat aged about nine years old; this photograph was taken shortly before he left India for South Africa.

## GROWING UP

3. Ahmed Deedat's father (far right) with some of his family.

4. Deedat (left) with a young friend in Durban.

5. Tall and good looking, Deedat gradually developed the confidence to take on the world.

## MARRIAGE AND FATHERHOOD

6. Deedat with his wife Hawa and their son Ebrahim, who was born in 1945.

7. A proud young father, Deedat shows off his firstborn son.

8. At the beach with his daughter, Ruqayyah.

9. The young Deedat family shopping in Durban.

## MOVING TO PAKISTAN

10. Close friends, the Deedat and Lutchka families, emigrated to the newly established state of Pakistan in 1949, expecting great things of leaders such as Liaquat Ali Khan (right) who was the head of state, pictured here with Jawaharlal Nehru, who was prime minister of India.

11. Deedat with his two youngest children in Pakistan.

12. Deedat (back row, fourth from the right) with friends and colleagues in Pakistan.

13. Hawa Deedat and Mrs Lutchka relaxing in one of Karachi's public parks.

## RETURNING TO SOUTH AFRICA

14. Disillusioned by the failure of Pakistan to evolve into the ideal Muslim state, the Deedat family returned to South Africa. Deedat's speaking tours began soon afterwards and on rare occasions his family would travel with him; here (from left) are Hawa, Ruqayyah, Yousuf and Ebrahim on an outing to Cape Town's Hout Bay Harbour in the 1950s.

15. Deedat's elder son Ebrahim (right) with two friends in Durban, c. 1956.

16. Although Deedat's work became an almost all-consuming passion, spending time outdoors with his family was one of his favourite ways of relaxing.

## DURBAN IN THE 1950s

17. The executive committee of the Natal Muslim Council; although this organisation never really got off the ground, it was the first serious attempt to form a body to represent Muslims in the province, and the influence of its members was clear in the later formation of the Arabic Study Circle and Deedat's own Islamic Propagation Centre.

18. One of Deedat's employers sent him on a public-speaking course with the Dale Carnegie Foundation which turned out to be the first one that Indians participated in. Shown here are Deedat's fellow class members; Deedat is named in the caption but was absent on the day the photo was taken.

19. Deedat with trophies that he won during one of the Arabic Study Circle's speech contests in the mid 1950s.

## THE EARLY DAYS OF THE ISLAMIC PROPAGATION CENTRE

20. IPCI founder members, G.H. Agjee and G.H. Vanker (circled), with a visiting teacher.

21. Deedat giving one of his first public lectures in a small hall.

22/23. One of the issues the IPC was concerned about was inter-religious marriages; Deedat provided classes and conducted nikah ceremonies for couples from mixed religious backgrounds. This young couple asked to be married at the IPC's offices in Madrasa Arcade.

24

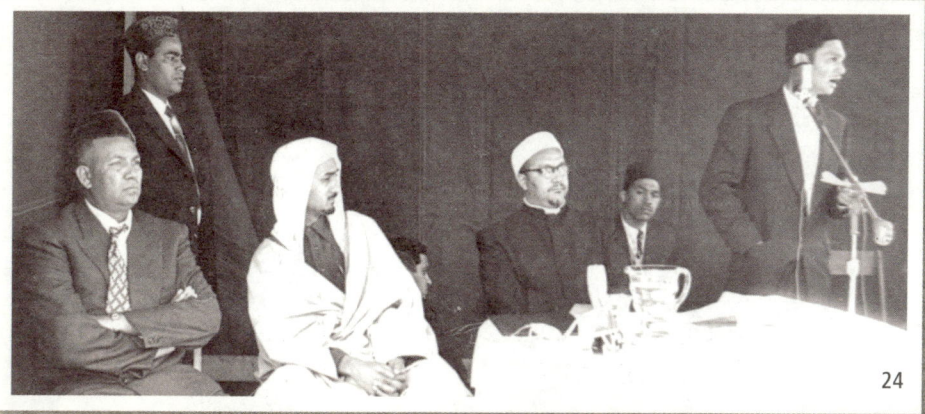

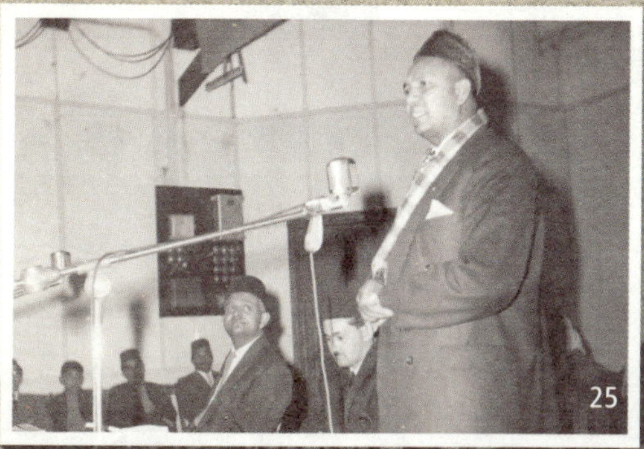

25

## DRAWING CROWDS IN THE CAPE

24–26. Deedat was regularly invited to Cape Town in the 1960s and 1970s; his reputation grew with each visit until crowds would regularly pack the vast City Hall to hear him speak.

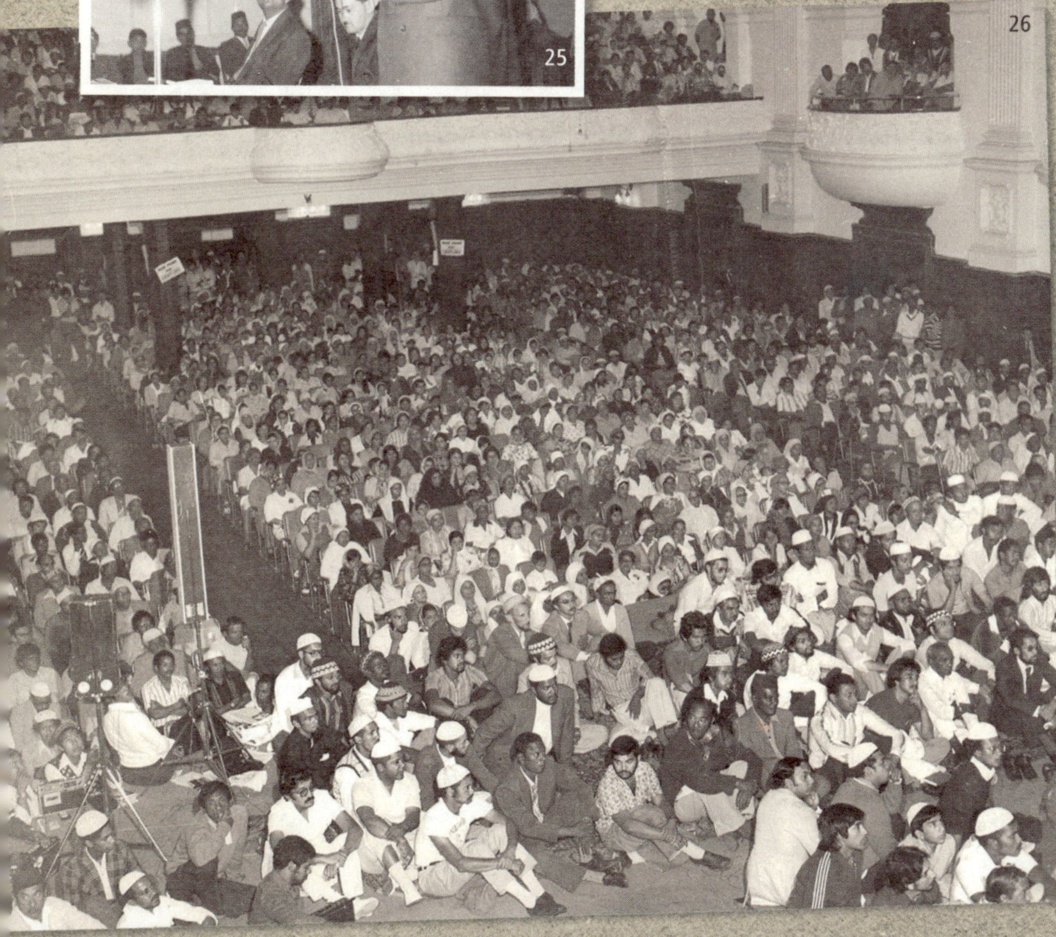

26

**BUILDING AS-SALAAM**

27. Deedat and his family dedicated many years of their lives to building a Muslim seminary near Braemar in rural KwaZulu-Natal.

28. Some of the seminary's young students in full uniform for Eid.

29. Prayer mats are laid; As-Salaam was the venue for the Muslim Youth Movement's important 1974 conference.

## TOURING AFRICA AND THE MIDDLE EAST

Even during his time at As Salaam, Deedat undertook lecture tours, but when he was freed from his responsibilities at the seminary, he travelled extensively, regularly visiting places such as:

30. Kenya and other African countries including Botswana and Tanzania.
31. Johannesburg and other major towns and cities in South Africa.
32. The Middle East.

## BECOMING AN INTERNATIONAL FIGURE

33. The United Nations' offices in New York, where Deedat offered the jum'a prayer and gave a lecture.

34. London's Royal Albert Hall, where he debated with evangelist Floyd Clarke.

35. Baton Rouge, Louisiana where he took on televangelist Jimmy Swaggart in what became his most widely publicised debate. During the debate, Deedat offered Swaggart $100 to quote Ezekiel 23 which, Deedat said, was pornographic and proved that the Bible could not be God's word. Swaggart took up the challenge, and here Deedat is seen paying the money, which Swaggart then returned to contribute towards the costs of hiring the venue.

36. Pakistan, where he met President Muhammad Zia-ul-Haq.

## MAKING INFLUENTIAL FRIENDS AND ALLIES

37. Deedat with renowned scholar Professor Ali Mazrui of Binghamton University, New York State.

38. Louis Farrakhan often expressed his support for Deedat and the IPCI; here Deedat presents Farrahkan with a collection of his videos and publications.

39. Dr Zakir Naik and Deedat were close friends; Naik followed in Deedat's footsteps and is well known internationally in the field of da'wah. He is also the founder and president of the Islamic Research Foundation.

## WINNING THE KING FAISAL INTERNATIONAL PRIZE

40. Deedat with fellow prizewinners on the night of the awards ceremony.

41. Durban's Arabic Study Circle hosted a reception for Deedat after he was awarded the King Faisal prize. Seated on Deedat's right is the Circle's president Dr Daoud Mall while Professor Salman Nadvi looks on, and Fareed Choonara is at the microphone.

42. The prize afforded Deedat opportunities to meet more dignitaries in the Middle East; here he is in discussion with Sheikh Zayed Bin Sultan al 'Nahyan, president of Al Aïn University in the United Arab Emirates.

## BEING A GRANDFATHER

43. Deedat's wife Hawa, with his daughter Rukhayya and his first grandchild, Sumayyah.
44. Deedat and Hawa with their son Ebrahim.
45. The older Deedats with their son Yousuf and his children.

**TAKING TIME OUT**

46–48. Deedat and his wife Hawa shared a life of mutual devotion and deep love for their grandchildren.

49. For a man who achieved so much in his life, time to really relax and switch off was a rare delight.

## NEARING THE END

50. On a visit to Mecca, Deedat climbed Jabal al-Nour to visit the famous Cave of Hira.

51. Confined to bed for nine years after a near fatal stroke, Deedat continued to enjoy the company of friends and supporters. Here, present chairman of the IPCI, Haroon Kalla, reads to him from *The Choice*.

# INTRODUCTION: THE ARGUMENTATIVE MUSLIM

I just gone through your website and came to know that Mr Deedat has left this world. I cannot explain how sad I am since I think his speeches have changed my life forever.

I first heard him speak some two years ago on Peace TV and it inspired me so much – even though I was born Muslim I was not a practicing one. After one of his speeches, where he said that we Muslims have just kept the holy Qur'an and did not bother to read it, I made it a point not just to read it in Arabic but also to read the translation both in English and Urdu. I also started praying five times a day, and made it a point to listen to every program that Peace TV showed where he was speaker.

May Almighty Allah give him a place in paradise and forgive him since I am sure his speeches have touched and changed millions of people like me.

Regards
Zubair Usman, Karachi, Pakistan

THE DURBAN-BASED Islamic Propagation Centre International (IPCI), of which Ahmed Deedat was a founding member, trustee, and president, continues to receive letters such as the one on the previous page almost daily from places as far-off as Mexico, Papua New Guinea, and Kazakhstan requesting copies of Deedat's books and recordings. A Google search in June 2011 threw up 1 170 000 websites containing the phrase 'Ahmed Deedat'. Many of these sites are polemical, with opponents and proponents debating his views with Deedatesque intensity and vigour, and holding tenaciously to their positions.

A cursory reading of Deedat's life circa 2001 stimulated an abiding fascination with the 'Deedat phenomenon', something that had its roots Durban, the city in which I grew up, and yet had a reach and influence that was undoubtedly global. Indeed Deedat epitomised the concept of 'think local, act global' long before this became common parlance in our rapidly globalising world.

Teaching commitments delayed my sustained entry into Ahmed Deedat's world. By the time I was ready to interview the man himself, sadly he had passed away. This book would have been richer had he been able to respond to the many issues raised in the course of my research, but this study does not rely on speculation and conjecture. I had access to a wealth of primary and secondary material, including audio and visual recordings and informants willing to share their views on Deedat. All of this partly compensates for the lack of direct

Deedat's first lectures in the 1950s attracted small audiences. By the 1960s thousands of people were filling auditoriums to listen to him speak.

input from Deedat himself. Audiovisual material was especially helpful in providing insight into Deedat's style of debate, the content of his talks, and the extent of his influence.

Oral testimony was important in reconstructing aspects of the story as this provided eyewitness accounts and first-hand experiences. Many historians and social scientists mistrust oral history because it rests upon memory, which is not always reliable. Respondents sometimes misremember things or even embellish, invent, and rearrange events in order to present a more interesting story or to appear as the 'good guy'. Some of these problems associated with oral history apply to written documents too. While acknowledging that memories are contingent and subjective, they remain an important method of recovery and a means of expanding the boundaries of historical research, and I therefore attempted to judiciously cross-reference events and views. Where it was difficult to discern the veracity of particular viewpoints, opposing voices have been allowed to speak against each other. In an effort to keep notes to a minimum, extracts from interviews have not been endnoted each time they are cited. Instead, all interviews are listed at the end of the book. Similarly, access to the IPCI's archives provided an invaluable source of information, and where correspondence cited has not been endnoted, the originals are housed at the IPCI's offices in Durban.

Ahmed Deedat progressed from being a retail assistant rummaging for reading material in the basement of a remote rural store to become a renowned figure in many parts of the Muslim world. He walked with kings yet spoke in a manner and language that appealed to ordinary Muslims. He was not loath to enter 'enemy territory', challenging leading evangelical Christians on their interpretations of biblical and scriptural precepts and teachings, often on their home turf. His legacy continues to echo and haunt his opponents both inside and outside Islam. And all this took place primarily during the time when South Africa was a global pariah because of apartheid. This makes Ahmed Deedat even more fascinating – here was a man who, while building a local dynasty that continues to function, strode the global Muslim stage.

Deedat's tours of various countries featured on primetime television news broadcasts.

Growing up in Durban one could not but be aware of the influence and controversy that surrounded Deedat. But one had to travel abroad to truly appreciate the extent of his global appeal. For example, it was at Indiana University in Bloomington in the mid-1980s that Deedat's transnational popularity really dawned on me. Students from Malaysia and Saudi Arabia, who constituted a large segment of the Muslim student population on the campus, would typically ask: 'Where from?' 'South Africa?' 'Aaaah! Deeeedat, Deeeedat.' 'Yes.' 'Gooood. Welcome, welcome.'

Such anecdotes are far from exceptional. Urologist Dr G.M. Hoosen recalls attending a medical conference in Buenos Aires in the late 1980s. On Friday, he wanted to offer the midday Jumu'ah prayer and called the Pakistan Embassy to check whether there was a mosque in the area. With the help of a taxi driver, he negotiated the tricky route to the distant and, to his amazement, large and beautiful mosque. When worshippers discovered that he was from South Africa, the first words uttered were 'Deedat, Deedat.' And when they heard that he had some pamphlets at the hotel they followed him all the way back to his room to lay hands on the material. The 'sheer delight' of these Argentinians left Dr Hoosen dumbstruck. Although he was a trustee of the IPCI at the time, even he confessed to not having appreciated the extent of Deedat's popularity.

By the early 1990s many South African Muslims travelling to the Middle East, Malaysia, Pakistan, or Indonesia found that one other figure had become synonymous with South Africa: Nelson Mandela. That these two men were often mentioned in the same breath reflects Deedat's stature in the Muslim world. His books and pamphlets, as well as video, audio, and DVD recordings were, and continue to be, widely disseminated.

A banner advertising a lecture to be held in Sydney's Town Hall in 1996.

## INTRODUCTION: THE ARGUMENTATIVE MUSLIM

The title of this chapter was inspired by a collection of essays by Nobel Prize-winning Indian economist Amartya Sen titled *The Argumentative Indian* that underscores the long tradition of argument, public debate, and intellectual pluralism that informs India's history. One dictionary's definition of argumentative is 'the presentation and elaboration of an argument' or 'deductive reasoning in debate'. Some may feel that 'contentious' is more appropriate in Deedat's case, that is, 'causing or likely to cause disagreement and disputes between people with differing views'. On the other hand, argumentation may often lead to contention and quarrels, but that is not necessarily intentional. Deedat believed that through methodical reasoning he could counter the arguments of missionaries. His belief in open debate was underscored by Somali journalist Bashir Goth shortly after Deedat's death in 2005:

> It is not important whether one agreed with Deedat or embraced his style of debate or the core of his beliefs. What one couldn't miss in him was his unparalleled belief in the power of the word. The Islamic world today is in dire need of men like Deedat…whose good character, good deeds, good knowledge and humane nature, instead of their booby-trapped bodies, can reach overseas shores. Deedat was a person who could smile and not frown before his Christian brethren, a person in whose presence one felt safe, without having to think about running for cover when he reached to adjust his skullcap.[1]

Deedat had a particular style of argument that aimed to strike at the core of the beliefs of many Christians:

> To me, the missionaries are all one-book professors. They only know the Bible. They say, my Bible says this, my Bible says that, my Bible says this, my Bible says that. So right, this is his Book. So I said I agree with what he says and when you start analysing his claim, amazingly, it's not what he's telling you. Now what he's telling you is that Jesus is God for example…So I say, look, you show me in your Bible, any version, they have a dozen different versions, where Jesus said, 'I am God' and I am prepared to accept him as God. I said I do not talk for my people, the Muslims, they make up their own minds, but I am prepared to put my neck on the guillotine, chop it off as you like, if you show me where he says 'I'm God'. Believe me, in forty years I've been talking like this to the Americans, the DDs or Doctors of Divinities, the bishops, some great men, giants of Christianity, and nobody has ever come along with proof. You ask that simple question, so simple, so straightforward, the request you are making [but] the guy doesn't know what is hitting him so he goes beserk, then he wants to attack the Holy Prophet. I said, look, please, I'm only asking you a simple request. Show it to me and you've got a convert, not only a convert, I said, but I'll try and convince my other brethren as well.[2]

At the heart of Deedat's method was polemics, the art of theological disputation that best suited his argumentative approach, and that was based on a wide-ranging knowledge of religious texts and a confrontational style of public presentation. He was a master of polemics, often rousing audiences with the crassness of his language and then seducing them with the power of his oratory, his knowledge of Christianity, and his unrelenting commitment to his mission. Deedat was very clear about his role in life. God 'has given you a way of life [in the Qur'an]...But the role everyone takes is of their own choosing. You want to be a doormat or a punch bag, this is your choice, not Allah's choice.'[3] Deedat was no punch bag.

An observation by American sociologist C. Wright Mills on the relationship between biography and history is instructive:

> Neither the life of an individual nor the history of a society can be understood without understanding both...No social study that does not come back to the problems of biography, of history, and their intersections within a society has completed its intellectual journey.[4]

To place Deedat in the context of his times, he lived in an age when the peoples of Africa, Asia, and the Middle East were trying to free themselves from the yoke of colonial oppression, while white supremacist ideology was being entrenched with renewed vigour in apartheid South Africa.

The colonisation of Muslim lands by imperial powers after the Renaissance was followed by the spread of Christian missionary movements in the nineteenth century. The policies of the colonial powers and the activities of missionaries impacted heavily on the economic, political, educational, social, cultural, and religious institutions of Muslim societies. Increasingly, relations between Christians and Muslims became focused on economic and political interests. The likes of Sayyid Jamal al-Din al-Afghani, Muhammad Abduh, Sayyid Ahmad Khan, and Rashid Rida responded in different ways to the challenges posed by the decline of the Ottoman Empire and the rapid expansion of Western colonialism in the second half of the nineteenth century. Al-Afghani wrote of a pan-Islamist Islamic revivalism while Rida promoted the idea of the Salafiyya movement that restricted what was regarded as 'correct' in Islam to the Qur'an and hadith.

Key twentieth-century thinkers of whom Deedat was certainly aware include two Egyptians, Hasan al-Banna, a schoolteacher who established the Society of Muslim Brothers, and Syed Qutb, an activist who was executed by the Egyptian government in August 1966. Sayyid Abul A'la Mawdudi followed a parallel intellectual trajectory on the Asian subcontinent and inspired many globally through his message that Islam was the central force for uniting Muslims. Iranian sociologist Ali Shariati was another important ideologue.[5]

Born in 1917, Deedat grew up on the crest of anti-colonial upheavals and worldwide revolutionary ferment. Like Deedat, many Muslims looking at the world in the mid-twentieth century felt that Islam was under attack from Christian countries that had 'clubbed together to liberate Christian peoples from Muslim rule [in Greece, Bulgaria, Rumania], merely because they were Christians ruled by Muslims'.[6] Add to this the perceived and actual collaboration during the colonial period between imperial governments and missionaries (whose 'holiest of books', the Bible, came, in Homi Bhabha's words, to be seen to represent 'the standard of the cross and the standard of empire'), the activities of Anglican missionaries on the Cape Flats, and the symbiotic relationship between the Dutch Refomed Church and the apartheid regime in South Africa, and one can understand why this sense of global attack also had local impulses. Ebi Lockhat, who worked for Deedat for several years, has no doubt that the colonial context was crucial in moulding Deedat's outlook:

> He came from an era where he was under colonial domination. He was a product of that British colony when he came to South Africa, and here we had this policy of segregation and later apartheid, especially with the Indian Muslim. We were not like the Cape Malay who had been here for three hundred years. We were just starting out. So we were always, 'Boss, we'll build a school, you send the teachers, we'll put up the building,' that type of thing, just to get something. 'Boss, why do you want us to get a permit to go to the Transvaal?' Now within that environment, what was the way to strike back? The only way to strike back – and he found it – was to stand up for, and not feel inferior about, his religion.

Even at the height of the Cold War when many Muslim countries were closely allied to the United States, Deedat argued that Christianity, not communism, was the greatest threat facing the Muslim world. Echoing Muhammad Ali's famous statement, 'No Vietnamese ever called me a nigger,' Deedat told a journalist in 1987:

> I live in an ocean of Christianity. It is the Christian who comes and knocks at my door to preach Christianity, not a communist. The Christian gives me his Bible – free. It is their gift – free – to all Muslims. You fill in a coupon and get their Bible – free. Communists have not given me their book, free or otherwise. Have you seen it? Has anybody else seen it? No communist has knocked at my door yet.[7]

If Islam was under attack, as many felt, then it needed a defender. Beyond that, it needed someone to counter-attack. The stage, in a sense, was set for Ahmed Deedat. Years of self-directed study, combined with his love of the podium, his 'gift of the gab', and his fearlessness, made him the pre-eminent Muslim public figure in South Africa from the 1960s to the 1990s. Deedat was the Muhammad Ali of the theological ring, boxing clever, defending his corner, taking the fight to his opponent.

Recollections by Deedat's contemporaries of his love of the stage, as well as recordings of his debates and lectures, all suggest that Deedat conducted his mission in much the same way that Nelson Mandela viewed boxing. Mandela, who was a keen amateur boxer in his youth, wrote in his autobiography, 'I did not enjoy the violence of boxing so much as the science of it. I was intrigued by how one moved one's body to protect oneself, how one used a strategy both to attack and retreat, how one paced oneself over a match.'[8] When he went into a debate, Deedat measured his opponents, used their arguments against them, went from smooth calm talker to aggressive counter-puncher, was always gracious afterwards, thanked Allah (SWT) for his 'victory', forgave his opponents for not knowing better, and was already looking forward to his next battle.

Where Deedat differed from most of his Muslim contemporaries was his focus on the Bible. Arguing that the Bible ought to be analysed to 'show the holes in it' rather than be bypassed, Deedat mirrored Edward Saïd's view that the classics of Western civilisation should be read against the grain rather than ignored. Mimicry was central to Deedat's strategy, and was used not simply to imitate, but to confront, to contest, to challenge, to debunk. To do this he often used his 'enemy's' tools. As he told a reporter from *Arab News* in 1989: 'I use Western techniques to beat my opponents at their own game. If they have a laser gun, I must have a laser gun. If they have a stick, I must get a longer stick.'[9]

Focusing on Deedat's debates and writings about Christianity, which tend to present him as a one-dimensional 'Bible-basher', masks the fact that he addressed a range of other issues in his lectures, debates, interviews, and writings, such as: the emasculation of Muslims under colonial rule; the relationship between culture, power, and resistance; the value-ladenness of technology; and the shortcomings of Muslims, including the persistence of racism and ethnicity.

Deedat implored Muslims to arm themselves with knowledge and shrug off their inferiority complex, as the West was

> brainwashing our children in such a manner that they [are] feeling inferior. The missionary, who knocks on your door, is militant. No matter what smiling face he comes with, he knows in his heart that he is better than you, otherwise he wouldn't dare knock on your door to tell you that you are going to hell, he wants to save us from hellfire. He tells you that all your good deeds are like filthy rags, all your fasting and your prayers and your zakat and your hajj is all a waste of time…This means the giver is superior to the taker.[10]

This idea of superiority and inferiority has been widely theorised. Edward Saïd, for example, stated that negative 'dispositions toward Islam, sedimented in the Western psyche, have their genesis in a long-standing tradition of scholarly and popular discourse on the inferiority of Muslim practices and doctrines.'[11]

Interviewed on Pakistani television during his tour of that country in 1987, Deedat emphasised the destructive impact of colonialism on the Muslim psyche:

> The European came with his superior gunpowder…with that he knocked into submission our people all over the world. That's when they conquered Indonesia, a handful of them. A handful of them, the Portuguese, captured part of this territory, our country; a handful of French did the same, then the rest was taken over by a handful of Britishers because they had the gunpowder and they ruled us…on the subcontinent [for] one hundred and fifty years. So during that period also we couldn't talk to them. They were our masters, our rulers. Now, once we got our freedom, we don't know how to talk because we lost the art of talking.

Others have theorised the impact of colonialism, a period marked by enormous social change on the cultural and intellectual life of the colonised, far more eloquently than Deedat. For example, in the 1950s Frantz Fanon wrote that colonial domination 'disrupts in spectacular fashion the cultural life of a conquered people…Every effort is made to bring

## INTRODUCTION: THE ARGUMENTATIVE MUSLIM

Deedat was the 'Muhammad Ali' of the theological boxing ring, taking the fight to his opponent.

the colonized person to admit the inferiority of his culture.'[12] Michel Foucault argued that 'dominant groups in society constitute the field of truth by imposing specific knowledges, disciplines and values upon dominated groups. As a social formation it works to constitute reality…also for the subjects who form the community on which it depends.'[13] In *Culture and Imperialism*, Edward Saïd wrote that 'the enterprise of empire depends upon the idea of having an empire', and in *Orientalism*, he argued that colonial discourse operated as an instrument of power.

Deedat, too, understood that underpinning imperialism was an ideology in which, beyond the goal of capital accumulation, the notion that the empire had to rule over 'less advanced' peoples to fast-track their 'progress' and 'civilisation' was implicit. This, to quote Rudyard Kipling's famous poem from 1899, was the 'white man's burden'. The cultures of colonised peoples were subverted through new legal systems, education, the expropriation of land and labour, and political ideology. Deedat urged Muslims to shrug off this deeply embedded yoke of inferiority. He believed that Muslims were at least morally better than their white Christian masters and urged them to free themselves mentally from subjugation and to expose the moral and intellectual weaknesses of their rulers.

In the introduction to *Muhammad the Greatest*, Deedat wrote: 'What is the cause of this sickness, this inferiority complex? Yes! We are an emasculated people. Dynamism has been wringed out of us.' European intrusion into Muslim lands, Deedat felt, was continuing into the present with 'migrant workers in the guise of "tent makers" [missionaries], as Saint Paul called them, [who] are beginning to convert us, if not by direct conversion then by subtle influence that their civilisation is superior to ours. We must...push back the frontiers of western encroachment.'[14] In *Is the Bible God's Word?* Deedat stated that his lectures were designed to

> sound out these slinking missionaries who 'attack' the home and hearth of the unsuspecting Muslim who goes about minding his own business. The lectures are also aimed at restoring the damaged dignity of the Muslim who has been ruffled by the ruthless attacks of the Christian peddler. Ask the poor Muslims of Chatsworth, Hanover Park or Riverlea as to how they are subjected to the tyranny of certain missionaries.

Deedat warned Muslims of the dangers associated with foreign aid:

> Islam does not prohibit us from getting technological knowledge but with this technology and knowledge, this material benefit, cultural invasion takes place, religious invasion takes place. In the guise of wanting to help you economically, the Western world wants to plant in us their norms, they are trying to subvert our people into thinking as they are thinking, behaving as they behave, so we have to be on guard with regards to that.[15]

Deedat was also emphatic that the Western world could teach Muslims nothing in relation to spirituality. For example, when asked what Muslims could learn from the West, he told journalist Keysar Trad, 'Mathematics, learn from him, space science learn from him. But... there is nothing you can learn from him about religion'.[16] While Deedat probably gives the West too much credit, for mathematics was not a Western invention,[17] his point that the Industrial Revolution and Western technological superiority made the West's conquest of the rest of the world both possible and inexpensive, in terms of material and human resources, is well taken.

The idea that the West has little to offer in spiritual matters has a long history in anti-colonial discourse, most famously in the works of Mohandas K. Gandhi. Partha Chatterjee's work makes the distinction between the inner/outer, spiritual/material, arguing that since the Enlightenment, the West has placed 'rationalism at the heart of its culture'. While this has helped to bring about progress and prosperity, it has offered little in the spiritual sphere. Pointing to slavery, colonialism, the two World Wars, racism, and the Holocaust, many have questioned the value of this 'rationality' and 'enlightenment' in a context bereft of spirituality and compassion.[18]

In taking on Christian missionaries it is unlikely that Deedat explicitly aimed to repudiate Orientalism, as Saïd sought to do. Instead, he seems to have acted more from instinct and bravado in what was perhaps a case of practice preceding theory.

While Deedat's polemic was strongly religious in nature, the fact that he linked Christianity with 'whiteness' in apartheid South Africa bolstered support for his work. Deedat often lamented that 'we, the Asians, are suffering from an inferiority complex. We are mentally impressed by whites.'[19] Racist ideology was central to the construction of inequality in South Africa, and Deedat's teachings gave hope to many Muslims who were mostly black (Indian, Malay, and African) and subject to the tyranny of the racist apartheid regime. While race does not have a scientific basis, as Frantz Fanon wrote, it is an objective psychological fact in people's lives. Black people received a psychological boost when Deedat derided his white opponents. This was part of Deedat's aim. In response to a question from a reporter in 1987 as to how many Christians he had converted to Islam, he said: 'That is not the real goal. The real goal is you [Muslims]. I am talking to the enemy, and if it can boost your morale then it is good.'[20]

Ebi Lockhat used a boxing analogy to emphasise the ways in which Deedat's debates were psychologically important for many Muslims:

> My sport used to be boxing and in those days, when we used to go to Curries Fountain, you had blacks and whites fighting separately, and then they started having those mixed matches at Westridge Park. The nature of boxing is that you have an upcoming boxer; it's got nothing to do with colour but reality is that you don't want to match him with somebody that you can't definitely guarantee the result. Black American boxers, they would come here to fight upcoming whites. They are fighting a white, Afrikaans boxer. You are sitting there, knowing the [black] guy is a journeyman, and yet we are sitting there and hoping that the black guy lands a knock-out even though it won't happen. It's the syndrome that we had pre-1994…We wanted the All Blacks to win so badly in rugby. So the same syndrome existed when Deedat spoke, here was someone that can take on the whites…and win.

As Kate Zebiri points out, most Muslim 'writings on Christianity…portray it as a more or less exclusively Western phenomenon'.[21] Christianity is perceived as a white religion, as part of the 'arsenal' of Western modernity, and therefore as part of the problem and not the cure.[22] This global dichotomy between Islam and Christianity, West and East, coloniser and colonised – a dichotomy clearly evident in South African society as it intersected with a number of other identities by which (mainly black) Muslims were cast as inferior, less intelligent, poor – was important, not only in the making of Deedat, but also for the supporters that he attracted.

The Qur'an, in Deedat's view, was the perfect manual and he advertised it as 'The Last Testament' and 'The Future Constitution of the World'. He believed that Muslims had failed to benefit from its richness because of the way they approached it:

> Go back to the Qur'an. Allah gives you directions on how to do the job…He is giving you example after example but the Muslim is not reading the book. They rattle it off, they memorise it, they recite it beautifully, they put people into ecstasy when they

recite it, but what are we reading? Is it the sound, the music, sawab [reward] that we are reading for?[23]

Deedat also criticised Muslims for hanging on to narrow racial and ethnic identities. He called on them to forge a universal identity that transcended race, ethnicity, and nationality, as demanded by the Qur'an.

> Allah tells you in the Qur'an, 'O mankind!' Notice that he is addressing the whole of Mankind and not just Muslims or Arabs. 'We created you from a single [pair] of a male and a female and made you into nations and tribes that ye may know each other (not that ye may despise each other).' This is the standard laid down by Allah (SWT) to judge you – not race, riches, language or colour, but your behaviour. And not only is this theory, but Islam has certain practical ways of bringing this about. Five times a day we go to the mosque and get together, rubbing shoulders, the African and the Indian, the Arab and the Malay, everybody, rubbing shoulders, using the same taps, using the same towels, no gaps left between one individual and the other...Stand shoulder to shoulder and no gaps. And on a bigger scale in the social environment, on Fridays the whole community met in the masjid, and the higher meeting was the Eidgah where you get people from all over the place, and in the universal level, the pilgrimage where you get the surprise of your life. 'This man is from Tamil Nadu, and he's a Muslim,' because in my country all the Tamils are Hindus. He's Tamil, he's Muslim; he's pitch black, from Ethiopia, he's Muslim, my brother; and this guy, blonde hair and blue eyes, from Norway, he's Muslim. There is a system. Five times a day you read Ṣalah and you end saying 'Peace and blessings upon Allah', and you turn to the right you see a man from Ethiopia, and next time you turn, a man from China, and then you see a man from Timbuktu. There's a system laid out by the Almighty to end racism. We still have it [racism] but that is a remnant from the past.[24]

---

Deedat's uncompromising stance continues to evoke mixed reactions. Iqbal Jassat of the Media Review Network described him as a pioneer who 'understood the strategic significance of communication skills. He expended enormous energies to develop and deploy such skills to promote and defend Islam...Ahmed Deedat's contribution to Islam in South Africa can never be ignored, nor denied. His role in defending Islam from malicious and hostile propagandists needs to be accorded due respect and honour. *Now!*'[25] Shortly after Deedat's death in 2005, Somali journalist Bashir Goth of *Khaleej Times* wrote:

> Deedat had a firm belief in the magic of words, not just because he was aware of his skill in debating, but because he was a man who understood that Islam had won hearts over the centuries through the peaceful strength of its spoken word and not through the hoofs of its horses...Unshackled by the traditional, elitist language of Islamic

academia and untainted by the jihadist rhetoric of the radical ideologues, Deedat adopted the simple and peaceful approach of the medieval Muslim traders who spread Islam through their character and their trading acumen.[26]

There are many similar, often hyperbolic, complementary narratives. The author Huda Khattab wrote to Deedat in 1985 that she found his booklets about Islam and Christianity very beneficial. 'As an ex-born-again Christian, I find it very valuable to learn the Islamic versions of the various subjects, and the way you present Christianity makes me laugh at myself and wonder how I ever believed all the stuff that the Christians preach!' Khattab was born Samantha Scott in Blackpool, England, and raised as a Protestant. She had been a regular churchgoer, but in her teens felt that many of her questions were unanswered. She studied various religions before embracing Islam in 1983. After completing a degree in Arabic at the School of Oriental and African Studies in London in 1986, she authored numerous books on Islam. Channel Islam International presenter Ebrahim Gangat provided the following anecdote:

> There's a brother in Qwa Qwa [a rural area in South Africa] called Yusuf Mothoe [who] is busy translating the Qur'an into Sotho. I asked him, 'Brother, how did you accept Islam?' He replied: 'I was in the library in Qwa Qwa when I came across a book by Ahmed Deedat. I began reading it and it was all set and match for me. It inspired me and I came into the fold of Islam.' I met another brother who lived in Sharpeville. I asked him how he came into the fold of Islam. He told me that he read four pages of Deedat's book, just four pages, and was convinced that Islam was the true way of life…Deedat's true influence cannot be quantified because numbers do not do justice to his influence and the inspiration he provided to so many.[27]

Even some who did not embrace Islam were moved by Deedat's writings, as was the case with renowned Finnish pianist and Lutheran minister Richard Järnefelt, who featured in the 1999 *Guiness Book of World Records* for having a piano repertoire of three thousand songs that he plays from memory. Upon learning of Deedat's death in 2005, he wrote to the IPCI:

> My mistake was that I never had a chance to meet Sheikh Deedat. Fortunately our correspondence reached him in time. I got to know a warm and caring person whose devotion to God and persistent efforts in God's name was exemplary to anyone in any religion all over the world if wishing to sincerely approach God Almighty. I felt grand sorrow after Sheikh passed away. I became acquainted with Sheikh Deedat's theology by chance. In 1990, the state of Qatar organised a fair in Finland. I was looking at one stand when a man from another stand came to me and very friendly handed me a beautiful Holy Qur'an. He thought I was a Muslim since I had a long beard. I explained I was not entitled to take such a gift and, besides, could not read any Arabic. Instead of the Holy Qur'an he gave Sheikh Deedat's book *The Choice*. When I returned home

I started to devour the book of Sheikh. It seemed to answer many questions very wisely and was well written. It kind of talked to the reader...In 2003, I started my studies again. When it came to do my Pro Gradu, the final examination, I had a topic: The presentation of the theology of Sheikh Deedat to Finnish theologians.

While there was enormous support for Deedat among millions (mainly Muslims) worldwide, he had many implacable opponents whose views are discussed where appropriate.

This study does not evaluate Deedat's theological arguments in any depth. His works, and those of his critics, are widely available for readers to obtain and make their own judgements. There seems little point in reproducing the two sets of arguments here. Instead, this study seeks to situate Deedat historically and weave the facts of his life and mission into a coherent narrative.

Biographical narrative is a not an easy genre to write, and I have tried to avoid being either hagiographic or creating a picture of Deedat as 'a character in a bad novel'.[28] Deedat was a complex figure who, while he seemed answerable to no one in the way he went about his life's mission, was clearly a man of the people; one whose simple lifestyle and use of ordinary language made him seem 'one of us'. The apparent contradictions in his life simply reflect the fact that most lives are incoherent. Transformation is central to Deedat's story, as the way that he imagined and reimagined himself and his mission changed with time, as did the attitudes of people towards him. There are broader issues to keep in mind as we examine Deedat's life: the relationship between culture and power; the importance of mimicry in religious discourse; the reading of texts against the grain; the nature of anti-colonial discourse in a context of subjugation; and, as Hirschkind asks, 'what kinds of religious argumentation can provide for religious coexistence within a democratic political arena that is not beholden to the secular principle of religious indifference?'[29]

In time, as South Africa's political climate changed and the ambit of his 'targets' widened to include Hindus who shared a similar (Indian) racial background to many Muslims, Deedat's approach made many Muslims uneasy. Many of his admirers began to question the wisdom of his approach when their relationships with friends and associates became strained. Others criticised Deedat's support for conservative Middle Eastern regimes.

This book, then, is a story about the choices that Deedat made, and the social, political, and economic context in which he made them. It is the understanding of both structure and agency, of Deedat as both a product and maker of history that this book seeks to understand. In addition to his many personal attributes, Deedat was helped in his mission by factors such as the growth of transnational organisations from the 1970s, the post-1973 oil boom, the emergence and influence of Muslim youth movements in many countries of the world, and especially the technological revolution, which allowed his message to circulate globally. Also crucial was the worldwide Islamic resurgence, the acme of which was the 1979

Iranian Revolution. While the context undoubtedly influences what is possible, Deedat was one of those individuals who by sheer force of personality influenced the course of events.

Deedat was always in the maelstrom of controversy, and opinion on his life and work remains sharply divided both inside and outside the Muslim world. In narrating Deedat's life, the advice of Patrick French writing about his biography of V.S. Naipaul was noted, namely that the biographer's aim 'should not be to sit in judgement'.[30] The words of former US president Teddy Roosevelt are also apposite here:

> It is not the critic who counts; not the man who points out how the strong man stumbles, or where the doer of deeds could have done them better. The credit belongs to the man who is actually in the arena, whose face is marred by dust and sweat and blood, who strives valiantly…who at the best knows in the end the triumph of high achievement and who at the worst, if he fails, at least he fails while daring greatly. His place shall never be with those cold and timid souls who know neither victory nor defeat.[31]

It is hoped that this book offers readers a deeper understanding of Deedat's life and legacy, and serves not to close but to open the debate on his contribution to the world. Deedat himself would have welcomed this. As this book shows, he was always up for a good argument.

# THE INDELIBLE THUMBPRINT

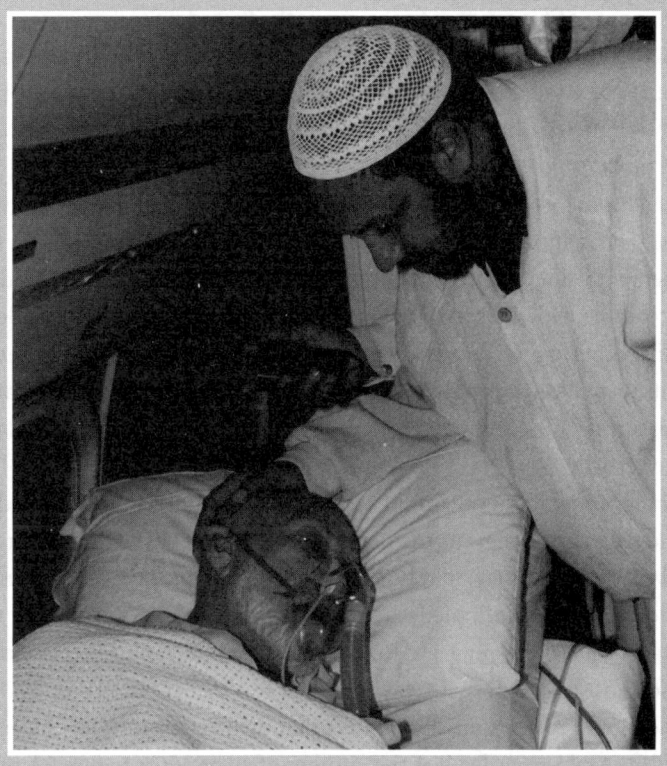

Given just days to live, Deedat's supporters in Saudi Arabia arranged a jet to fly him to a specialist hospital in Riyadh. Several months later, although severely paralysed, Deedat recovered enough to return to South Africa where he lived for another nine years.

In the Qur'an there's an ayah [verse] where Allah says that the believer should ask for no exemption from turmoil. The Prophets went through it. If you want to do Allah's work there is no exemption. And He says He will give glad tidings to those who patiently persevere, and who say when they are afflicted with calamity verily 'we belong to Allah and to Him we return'. So this is His, and He gives it and He takes it. I am reconciled with that.

– Ahmed Deedat[1]

ON FRIDAY 3 MAY 1996, two days after his return from a controversial tour of Australia where he had been threatened with deportation, and after a tense five-hour trustees' meeting, seventy-eight-year-old Ahmed Deedat left the headquarters of the Islamic Propagation Centre International (IPCI) at the corner of Queen and Grey streets in central Durban. It was just after five o'clock. Deedat made his way to the Nicol Square garage a few blocks away. He was by now a near mythical figure in the city, and many took note of his journey to the car park. According to eyewitness accounts, the one-time amateur boxer and weightlifter stumbled and was visibly struggling to walk as he reached Commercial Road. Deedat, however, displayed his trademark fortitude by proceeding to drive thirty kilometres through peak-hour traffic to his home in Verulam on KwaZulu-Natal's north coast.

On reaching his driveway, he finally succumbed to the pain and called his wife Hawa on the car phone. She helped him into the lounge, settled him in his favourite lounge chair, and called the family doctor, Dr Rajmahomed. The doctor realised that Deedat was in the throes of a stroke and had him speedily transferred to Wentworth Hospital in South Durban. The prognosis was not good. Locked-in syndrome had set in as a result of the stroke. This meant that although Deedat could be aware and awake, almost all the voluntary muscles in his body, apart from those in his eyes, were completely paralysed; he could not move or communicate verbally.

Abdul Karrim, a member of the Bin Ladin family of Saudi Arabia who had contributed liberally to the IPCI coffers, flew to Durban in his private jet to spend an hour with Deedat. He promised that no expense would be spared to provide the best available medical care.[2] Deedat was flown in a G3 Saudi Medevac army jet with a team of six doctors and nurses to the King Faisal Specialist Hospital and Research Centre in Riyadh. He was accompanied by his younger son Yousuf and his wife Hawa. Deedat was met at the airport by Saudi officials and the head of South Africa's mission in Riyadh, Garth Frieslaar.[3] Yousuf Deedat later told reporters that the Arabs regarded it as the 'mother of all honours to care for my father, who in their eyes is a soldier of Islam'.[4]

By the end of July, Deedat was able to 'speak' via a communications board operated through a special computer imported from the USA. As he could not sign cheques, local (South African) banks accepted his thumbprint.[5] Deedat was visited by diplomats, lawyers, scholars, teachers, and students. Nelson Mandela, South African president at the time, was one of many leaders to send greetings. His message was conveyed on 11 October 1996 by the ambassador of South Africa, Samuel Motseunyane, who told the *Riyadh Daily*:

> Mr Mandela is concerned about any South African living in any part of the world but the case of Deedat is special as he is highly respected, not only in South Africa, but in the world, for his dedication and hard work in the preaching of Islam during the past fifty years...I was also excited by the warm welcome extended to me by Shaykh Deedat.

Deedat presented the ambassador with a thumb-printed copy of *The Choice*,[6] an anthology of his key works.

Mandela and Deedat had spoken on the telephone once before. In October 1994, Deedat received a call from Saudi Arabia at his office. When told that that it was Nelson Mandela, the new South African president, Deedat recalled: 'At first I thought it was a crank call, and did not take the matter seriously. However, when I realised that it was indeed the State President, I nearly fell off my seat.' Mandela, who was on an official visit to Saudi Arabia, told Deedat that wherever he went people asked whether he knew 'Mr Deedat'. He suggested that they meet on 6 November 1994 during Mandela's visit to Durban. The meeting did not materialise because Deedat had to travel abroad, but he told reporters that he was 'greatly honoured and humbled at receiving the almost unbelievable telephone call from the President. It was the greatest thrill of my lifetime and I still cannot believe my good fortune.'[7]

South African diplomat Ashraf Suliman, upon assuming his post as Consul General at the South African Embassy in Riyadh, regularly visited Deedat in hospital. One thing that impressed him greatly was 'the dedication of his wife, Hawa. She was with him throughout his stay. She, to my mind became the ideal nurse and fulfilled that role remarkably.' Cassim Peer, who was the consul general of South Africa in Jeddah, described his visit to Deedat as 'a very sad and moving experience because Shaykh Deedat cried a lot when we were introduced to him'. Peer added:

> Shaykh opened many doors for me in Saudi Arabia. Wherever I went, whether it was a political, commercial or social meeting, people always asked about him and were pleased to co-operate with me and support me simply because I was a compatriot of Shaykh Deedat. Shaykh Deedat probably did more for tourism promotion to South Africa than I could have done with all my tourism workshops and conferences.

Deedat's many distinguished visitors in hospital included Professor Wajahat Ashraf Qazi, principal of the prestigious Pakistan Embassy School, who read a letter of commendation and prayer: 'We are greatly concerned about your health and pray to Almighty Allah to give you health. It is our hopeful desire to see you active again. You have been a source of great inspiration for Pakistanis. You have already created an army of many charged young Deedats who are looking forward for your able guidance.'[8] Ethiopian ambassador Mohammed Ali Ebrahim wished Deedat 'good health and a speedy recovery'. According to Ebrahim, Deedat was a respected figure in the whole African continent where his 'wisdom and knowledge on comparative religion were admired'.[9]

Deedat returned home after spending approximately nine months in Saudi Arabian hospitals. Many of his followers found it hard to reconcile the image of a bedridden Deedat at his modest Verulam home with the colossus who was a familiar figure across the Muslim world. His spirit remained buoyant, however, and is perhaps best summed up by the Qur'anic verse that he asked to have fixed to his bedside mirror and which remained there until his death:

> And [remember] Ayyub when he cried to his Rabb [Lord], 'Truly distress has seized me, but You are the Most Merciful of those that are Merciful'.
>
> – Surah Ambiya: 83

Deedat remained in command of his mental faculties and he held conversations by blinking his eyelids at an alphabet board to form words. His memory was excellent to the end. One of his visitors was long-time associate and current trustee of the IPCI, Ebrahim Jadwat, who told the *Saudi Gazette* that Deedat's memory was 'remarkable and people continue to benefit and get inspiration from him...His mind is a hundred per cent intact and he remembers everything.' Jadwat related that when he and his father, Mohammed, visited Verulam, Deedat told his father that he would 'replace the cricket bat', referring to a game that had taken place seven decades earlier when he had broken Jadwat senior's bat during a game of street cricket.[10] Nigerian Bala Muhammad, who was studying at the University of Natal in 2001, observed that Deedat's 'brain is as sharp as it had always been. He can see and hear, he can laugh and cry, and he can blink and nod. And more than all of these, he can also reason. He is also surprisingly sensitive to touch, for he can feel the warmth of human hands when they shake his.'[11]

Given Deedat's status in many parts of the Muslim world, newspapers and magazines periodically sent journalists to report first-hand on his health. Thus Muhammad Caravello of *Islamic Voice* described Deedat's physical condition, medication, and feeding method for his readers who 'were keen to know everything about the Shaykh':

> He obtains his nutrition via a pipe through his stomach. His wife has looked after him remarkably well considering that he has no bedsores whatsoever. Although his body is totally paralysed apart from his nose upward and he cannot eat, drink, speak or swallow anything, he is fully alert and can communicate via a chart. Subhan'allah, he is paralysed but he hears whatsoever is conveyed to him, understands and answers back using the chart.[12]

Tanzanian, Mohamed Said, who visited in June 2000, told Deedat about his impact on ordinary Tanzanians whom he continued to inspire. 'Shaykh Hafidh who had escorted me told me that my words about Christians reverting back to Islam had touched his heart and that Shaykh Deedat was crying with happiness.'[13] Bala Muhammad explained how the communication board worked:

> The 26 letters A to Z are grouped into five lines, each given a number from one to five. In this method A to E, for example, fall in line one, F to J in line two, and so following. So, if for example the Shaykh wants Yousuf to call someone with the name Jabir, the Shaykh would indicate with his eyes that he wants to say something. Yousuf would then ask: Line one? and the Shaykh would shake his head, meaning no, as the first letter of the name Jabir does not fall in line one. Line two? The Shaykh would nod his agreement as 'J' is in Line two. Yousuf would call out the letters F, G, H, I, J?

After visiting Deedat's bedside, Louis Farrakhan told reporters, 'He's a hero of mine. I came from his bedside inspired, uplifted.'

On the correct letter, the Shaykh would nod yes. Back again to line one for the next letter. By the time Yousuf spells J, A, he knows that his father wants Jabir.

Muhammad felt that he was 'having a normal conversation with the Shaykh'. Muhammad noted that all 'types of people, Muslims, Christians, Jews, Europeans, Asians, Africans', visited; and that Deedat's memory 'was still very sharp, as he could remember that many Nigerians, including Kabiru Yusuf of *Weekly Trust* who was in Durban for the 1999 Commonwealth Summit, and another brother who had also published a similar story in a past *Weekly Trust*, had visited him not too long previously'.[14]

International well-wishers were regularly taken by IPCI staff to pay their respects to Deedat. Some, such as al-Haji Corr of Gambia who worked for the World Health Organisation, arrived in South Africa, visited Deedat on the same day, and left the following morning. Yusuf Islam (formerly Cat Stevens), Zakir Naik, and Louis Farrakhan of the Nation of Islam in the USA were among a host of renowned visitors.

According to Mahomed Khan, who has worked for the IPCI since the late 1980s, Farrakhan visited Deedat on 25 October 2002, and commented that Deedat was mentally much stronger than when they had met previously in Chicago in the 1980s. Farrakhan told a well-attended public meeting in Durban:

> Last night I had the good luck of visiting one of my heroes. Ahmed Deedat is truly a champion of Islam. He's a hero of mine. We had shared many days together, and I saw him in the days of his strength, and last night I saw him even stronger. I saw him laying on the bed, having suffered a severe stroke, being unable to speak…With that chart he formed words just with the use of his eyes and he said, 'Dear brother, I watched you on SABC television and I was very impressed that you said to them that they should have mentioned God in their deliberations.' His brain is sharp. He can see, he can hear, he can think, he just can't speak but his faith is strong. I came from his bedside inspired, uplifted and I said, 'Father, when I go back I will tell the brothers of your great work. Do not worry, you will never be forgotten. For as long as those who love Islam live, Ahmed Deedat will live.' I looked at my brother and said, truly there must be another life where God gives reward to those who suffer in his cause because this man fought hard and from his bed he is not saying, 'O Allah, I fought for you, why did you allow this to happen to me?' Never doubt Allah's goodness because trials have come into your life. God is good and He is the Master of us but He tries us with all kinds of tests. If you can only go out to sea when the weather is calm, you are not a good sailor, but if you can match your ship in all kinds of weather then you are truly a man of the sea.[15]

When Raihan, the internationally renowned Malaysian singing group, visited South Africa in October 2002, band members insisted on meeting the 'powerful soldier of the deen [faith] of Allah.' In conversation with Yousuf Deedat, Raihan's director, Amran Idris, said,

> We were honoured to meet a missionary known worldwide…We were also thrilled when he knew who we were. It was an honour for us to sing a song that touched his heart and brought tears to his eyes. This was a heartfelt experience for all of us. We were motivated by him to pass the message of Islam to others. He said it would be accepted by many people, irrespective of race, culture, nationality, space, or distance because Islam is a universal religion.[16]

The visit of internationally renowned scholar Dr Zakir Naik in May 2000 was charged with emotion. Together they watched the DVD *On Becoming a Da'ee* which opens with a lecture by Naik. As the bedridden Deedat watched, he was totally overcome with emotion, and through his computer, told Naik, 'My son, what you have done in four years, it took me forty years to accomplish.' Naik responded:

> It was because of your forty years hard work that that was possible. You have to make the basement first and that takes time and then the building comes up…You gave me

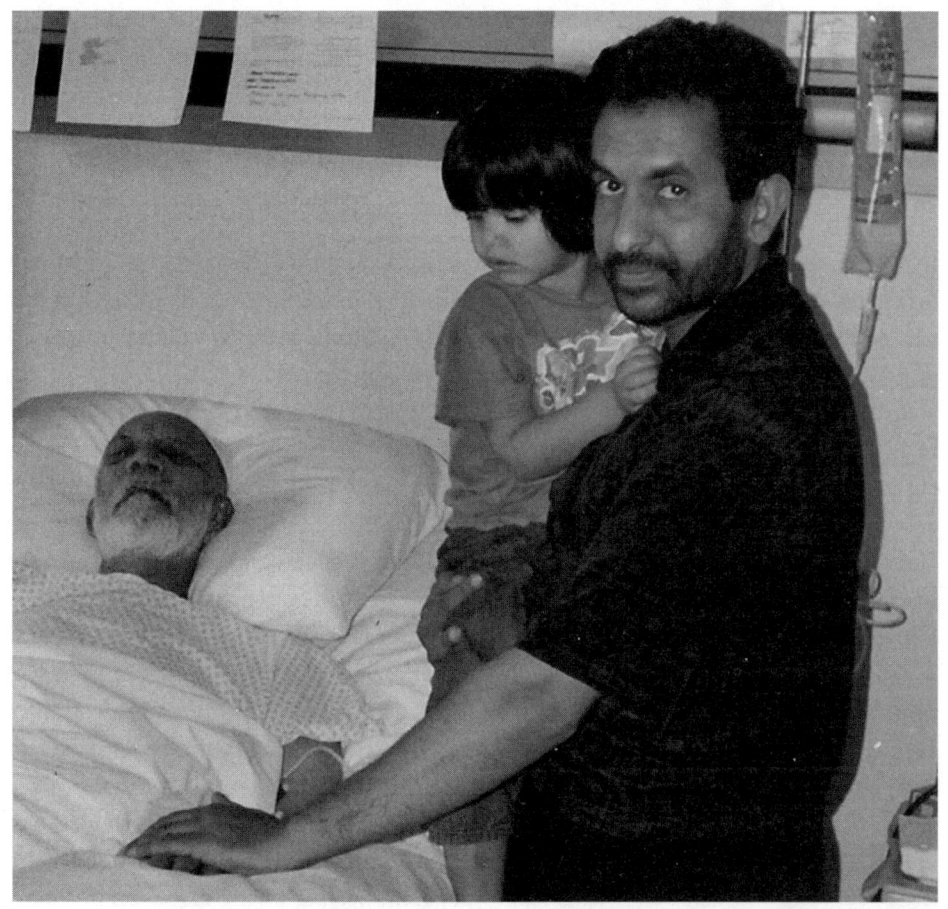

Mr Ashraf Suliman, then South Africa's Consul General to Saudi Arabia, regularly visited Deedat in hospital in Riyadh.

everything on a platter. If you weren't there then I would have taken forty-four years but because of Allah and guidance from Him, that you did all this foundation work for forty years, has made it possible for us to do this in such a short time.[17]

Deedat inspired many, even during his illness. Sabiha Doolarkhan wrote to him every month. Her discussions with Deedat were vital in her decision to embrace Islam in the 1980s. 'I was in awe of the stately man who sat behind the desk,' she wrote in one of her letters to Deedat, 'you epitomised what I expected Islam to represent – your calm demeanour and comfortable disposition encapsulated the essence of the dignity of Islam – and I left positively and pleasantly imbued with the spirit of Islam.' Deedat inspired Sabiha as she reflected after one of her visits: 'No one can look as majestic or profound as you do on a sick bed…surely that in itself is evident that Allah is indeed well pleased with your life's work.'[18]

Bala Muhammad, like many other visitors, was also full of admiration for 'sweet old Mrs Hawa Deedat, who doubles as his doctor and nurse. She has looked after him remarkably well':

The last doctor to visit the Shaykh came many years ago, as she has learnt all there is to treat her husband: she is now very familiar with all things intravenous and intramuscular, she feeds the Shaykh through a tube directly inserted into his stomach, and prepares all the necessary medicaments. (Before I left, I felt she deserved to be called Dr Hawa Deedat.) One other 'miracle': Mrs Deedat is said not to have even once stepped out of the house since the Shaykh returned from Saudi Arabia.[19]

In an interview with Channel Islam International in 2003, Yousuf Deedat told listeners that his eighty-year-old mother had not 'left the household for seven years. She sleeps on the sofa next to him [Deedat]. She gets up at dawn every morning to give my father four injections, insulin and heparin. She bathes him, she feeds him.'[20]

In 2003, Fatima Asmal recorded that several Christian missionaries also visited Deedat in an attempt to 'save' him.[21] Deedat's son, Yousuf, told Asmal that 'people from different faiths visited or wrote regularly to preach their religion [but] in every instance he [threw] a 'scud missile' at them.'[22] Fatima Asmal recalled Deedat's 'infectious laugh,' which she described as 'almost a guffaw – a mixture of a wheeze and a groan,' when she asked him whether he was ever swayed by the arguments of his Christian opponents.[23] Some Christian evangelists viewed Deedat's stroke as punishment for his critique of Christian doctrine. David Foster, for example, wrote that Deedat's 1992 booklet *Combat Kit* 'marked the beginning of the end…A small group of Christians prayed about these provocations.' Deedat failed to repent and was struck down four weeks after his controversial Australian lecture tour, which climaxed on Good Friday, a Christian day of mourning over the sacrificial death of Jesus (PBUH). Foster visited Deedat and prayed for him, 'without any apparent healing taking place. On our next visit we asked him whether he was now prepared to admit having done wrong. Deedat spelt out his emphatic reply, one letter at a time, "I have no guilt on my head."'[24]

For Muslims, however, illness is seen as a blessing. The Qur'an emphasises good relations among Muslims, 'the believers are nothing else than brothers, so make reconciliation between your brothers, and fear Allah, that you may receive mercy' (Qur'an 49:10), while the Prophet (PBUH) is reported to have said that it is 'not lawful for a believer to forsake a believer beyond three days, and whosoever does so more than three days and

Deedat's wife, Hawa, nursed him with unfailing devotion during the long years of his illness.

then dies, shall enter Hell.' Deedat's relations with some of his fellow Muslims had ruptured over the years, and the fact that he was bedridden gave him and his erstwhile opponents an opportunity to repair damaged relations. From a Muslim perspective, Deedat's stroke can be interpreted as a blessing.

Ahmed Hoosen Deedat was eighty-seven when he passed away shortly before seven o'clock on the morning of 8 August 2005. According to Yousuf, his father was listening to the recitation of Sura Yasin, considered the heart of the Qur'an, on Channel Islam International. He had become seriously ill about three weeks before, suffering cardiac problems and kidney failure. Hawa and Yousuf Deedat were at his side when he died. The funeral was covered live on Channel Islam International while Qatar-based television news station Al-Jazeera covered the funeral procession on its news segments, a sign of Deedat's popularity in the Middle East. The janaza prayer was said at the Wick Street Mosque in Verulam.

The headlines in Durban's daily newspapers, 'Fiery Muslim missionary dies after long illness', (*Natal Mercury*, 9 August 2005) and 'Controversial Muslim icon passes on' (*Daily News*, 8 August 2005), point to the storms that Deedat had created. The IPCI issued the following statement:

> Early this morning, 8 August 2005/2 Rajab 1426, Shaykh Ahmed Hoosen Deedat passed on to meet his Creator. This was after succumbing to a severe stroke that left him paralysed for more than nine years. Throughout this period, he gracefully persevered under the most difficult personal conditions; however, not forgetting his task as a da'ee [Islamic worker] and an ambassador of Islam, he continued to inspire, educate, challenge and inform people about the universal message of Islam. It is on this solemn occasion of his demise that we salute the courageous spirit and phenomenal work of this world-renowned personality, a hero of the Muslim World, nay, a true hero of believers all around the globe!

The IPCI was inundated with several thousand tributes expressing a deep sense of loss, of which just a small selection are quoted below.

- Abdul Salem Al-Sulaiteen of Qatar praised Deedat for 'defending the noble cause of Islam before the challenges and misunderstandings created by Christian missionaries worldwide. Shaykh Deedat's death is a personal loss to me as is the case with so many here in Qatar' (13 August 2005).

- For Khaliluddin of Birmingham in the United Kingdom, Deedat's 'passing away is a huge loss to the Muslim Ummah, especially at this day of age, where non-Muslims are going out of their way to torment and batter the book of Allah by misquoting and misinterpreting the book and the Sunnah in a way to disunite the Muslim Ummah' (12 August 2005).

- Faiz expressed sadness that God had 'called back a great scholar' who had served 'with candour, pizzaz, oomph, charm, and true self for the stormy and blazing part of his life. He has always inspired me to the utmost. I wish I could follow in his footsteps or even in the shadows of his shadow' (10 August 2005).

- For Muhammad El Usman of Nigeria, Deedat 'demonstrated the real meaning of the adage that the purpose of life is to live a life of purpose' (11 August 2005).

- Abubakr Karim of Toronto, Canada, wrote that Deedat's death 'left a gap that can hardly be filled. He was a humble and decent human being. When he visited Toronto in 1995 I attended almost all his lectures trying to benefit from him. Although he was old he had the energy of a young soldier' (9 August 2005).

- According to Uthman Chilungo, South African Muslims 'will never know the stature of Ahmed Deedat in the minds of Muslims from the rest of Africa and beyond. Indeed, for that matter, his name brought awe to many a crusading missionary. One incident which comes to mind happened a few years ago. A local Da'wah office in my hometown approached the principal of a missionary secondary school who agreed to put literature in the school's library for the sizeable Muslim studentship there on condition that Shaykh Ahmed's series would not be part of the collection' (10 August 2005).

- Adnan Mohammed Al-Jame of the World Assembly of Muslim Youth wrote that 'It is a great loss for Muslim Ummah as a whole and a great personal loss for the thousands of budding da'ees who took inspiration from him' (9 August 2005).

- Zakaria Abdullah of Kuala Lampur, Malaysia, was an 'avid reader' of Deedat's writings to 'combat the Filipino Christians working with us here in Malaysia…We want to preserve and expand the legacy of Sheikh Ahmed Deedat as far and wide as possible. The Islamic world owes him a debt of gratitude for making Da'wah efforts and process much easier. He has laid the groundwork for modern da'ee to use as guide and to emulate' (9 August 2009).

- Gary Dargan was an Australian Muslim who 'had the pleasure of being involved in his only Australian tour. I was the MC for his two Sydney tours. It was an amazing time and many of us were inspired by his forthright speech and his engaging manner with people…There have been few great advocates for Islam in our time. Ahmed Deedat was one of them. While we could say that his passing has left the Ummah poorer, his example has inspired a generation of younger Muslims to get out and emulate him in working for Islam. This is a significant legacy' (11 August 2005).

- Noura Al-Noman of Sharjah, who met Deedat during his visit to the United Arab Emirates in 1986, described him as 'a great Muslim hero. I can never forget his kindness and his generosity. He asked me to call him "uncle" and that was the greatest moment of my life' (10 August 2005).

- Iranian Mohammed Reza Sadeghi wrote that 'brother Al Haaj Ustaaz Sheikh Ahmed Deedat…was definitely a figure of importance for me when I started to learn about comparative religion. He made so deep contribution to this discipline. It is a part of me, which leaves, I miss him' (9 August 2009).

- From Spain, Omar Ribas, Secretary of the Associacio Catalana d'Estudis Islamics, prayed 'to Allah for the eternal blessings and happiness of the Sheikh in the Janna near the beloved of Allah' (9 August 2005).

- Badia of Medina could not 'stop my tears, my heart feels as if I have lost a father in all means. I am married to Italian man, your good father teach me a lot and I take advice and knowledge. I feel I am lost. We need people nowadays to show the world what is Islam' (9 August 2009).

- Renowned scholar Professor Ali Mazrui of Binghamton University in New York state was 'truly saddened to learn about the death of our beloved Ustaaz, a true Ambassador of Islam for decades. He has definitely left his mark upon Islam in Africa. May the Almighty guide him by the hand to the gates of paradise, Amen. I was greatly honoured to know him when he was alive and well. I was both saddened and inspired to see him in his bedridden days' (9 August 2009).

- Syed Nasiruddin Kazi of India had been an 'ardent admirer' of Deedat 'since my childhood and will continue to be till my last breath.' He had attended two of Deedat's lectures in Jeddah in 1988 and 'remember his energetic composure in these two grand majestic halls which left me spellbound only to kindle a strong desire to follow in his footsteps. I was eleven or twelve years of age at that time and got captivated by this magnetic personality. Our household has lost our personal mentor and one of our closest kin' (18 August 2005).

The thousands of letters of condolence included those from Abdul Wade, president of the Republic of Senegal (9 September 2005), and Dr Abdullahi Adamu, governor of Nasarawa State in Nigeria (9 August 2005). Even former 'foes' were effusive in their praise. Ashwin Trikamjee, president of the South African Hindu Maha Sabha, stated that he was saddened by Deedat's death, noting: 'He was a great scholar of the religion of Islam and, although he was controversial, he has made a huge contribution to the religious community of South Africa.' Anglican bishop Ruben Philip extended his condolences to Deedat's family and hoped that dialogue between Christians and Muslims would continue.[25]

Deedat's friends, supporters, and relatives gathered at his Verulam residence to pay their final respects. Shafa'at Khan, a presenter from Chanel Islam International, vividly remembers the scenes and recalled that 'Verulam came to a standstill. It was as if a mini-hajj was taking place.' Iqbal Essop, an employee of the IPCI since the 1980s, observed that this was the first time that the mosque had been packed to capacity for a janazah prayer. 'People were praying in the car park. Walking in the procession to the graveyard hurt, and I am still moved to tears when I think about it.' Mahomed Khan, who had worked for

Deedat since he was a teenager, felt 'distraught' and was hurt that many of those who were 'at the funeral praising him could not appreciate him when he was alive.' Mufti Menk of Zimbabwe, who happened to be visiting Durban at the time, performed the janaza. Deedat was laid to rest at the Verulam Muslim Cemetery.

Commemorative events were held simultaneously in several countries around the world. In Riyadh, for example, the Islamic Research Foundation organised a 'Condolence Meeting and Funeral Prayer' at the Khayyam Hotel on 12 August 2005. Mosques in Tanzania held janaza prayers in absentia in Deedat's honour. The Tanzanian scholar Mohamed Said wrote that when news of Deedat's death reached his country, mosques in Dar-es-Salaam and other places offered janaza for him while 'in deep anguish and as remembrance'. His obituary was published in *Al Hudabore*, one of Tanzania's leading Muslim newspapers. And in Colombo, Sri Lanka, where Deedat had officially opened the Centre for Islamic Studies's bookshop during his visit there in 1987, the Centre organised janaza prayers for Deedat at all the mosques and announcements were made via the state media's Rupavahini channel.[26]

Ahmed Deedat was one of the most renowned and controversial South African Muslims of the twentieth century. More of a populist and polemicist than a theologian, his international popularity exceeded by far that of any contemporary South African (Muslim) religious figure. Deedat was a complex man who stirred strong passions for and against his mission. Rarely were people indifferent to him. Descriptions of Deedat run the gamut from 'gentle and caring' to 'dogmatic and contentious'. Hundreds of thousands of his pamphlets, books, videos, and audio recordings have circulated globally. Deedat evolved into a transnational Islamic personality by building a reputation as a 'defender' of Islam against evangelists through his booklets, lectures, and interreligious debates with Christian scholars and missionaries.

# 3
# FROM ADAMS MISSION TO AHMED'S MISSION

Deedat in the mid-1930s.

> In former times when the Christians were not in power, and the noisy violence of their abrogated religion was therefore concealed, our Professors seldom turned their thoughts towards its refutation; but upon the learned of this age, it is incumbent and their sacred duty to use every endeavour to overturn their faith, otherwise these people by their insidious efforts will gradually mislead whole multitudes.
>
> – Sayyid Abbas Ali, 1845[1]

DEEDAT'S JOURNEY began quite by chance when he came across a book chronicling a nineteenth-century debate between a Mawlana and a missionary. That book was *Izhar-ul-Haq: Truth Revealed*.

It is ironic that Adams Mission, the home of Christian missionary education, inspired Deedat to challenge the authenticity of the Bible. As in most colonial settings, Christian missionaries were active in Natal from the earliest days of white settlement. The American Board Mission dominated the missionary field in Natal from the 1830s, and its medical missionary, Dr Newton Adams, settled in Umlazi in 1836.[2] Adams College, which offered a liberal Christian education to African students, was opened in 1853.[3] Situated about forty kilometres south of Durban it has produced a stream of outstanding graduates, most notably Nkosi Albert Lutuli, who became president of the African National Congress and was awarded the Nobel Peace Prize in 1960.

It was the two years that Deedat spent at Adams Mission in the late 1930s, during the awkward transition from teenager to adult, that gave him his life's calling. At the time, Deedat worked as sales assistant at O.N. Mahomed, a small general dealer that serviced the students of Adams College and the African communities living nearby. Deedat later claimed that the students at Adams College had served as a catalyst for his own mission. He told a reporter in 1986 that he was 'driven by the challenges of Christian missionaries in his boyhood, who questioned his early Islamic faith, to read and study his religion and the Christian faith as well'.[4] Students and teachers from the mission taunted him about Islam as they sought to prove the superiority of Christianity. Deedat was often unable to respond to the challenging questions of prospective missionaries. As he explained:

> These missionaries would come and question us if we knew how many wives our Prophet (PBUH) had. I did not know a thing about that. They also asked us if we knew that our Prophet spread Islam at the point of a sword or that the one who did not accept Islam had their heads chopped off. They also used to ask us if we knew that our Prophet copied his book from that of the Jews and Christians, and I knew nothing about that. We were like sitting ducks and targets for these missionaries, who were well trained while we, even being Muslim, did not know much about our religion. The only thing the entire staff of that shop and myself knew about Islam was that we were Muslims and not what made us Muslims! We thought that the Kalimah made us so. In fact, what Kalimah meant was not known to the bulk of the people. We prayed and even fasted, without really understanding much about Islam. It was harassment, constant harassment for us, and pleasure for those missionaries.[5]

'Being a sensitive young man of twenty,' as Deedat explained in his preface to *Is the Bible God's Word?* he 'spent sleepless nights in tears for not being able to defend the one dearer to me than my own life, that mercy unto all mankind – Muhammad (PBUH). I resolved to study the Qur'an, the Bible and other literature.' Deedat's early experience at Adams Mission is part of folklore and has earned the sympathy even of some who did not agree with his methods, such as Salman Nadvi, professor of Islamic studies at the University of Durban-Westville for almost three decades from the mid-1970s:

> I was not positively inclined towards his debates but you must understand that Ahmed Deedat came into this whole thing as a result of a personal experience. That personal experience is one we were all familiar with because Christianity is a missionary-orientated religion. Their missionaries are paid to propagate and convert, which is exactly the opposite of Islam. In Islam, we don't have paid missionaries to convert people but each Muslim should have, in him or her, Islam in a practical sense, which itself works as an invitation to Islam. So, I was not very favourably inclined towards debating Islam, especially [Deedat's] rough language and the jokes or satire that he employed. But Ahmed Deedat himself related to me his early life, how he got into this, so I could understand the logic which forced him to get into it because that was his personal experience.

Deedat had been obsessed with reading from a young age. While still in Durban he often found refuge in the Gandhi Library, which housed a large collection of books in English, Gujarati, Tamil, Hindi, and Urdu, as well as numerous newspapers. Deedat spent hours browsing through magazines, newspapers, and books. He had a youthful openness to the written word, and took in everything from *Sinbad the Sailor* to the works of Louis Pasteur. When working as a shop assistant at O. N. Mahomed, his passion for reading extended as far as reading the old newspapers that were used to package sugar, flour, and salt. When making these parcels, Deedat would read the articles, sometimes oblivious of the waiting customers. He eventually tired of newspapers and discovered the shop's basement where old books and magazines were stored. Deedat's rummaging was initially disappointing as he spent most of his free time setting aside piles of magazines such as *Farmer's Weekly* and *Personality* that were of little interest to him. He was keen to read about politics, colonialism, and Islam.

One is reminded here of Deedat's predecessors in nineteenth-century India who were searching for solutions to the challenges posed by missionaries. The Reverend T.G. Clark described one such individual who 'night after night, by the toil of the lamp…ransacked every book within his reach from which the admission of "various readings" might be plausibly construed into the announcement of irremediable corruption; and placing the results of his researches in the possession of the molwi, or Mahommedan teacher…in expectation of finally overwhelming the Christian cause'.[6]

Deedat's life changed one afternoon when he came across a worm-eaten book full of mildew that caused him to sneeze uncontrollably. It was Mawlana Rahmat Allah Kairanawi's *The Ijaharul Hakk*, now more commonly known as *Izhar-ul-Haq*. Noticing the English translation, *Truth Revealed*, in parenthesis on the cover, Deedat immediately began reading. When the store closed, he took the book back to his room and read it from cover to cover. Half a century later, he was to tell reporters that the book transformed his life.[7]

*Izhar-ul-Haq* is based on a debate between Mawlana Kairanawi and the Reverend Carl Pfander in the city of Agra in India in 1854. Theological debates between Muslims and Christians have taken place since the time of the Prophet Muhammad (PBUH) in the seventh century but, as author Avril Powell points out, 'common roots in both history and doctrines, have failed to reconcile incompatible interpretations of divinity, revelation, and prophethood.'[8] For Christians, Islam is a heresy because it denies the divinity of Jesus, while Muslims regard the Christian teachings relating to the Trinity as a deviation from the belief in one God.[9]

Muslim scholars such as Ibn Hazm (994–1064) and Ibn Taymiyya (d. 1323/728 AH) produced extensive studies of biblical criticism. Ibn Hazm, a Cordoban who lived in al-Andalus, Muslim Spain, produced a mammoth five-volume study called *Kitab al-fisal fi'l-milal wa'l-ahwa wa'l-nihal*,[10] which earned him the title 'Father of Comparative Religion'. The study provided a critical assessment of Jesus, and anticipated objections to the Bible by nineteenth-century critics.

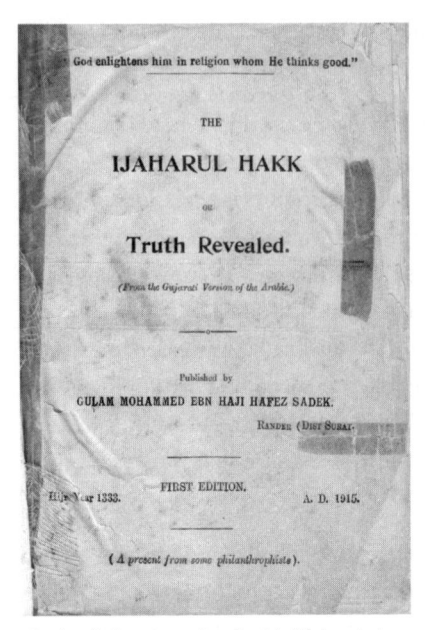

The book that gave Deedat his life's mission

Ibn Taymiyya is a towering figure in Islamic intellectual history. He was born in Syria and died in Damascus. During this period, the Islamic world was under threat from Christian crusaders as well as Mongols who had virtually destroyed the eastern Islamic empire when they captured Baghdad in AD 1258 (656 AH). Of his major works, *al-Jawab al-sahih* critiqued the Christian doctrine of the Trinity, while *al-Sahih Ibn Taymiyya* argued that Christianity was an aberration of Jesus' true message and consisted of an eclectic blend of paganism, myth, mystery, and prophetic half-truths.[11]

By the nineteenth century, Muslims were in retreat while European imperialism was making inroads in many parts of the world. Oriental cultures and traditions were systematically studied to confirm the epistemic authority of the West. The expansion of European power gave rise to the concept of Homo Islamicus ('Islamic Man'), which peddled the idea that Muslims belonged to a civilisation different from and inferior to that of the West. European political, intellectual, moral, and cultural power was spread in this way.[12] In the words of Reverend Carl Pfander, who was based in India, Christians were apparently 'superior in learning, in arts, in civilisation and in political power to all the other nations of the earth…Christianity will supersede all other religions and fill the whole world.'[13] While Europe was civilised, enlightened, and godly, Islam was perceived to be barbaric and its civilisation engulfed in darkness.[14]

The confrontation between Muslims and the British in pre-Mutiny India (1857) took on a religious dimension as Christian missions, 'representative of evangelical revivalism in its first and boundlessly confident phase of overseas activity', increased their activities.[15] With government support, missions were established throughout the country and the Bible was translated into several Indian languages. Supported by British funding, military power, and media propaganda, missionaries, according to Deedat, went all-out to demonstrate that Islam was a false religion. Deedat believed that Islam was as much under attack as it had been during the Crusades:

> The British realised that if anybody could give them trouble, it would be Muslims. That was because power and rule had already been tasted by Muslims. The Hindus, on the other hand, were as docile as the cows they were worshipping, so there was no fear from that quarter. The British wanted to convert Muslims so that they could rule India for a thousand years. So they started pouring in their missionaries, like frogs in the rainy season.[16]

Muslims countered missionary activity by publishing literature, delivering speeches in public spaces, opening religious schools, participating in the Mutiny of 1857 and, above all, debating with missionaries. These 'verbal, face-to-face interchanges' were termed munazara, an Urdu term commonly used in the nineteenth century to refer to religious debates. The term is derived from an Arabic word meaning 'to evaluate'.[17] Deedat told a reporter in 1987 that such debates did not take place in the formative years of the missionary presence in India, because Muslims

> did not know the English language and since they were only recently conquered by the British their militant views could send them to the dreaded Kala Pani [into exile across the sea, the 'black waters']. The Muslims kept themselves out of harm's way, by not debating religion. Then these missionaries started mastering our languages and started challenging Muslims to debate in their own language.[18]

The likes of Mawlana Kairanawi, Muhammad Qasim Nanautavi, Abul Mansoor, and Dr Wazir Khan countered with a vigorous intellectual defence of Islam. What is generally described as the 'greatest' munazara took place in Agra in 1854 between Mawlana Kairanawi and Reverend Carl Pfander, the pre-eminent Christian missionary in the Islamic world at that time. He was a Protestant missionary born in Germany, and proficient in spoken and written Arabic and Persian. Shortly after arriving in India in 1839 he translated his book on Islam, *Mizan-ul-Haq* [Balance of truth], into Urdu. The book remains, according to Powell, 'the single most provocative Christian contribution to Muslim–Christian polemical interchange'.[19] Pfander described Islam as 'a system of falsehood' and Muslims who rejected Christianity as liable to 'soon turn as a dog to his own vomit, and wallow afresh in the mire from which he has been washed'. Pfander was convinced that he would 'witness the conversion of the Islamic world in his own lifetime'.[20]

The setting for Pfander's confrontation with Muslim scholars was Agra, which had fallen into decline after the British conquest but was gradually regaining its economic and political importance. The Taj Mahal and Emperor Akbar's red sandstone fort were evocative reminders of past Mughal glories. In 1837 a drought which led to half a million deaths triggered large-scale missionary activity in the guise of relief societies. The Mughal tomb close to Emperor Akbar's mausoleum in Sikandra was used as an orphanage for boys, and around sixty Hindu and Muslim boys were converted to Christianity. Pfander was sent to Agra in 1841, and began distributing *Mizan-ul-Haq* to the 'ulama and 'respectable native residents' such as Professor Nur al-Hasan of the Anglo-Oriental College; Sir Sayyid Ahmad Khan, then a rising star in the British East India Company and founder of the Aligarh Muslim University; and Kazim Ali, sajjada nashin (keeper) of the tomb of Shaykh Salim Chisti at Fatehpur.[21]

Pfander had thrown down the gauntlet. Muslim scholars began studying Arabic and Persian copies of the Bible that had been translated by Henry Martyn, as well as Bible criticism written by various Christian theologians.[22] However, there was no comprehensive refutation of *Mizan-ul-Haq* until the emergence of Mawlana Kairanawi.[23]

Mawlana Kairanawi (1818–1891) was one of the outstanding scholars of his generation. He studied under his father, Mawlana Khalil Ahmed, until he was twelve, and then with such great scholars as Mawlana Muhammad Hayat and Shah Abd al-Ghani in Delhi and Lucknow. He challenged Pfander to a munazara, which took place on 10 April 1854 at the Agra bazaar. Mawlana Kairanawi was the first member of the 'ulama fraternity to make extensive use of contemporary biblical criticism by Richard Mant, Thomas Horne, Richard Wilson, and Thomas Scott.[24]

Newspaper editors, 'ulama, and prominent Muslims attended the munazara, as did high-ranking diplomats and dignitaries such as Sir William Muir, Secretary to the Indian Government; Mosley Smith, a judge at the Sadr Court (a high court in British and Mughal India); George Christian, Secretary to the Sadr Board of Revenue; local missionaries such as T.G. Clark of the Free Church of Scotland Missionary Society; Mufti Riyaz al-Din, the Chief Mufti of Agra; Mawlana Muhammad Asadullah, the Chief Qadi ; and Mawlana Qamar al-Islam, Chief Imam of the Jami' Mosque in Agra. In the build-up to the munazara, Mawlana Kairanawi boldly promised to convert to Christianity if he failed to respond satisfactorily to Pfander. The debate was to cover five subjects: naskh (abrogation) and tahrif (corruption) of the Bible, taslis (the Trinity), risalat-i-la Muhammad (the prophethood of Muhammad, PBUH), and, finally, the Qur'an.

In his opening argument Mawlana Kairanawi got the Reverend Pfander to admit that he had misrepresented the Qur'anic view of the abrogation of the Bible in his works, thus immediately 'reducing his credibility in the eyes of the audience'. He then drew upon the works of George D'Oyly and Richard Mant to argue the possibility of the abrogation of the Bible. When Pfander asked Mawlana Kairanawi, who was assisted by Dr Wazir Khan, to show him any passage in the extant editions of the Gospels that was not present in original manuscripts, they pointed to verse seven of the fifth chapter of John's first epistle.[25] According to reports, pandemonium broke out among the audience. Pfander insisted that this 'small alteration does not affect the Holy Book of the Heavens!', to which the mawlana replied, 'Since you admit that the Bible has been altered in seven or eight places, how can you claim that it is true and how can you believe in it?' Local newspapers immediately published Pfander's 'admittance' and forecast 'impending victory'.

The following day Pfander tried to use Qur'anic verses to prove that the Bible in circulation at the time of the Prophet (PBUH) was authentic. Mawlana Kairanawi contested this so Pfander refused to continue the munazara. Muslims claimed a victory.[26] Reverend Pfander's transfer to Peshawar fuelled speculation that he wanted to avoid another munazara. According to British Muslim scholar Abdur Rahim Green:

> the Kairanawi–Pfander debate came at a time when Muslims needed the intellectual spark to defeat the Christian missionaries on their own home turf, that is, the Bible. [It] changed the landscape of Christian missionary attitudes towards Muslims especially in the Indian subcontinent with a much wider impact on the world too in the 19th century and early part of 20th century.[27]

Some Muslim commentators have argued that this debate was partly responsible for the brutality of British aggression against Muslims during the 1857 Mutiny, during which many Muslim scholars were killed. Mawlana Kairanawi was placed at the top of the British army's 'most wanted' list. He was forced into hijra (migration) and made his way to Makkah where he established the Madrasa Saulatia, while his family's estates in Kairana and Panipat were confiscated by the British. His magnum opus, *Izhar-ul-Haq*, was published in 1864 and translated into six European languages. The book argued that the Bible was not God's word because it was factually incorrect, inconsistent, textually arbitrary, and historically inaccurate.[28]

---

Deedat told a reporter in 1990 that he had been 'very impressed' and 'overawed' by the book's logical argument. 'This particular book seemed to be the answer to my own frustrating situation. I went through it in detail. I read about Matthew, Mark, John, and how one commentary contradicted the other.' On his next visit to Durban, Deedat purchased a copy of the New Testament.[29] G.H. Agjee, Deedat's nephew and a founding member of the IPCI, recalled that Deedat highlighted contradictions in the Bible in crayons of various shades, and simultaneously recorded these on thumb cards which he studied intensely. Armed with this knowledge Deedat began challenging seminary students at Adams Mission. In his words, he 'went on the offensive' and 'confused' them with awkward questions. He would even visit students in their living quarters to engage in debate. As he would later point out, the students learnt that if they 'gave one blow against my religion I would give ten. That's the only mentality I had as a young man. This became my hobby and pastime. It was pleasing to see that what they did to me, I was able to do to them.'³⁰ Deedat wrote in *Is the Bible God's Word?*:

> *Izhar-ul-Haq* was the turning point in my life. I was able to invite the trainee missionaries of Adams Mission College and cause them to perspire under the collar until they developed a respect for Islam and its Holy Apostle. It made me ponder as to how so many unwary Muslims are being constantly assaulted by Christian evangelists who carry out a door-to-door campaign, and being invited in by the proverbially hospitable Muslim. I thought of how the merciless missionary munched the samoosas and punched the wind out of the Muslim with snide remarks against his beliefs. Determined to bring home to Muslims their right to defend themselves and to arm them with enough knowledge to counter the hot gospeller, the door-to-door pedlar of Christianity…I humbly undertook to deliver lectures to show the Muslim masses that they had nothing to fear from the assaults of the Christians.

As his confidence grew, Deedat sought out 'bigger debates'. When he visited Durban on weekends, he would 'go around looking for churches and debate with the church fathers'. Deedat thrived on these exchanges and took advantage of every opportunity to 'stump' Christians.³¹ He developed his debating skills and deepened his knowledge of Christianity through these exchanges. Deedat's contemporaries, such as G.H. Agjee and his half-brother, Abdullah Deedat, observed that he had a 'passion' for debate and thrived on stage. When asked what drew Deedat into a life of public debate and teaching, Ebi Lockhat commented that 'it was his love for debate, because if you analyse him, he loved debating from school, from learning other people's speech, to acting in plays. He told me that he even boxed at one stage.'

Deedat would become a transnational figure in his late sixties. Before then, his travels took him from a remote village on the Indian subcontinent to the tip of Africa, to various parts of rural Natal, back to the subcontinent shortly after his 'homeland' was partitioned, and returned him to Africa following his disillusionment with Pakistan. His 'greatness', folklore has it, was predestined.

## 4

# THE BEGGAR'S PREDICTION

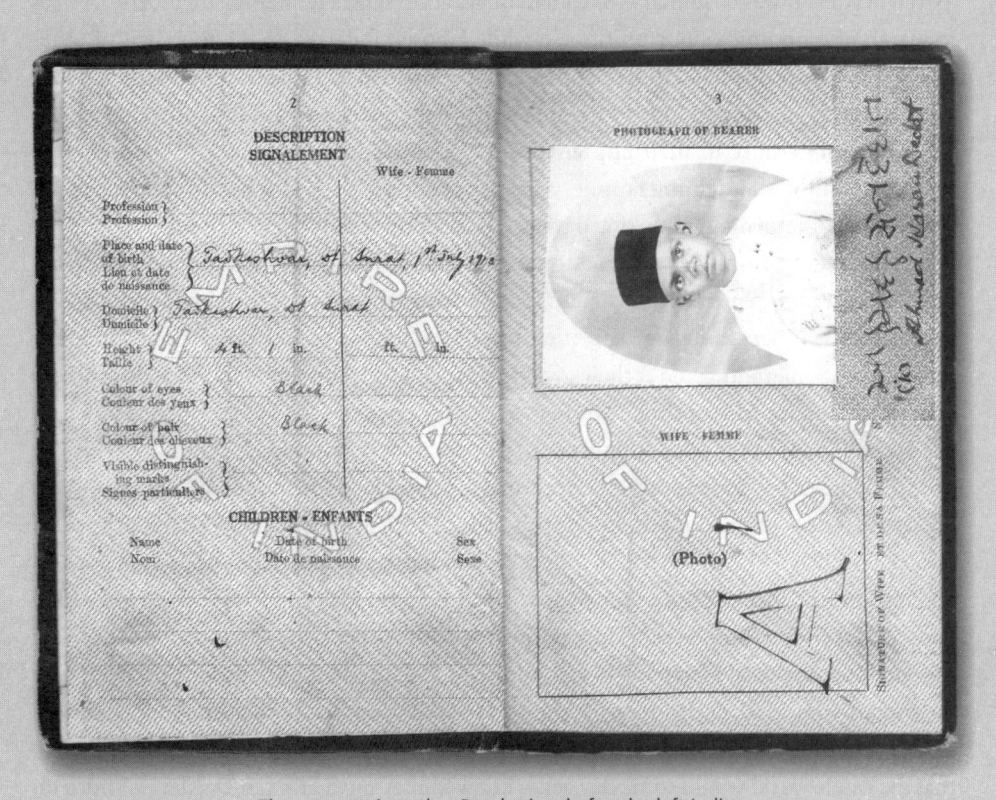

The passport issued to Deedat just before he left India.

Life means a passionate burning, an urge to make,
To cast in the dead clay the seed of heart.

– Allama Iqbal

FATHIMA DEEDAT was pregnant with her second child in 1917 when her husband Hoosen left her and their daughter Rassool in the village of Tadkeshwar, Gujarat, and went in search of greener pastures. This was the year of the Bolshevik Revolution in Russia but the British continued to believe that their rule over India would be permanent and drained the colony economically. Many of the villagers of Gujarat made their way to South Africa where, they were led to believe, the streets were literally 'paved in gold'. It was customary for Indian migrants to send a few family members overseas in search of economic opportunities. So while Hoosen followed in the footsteps of other villagers, his elder brothers Ahmed and Suleman remained in Tadkeshwar with their father Cassim. It was also common for migrants to leave their wives and children behind on the subcontinent because of their apprehensions about settling in a new environment, the financial costs of maintaining families with uncertain incomes, and because most held on to the myth of returning home one day even though this rarely materialised.

Indentured labourers were introduced into Natal in 1860 to work mainly on the sugar plantations. Entrepreneurs from Gujarat followed from the early 1870s. Some sailed straight to Natal while others came via Mauritius and Mozambique. Unlike indentured labourers, these Gujarati migrants came at their own expense and were initially subject to the ordinary laws of the colony. Migrants like Hoosen were a far cry from the large traders and barely eked out their livings as sales attendants.

With Hoosen having left, Fathima worked as a cleaner for affluent members of her village. She washed dishes and clothing in return for meals. According to Ahmed Deedat's friend and fellow villager, Yakoob Mehtar, village legend has it that one day just as Fathima was about to eat the meal that was her wage for a day's labour, a crippled beggar approached and asked for something to eat. Though pregnant and hungry, she spontaneously gave her meal to him. A few days later, the beggar returned and repeated his request. She again gave her food to him, washed the utensils, and this time also washed his clothes because he was unable to use his hands. The beggar told her that the child in her womb would be a boy, and that the whole world would some day get to know him. Ahmed Hoosen Deedat was born on 1 July 1918. Soothsaying and fortune telling are not part of the Islamic belief system, and the beggar's statement may have been more of a prayer offered for Fathima in exchange for her kindness to him, but Yakoob Mehtar's mother shared the story with him in about 1945 when he returned home from work one day and told her that he had befriended Ahmed Deedat, a gaam waaro (a Gujarati term that means 'fellow villager' and implies an unusual degree of affinity). Several variations on the legend circulate in Durban. For example, Ebi Lockhat, who worked for the IPCI in the early 1990s, remembers being told that

> Deedat's mother, because they were living in subsistence in India, when she was pregnant, she used to take on dhobi work, laundry. And there was an out-of-work or one of these kind of guys that nobody will look at, so when she washed his clothes he predicted that she was carrying a son that was going to do something great. That's the story told to me.

Although the details surrounding the legend remain a mystery, the poverty Deedat experienced as a child is well known. Ebi Lockhat recalled Deedat telling him that as a child 'we sat on the ground, we ate on the ground. We were so poor that I didn't know that you didn't normally do that.' Deedat related that he would have 'rice and tea for lunch and supper if he was lucky, and he would mix it'. In the decades that followed, Yakoob Mehtar and many others witnessed Deedat's incredible journey from being an unknown furniture salesman to becoming a renowned figure in the Muslim world.

While Fathima Deedat remained in Tadkeshwar with her children, her husband Hoosen began his immigrant life in Durban working for a local Muslim trader. He subsequently opened a small sewing business in Madressah Arcade, next to the Jumu'ah Mosque in Grey Street in the heart of the 'Indian quarter'. A.S. Ballim, Deedat's neighbour in Saville Street for several years and a founding member of the Arabic Study Circle, recalls that Hoosen 'was very poor and had a small repair shop, mending torn clothes for his mainly African clientele'. He spent his last years working in Overport for Reunion Clothing Manufacturers. Yakoob Mehtar, Ebrahim Jadwat, Ismail Manjra, Moosa Paruk, and others described Hoosen Deedat as 'down-to-earth', 'hardworking', and 'not overly ambitious or given to material advancement'. He was content to earn just enough to support his family. In local parlance he was a 'battler'.

---

Ahmed Deedat spent the first nine years of his life in Tadkeshwar with his mother and sister, whom he remembered as 'very nice and warm-hearted'.[1] The absence of his father clearly impacted on him, and he remembered running away from school almost daily by jumping out of the classroom window onto a rubbish heap, and making his way home.[2]

His mother struggled to make ends meet, so much so that her son was eight years old before she was able to afford the one rupee required by a professional barber from a neighbouring village for Deedat's khatna (circumcision). Deedat had a clear recollection of this painful procedure years later when he laughingly related to a reporter, at the ripe old age of seventy-five, how the barber would distract the boys from the pain by telling them to look at a non-existent 'golden bird' at the crucial moment. He added with a wince that it did not work.[3]

Deedat was nine when his father sent word instructing Ahmed to join him in Durban. He, with a group of village boys of roughly similar age, duly left Tadkeshwar and made the exhausting journey by ship in the company of a distant relative, a Mr Rawat, whom the boys referred to as 'Uncle'. Deedat's mother passed away nine months after his departure.

Deedat lived with his father in a hostel for Muslim bachelors in central Durban's Prince Edward Street (now Dr Goonam Street).[4] He spoke about these early days to Ebi Lockhat:

> His father brought him to South Africa with the intention of bringing his mother later…His father held his hand when he got off the docks and said, 'We'll take the bus.' He assumed that the bus belonged to his father because he said he hadn't seen that

kind of bus before – it was a double-decker, probably a tram. He was brought somewhere in the Prince Edward Street area to a Musafir Khana and he stayed there with his father. He used to think quite often about his mother until one day he got the message that she had passed away and for many months after that he used to dream about her and think about her. He said that they would look for the *Karanja*, which was [a] very famous [ship] in those days. If a naval ship came they would walk to the harbour to view it because it meant a good meal, that's what they would do on Sundays.

Some time after the death of his wife in India, Hoosen Deedat married Hamida Parkar, the daughter of Shaykh Ally Ismail Parkar. They had four sons, Mohamed, Abdullah, Cassim and Umar, and six daughters Bhen Goree, Amina, Rabia, Zubeida, Halima, and Khadija.

The Deedat household was fairly religious. According to Yakoob Mehtar, Hoosen Deedat belonged to an informal grouping known as Aashike Rasool, literally meaning 'Lovers of the Prophet (PBUH)'. Hoosen's contemporaries regarded him as 'fervent' in his love for the Prophet (PBUH) and his defence of a populist expression of Islam that emphasised celebration of urs (death anniversaries of various saints), the birth of the Prophet (PBUH), and the offering of communal salutations. A.S. Ballim recalls that Hoosen Deedat 'was engrossed in Aashike Rasool, and it was well known that he would cry whenever the Prophet's name was mentioned'.

Hoosen Deedat in his later years.

---

Deedat did not know a word of English when he arrived in South Africa but he had a flair for languages and quickly mastered English. He attended the Crescent Islamic School in Pine Street. G.M. Randeree, who attended the school in the 1920s and 1930s, recalled that they 'were taught Arabic, Urdu, Gujarati, and elementary English. The focus was the Qur'an and Sunnah, with a little secular education'. Deedat transferred to the Hindu Tamil Institute a year later and from there went to the Higher Grade School in Carlisle Street.

Deedat struggled during his initial period of schooling. Years later he recalled a history examination at the Hindu Tamil Institute in which he encountered the question, 'What are the aboriginal races of South Africa?' He answered 'horse race, dog race, and donkey race'. Not surprisingly, he scored the lowest mark in the class, but he soon impressed teachers with his avid reading and quick mind. By the time Deedat reached Standard 4, he was the most fluent reader in his class and scored the highest marks in mathematics, poetry, history, and drawing. When he finished first in the mid-year examinations, he was immediately promoted to Standard 5. By the end of that year he was again top of his class. This prompted his father's friend Ahmed Mukhtar, an Imam at the Grey Street Mosque, to praise Deedat in the presence of an affluent visitor who promised that if Deedat passed Standard 6 he would pay his tuition fees at Sastri College.[5]

The Deedats had moved to Cato Manor after Hoosen remarried. Hoosen Deedat could not afford the two-penny bus fare to Carlisle Street, so Ahmed Deedat walked to and from school each day. He sometimes arrived at school on an empty stomach and, when students were required to stand in class, he sometimes felt dizzy and would inhale and exhale deeply to avoid fainting. He was asked to leave school several times because of his father's inability to pay fees and purchase books. This problem was temporarily resolved when Deedat found work as an 'errand boy' for teachers at Sastri College. During the lunch break, he would collect food from the Sastri College hostel and deliver it to the Indian teachers at the school. In the evenings he would again collect food from the hostel and deliver it to the homes of some of these teachers.[6]

Despite his personal difficulties, Deedat excelled in his final year of primary school and gained admission to Sastri College, which, at the time, was the only high school for Indian children in South Africa. Finding the money for fees was a problem, though, so Deedat visited the businessman who had promised to sponsor him. The offer never materialised, however, and Deedat had to abandon high school after three days, his dream of a solid education abruptly shattered.[7] He told Ebrahim Jadwat of his educational struggles:

> Most important – and I think this is the inspiration for youth – he discovered the Gandhi Library and this library was his pastime. For his age, he was very highly read because he was reading books on subjects that were beyond his years. And that's what improved his English, and gave him those double promotions. So, although when he came here at the age of nine, he started school later than the others, he surpassed them with a series of those double promotions. When he went to high school his father couldn't afford the fees and that's where this love for reading helped his self-education. He had an immense power of concentration.

Deedat did not have much time to grieve over his fate. Soon after he left school, his family moved from Cato Manor to Saville Street in central Durban. His new neighbours included A.S. Ballim[8] and Hafidh Goolam Darjee, who had an important influence on Deedat and whose son, Yusuf Ally, was pivotal in Deedat's later life. Deedat began working at a café on Durban's Umgeni Road in return for meals and a place to sleep. For the next decade he lived a nomadic life, travelling to various parts of the country in search of secure employment.

After leaving Durban, his first stop was Waschbank in Northern Natal, where he secured a job with the Mall family. Waschbank is located at the hub of Natal's coal industry. The mines at Dundee, Waschbank, Elandslaagte, and Talana employed large numbers of Indian and African workers. Saleh Mall arrived in Natal in the late 1880s and established the firm of S.I. Mall where Deedat obtained work. His starting salary was £2.10 per month but he worked so hard that his employer soon doubled this amount.[9]

After some time, Deedat became homesick and returned to Durban. After a few months he met a businessman who offered him a job in Greylingstad, a small farming town west of Standerton in present-day Mpumalanga. Deedat made the long journey to Greylingstad with the businessman. But when it was time to claim his salary, he was told that he would not be paid because he did not speak Afrikaans. Deedat pointed out that his employer was aware of this prior to employing him. The employer then changed their verbal contract, and insisted that the agreement had been that Deedat would tutor his children. Deedat explained that he had begun teaching the children volutarily during his spare time. In the end, he was never paid but was given a one-way third-class train ticket to Johannesburg. Deedat did not reveal the name of this businessman to avoid embarrassing the man's family.

In Johannesburg, Deedat moved in with a friend from Durban, Hyder Khan, who stayed in a ramshackle backroom and worked as a tailor. Deedat approached the well-known 'Maulvi' Mia for a job. The maulvi asked Deedat if he was married or engaged. When he replied 'neither', the maulvi advised him in Gujarati: Namaaz paro karo; kaam tayjaahe ('Keep praying, you'll find work'). A few weeks passed and, with his job prospects no brighter, Deedat swallowed his pride and visited the maulvi again. This time, Maulvi Mia offered him food and accommodation in his staff quarters, and a few days later sent him to the retail firm of A.M. Desai where he was given a job and paid £6 per month.

Deedat's good fortune came to an abrupt end after about six months when his boss was away in Durban. A tall white 'customer' walked in and began firing questions at Deedat: 'Where are you from?' 'Greylingstad.' 'And before that?' 'Durban.' 'Where's your permit?' Deedat responded that he did not know what a permit was. At that the stranger revealed that he was an immigration inspector and said Deedat had to accompany him to the police station in Market Square. At that time, Indians required special permission to enter the Transvaal – a law that remained in place until the 1970s. Deedat stalled the man, saying that he could not leave the shop as his boss was away, but promised to meet the inspector the following day when Mr Desai returned. As soon as the man left, Deedat left for Natal to avoid imprisonment.

Deedat's next port of call was Greytown in Natal, where Muslim traders had settled from the 1890s. Deedat worked at M.E. Lakhi, a shop on the corner of York and Bell Streets. The owner, M.E. Lakhi, who was originally from Panoli, had arrived in 1883. Deedat spent several years with Lakhi. Working for Lakhi and for S.I. Mall, two of the most prominent Indian businessmen in Natal, helped Deedat develop his skills as a salesperson. Later in life, he referred to Lakhi and Mall's businesses as 'universities of commercial trade' and spoke proudly of having graduated from both. Keen for a new challenge, he then accepted a job as a shop assistant at O.N. Mohamed, the general dealer at Adams Mission, south of Durban. It was at the mission that his life took an unexpected turn, as shown in the previous chapter. Deedat described these early days to Baboo Jadwat:

He said he spent a lot of time reading and just doing a ritualised Islam [with] no interest in religion until he started working. Deedat was a counter hand, and there was a big demand for such people's services in the farm stores, and that is where Ahmed Deedat started off.

While living at Adams Mission, Deedat would visit Durban on his weekends off where he made a point of attending gatherings of the Kemal Study Group with his close friend Ahmed Hoosen Lutchka. During one of these visits, Lutchka implored: 'You're wasting your time there – why don't you come and work here in Durban?' Lutchka felt that Deedat's career prospects would improve in Durban and suggested that he approach Mr Moosa of Simplex Furniture who was from the same village as Deedat. These common origins carried a lot of weight when it came to employment. Lutchka insisted that Deedat remain in Durban, assuring him that if he did not get a job, he (Lutchka) would assist him to make a start as a fruit and vegetable hawker.

Deedat heeded Lutchka's advice. He visited Hafidh Amod Haffejee Moosa the following day. Moosa had arrived in Natal in 1892 and established A. H. Moosa & Sons in Commercial Road. He and his sons, Ismail, Mohammed, and Moosa, laid the foundations of what was to become a significant business empire. On meeting Deedat, Hafidh Moosa's immediate reaction was that there were no jobs available. Deedat appealed that he would do 'anything', even sweep, for a living. Hafidh Moosa queried whether he could drive. Deedat replied in the negative but said that he was a quick learner. Impressed by the young man's determination, Hafidh Moosa sent Deedat to his son-in-law, Goolam Agjee, the manager of one of his businesses, to help him get a licence. Deedat soon obtained a learner's licence and landed a job as a driver.

Abdul Kadir Saleh Mall.                    Mahomed Ebrahim Lakhi.

The Simplex Furniture Factory in Durban, where Deedat worked during the 1940s, rising from driver to dispatch clerk, salesman, and finally to branch manager.

One of his new colleagues was Yakoob Mehtar, who remembers:

> The building of the Simplex Furniture Factory was a big warehouse in which there was a furniture showroom. Ahmed Deedat used to organise the dispatches. Whatever goods were sold had to be delivered. He used to be at the door and at lunchtime he would lock up, open again at two o'clock; and at five o'clock, close and take the key home. He was solely responsible for this door. He was given this responsibility because he was an honest man and the boss realised that with him holding the door key, there will be no pilfering.

Deedat soon qualified as a driver and was later promoted to lorry driver, then dispatch clerk, clerk, salesman and, finally, branch manager. Yakoob Mehtar's first encounter with Deedat was in the canteen. When Deedat discovered that Yakoob was the son of Chota Mehtar, Deedat told him that when he had arrived in Natal, migrants from Tadkeshwar would meet every Sunday at Chota Mehtar's home in Queen Street to share village folktales and the latest news from their village. Yakoob excitedly related this to his mother who affirmed the story. What had stuck in Mrs Mehtar's mind, though, was the fondness that Hoosen Deedat had displayed for the young Ahmed at these meetings. Although Ahmed Deedat was a 'big strapping boy', his father would sit him on his lap and tell others proudly that 'my boy' carries the Prophet's name.

Yakoob Mehtar invited Deedat home for lunch and they formed a lifelong friendship. Mehtar recalled that Deedat was a keen 'physical culturalist', as weightlifters were called. At five o'clock each evening he would go to Jackie Naidoo's gymnasium in Victoria Street near the Indian Market. Deedat was tall and strong, and took great care of his health. Deedat was also keen on spreading the message of Islam. His first convert was fellow worker Dedan Bhengu. Yakoob Mehtar mentioned that Deedat would 'get stuck into anyone, whether at home, work, or gym'. Deedat spent his own money to print cards about Islam in Zulu. A few have survived and can be viewed at the IPCI archives. They state his home address: 45 Hoosen's Building, Queen Street, Durban, and phone number.

Although he initially held relatively lowly positions at Simplex, Deedat never kowtowed to management. Yakoob Mehtar remembers that one day Deedat told his manager that he might be slightly late in returning from his lunch break as he required a haircut. When Deedat returned, the company's boss happened to be standing in the dispatch area and asked him why he was late. When Deedat told him that he had obtained permission from his manager, the boss said furiously: 'Deedat, don't cut your hair in my time.' Deedat responded, 'But my hair grows in your time!' Ebi Lockhat remembers hearing a slight variation on the same tale many years later:

> One day I was having lunch and a gentleman walked into Deedat's office [at the IPCI], a white-haired Asian gentleman. He promptly pulled up a chair and opened a lunchbox and started eating. So, in my diplomatic way I asked him if I could help him and just as abruptly he said, 'No, you can't, I'm waiting for Ahmed'. A few minutes later when Deedat walked in, there was a warm embrace. They sat down and started talking and sharing their sandwiches. I asked Mr Vawda, which was his name, 'Was Mr Deedat always like this, argumentative, etc?' So he said to me in Deedat's presence, 'You know this Ahmed, he's always been like this. Both of us worked at Simplex. He was the driver and I worked in dispatch. In those days we had very strict bosses. There was a Mr Moosa in charge of us and Deedat said to me that he was going to ask him for time to have a haircut. Deedat goes to this office and says that he wants to go for a haircut and Mr Moosa roars, "What's wrong with you people. Why don't you have a haircut in your time?" Deedat answered on the turn, "because the hair grew in your time". That was the type of sharpness Deedat showed at an early age.'

> One day he explained that in one of the places that he worked, somewhere in Northern Natal, there was a practice and it happens until today. During the month of Ramadan when people come for collection – the Muslim community, they're good givers – but instead of telling a person, 'I've already given,' if they see somebody coming in and they can't help the guy, they point to a staff member and say, 'Go and speak to him, he's the boss.' And it's an unspoken language: nobody says 'I'm not the boss.' They listen to the guy's story, open a book and [say], 'Sorry, all's given.' [The boss] uses him as the send-off. So Deedat tells me this was really getting on his nerves…and he decided to put a stop to it. So I asked, 'Uncle, how did you do that?' He says, 'Well, a group of guys walked in. The boss pointed to me and said, that's the boss, go and see him. I took one look at the guy's book and then looked back at my boss and said, "Give him £5, give him £5, open the till and give him the money". The boss had to give the money. He couldn't tell them now that he was the boss.' He never sent anyone to Ahmed Deedat again.

Hawa Gangat became Deedat's devoted and lifelong companion.

With a steady job and decent income at Simplex, Deedat actively pursued marriage. It is common knowledge in Deedat's circles that he was turned down by thirty-three prospective fathers-in-law before Suleman Gangat of Glendale in Northern Natal accepted his proposal for his daughter, Hawa. The first time Deedat set eyes on Hawa, she had entered the room for a few moments only, carrying a tray of tea and treats and left almost immediately, in keeping with tradition. For Deedat, it was not a case of love at first sight, and he had to be persuaded to go ahead with his proposal by Mohamed Essack Noorgat of Stanger, a mutual family friend and 'go-between', who had accompanied him to the Gangat household.

Like the Deedats and Gangats, Noorgat was also from Tadkeshwar. The prospect of bringing together two young villagers was too good an opportunity to miss. Noorgat was adamant that Hawa was the perfect match for Deedat and implored him to propose. Deedat accepted Noorgat's counsel. It was a decision he did not regret, as the marriage was an extremely happy one. During interviews, Hawa Deedat often spoke of her husband's gentle nature and generosity. She fondly related how he would offer to buy her anything she admired and would eat whatever she cooked without complaining. She even chose his clothing since he was reluctant to 'waste' money. These insights offer a window into a side of Deedat far removed from his tough-talking public persona.

Their son, Yousuf, recalled that his mother 'never ate alone'. And when Deedat spoke at public meetings, she would sit in the front row even though she did not follow a word because she did not speak English. We would have supper afterwards and he would ask 'How was my lecture?' 'Very good. Excellent,' she would say. 'What part did you find interesting?' he would ask, smiling. 'Why don't you keep quiet and eat the food?' she would respond. Deedat's nephew, G.H. Agjee, often visited the newly married couple at their apartment to read his uncle's books and remembers well the affection that the couple showed for one another.

It was perhaps in the years following Deedat's stroke that the love 'Ma', as Hawa was fondly called, had for her husband and her sense of loyalty to him was most evident. Visitors recalled Hawa at Deedat's side, wiping his mouth or straightening his pillows. She spent much of the nine-year period after his stroke sleeping on a couch at the foot of his bed, with the cats that she so adored as company. Visitors were warmly welcomed at the door and invited in with grace and hospitality.[10] After a visit to Verulam, Deedat's longtime friend

Deedat's close family members all remember his gentle and generous nature, far removed from his tough-talking public persona.

Saleh Mohamed of Cape Town wrote to him on 29 August 1997:

> I really have lots of admiration for Aunty's dedication. I attribute your good health to her caring and devotion. May the Almighty reward her for all that she is doing.... When you indicated that should you resign [from the IPCI] ... '[must I] live on fresh air?' I was taken aback by Aunty's comment that Allah will provide and that she would even sell her jewellery in order to come by. It definitely shows the amount of confidence instilled in her, something which you've always praised her for. The backbone of the Deedat Family, no doubt, even in times like these!

Deedat and Hawa had two sons, Ebrahim and Yousuf, and a daughter, Ruqayyah. Ebrahim was born in 1945, Ruqayyah in 1946, and Yousuf in 1953. Ruqayyah married Mohammed Akoon in June 1971, and they had a daughter Sumayyah, born in 1973. Ruqayyah and Akoon's troubled marriage ended in divorce in 1978, and Ruqayyah succumbed to cancer two years later. Ahmed and Hawa legally adopted Sumayyah when she was six years old. In later years, they took Sumayyah on various overseas trips, which is how she met Essam Mudeer, son of a Jeddah businessman, who was a regular at Deedat's lectures and got to know the Deedat family personally. Sumayyah and Mudeer were engaged in Verulam in November 1993 and married on 29 January 1994.[11]

Deedat's eldest son Ebrahim was described as a 'genius' by Jamaluddin Ahmed. 'He was brilliant and could have been anything.' Saleh pointed out that as a child Ebrahim 'yearned to be like his father. He would walk like uncle [Deedat], sit like him, and talk like him.' He wanted to be a photographer and went to study in Cape Town at the age of eighteen. After his return to Durban and a troubled marriage, Ebrahim experienced serious health problems and was institutionalised for a while. He died from a snake bite in October 2011 while visiting his daughter and newly born grandson in Pakistan. Deedat's younger son Yousuf features prominently in this story, and enters the discussion at various points.

Throughout his early years, though, Ahmed Deedat was restless and searching for his life's mission.

# 5

# PAKKA MUSALMAN

Deedat in Karachi; believing it would become a model Muslim state, Deedat and his family emigrated to Pakistan in 1949.

The formation of a consolidated North-Western Indian Muslim State appears to me to be the final destiny of the Muslims at least of north-west India. We are 70 million, and far more homogenous than any other people in India. Indeed, the Muslims of India are the only Indian people who can fitly be described as a nation in the modern sense of the word.

– Allama Iqbal, 1930

DEEDAT WAS PASSIONATE about all forms of knowledge, and was fortunate that his position at Simplex allowed him to enrol for various short courses. The first of these was in radio servicing, which he found himself failing. Shocked by this, his first experience of failure, and attributing it to the fact that he had not done his homework, Deedat hunkered down and put together a regimen of long hours of study. The following year he passed all four examinations and was one of only three students to pass engineering drawing. Deedat also attended a Dale Carnegie course on public speaking that stood him in good stead in future years. Tests preceding that course revealed that he had an extraordinary memory, which explains how he was able to remember and profusely quote chapters and verses from the Bible.

Deedat delivered his first public lecture, 'Muhammad: the Messenger of Peace', at the Avalon Theatre in Durban in the early 1940s under the banner of the Kemal Study Group. The lecture went off smoothly and was well received by the mainly Muslim audience. Deedat's wife Hawa was shocked to see her husband on stage: 'I thought, can this man talk?' Deedat's half-brother Mohamed was among those present at the first lecture:

> The pride started with Ahmed Deedat when I was a boy of twelve, then he gave his first lecture in a cinema known as Avalon in the year 1939 or 1940. I was very, very proud of him – every lecture, wherever, I was always present there. Many Muslims, Indian Muslims of Durban, objected to Ahmed Deedat [saying] that he should not discuss religion and bring friction between Christians and Muslims. They even asked Ahmed Deedat, 'Ahmed, Stop this, let's not be enemies, please don't go on the platform.' A.I. Kajee and many other Muslims told him, 'We will go and tell them that you are young and your blood is hot and you just got on to the stage to say something but you found that you cannot do it, so please step down.' But Ahmed Deedat says, 'No, I will do what I want to do.'[1]

Deedat's energy impressed members of the Theosophical Society in the audience who invited him to speak at a seminar hosted by the society. He accepted the invitation and spoke on 'What the Bible Says about Muhammad'. By his own admission the lecture was a 'damp squib' because he had chosen the wrong topic for an audience that was more interested in the philosophy of religion than the Bible. Despite his misgivings, the society extended another invitation to Deedat a few months later. This time he spoke on 'Reincarnation: Fact or Fiction', and described the second lecture as a 'stupendous success'.

Deedat prepared meticulously for his public lectures. According to Mustacq Saleh of Cape Town, whose family worked closely with Deedat, he used colleagues and friends as 'punch bags', discussing topics with them, sharing ideas and gauging their reaction to assess how the public might receive the lecture and the kinds of questions that could be posed. Dr G.M. Hoosen remembers that 'Deedat would practise his talks on me. He put a lot of effort into it. Whenever he got a chance, he grabbed people to practise. He was totally focused. He was highly motivated and nothing could stop him once he decided to do something.'

A.S. Moola recalled that travelling with Deedat could seem like 'an examination' as he would pose a barrage of questions and bounce his ideas around. Hawa Deedat noted that her husband 'used to lecture in the house a lot and I used to complain, "You're making a lot of noise, you're a very noisy man."'

According to Moola when Deedat lectured in Ladysmith, he would send 'two hundred posters even though there were only a hundred poles in the town. He would arrive four or five hours early, check that all the posters were up, the sound system was adequate, the stage was to his satisfaction, and so on.' Contrary to what one might expect, Deedat often became nervous before a debate. According to Saleh he would recite verses of the Qur'an to calm him down and allow him to concentrate. Shafa'at Khan pointed out that Deedat always carried around little thumbcards, containing quotations from the Qur'an and the Bible, which he studied in his spare time.

Eager to learn, Deedat soon developed a desire to teach. When he could not find anyone to teach Arabic, he acquired a book on Egyptian Arabic and formed a class that he taught after the nightly 'isha prayer. By teaching, he felt, he was also learning. He soon tired of teaching and convinced a senior figure from within the Kemal Study Group to take over. One evening the teacher did not turn up. The group waited for a while before deciding to go home, and were surprised to run into the teacher returning from the cinema. The incident affected Deedat, who later said that it had 'really broken my spirit'. The Arabic lessons ceased shortly thereafter.

Meanwhile Deedat had been following the anti-colonial struggle in India with increasing interest through the 1940s. When Pakistan was created, he decided, with his friend Ahmed Lutchka, to emigrate to Pakistan to become a 'pakka musalman' (Urdu for 'proper Muslim'). Pakistan was established as a state on 14 August 1947 as one of the two parts of the partitioned British India. In 1930 the poet and philosopher Sir Allamah Iqbal first mooted the idea of an independent Muslim state while Muhammad Ali Jinnah, Pakistan's first governor-general, convinced the Muslim League to adopt the Lahore Resolution of 1940 that espoused the two-nation theory. Jinnah, who is revered as Pakistan's Quaid-e-Azam (great leader), was an inspiration to many Indian Muslims because of his role in ending colonial rule in India and Pakistan. Deedat regarded Jinnah as his hero but never saw him in person as Jinnah died before Deedat settled in Pakistan.

Deedat moved to Pakistan because he wanted to live in an Islamic state. He told a journalist in 1987 that during the 1940s he had engaged in many debates with Muslim members of the Natal Indian Congress (NIC) who worshipped communist 'Russia as their hero and thought of Pakistan as a mad man's dream. But I was convinced that Pakistan would be achieved and would be a stronghold for Muslims – a place where a Muslim could practise his way of life far more easily.'[2]

When Deedat announced his impending emigration, he was warned that the cost of living would be prohibitive and that he would struggle financially. He replied that if he could not find accommodation, he would live in a tent. He suggested to Hawa that she remain in South Africa until he found a suitable job but she insisted on accompanying him. Deedat prepared for the move months in advance. Earning an income was his first priority and he considered various ways to do this. He owned a typewriter and was an efficient typist, and considered acting as an agent for South African companies in Pakistan. He wrote to potential partners in South Africa and to businesses in Pakistan, but to no avail.

Nevertheless, in March 1949, Deedat and Hawa boarded a ship to Pakistan with Ebrahim and Ruqayyah, who were four and three years old respectively. The Deedats were accompanied by Deedat's friend Ahmed Lutchka (father of future IPCI trustee, Dr G.M. Hoosen) and his family. G.M. Hoosen was ten when they made the voyage and remembers the journey by ship as a nightmare. Short of money, the two families went as 'deck passengers' in the cargo hold. There each family was entitled to one piece of wood, six feet by six feet, which was attached to the inner wall by a rope. At night they drew a 'curtain' for privacy and the entire family had to sleep on this single piece of wood. There was no view or ventilation. 'We were literally like animals in a pen,' said Hoosen.

Shortly before the ship reached Mombasa, a passenger named Abu Bakr Murdoch asked Deedat if he would type a letter to his father-in-law in Karachi to inform him of his impending arrival. Deedat obliged, but when he got to the end of the letter, he asked Murdoch whether he could include a short footnote asking for assistance for himself. Murdoch agreed. So Deedat added, 'I have a friend and two children. He's coming with me. Please try to find some accommodation for him. He's even prepared to stay in a tent.' As Karachi approached, other passengers began to ask Deedat where he was going. Although he kept replying in Gujarati, 'Allah bo Motho che' (God is very great), at the back of his mind he was asking himself the same question. He later recalled that as Karachi became visible in the horizon, the hairs on his neck began to tingle at the possibility of what might happen if the authorities discovered that he had neither accommodation nor a prearranged job.

As soon as the ship docked, however, Murdoch and his father-in-law, Ebrahim Kassim, approached Deedat and informed him that the family could stay at Kassim's apartment. Although the apartment did not have electricity, Deedat was more than satisfied, reasoning that anything was better than nothing. When he asked about rent, Kassim replied that he was his guest. Kassim's family was in India and he wished to reciprocate the assistance Deedat had given to his son-in-law. He thus offered to stay with friends until Deedat found suitable accommodation. Kassim's friends then carried Deedat's luggage and helped him through customs. This took until well after midnight and the group then made their way to Manora, a small peninsula just south of Karachi. They spent the night there and moved to their new home in the nearby town of Kiamari the following day.

Deedat began looking for work almost immediately but most companies were wary of employing foreigners who were clueless about Pakistani business customs and practices.

*Deedat's friend Ahmed Lutchka with his family at Beira en route to Pakistan.*

Deedat's big break came when, at the end of one interview he was asked the customary question 'When can you begin?' Afraid of being turned down again, he reversed the situation by telling them that he was considering a few offers and would 'let them know'. This seemed to do the trick, and Morgan Milton Pakistan Ltd offered him a position. The company specialised in wholesaling gramophone equipment. Deedat earned 300 rupees per month. He also did the correspondence of Jahangir Textile Mill and other businessmen on a part-time basis, which yielded an additional hundred rupees per month.

After a few months, Deedat and his family moved into a rented apartment in Karachi. On four hundred rupees per month, the family led a comfortable life. They would eat out on Sundays and were able to tour much of the country. Deedat was surprised when Muhammad Moosa from Simplex visited Pakistan and asked if they could meet. Moosa said that the family were starting a business in Pakistan and would like Deedat to work for them. Deedat agreed, and helped to choose the site where the company established its Star Textile Mill. Deedat worked for Moosa until his return to South Africa nearly three years after his departure. Deedat had become disillusioned with the new Muslim country's largely secular constitution and orientation. Lutchka shared this sentiment as his son, G.M. Hoosen, recalled.

Lutchka and Deedat had keenly followed the formation of the state of Pakistan, and wanted their children to grow up in an Islamic state. Their first shock was finding a shop openly selling alcohol in Karachi but they were willing to give the nascent state a chance. Matters did not improve and Deedat became very disillusioned, as he told a Pakistani reporter in 1987: 'It was the best part of my life materially. I had a lovely time and, in that area, I don't have anything to complain about at all. [But] the main reason for my migrating to a Muslim country had been left unfulfilled…I got disgruntled with the spirit of the nation.'[3]

Two things about Pakistan left a deep impression on Dr G.M. Hoosen. The first was the turmoil in Karachi, a city that could accommodate around two hundred thousand people but harboured over a million inhabitants. An influx of refugees meant that people were living in shacks, on the streets, in parks, even in schools. Hoosen remembers that half the classrooms in his school housed refugees. The second thing that struck Hoosen was the poverty his family had to face. His father tried his hand at several things, manufacturing hair oil, moulds for shoes, and eventually working as a receptionist at a hotel, but his wages barely covered their rent and they lived on his 'tips'. Every anna of every rupee had to be accounted for. Ahmed Lutchka too decided to return to South Africa with his family.

Deedat left Pakistan about a week before its first prime minister, Liaquat Ali Khan, was assassinated on 16 October 1951. He was asked about his Pakistan sojourn during his 1987 tour of that country and said that, in hindsight, he saw his return to South Africa as a blessing in disguise:

> *Interviewer:* You saw Pakistan in the 1950s and what you are seeing now in the 1980s, there must be a world of change. What are the most significant elements of this change that you as an outside observer have seen in your recent stay in Pakistan?
>
> *Deedat:* You see materially, Pakistan has progressed tremendously industrially. I happened to be here in 1949, 1950, 1951…But, you see, I came for a special purpose. I migrated from South Africa where I had a settled life, a good job, good home and I was moved by the spirit of an Islamic state, that I want to go to Pakistan with my wife and children. I wanted to be a good Muslim, that's what brought me here. I wasn't forced by any circumstances because when this Pakistan idea came into being around the 1940s, I was very young but I was for it. They wanted to establish an Islamic state. We had no Islamic state where we could permeate Islam. So, with that enthusiasm, I came here and I lived here for three years. I had a good job and if I kept in that field I might have been a small industrialist doing very well. But somehow I got disappointed, and several days before the Prime Minister Liaqut Ali Khan was assassinated, I left Pakistan. I was about reaching Mombasa when we got the news on the radio. But that must have been a blessing because if I didn't go away, I wouldn't have come to this comparative religion, instead of having a luxurious life in some mansion.[4]

Ebrahim and Ruqayyah Deedat (left) with the Lutchka children, Goolam Hoosen, Ayesha and Anwar, outside Frere Hall, a historic landmark in Karachi.

Deedat often spoke about his disappointment with Pakistan:

> So I went disappointed in 1951 and now, when I come back, this is about my third trip now, and I'm dissatisfied. Economically I'm satisfied. The food is good and relatively cheap compared to my country. And the community is virile and healthy, strong compared to our brethren across the border, you know, lots of energy. But, you see, when I left Nairobi on Friday 2 October [1987], in the Pakistan Airlines coming to Karachi, we were given Pakistani newspapers. I found something there that really hurt me. There was an article on the first language of schools, what shall it be? Should it be Urdu or Sindhi? And what other language? You are debating now for forty years what should be the language at school? After forty years they haven't settled that yet. So naturally it hurt me. In forty years, unfortunately forty years have gone, we haven't even become Pakistanis. We are supposed to be good Muslims, that will take a little longer, but we haven't even become Pakistanis yet. How is it that for forty years you have not been able to bring these people together as a unit, as a people, one nation? The sacrifices that we make simply have been all in vain – that hurts me at the heart.[5]

Many of Deedat's generation were bitterly disillusioned with Pakistan. The euphoria of independence was followed by the disappointment of the reality. Writers whose powerful words had helped to create the new state were among its most vocal critics. Faiz Ahmed Faiz, one of Pakistan's greatest poets, was imprisoned as a dissident in the 1950s; his poems

'Freedom's Dawn', 'August 1952', and 'Bury Me Under Your Pavements' capture the pain of the bruised ideals that the likes of Deedat and Lutchka had aspired to. The following lines are from 'Freedom's Dawn':

> This leprous daybreak, dawn night's fangs have mangled –
> This is not that long-looked-for break of day,
> Not that clear dawn in quest of which those comrades
> Set out, believing that in heaven's wide void
> Somewhere must be the stars' last halting-place,
> Somewhere the verge of night's slow-washing tide,
> Somewhere an anchorage for the ship of heartache.
> Let us go on, our goal is not reached yet.[6]

In retrospect, Deedat's Pakistan venture was always going to be fraught with difficulties. The partition of British India had resulted in riots across India and Pakistan that left around half a million people dead, while an estimated eight million Muslims moved from India to Pakistan, and around ten million Hindus and Sikhs moved in the opposite direction. Disputes over princely states such as Jammu and Kashmir led to war in 1948, which ended with Pakistan and India each occupying parts of Kashmir. In East Bengal, which had more than half of Pakistan's population, there was increasing dissatisfaction with the federal government in West Pakistan. While India inherited most of the British administrative machinery, Pakistan started with practically nothing; records and Muslim administrators were transferred from New Delhi to the makeshift capital at Karachi. The liberal statement of constitutional principles promulgated in 1949 by the largely English-educated founders of Pakistan ran into strong orthodox Muslim opposition. It can be argued that the country has never recovered from this false start.

While Deedat was glad to return 'home' in 1951, he was soon frustrated by the state of Islam in South Africa.

# 6
# DISCOVERING DA'WA

Deedat giving one of his early lectures.

Allah commands in the Qur'an, 'who is better in speech than he who invites people to Allah's ways'. There is no better speech than if you invite people to Allah's ways. This had become my favourite pastime. I couldn't help talking and talking. Gradually people discovered me and thought me to be the guy who could stand up to the Christian missionaries…Obviously, I loved it.

– Ahmed Deedat[1]

BY THE TIME Deedat returned to South Africa from Pakistan, the Afrikaner-dominated National Party, elected in 1948, was firmly entrenched. It had immediately set about segregating the population on the basis of skin colour. Indians, whites, coloureds, and Africans were made to live in separate areas, attend different schools, and even swim in different parts of the ocean. Indians, like coloureds and Africans, the other so-called non-white groups in the country, were denied the vote and given access to inferior schooling, health services, and residential areas.

There were approximately 367 000 Indians in South Africa in 1951. This included 79 000 Muslims. Only 6 per cent of these regarded English as their home language. Education was a luxury and few Muslim children, and virtually no girls, had access to secondary schools. The earliest Islamic organisations were formed by the children of the wealthier traders and those with access to education.

By the 1930s, groups such as the Iqbal Study Group, the Orient Islamic Educational Institute, the Young Men's Muslim Association (YMMA), the Kemal Study Group, the African Muslim Society, and the Natal British Moslem League catered for small numbers of Muslims. Muslim society was largely in the grip of ulama, whose focus was on rituals and rote learning of the Qur'an. Many young Muslims felt intellectually barren as they groped for meaning in Islam in their everyday lives. According to A.S. Ballim, young Muslims who were interested in the anti-imperialist struggle worldwide and the emerging conflict over Palestine, or those who were becoming familiar with the works of the poet philosopher Allamah Iqbal or the Muslim revivalist Mawlana Mawdudi, found little to stimulate them.

The YMMA, which was established in 1932, was the most active Islamic organisation during the 1940s. From 1944 to 1953, it published a monthly journal named after Mawlana Mawdudi's *Risala diniyat* [Towards understanding Islam]. The YMMA serialised Mawdudi's book and published special issues on Muharram, sawm (fasting), and hajj. Long before Deedat came on the scene, the YMMA published calls for South African Muslims to train propagandists 'in the same way as Christians do' and establish a Muslim missionary settlement 'where an education centre could be inaugurated for training of our children and proper Islamic mission work could be based'. Prominent members included Mohammed Vawda and A.K. Simjee.

The Kemal Study Group, which Deedat belonged to, was formed in the late 1930s. Oral recollections suggest that its formation was inspired by the visit of Khwaja Kamaluddin, founder of the Woking Mosque in England and the journal *Islamic Review*, to Natal in 1926. Taking their cue from Kamaluddin, the Kemal Study Group attempted to make Islam relevant in the contemporary period. Its members included Goolam 'Sittar' Jamal, A.S. Ballim, Ahmed Lutchka, Hafidh Darjee, Suleman Seth, I.C. Shaykh, Secunder Amod Murchie, and A.K. Simjee. They established a library in Durban's Madressa Arcade, which is near the Jumu'ah Mosque in Grey Street. The group seems to have disbanded in the early 1950s.

The establishment of the Natal Muslim Council (NMC) in 1943 marked the first serious attempt to form an organisation that would represent Muslims. It was formed by advocate

Kemal Study Group members (standing, from left) Ahmed Lutchka, Ahmed Jeewa, Hafidh Goolam Darjee, IC Shaykh, and M. Fakir, with members of the Rampool Regiment which passed through Durban during the Second World War. The Indian regiment's members were feted by the local Indian community during their stay in South Africa.

Ibrahim M. Bawa, politician A.I. Kajee, who was elected president, and merchants such as M.S. Badat, M.A. Motala, A.M. Moolla, E.I. Haffejee, and A.B. Moosa. The NMC faded away because of the scepticism of Muslims, who adopted a 'wait-and-see' attitude.[2] A fresh attempt was made to organise Muslims when Mawlana Abdul Aleem Siddiqui visited Natal in 1952. He convened a conference of thirty Muslim organisations that agreed to resuscitate the NMC. Ibrahim M. Bawa was elected the new president and Dr Daoud Mall was made vice-president.[3] But by the late 1950s, the NMC had once again fallen dormant.

According to a report on Islamic education as presented to the Orient Institute on 29 September 1958 by M.A.H. Moosa, Islamic education was poorly organised and needed urgent remedying. A committee comprising Dr Daoud Mall, A.S. Ballim, Mohamed Mahomedy, and M.A.H. Moosa met with A.M. Moolla of the Orient Islamic Institute and warned him that Islam would be 'lost' in South Africa because 'the poorly equipped madrasas did not create an understanding of Islam'. The committee suggested to Moolla that they import someone from overseas to train local Islamic teachers. Moolla concurred

Deedat being awarded a prize in one of the Arabic Study Circle's Annual Speech Contests in the 1950s.

and wrote to Aligarh University. Professor Ishrat Hussain, who was fluent in Urdu and Arabic, and had an MA in English, was sent to Natal. He was followed by Wahajul Rasool, a Bengali who joined the staff of the Pine Street Madrasa.

Professor Hussain prepared a report on religious education after visiting fourteen madrasas in Durban. He concluded:

> Madressa education does not go beyond the learning of the Holy Qur'an 'Nazerah', bare meaningless recital, that does not enable the learners to be familiar with even the real function of the Holy Qur'an as a true and practicable 'Code of Life' which if rightly followed is truly capable of putting the Muslims higher than the best standards of life attained by man... The learning of religion has been reduced to the memorising of a few rituals. The pupils are equipped with neither the past achievements of the Muslims nor the future aspirations of the nation.

Nothing came of this report as 'ultra-conservative elements', in Ballim's words, nullified the work of Professor Hussain.

The first organisation that sought to break the mould was the Arabic Study Circle, which was formally constituted in 1954 with Dr Daoud Mall as president. The Circle promoted the study of Arabic so that Muslims could consult the Qur'an directly instead of following Islam ritualistically. It organised annual speech contests from 1954. Participants at the inaugural contest included Ahmed Deedat, G.H. Vanker, Yakoob 'Nash' Meer, and Kader Asmal.[4] Asmal emerged victorious in the contest adjudicated by a well-known stage person-

Joseph Perdu's approach to Islam inspired Deedat enormously; they lectured together in Durban.

ality, Elizabeth Sneddon. Deedat was awarded second prize.⁵ Shortly after the formation of the Circle, a group of Muslim women, led by Zuleikha Mayat, formed the Women's Cultural Group in March 1954. This was groundbreaking at a time when women were not expected to participate in the public sphere.⁶

Deedat's return from Pakistan in the early 1950s coincided with this Islamic 'renaissance'. He participated in the Circle as he believed that Muslims had to learn Arabic, as he told a journalist in 1987:

> The existing education system of teaching Arabic was invented for new converts, and most of us are new converts to Islam. In most cases, our background is Hindu. By asking the potential convert to repeat Kalimah Shah dah, a Hindu turned into a Muslim. The new Muslim was advised not to eat pork, not gamble and drink...My father never read Arabic, but just by the sound he was able to correct me. So the next generation continued to follow a similar way of practicing Islam, that of reciting the Qur'an beautifully, without really understanding the message...I did the same and even my grandchildren will continue to learn through this system of new converts. What's wrong with us? When will we really become Muslims? All the 'alims, can't they see that?...We still do not know a word of the Qur'an. Therefore, we are in a mess. Five times a day you offer prayers if you are a good Muslim. And as soon as you come out of the mosque your backbiting and slandering starts. That's because you do not actually hear what Allah wants of you and you listen to Him through the Imam.⁷

The 1950s in Durban were marked by both vibrancy and controversy in Islamic circles. The controversy started when the Arabic Study Circle invited Joseph Perdu, a French Christian convert to Islam, to live and lecture in Durban. Perdu organised Qur'anic classes where Deedat usually read an extract from the Qur'an, on which Perdu provided tafsir (exegesis). Perdu had a considerable impact on Circle members. Deedat told *Indian Views* that he had 'learnt more from Mr Joseph Perdu than I had learnt in the previous thirty-eight years of my life'.[8] According to A.S. Ballim, if *Izhar-ul-Haq* was the spark that lit Deedat's interest in comparative religion, Perdu was 'the lightning rod'. Perdu later became a source of controversy when rumours surfaced that he might be a member of the Bahai faith.[9]

Perdu departed for Brazil shortly after the controversy broke, but his short stay sharply divided Muslims in South Africa. In Durban, those who objected to Perdu coalesced around Adam Peerbhai and Mohammed Makki. Relations became highly antagonistic and, in the case of Makki and Deedat, they remained permanently strained. Those who attended Perdu's lectures argue that he influenced them because of his intellectual approach to Islam and that he did not contradict their beliefs in any way. A.S. Ballim described Perdu 'as a breath of fresh air. The logical manner in which he explained the Qur'an moved us without compromising our beliefs. To us, he was a true scholar.' Abdullah Deedat made a similar observation; the thirst for knowledge and absence of suitable teachers meant that the Muslim community 'would have hung on to anybody who was different as long as they spoke sense'. G.H. Agjee remembers being 'spellbound, like Oliver Twist. Perdu was a charismatic figure. We wanted more…I remember he gave five lectures at Orient Hall. Each was a masterpiece. He had a magnetism to capture your attention.'

Perdu's departure left a void that was filled briefly in early 1957 by a visitor known only as Reverend Fairfax, an English convert to Islam, who taught his eager 'apprentices' to expound the Bible for the benefit of Muslims. However, he left South Africa abruptly after delivering just three lectures, with some financial issues hanging over his head. Little more is known about the mysterious Fairfax, but Ahmed Deedat volunteered to continue the classes. According to G.H. Agjee, this was a blessing in disguise as 'Deedat knew more than Fairfax. However, Fairfax gave us the impetus that we needed…he got the ball rolling.' Agjee remembered vividly that Deedat's first lesson was on Deuteronomy 18:18, a Bible verse interpreted by Muslims as a prophecy about the coming of the Prophet Muhammad (PBUH).[10]

The desire among younger Muslims to learn more about Islam and Christianity was influenced by both local and international factors. Locally, it had to do with the entrenching of apartheid segregation as well as the growth of Christian missionary work, particularly the Jehovah's Witnesses who, locals felt, were targeting Indians as they went from door to door preaching their brand of Christianity. Internationally, the rise of the USA and the Soviet Union as superpowers, the decline of Muslim power in the Middle East, and the upsurge of nationalism in the Third World, lit a fire among many younger Muslims who felt an urge to 'defend' Islam against theological attacks and to contribute to its resurgence. G.H. Vanker recalled the ferment of the 1950s in a letter to Rabitat al-Alam al-Islami (the Muslim World League[11]) when he wrote:

> In those dark days, since no organisational Muslim voice existed in South Africa, the mass media created havoc in the minds of the Muslim people. They [Muslims] had no knowledge of comparative religion study and hence were a target of malicious propaganda…Because of the silence of Muslims, Christianity had an upper hand on the millions of people, both blacks and whites in the country…Christian missionaries, besides the mass media, were playing a major role directly and indirectly to undermine Islam by misrepresenting it by malicious anti-Islamic propaganda to Muslims as well as the twenty million inhabitants of the country.

This perception was widespread among Muslims. G.H. Agjee remembers:

> Internationally, there were more conversions in the colonies after the British left. Jehovah's Witnesses were going around the country preaching Christianity from house-to-house…Our wives were giving samoosas and cakes to them while they were hammering us. Deedat arose at the right time. A Salahuddin sent by God without a sword. Deedat was not a great Mawlana but he stood up to the Christians. He taught us that we must fight back blow-by-blow. He gave a sense of respectability to Muslims.

South African Muslims viewed the Jehovah's Witnesses as a major irritation. The organisation was started in 1872 by Charles Russell, a young Pittsburgh Presbyterian who rejected the idea that a loving God would create Hell. He taught that Jesus had returned to Earth in 1874 in non-bodily form and that God (Jehovah) would bring the world to an end in 1914. Russell published the *Herald of the Morning* which he renamed the *Watchtower* in 1884. The magazine is still published, and in 2000 had a daily circulation of around 800 000 copies. Jehovah's Witnesses go systematically from door to door in an area, trying to convert anyone who will listen.[12]

Deedat felt that local Muslims, many of whom lacked a good command of English, and were in awe of whites because of decades of racism, and who were by nature courteous and hospitable to visitors, would be vulnerable to missionary advances. Not only did Deedat want to counter this, but, according to Ebi Lockhat, he wanted to spread the message of Islam:

> He used to say to me, 'We want to keep our religion to ourselves. We have an idea that we want everybody to make themselves right before we tell our neighbours. I want to ask you a question Ebi' – he was very questioning – 'can you tell me which day a thousand million Muslims are going to stand up and say, "we are alright now, we must start doing da'wah?" Today you must be talking to everybody.' So he believed in his mind that we were under threat and he had to negate that by propagating his message. He pursued that with a passion, he believed in that.

Deedat's question to Lockhat as to when Muslims would be 'alright' must be understood in the context of developments within Islam in South Africa since the 1960s. Most South African Muslims were broadly termed 'Tablighi' or 'Barelwi'. The Tabligh Jama'at was a transnational religious movement founded in Delhi in the 1920s by Mawlana Muhammad Ilyas and was introduced to South Africa in the early 1960s. Those who follow the Tabligh methodology believe that they should minister first to fellow Muslims and turn their attention to non-Muslims after Muslims have perfected their religion. Deedat felt that this was an elusive utopia and that Muslims should preach the message of the Qur'an without delay.

Deedat also opposed populist practices that emphasised rituals and the intercessionary powers of saints. Deedat was a man of action, and told an interviewer in 1986 that the Sufi practice of cutting oneself off from society was 'a luxury. Why should there be such practices when the bulk of the Muslims find it hard to carry out the outward duties of their faith? What is the use of this spiritual exercise when physically they cannot walk? You know who a Sufi is? A Sufi is any Muslim who can fulfil his obligations, not someone who cuts himself from the community. A good humanitarian is a Sufi.'[13]

Deedat implored Muslims to act on the message of the Qur'an. He told journalist Keysar Trad that while South Africans were 'good' Muslims in many respects they had one crucial failing:

> We Indian Muslims in South Africa are sending more hajjis for hajj than many Arab countries on a pro-rata basis; we send more Tablighis to the Tabligh Jama'at than Pakistan on a percentage basis. There are more Muslims who keep beards in South Africa on a percentage basis than Muslims anywhere else in the world. In South Africa, we are less than two per cent, but every sheep and cow that is slaughtered in the major cities of Durban, Johannesburg, or Cape Town is made halal because of us. Eighty-five per cent of all chicken in the country is made halal because of two per cent of the population. The Muslims that you see in the masjid, ninety-five to ninety-nine per cent have something on their heads when they go for salah. This is how we were brought up. So we are strict and good Muslims, but we didn't do da'wah and that is our drawback.

Most of the ulama in South Africa the 1950s had been educated on the subcontinent, lacked a good command of English, and were unfamiliar with local conditions. The challenge posed by modernity and the activity of Christian missionaries was taken up by men such as G.H. Vanker, G.H. Agjee, Ahmed Deedat, and Dr Daoud Mall, who soon tired of occasional lectures and decided to coalesce into a formal organisation to mount a sustained challenge to missionary activity.

# 7
# THE ISLAMIC PROPAGATION CENTRE AND ITS FOUNDERS

IPCI founder members G.H. Vanker and G.H. Agjee (left), and Arabic Study Circle members A.S. Ballim (centre) and Ismail Manjra (right), chat with visiting Islamic scholar, Masood Yaar Khan.

Invite (All) to the Way of thy Lord with Wisdom and Beautiful Preaching; and reason with them in ways that are Best and Most Gracious.

– IPC letterhead

AS THEIR LECTURES grew in popularity, Deedat and Vanker decided to establish a formal organisation. They convened a public meeting on 17 March 1957 at the Pine Street Madrasa which was attended by the likes of A.S. Ballim, Dr Daoud Mall, Muhammad A.H. Moosa, M. Nazeer Ali, Suleman Shaikjee, Hassim Kajee, G.H. Agjee, C.S. 'Whitey' Vanker, A.S. Noorgat, A. Chohan, A.K. Salejee, and Abdul Khalek Christy (Yesudas). One of the first issues discussed was whether it made sense to start another organisation in addition to the Arabic Study Circle. The consensus was that their focus on combating missionary activity would be different to the core activity of the Circle, which was to promote Arabic, and that they should, in A.S. Ballim's words, 'go for it'. Ismail Manjra, then secretary of the Circle, recalled that it was left to individual members of the Circle to decide whether they wished to join the new organisation.

Thus the Islamic Propagation Centre (IPC) came into existence. G.H. Vanker was elected president, Deedat was appointed secretary, A.K. Salejee treasurer, and A.S. Noorgat registrar. Shaikjee, Kajee, Agjee, 'Whitey' Vanker, and Vally Mahomed were elected as committee members. At the IPC's second annual general meeting on 7 September 1959 Deedat was elected president with Vanker becoming secretary-general. The reason for swapping portfolios was that members felt that Deedat was more suited to 'selling' the organisation and Vanker to administering it. In the early to mid-1960s, the IPC committee included the likes of Vanker, Deedat, S.A. Lockhat, M.N. Alli, E.H. Ismail, and G.H. Agjee.

Reverend and Mrs Fairfax received a great welcome when they arrived in Durban; they were met by (from left) Abdullah Khan, Deedat, G.H. Agjee, E.H. Ismail, Secunder Murchie, and G.H. Vanker (extreme right), among others.

According to the IPC's constitution, which was adopted in 1959, the organisation had been formed to promote Islam among Muslims and non-Muslims through lectures, publishing, and the dissemination of literature; establish an institution to train Muslim missionaries; provide assistance to new Muslims to adapt to an Islamic way of life and integrate into Muslim society; build schools, colleges, and orphanages to further the cause of Islam; undertake social, welfare, and religious work; and co-operate with other Islamic organisations to further these objectives.

The original letterhead of the IPC carried the Qur'anic verse 'Invite (All) to the Way of thy Lord with Wisdom and Beautiful Preaching; and reason with them in ways that are Best and Most Gracious'. In time, this seemed ironic to Deedat's critics, who accused him of causing offence to non-Muslims through his confrontational approach. Deedat held a grudging admiration for the dedication of Christian missionaries, as he told one reporter:

> In Karachi in the 1950s, living in Pakistan, Katcheri Road, second floor, I get a knock at the door early in the morning. I open the door and a Caucasian, a white man, says, 'Good morning.' I say, 'Good morning, what can I do for you?' The man says, 'Look, I've got some literature for you.' I said, come inside. He comes in. Sits down. I say, 'Where do you come from?' He says, 'I come from England.' A few days later, another knock at the door. I open the door and another white man. This is right in the centre of Karachi. I say, 'What can I do for you?' 'I've some literature for you.' 'Where do you come from?' 'America.' This guy's coming from six thousand miles, that guy's coming from ten thousand miles to preach to me in my country. I want to know what am I doing? Nothing. Nothing. It is an obligation of the Musalman to deliver the message long before Salah, zakah and hajj became fard [obligatory]. Allah tells his prophets and through him, he's telling us, 'You deliver the message because it is your duty.'[1]

As impressive as the commitment of individual missionaries was the machinery behind them:

> They have produced this Bible. This is their proof, authority. They have produced it in two thousand different languages...it's hard to imagine, two thousand different languages! They have the Bible in Urdu, Gujarati, two Gujarat dialects, they have eleven different Arabic Bibles. There's something unimaginable that they have eleven different Bibles for Arabs alone. What do you do with eleven different Bibles? Because there are different dialects, they have different scripts. I didn't know that. To me the Arabic of the Qur'an is the only Arabic I was thinking that existed and I thought every Arab was speaking that Arabic. He says, 'No, there is the Tunisian script, Moroccan script, Syrian script, Palestinian dialect, there is a South Sudanese dialect and on and on, eleven different Arabic dialects. They have the Bible in 107 African languages, complete Bibles, and in another 117 African languages the New Testament alone.[2]

Deedat often lamented the fact that Muslims had given up on this duty. He told an interviewer on Pakistan TV in 1987 that

Allah (SWT) blessed the Muslims so abundantly that they spread throughout the world and became masters of half the known world but when they became masters they stopped preaching and said, 'you can see Allah has blessed us. If you want to be one of us you are welcome,' but he wouldn't go out of his way to deliver the message.³

The IPC was the vehicle through which Deedat, Vanker, Agjee, Salejee, and others hoped to combat missionary activities while conducting da'wah. As the work of the IPC gathered pace, premises were rented at Madressa Arcade in Grey Street in the very office that had once been the home of the YMMA; two adjacent offices were rented as the organisation grew. By the time the IPC left Madressa Arcade in 1986, Deedat was a household name in the Muslim world and the IPC had been transformed into a transnational organisation.

Among early members, A.K. Salejee was only active for a short while. He was born in Umzinto in 1928, and moved with his family to Isipingo where they opened the Reunion Trading Company. Salejee attended public lectures organised by the Arabic Study Circle and those by Deedat, and was appointed as a trustee of the As-Salaam Trust. When Salejee went on hajj in 1964 he was influenced by the nascent Tabligh Jama'at movement and helped it take root in South Africa. He quietly ended his involvement with the IPC.

E.H. Ismail was a prominent retailer who owned stores in Commercial Road and Field Street, called Up-to-Date Dealers and Empire Tailors respectively. He was well known for his distinguished attire, which included a suit and red fez. E.H. as he was addressed, was involved in a host of sporting, religious, and social welfare activities. It was he who first suggested that the Arabic Study Circle hold its annual speech contest. He served as a committee member of the IPC for several years. During the 1950s he arranged for Qur'an reciters from Cape Town to perform at the Queensbridge Mosque in Durban.

IPCI founder member E.H. Ismail.

IPCI founder member Secunder Amod Murchie.

Secunder Amod Murchie, born in Kosad in 1915, joined his father Ahmed in Natal in 1924. He studied at Sastri College and taught English on the south coast, and was later active in both the Pine Street Madrasa and the Anjuman School in Leopold Street which he helped to establish with A.I. Kajee and A.M. Moolla. Murchie was also involved in his wife's family's business, I.C. Shaikh's in Grey Street, and it was his knowledge of accounting and experience on the south coast that led to his recruitment by the Kadwa family as treasurer of the As-Salaam Trust. Later in life Murchie lived in Mount Vernon and was treasurer of the Umhlatuzana Mosque until his death in 1980.

G.H. (Goolam Hoosen Yusuf) Agjee played an important role in the IPC. Deedat's sister Rassool was left a virtual 'orphan' when her mother died, and her paternal uncle Suleman Deedat arranged her marriage to Essop Agjee of Port Shepstone on the south coast of Natal. Essop travelled to India for the nikah (marriage) ceremony. Such transnational marriages were common in the formative years of Indian settlement because of the shortage of women, particularly from one's village of origin, in South Africa. Essop Agjee became ill when Rassool was pregnant and died shortly before Goolam Hoosen was born, while Rassool passed away when he was two.[4] Goolam Hoosen, who would be a pivotal figure in the cause of his maternal uncle, recalled their first meeting:

IPCI founder and Deedat's nephew, G.H. Agjee.

It was in the year 1944 that my uncle [Deedat] came to see me in Port Shepstone. I was told by my uncle Dawood Agjee that my mother's brother was coming to meet me. I was greatly impressed by seeing a young handsome man of about twenty-five years of age, while I was about fourteen years old. He took my hand and shook it firmly and then hugged me with a firm embrace. For an orphan who had lost both parents by the time I was two years old, this meeting of an uncle and nephew was emotionally most fulfilling. We saw each other for the first time, yet we were only eighty miles apart. Uncle Deedat and I took a walk to a hilltop overlooking the Indian Ocean and the Umzimkhulu River. There, in full view of the beautiful scenery we talked as uncle and nephew. Before departing for Durban, he presented to me a book on the life of the Prophet Muhammad (PBUH). Thus started my own journey in earnest in Islam.[5]

# The Second Annual General Meeting

OF

## The Islamic Propagation Centre

will be held at

### Pine Street Madressa Hall Durban

on Monday (Settler's Day) 7th Sept, 1959 at 10 a.m. Sharp

AGENDA:

1. Minutes
2. Secretarial Report
3. Treasurer's Report
4. Election of Office Bearers
5. Amendments to Constitution
6. General

---

**All MUSLIMS ARE INVITED TO ATTEND**

| A. H. DEEDAT | A. K. SALEJEE | G. H. E. VANKER |
|---|---|---|
| President | Treasurer | Secretary |

P.O. Box 2439 — 47 Madressa Arcade, Durban — Phone 27054

Born in Port Shepstone on 6 September 1929, Agjee was raised by his grandfather Ebrahim Agjee after his mother's death. At the age of seven, he and his grandfather boarded a ship bound for India but his grandfather suffered a heart attack and died while they were at sea. In India, the young Agjee spent a few months at his grandmother's village of Karod and then moved to Tadkeshwar, his father's village, where he lived with a paternal aunt. He studied Urdu, Gujarati, and the Qur'an at the local darul 'ulum (seminary). Agjee returned to South Africa in 1939 as the first shots of the Second World War were fired. Agjee's Islamic education continued under Soofie Desai, Mawlana Panchbhay, and Munshi Mehboob Khan in Port Shepstone.

After Panchbhay's death, the madrasa was supervised by Hafidh Ismail Padia, the father of Bhai Padia who led the Tabligh Jama'at in South Africa from the 1960s. Agjee memorised the Urdu *Farhanq*, a dictionary that permitted the learner to understand Urdu books of jurisprudence. Agjee credits these years for the confidence that he later displayed in da'wah-related activities. By the time he was fourteen, Agjee was delivering the khutba (sermon) before the Friday prayer, leading the congregation in prayer, and delivering speeches at weddings.

Schooled in orthodox Islam, Agjee's Islamic horizons broadened when he came across a copy of the *Islamic Review* at the home of a friend in Port Shepstone:

> When I picked up the first copy I could not put it down. This was a different world from what I had been used to. My Islam was very orthodox. We never focused on other religions. Suddenly I was reading about things like 'Trinity: Fact or Fiction?' These reviews were challenging Orientalists. I read articles by the late Khwaja Kamaluddin and Mawlana Muhammad Ali and could not put these books down.

Agjee's interest in what he himself described as 'a more introspective Islam' developed further when he attended Pakistani Mawlana Nurul Haq's Qur'anic tafsir classes at the West Street mosque:

> For those of us who were brought up on rituals, the Qur'an was talking to us for the first time. It was liberating...I loved going to the classes [because] there was meaning in Allah's word for the first time...while the rest of the Mawlanas were talking moral issues, the do's and don'ts.

Agjee obtained a full set of copies of *Arafat*, a monthly magazine published by Muhammad Asad during 1946 and 1947. Like Deedat, Agjee was inspired by Asad, whose message was summed up in the editorial of the first issue:

> A world in upheaval and convulsion: this is our world; an embittered all-round fight for new ways of life...At a time like this, we Muslims must take stock of our cultural holding. It is not enough to say we are Muslims and have an ideology of our own. We must be also in a position to show that our ideology is vital enough to stand the pressure of the changing times...The upheaval offers tremendous possibilities for

better or worse...We can if we so desire make a new start in terms of the Islamic Programme and thus resurrect our society from the cold ashes of convention and decay. It is up to us to decide whether we shall build our future on the real values of Islam or entirely drift away from Islam and become passive camp-followers of Western civilisation.[6]

Agjee read every copy of *Arafat* from cover to cover and retains 'in my possession all copies neatly bound'. He also attended Joseph Perdu's classes and joined the Arabic Study Circle to increase his knowledge of Arabic and thus gain direct access to the Qur'an. The intellectual challenges of inter-religious discourse appealed to him and he became a vital cog in the IPC. Ahmed Mustacq Saleh of Cape Town, who had regular contact with Agjee over many years, described him as 'very dedicated. He was highly organised and an intellectual in every respect.' A.T. Rasool regarded Agjee as 'aggressive, but he did not say anything to Deedat who was his uncle. He was very, very bright. While he did not say much when he stood up to talk, it was hard to get him to sit down [laughs].' Agjee stood by Deedat's side to the end. Even in his eighties, he remained in awe of 'Uncle Deedat'.

Mahomed Khan is one of the unsung heroes of the IPC. Khan, one of five children of Ahmad Khan and Katoon Bi, was born in 1925 in Sea Cow Lake. His father worked as a labourer in Shire's Quarry in Riverside and on weekends taught madrasa classes at the Soofie Saheb Mosque in Sea Cow Lake. Khan attended Umgeni School in Briardene where he completed Standard 6. An avid sportsman, he played golf, participated in competitive cycling, played cricket and soccer, and was a keen swimmer. He married Zulaka in 1956 and they had three children, Ahmed, Shabaan, and Misbanoor. Shabaan worked at the IPC on weekends and during school holidays from the age of ten until he qualified as a teacher in 1983. Later appointed the principal of the Jumu'ah Masjid School in Durban, which is situated opposite the IPCI building, Shabaan witnessed the rise and later implosion of the IPCI first hand.

Mahomed Khan worked for the IPCI for over four decades.

Khan took on a series of odd jobs after leaving school and was a cashier at a theatre in Victoria Street. When he joined the IPC in 1959, his employer A.B. Moosa wrote in a testimonial that Khan 'was intelligent and punctual. He performed his duties very well. He is very enthusiastic and keen.' While he was working in Victoria Street, Khan had got to know Vanker and occasionally attended Deedat's public lectures. Vanker and Deedat convinced him to join the IPC in 1960, as he explains:

> Mr Vanker and Mr Deedat said they wanted a typist. I'm a touch typist, right, so they said, 'Come and join us, we need people like you.' I said I can't, I must wind up early, give me a month's chance. So I handed over and joined them in 1959. Deedat was nice but demanding, a stern man. When he wants a job done, it must be done. That's how his work was. You can't fool around with him, don't ask questions.[7]

The hours were long, the work hard, and the pay poor. He lived in mainly working-class areas. Before he received a council home in Shallcross, he lived for six months in a wood-and-iron shack in Tin Town. In Shallcross, Khan dedicated his life to welfare work. His wife Zulaka ran a madrasa while he was a volunteer case investigator for the Darul Yatama orphanage. He also assisted the local burial society and was a member of the Glenridge Islamic Society. Khan's home was known as the 'Muslim Welfare Centre of Shallcross'.

At the IPC, Khan attended to correspondence, saw to accounting and financial matters, made sure that fundraising appeals went out timeously, and travelled with Vanker and Deedat throughout Natal during Ramadan to raise funds. Jamaluddin Ahmed remembers Khan as 'a wonderful old chap… a remarkable man, an innocent human being' who was under a lot of pressure as the IPCI grew in size and scope. Khan gave almost four decades of loyal service. Described by Yusuf Ally as 'simply the most honest and dignified man I knew', Mahomed Khan passed away on 22 June 2007 at the age of eighty-two.

While all these members played an important role in the IPC, one man stood apart in the eyes of most observers. Jamaluddin Ahmed (see Chapter 24) described him simply as 'a saint':

> G.H. Vanker was a remarkable man, beautiful person, tremendous personality, a Saint, I would call him. He was the only Muslim teddy bear that I met – and I mean that in the nicest possible way – because he was huggable when you needed him…He was not interested in power, and when things were not going as he would have liked, he quietly withdrew and carried on in his bookstore…What an honest man! I would sometimes choose a book at his bookstore but he would refuse to sell it to me because he said that I would not enjoy it. I would insist on getting the book. We would eventually compromise that I could read the book and buy it only if I liked it.

Goolam Hoosen (G.H.) Vanker was an appropriate choice as first president of the IPC given his commitment to da'wah and the high esteem in which he was held by Muslims across the spectrum. He played a crucial role in the IPC's development, initially as president and for almost three decades thereafter as secretary-general.

Vanker was born in Durban on 1 August 1924. His grandfather Ahmed Vanker had come to South Africa from Kathor and established a business in Umgeni Road. G.H., the second son of Ebrahim Vanker, was brought up by his grandparents after his parents separated. He joined his mother in the Transvaal in 1941, and found employment as a shop assistant in Waterval-Boven, a small country town in what was then the Eastern Transvaal. Vanker would later claim that his study of the Bible began on a bus in Johannesburg in 1948 when a Christian priest's offer of a Bible caused him to wonder how many Muslims would be susceptible to this type of proselytising. Also in 1948, he married his cousin Khadija Vahed. Their third son, the late Ahmed Farouk, followed in his father's footsteps, completing a higher degree in Islamic studies and lectured at the University of Durban-Westville.

Due to strict restrictions on the inter-provincial movement of Indians in South Africa, Vanker went by the name of Jazbhai in the Transvaal. But after the National Party came into power in 1948, the authorities became more vigilant and, rather than risk arrest, he and his wife returned to Durban in 1951. Vanker found work as a travelling salesman with Kazi Agencies and joined the Arabic Study Circle whose president, Dr Daoud Mall, recalled his first glimpse of Vanker:

> It was in 1954 where he was a contestant at a speech contest...Dressed in a loosely fitting suit with a red fez on his head, he was gently swaying to the rhythm of his own oratory. The fervour, glint in the eye, mannerisms and broadly sprawling beard reminded me of the zealous evangelist and what completed the picture was that at times he clutched the long stem of the microphone. At such times he was veritably a shepherd with his staff herding the lost sheep, and perhaps that is how Mr Vanker saw us in the audience – as so many lost sheep who must be brought back into the fold.[8]

First president of the IPC, G.H. Vanker, had a formidable knowledge of Islam and a splendid sense of humour; seen here in conversation with Mawlana Ansari, imam of Durban's West Street Mosque.

According to Vanker's wife, Khadija, her husband met Ahmed Deedat through the Circle, and Deedat first visited their tiny apartment in Warwick Avenue in the mid-1950s. After several long discussions Deedat and Vanker agreed to form the IPC. From the beginning, the two men personally visited Muslim businessmen and persuaded some of them to commit to a donation of twenty-five cents a month. Vanker joined the IPC on a full-time basis even though he was offered a partnership in Kazi Agencies. This came at considerable personal cost, as Dr Mall would later recall:

G.H. Vanker.

> Knowledge allows one no rest. It kindles many latent fires. Mr Vanker was soon consumed by the flames of his interest and he gave up his work as a travelling sales agent that earned him his livelihood. With his colleague Mr Deedat, they voluntarily started the Islamic Propagation Centre. To a man with a growing family and no private income, what it must have cost to launch out in the new untried field, can best be imagined. But truly has it been said that God looks after his own 'special sheep', for today the 'Centre' is the hub where the people of many faiths converge to eke out information.[9]

G.H. Agjee recalled that Vanker's wife often sewed late into the night to make ends meet. Khadija too remembered the strains and hardship, pointing out that at the time of Vanker's death in 1987, even though the IPCI was flush with petrodollars, his salary was a mere R350 a month! 'I am doing this for Allah' was his stock reply when anyone queried his modest economic circumstances. Shortly after Vanker passed away, Essop Kajee, well known for his work for the *Daily News* Milk Fund, wrote to Deedat and Agjee on 27 August 1987:

> The tragedy of this week was losing a real Brother – a Father Figure – Advisor – and above all, a 'Simpleton', as we knew him. Late Brother Goolam Hoosen Vanker was a very dear person to me. He was in my company in the Old Days. Goolam was my friend of those years. Together we also went to the struggles of those yesteryears. He lived in Warwick Avenue which in those days was known as 'Ducheens', an area where the lowest of the low lived; prostitution thrived and so did gambling. It was the birthplace of 'Fafee' running; the illegal bookies' bucket shop of the Turf; the dagga pedlars. The Ducheen Gang, the Crimson League, all took birth here. And it was amongst this squalor where Brother Vanker lived. In his own small way there, he was able to reform a small section of his neighbourhood. And in so doing he reached a stage where everybody referred to him as Bapoo. But with Allah's help we all survived. Some even up to today say that Vanker was the Father of all the orphans in Warwick Avenue. Brother Vanker had a very strong weapon and he used it quite often in his lifetime – that weapon was humility.

From 1962 to 1972, while Deedat was at As-Salaam (see Chapter 11), Vanker managed the central office of the IPC in Durban. He was active in public life, delivering papers at Islamic conferences, preparing an Arabic reader for children, and compiling several poems, the most popular of which, 'Operation Death' and 'Great Sacrifice', were recited by thousands of school children. He also published *The Propagation of Islam*, a manual on how to transmit the beliefs of Islam. Vanker was one of the first persons that Professor Salman Nadvi met when he arrived in South Africa in 1973 to take up a professorship at the University of Durban-Westville: Nadvi recalled:

> At the time he was running his bookshop and also involved with the IPCI. He was a very friendly person, a very lively person. I would often go to his shop just to visit him and talk to him. He was very knowledgeable about Islam but he was also very friendly, full of jokes, a very lively person indeed.

Dr G.M. Hoosen described Vanker as 'a giant amongst us, absolutely unassuming, he never cared for the world…[he] spent a lot of time developing the material that Deedat used so effectively'. A.T. Rasool remembers Vanker as 'quiet but formidable', recalling an interfaith forum at Natal University in the 1950s: 'One aggressive Christian attacked Islam by ranting and raving. Vanker calmly cut him down to size. The whole house, Christians, Muslims, and Jews, gave him a standing ovation.'

Children from the Islamic seminary that Deedat and the IPC established at As-Salaam were part of the Fourteenth Centennial Anniversary celebrations of the revelation of the Qur'an in 1968.

Stories of Vanker's sympathy and understanding are legendary. Dr Yusuf Osman reminisced:

> I was a student at Natal Medical School. We went through our intellectual struggles with religion, socialism, politics, etc. Fortunately, we had someone like Mr Vanker with whom we could engage on almost any topic associated with Islam. Mr Deedat we found sometimes too fixated on the comparative aspect which was not the need of the hour for us then. I would often go to the Upstairs Bookshop and spend many happy hours there with Mr Vanker. I say happy because Mr Vanker really had a splendid sense of humour with numerous light-hearted anecdotes to accompany his presentation. Mr Vanker knew his comparative religion on Islam, Christianity, Judaism and Hinduism as well as Mr Deedat. I remember one quote that he had hanging in his office. Paraphrased, it read: 'There is no limit to what one can do, if one does not mind who receives the credit.' I feel that this embodied his philosophy. He silently did his research, gave lectures, and participated in debates and engaged people in ideas at his office. Yet he lived in the shadow of Mr Deedat. I believe Mr Vanker honestly did not care who received the credit.

Mustacq Ahmed Saleh of Cape Town, whose family ran the Cape 'chapter' of the IPC, described Vanker as a 'gentleman in every sense of the word. He had a sober influence on Deedat. He planned thoroughly and did most of the spadework.' G.H. Agjee also emphasised their contrasting personalities. Deedat was aggressive while Vanker was a 'gentle individual who got his way through persuasion and logic'. In Shabaan Khan's opinion, while Deedat was direct, Vanker was diplomatic. 'One-on-one he could convince you more easily. Their styles actually complemented each other.'

An example of Vanker's diplomatic approach occurred shortly after the IPC was formed. A pamphlet titled *al-Hidayah* was published by a certain Abdul Masih in January 1959 in response to a lecture by Deedat on 'What the Bible says about Muhammad'. Masih was a Christian who urged Muslims to convert to Christianity in order to be 'saved'. The tactful Vanker wrote:

> We genuinely appreciate your motives and concern for those of our faith...It is not our intention to quarrel or upset those that have views that are divergent to ours. On the contrary we feel that both Christians and Muslims can learn a great deal from each other. The only way this is possible is by *direct contact*. We wish to extend to you, in all good faith, an invitation to address us on your views. We also would appreciate an invitation from you at a venue and time suitable to yourselves when we too, can in a friendly and charitable manner put forward what we consider are facts with which no reasonable Christian would find fault.

Masih did not take up the offer, nor did he challenge Deedat at any of the public lectures as the adverts encouraged Christians to do.

Vanker remained a vital cog in the IPC, 'the oil that made it run smoothly', according to Shabaan Khan. He made sure that Deedat's ideas came to fruition. This was important because Deedat was 'impulsive' and rarely did a cost–benefit analysis. According to G.H. Agjee:

> When Deedat got an idea, he just went ahead and would never back pedal. This was his strength and weakness. It sometimes got us into trouble but it also achieved a lot of things that would not otherwise have happened…Uncle [Deedat] often got ideas to publish something. The IPC, particularly in the early days, did not have the money for his projects but he would go for broke. If the IPC could afford 500 pamphlets he would order 5 000, and he would go out and find the money, even if he had to plead from door-to-door.

With Deedat in As-Salaam for most of the 1960s Vanker and Khan saw to the day-to-day running of the IPC. Vanker was a persuasive speaker in his own right. For example, he received a letter of gratitude from I. Luden of London, dated 18 February 1975:

> On behalf of my wife and daughter and our friends from England, I would like to express our thanks and appreciation to you for the wonderful manner in which you received us in your holy place of worship [Grey Street Mosque] on Sunday. As a result of your informative and absorbing lecture you have, unfortunately [for us], sowed the seed of doubt in our minds regarding the five points on which Islam differs from our religion. The Muslim version appears to be the correct one. Your vast knowledge of our holy scriptures and your intimate knowledge of Islam leaves us feeling very ignorant and unsure of ourselves. What worries me personally is the utter simplicity and pure logic of Islam, which cannot, by any thinking person, be denied. I write as a communicant member of the Anglican faith [and who until now has never doubted that faith] and as one who in all probability will adhere to that faith until the day I die. However, I must in all honesty acknowledge that you have considerably shaken me [and the others] in our beliefs. Once again a very sincere and appreciative thank you for the experience and your valuable time. May God bless you in all your endeavours and may peace be with you.

In 1968, the IPC played an important role alongside the Arabic Study Circle and local madrasas in organising local celebrations of the Fourteenth Centennial Anniversary of the Revelation of the Qur'an that took place in August of that year. The IPC offices were used for planning meetings, and, as one of the main organisers, Vanker was made honorary secretary of the Centennial Society. Twenty thousand Muslims gathered at Curries Fountain to celebrate the occasion. The colourful event saw Muslim children dressed in costumes representing countries such as Pakistan, Burma, Kashmir, Mughal India, and Egypt. Boys and girls sang qasidas in honour of the Prophet (PBUH) and the Overport Muslim Brigade rendered a military display and led the crowds in a procession through the streets of Durban.

The Friday prayer was performed in the open at Curries Fountain.[10] Shabaan Khan recalled that the celebration was 'spearheaded' by Vanker who worked late most nights to make a success of what he described as 'the greatest day in the history of Muslims in this country'.

Vanker also ran a small Islamic bookstore in Madressa Arcade called the Anchor Mail Order House from 1977. It had belonged to his long-time friend Cassim Moolla whose wish it was that he should take it over because he knew that Vanker would remain loyal to his ideal of providing good quality Islamic material at affordable prices. Vanker was apprehensive as he did not have capital, but local business houses such as Sartaj filled the shop with books on the understanding that Vanker would 'pay when able'. Vanker employed a cousin to run the shop (now known as the Upstairs Bookshop). Despite his failing health from the mid-1970s, Vanker remained devoted to the IPCI until two heart attacks forced him to 'retire' in the 1980s.

When the IPCI established a Board of Trustees in 1985, Vanker was appointed life trustee, which he remained until his death on 24 August 1987 (10 Muharram in the Islamic calendar, which was also his Islamic birth date). In his later years, due to a combination of factors including ill health, Vanker became less and less involved in the day-to-day running of the IPCI, and quietly faded into the background. It was difficult to establish exactly what happened because Vanker did not discuss this issue with anyone. As his wife Khadija points out, he 'never brought his work home, not even a pen', and she 'had no clue what was going on'. One of the items on the agenda of a trustees' meeting on 23 January 1987 was 'Vanker's resignation'. It is not clear, though, whether this was discussed and what the outcome was, as there are no minutes and none of the interviewees was prepared to discuss the issue.

Several local organisations, including the Arabic Study Circle, the IPCI, and the Muslim Youth Movement, arranged a 'Special Evening' in Durban to honour his contribution to the Muslim community. For Rasool,

> G.H. Vanker was the nearest I came to seeing a saint. People would come to the shop, some had no rent money, some had no food. He would give them a note and send them to A.H. Grocers for food and put it on his account. That's where the money from the shop went. He never wanted the headlines and never went forward into the limelight.

Zuleikha Mayat of the Women's Cultural Group sent a letter of condolence to the Vanker family on 14 September 1987:

> Please accept the condolences of the members of the Women's Cultural Group on the demise of your late husband. Our association with Mr Vanker goes back a long way. We knew him from the time that he used to participate in the Arabic Study Circle Speech contests and in so far as the Islamic Propagation Centre, well, all we know that that was his life work. One can well say that he was the man behind the organisation, quietly going about his work, without the fanfare and publicity.

Shareek-e-Gham ('Sympathiser') Raaghib Murada-baadi, a Karachi-based sha'er (poet) who had met Vanker during a visit to South Africa composed the following tribute:

> Departed the respected Ghulam Husain
> Towards the Paradise, leaving the world.
> In piety and in fearing Allah, the life that was spent
> On the Day of Judgement will receive its reward.
> The fear of Allah remained in the heart
> By the grace of the Lord of Madinah [Prophet Muhammad, PBUH]
> His habit or manner was the propagation of deen
> He was *the* propagator of this kind in the country
> Successfully propagating for thirty years
> Is there anyone like him in Durban, today?
> From the books written by him
> The entire community benefited
> He was a believer [mu'min] of firm and sincere doctrine
> By Allah, the community is proud of him.
> Humble nature, warm-heartedness, sympathetic
> He was blessed by Allah with these attributes
> He was generous by the grace of Allah
> When did stinginess ever come near him
> Why should one not feel the grief of his death?
> When one cannot see another person of his kind.
> Even though Vanker is no longer present
> Nevertheless he is the source of discussion all over
> By the intervention of Prophet Muhammad of Arabia
> He must be forgiven, O, my Allah
> This was indeed the desire of Unus Meer
> That Raaghib composed this elegy
> Also praying for his blessing is this 'sha'er'
> Grieved by the death of Vanker.
> Go to his grave, O Raaghib
> Read Fatihah and raise your hands in prayer

# 8

# IS THE BIBLE GOD'S WORD?

Aiming to counter the millions of copies of evangelical Christian magazines that flood the world each month, Deedat began writing his own publications.

The Christian has already reproduced the Bible in over a thousand languages and broadcast it to the four corners of the globe, terrifying the nations of the world to accept the '*Blood Of The Lamb*', that Christ died for the sins of mankind, that he [Jesus] is the only saviour. All this is against the clear evidence of his own Holy Book. We must free him from his illusions, and there is no better way than to use his own evidence, his own logic, to refute his claims.

– Ahmed Deedat[1]

'IQRAA!' (READ!) was the first word revealed to the Prophet Muhammad (PBUH). Deedat realised the importance of da'wah through the written word early on in his mission. He often reminded Muslims that Christian agencies were spending millions of dollars on the 'free, glossy and multicolour' *Plain Truth* magazine. In addition, as he told a journalist in 1987: 'Look at the 15 May issue of *Watchtower*. See inside here – it says: average printing: 12 million. Just imagine, 12 million in 103 languages. The same group has another magazine called *Awake*, also monthly, with an average printing of 10 million.'[2]

Deedat sought to counter what he perceived as a propaganda offensive, but admitted that he was initially 'terrified of the printed word' due to his 'limited educational background'.[3]

He overcame this fear and went on to flood the world with his literature. He told Pakistani journalist Abul Kalaam that

> no agency, no medium, no means of communication can penetrate the heartlands of Islam more deeply than the printed page; and no agency or medium abides so persistently as the printed page; and no agency or medium can criticise so daringly as the printed page; and influence so irresistibly as the printed page.[4]

According to Ebi Lockhat:

> Deedat was a very big exponent of the written word. He would always say to me, 'You are a writer, writers write, and you must write a book but better than a book is a booklet and better than a booklet is a leaflet.' He was a great exponent of putting things in writing because…(of course he was not in the email era) but he said there's no border that can prevent a letter from reaching your home, and that you've got to flood the world with literature. Send leaflets and booklets because books are too long to read. His booklets were very popular because I think he had a winning formula. He said that people don't want to read long academic books – keep a long story short, sharp, incisive, to the point. And you can see the difference. His booklets are widely read.
>
> There's another little anecdote. I once suggested to him that now that we are entering the computer era, why don't you get a computer? He said that he can't use it. He said that he hates electric typewriters too. He said that when he writes he's got to hear the keys and the clangs of the old typewriter, and that's the way he wrote. And some of his best writings were produced when he put his mind to something and said, 'I think I'm going to go home and finish this booklet.' He would sit, concentrate and produce something really outstanding.

The IPC distributed booklets virtually from its inception. Printing costs increased gradually over the years and ran into hundreds of thousands of rand by the late 1980s. The most widely distributed booklets in the early years were:

- *What was the Sign of Jonah?*
- *What the Bible says about Muhammad*
- *Who Moved the Stone?*
- *Resurrection or Resuscitation?*
- *Is the Bible God's Word?*

Titles such as *50 000 Errors in the Bible, Crucifixion or Cruci-fiction?* and *Resurrection or Resuscitation?* are examples of what Phillip Lewis describes as Deedat's 'vituperative style'.[5] Aside from polemics, Deedat also focused on social and moral questions, including alcoholism, gambling, prostitution, and homosexuality in Western societies, proposing Islam as a solution for this 'decadence'; and Muslims marrying outside the faith.[6]

According to Professor Salman Nadvi, Deedat's ideas resonated widely among Muslims:

> Muslims were impressed because Ahmed Deedat was arguing back with Christians. Everybody was impressed, even the literate person, even scholars were impressed with Deedat's knowledge of the Bible which we didn't know anything about. So the scholars who were steeped in Islamic knowledge could not rebut Christian arguments as such. Nobody went into depth studying Christianity. In the early days of British rule in India, Christianity was part of the syllabus in Islamic education so Muslims knew something about it. Islam and Christianity were together for a very, very long time in the Middle East but Muslims did not spend time studying what it was all about and how to rebut its arguments.

Deedat drew on biblical hermeneutics and secular criticism which challenged the idea that the Bible was the literal word of God. He highlighted textual differences between different versions of the Bible and showed that in places the same event is described but different information is given.[7] In *The Bible: The Biography*, Karen Armstrong concludes that 'disparate influences' shaped the Hebrew Bible and New Testament. The Bible does not have a single message because the editors who fixed the canons 'included competing visions, and placed them, without comment, side by side'. Biblical authors saw the Bible as 'a template for the problems of their time [and] felt free to change it and make it speak to contemporary conditions'.[8] The Bible was not seen as a system of 'rigid doctrines, unchangeable legal principles...but as a living message, repeatedly perceived anew in its recitation as the great prophetic testimony to the one and only powerful and merciful God'.[9]

During what has become known Age of Reason in seventeenth-century Europe, philosophers and scientists became suspicious of intuitive modes of thought and sacred traditions, and demanded that 'Truth' be demonstrated empirically. The emergence of so-called Rational Man changed how the Bible was read. Many scholars became suspicious of religion and applied their critical skills to the Bible. Baruch Spinoza, for example, pioneered biblical criticism and concluded that the 'obvious inconsistency' in the Bible meant that it could not be of divine origin. Spinoza was excommunicated in 1656. William Whiston published a version of the New Testament in 1745 from which he erased all references to the Incarnation and the Trinity, which he claimed were church teachings rather than God's word. Johann Gottfried Eichhorn, a professor of Oriental languages at Jena University in the 1800s, argued that there are two main authors of the chapter of Genesis, one who called God 'Yahweh' and the other who used the title 'Elohim'. This, he argued, is why there are two accounts of creation in that chapter. Wilhelm DeWetter argued that the the first five books of the Old Testament were a combination of four independent sources. Julius Wellhausen went a step further and suggested that there had been additions to the four sources before they were combined into a single narrative.[10] These revelations did not affect most practising Christians and Jews, many of whom considered revelation to be an ongoing process in which 'exegetes continued to make the Word of God audible in each generation'.[11]

This changed in the nineteenth century when the works of Charles Darwin, Karl Marx, and Thomas H. Huxley were viewed as an assault on religion. The publication of *Essays and Reviews* by seven Anglican clergymen in 1861 made biblical criticism available to the wider public who were 'now informed that…Moses had not written the Pentateuch, nor David the Psalms. Biblical miracles…should not be understood literally, and most of the events described in the Bible were clearly not historical.'[12]

Around the turn of the twentieth century, Catholic intellectuals such as Maurice Blondel, Lucien Laberthonniere, Baron von Hugel, and George Tyrrell sought to reconcile Catholic tradition with contemporary ideas. The denunciation of 'modernism' as hostile to the Catholic Church by Pope Pius X's *Pascendi dominici gregis* (1907) paved the way for repression, dismissals, and excommunication, all of which stifled independent thought in the church.[13] As far as conservative Christian thinkers were concerned, biblical criticism, also known as 'Higher Criticism', symbolised all that was wrong with the post-Enlightenment world.[14]

The *Scofield Reference Bible* published in 1909 was categorical that 'there was no hidden truth [in the Bible], accessible only to a learned elite'. The Bible, it argued, meant exactly what it said. This fundamentalist emphasis on the literal, Armstrong concludes, was 'a breach with tradition, which usually preferred some kind of figurative or innovative interpretation'.[15] Nevertheless, many Christians, especially those from evangelical Protestant groups in the USA, such as the Mormons, Jehovah's Witnesses, and Seventh Day Adventists, came to hold that the Bible was 'in every respect – linguistic, stylistic, logical, historical, scientific – a miraculous, absolutely perfect holy book' in which the scriptures not only contain but are the Word of God, and in which 'every biblical statement on any subject was absolute truth to the facts'.[16]

Deedat challenged the concept of biblical inerrancy. He drew on existing biblical criticism and packaged it in his own unique way to argue that the Bible was in fact corrupt.

David Westerlund, professor of religious studies at Södertörn University in Stockholm, summarised Deedat's theology through an analysis of his core works: *Is the Bible God's Word?*; *al-Qur'an: The Miracle of Miracles*; *What is His Name?*; *Christ in Islam*; and *Muhammad: The Natural Successor to Christ*.[17] According to Westerlund, Deedat's views on Jesus, the Prophet Muhammad, the Qur'an, and the Bible fall within the 'orthodox tradition' and are similar to liberal Protestant theology.

Deedat saw the doctrine of the Trinity as evidence of shirk (polytheism) and, seeing this as the foundation on which Christianity was built, he sought to refute it. He remained wedded to the classical Islamic idea of the ahl al-kitab ('people of the book', that is, Christians) as a people who received divine revelation through Moses and Jesus but subsequently distorted part of God's messages and neglected other aspects. He argued that Christians and Jews had deviated from their received texts to such an extent that their only salvation lay in their conversion to Islam.

In *Who Moved the Stone?* Deedat wrote that the Christian mind 'has been programmed from childhood to accept dogmas without reasoning. Today, the Christian is groping for the Truth [and] asking questions which he did not dare to ask a few centuries ago.'[18] He articulated the Muslim view about Jesus and Christianity, namely that: sin is not inherited; the doctrine of the Trinity is a fabrication; Jesus was not God; God does not beget children; Jesus was not killed or crucified; Christian texts have been falsified; and Qur'anic beliefs are a logical fulfilment of Jesus' teachings.[19]

In *Is the Bible God's Word?* Deedat argued that while the Bible contains the words of God, the prophets and accounts of historical events – and therefore has divine origins – the existence of several early manuscripts and translations and the inclusion of the words of human beings raised doubts about its validity as a record of Jesus' life and teachings.[20] In view of various discrepancies, Deedat argued that the Bible cannot be taken as the literal word of God. On the other hand, Deedat claimed in *al-Qur'an: The Miracle of Miracles* that the Qur'an, which Muslims regard as the 'foundation document of God's final revelation',[21] has divine origins and contains the unchanged word of God. When Deedat toured Switzerland he was interviewed on World Radio Geneva's 'Freely Speaking' programme on 16 March 1987 and was asked about the authenticity of the Qur'an. He replied as follows:

> We believe that God chooses His messengers, and this choosing is not of our standard, like He chose Moses, who had killed an Egyptian, was a stutterer, but God chose him to be his mouthpiece. He chose Jesus, a person without genealogy, a man without a father that he can point to, but God chooses a man like that and of poor background. Why? That's His business. Then He chooses Muhammad, a man who was absolutely illiterate, a person who didn't know how to read or write, a man who couldn't sign his own name, and He chooses a man like that…That one man, illiterate man, He brought about this book which in its material magnitude outshines any author of the

Holy Bible. The Holy Bible consists of some sixty-six books of the Protestant Bible and seventy-three books of the Roman Catholics. These sixty-six books are authored by forty different persons and the most voluminous writer is Paul who wrote fourteen of the twenty-seven books of the New Testament. But when you take those fourteen books, sometimes half a page, one page, it is a little thing. If this Qur'an is Muhammad's job, a one-man job and from an illiterate man, he outshines every author that you can think of. So I say, where did he get it? He says that it's given to him by inspiration from God, he takes no credit for it and when you look at it, you find he's not talking about himself at all. He dictated it. As he was moved, inspired, he dictated it and it was preserved. He was dictating it to people to write it down, and have it read to him again, and he used to confirm that it was correct. And this is now part of the scripture. The twenty-three years of his prophetic life was given by God, is now contained in this volume called the Holy Qur'an.[22]

In *Christ in Islam*, Deedat outlined the special status that Jesus occupied in Islam. Christians, he points out, 'do not know that the true spirit of charity which the Muslim displays, always, towards Jesus and his mother Mary springs from the fountainhead of his faith – the Holy Qur'an…Jesus is mentioned in over a hundred verses in the Qur'an and regarded "with great reverence and sympathy".' However, while accepting Jesus' miraculous conception and numerous miracles, Muslims believe that these were performed with God's permission and that Jesus was the servant rather than the son of God. In *The God that Never Was*, Deedat listed passages from the Bible that describe Jesus' human characteristics to argue that he was not divine. To regard Jesus as the son of God implies that 'God was born, had a family, developed spiritually, was tempted by the devil, hungry and thirsty, on the run, captured and killed'. Deedat's style in this booklet, as in many of his works, is caustic. He has sections titled 'The Strong-Arm Method of "God"', 'The Sabre-Rattling "God"', 'The Dumb and Docile "God"', and 'The Obituary of the Late and Lamented "God"'. Deedat aimed to show that if Jesus was God, then these human characteristics portrayed in the Bible must also be God's qualities.

In *Muhammad (PBUH) the Greatest*, Deedat reiterated his argument that Jesus was a prophet sent by God whose message was distorted by Paul, the main author of the New Testament. Deedat went on to show that for Muslims, 'irrespective of cultural, geographical and political differences, Muhammad (PBUH), is Allah's greatest creation…*But what of the non-Muslims?* Surprisingly, over the centuries many an eminent non-Muslim has rated Muhammad (PBUH) most highly and given due recognition to his greatness.' Deedat admonished Muslims for their inferiority complex when he explained how the booklet originated:

> I received a phone call from the Muslim community in Dannhauser, a small town in Northern Natal, who were organising a birthday celebration of the Holy Prophet. They invited me to give a lecture on that auspicious occasion. I deemed it an honour and a privilege [and] readily agreed. When they inquired, in view of their advertising needs, as to the subject of my lecture, I suggested…'Muhammad (PBUH) the Greatest'. On

my arrival in Dannhauser, I noticed a lot of posters advertising the meeting which in essence said that Deedat would be lecturing on the subject 'Muhammad the *Great*'. I was somewhat disheartened and, on inquiring was told that the change in the title was due to a printer's error...Some two months later, I got another, similar invitation from the Muslim community of Pretoria, the administrative capital of South Africa. The subject I had mooted was the same – 'Muhammad (PBUH) the Greatest.' To my dismay the topic was again changed to 'Muhammad the *Great*'. Identical reasons and excuses were given. Both these incidences happened in South Africa, my own country. What is the cause of this sickness? This inferiority complex? 'Yes!' We are an emasculated people. Dynamism has been wringed out of us, not only by our enemies, but by our own spiritless friends.

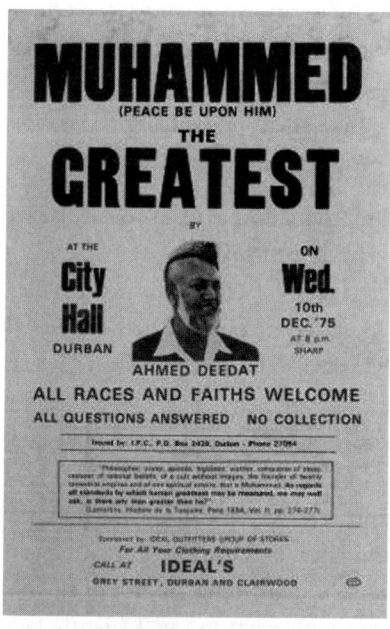

Deedat cited the works of Western non-Muslim writers who had written favourably about the Prophet Muhammad (PBUH) and Islam, such as George Bernard Shaw, A.J. Arberry, Thomas Carlyle, Jules Masserman, and Michael H. Hart who, in *The 100: A Ranking of the Most Influential Persons in History*, placed the Prophet (PBUH) in first place.[23] In *Muhammad: The Natural Successor to Christ*, Deedat draws on the Bible to argue that it prophesied the coming of Muhammad. He interprets Deuteronomy 18:18 and a reference in John's Gospel to the 'Comforter' or 'Helper' as prophecies about the Prophet (PBUH).[24] In 1984, Deedat wrote that, in the battle for hearts and minds, the '"crucifiction" is the only card the Christian holds. Free him from his infatuation and you will have freed the Muslim world from missionary aggression and harassment.'[25]

By 1975, Deedat no longer had to worry about 'printing errors' on the posters advertising his lectures.

In *Crucifixion or Cruci-fiction?* Deedat wrote that his study of this vexed subject 'was thrust upon me by those of the Christian faith who claimed to be my well-wishers. I seriously took their concern for me to heart and studied and researched objectively. The results you will agree are astounding.' Deedat's hypothesis was that Jesus was put on the cross, but did not die. Instead, he argues that Jesus fainted (swooned) and the Romans thought that he was dead. He revived later and a rumour started that he had risen from the dead. Deedat used verses of the Old and New Testaments to argue that Jesus was not on the cross long enough to have died. Noting Paul's message that salvation can only be obtained through the death and resurrection of Jesus, Deedat argues that 'if Jesus did *not* die, and he was *not* resurrected from the dead, then there can be *no* salvation in Christianity! In a nutshell: *no Crucifixion*, *no Christianity!'* The South African Directorate of Publications wanted to ban *Crucifixion or Cruci-fiction?* in 1985 on the grounds that it was 'offensive and blasphemous'. The Appeals Board ruled that the booklet was not undesirable even though its tone was 'harsh'.[26]

Many of the issues raised by Deedat had already been articulated within the tradition of biblical criticism. However, the way in which Deedat packaged his message appealed to many and affronted others. Deedat's publications had bold graphics and were easy on the eye and mind. His literary style was 'characterised by clearness and simplicity. It lacks academic complexity and jargon,' and includes both 'humour and human interest', making it accessible to a wide non-academic readership.'[27] The following extract from *Is the Bible God's Word?* is a good example of his style:

> While I was still formulating the theme of this booklet [in 1980], I heard a knock at my door one Sunday morning. I opened the door. A European gentleman stood there, grinning broadly. 'Good morning,' he said. 'Good morning,' I replied. He was offering me his *Awake* and *Watchtower* magazines. Yes, a Jehovah's Witness! If a few had knocked at your door previously, you will recognise them immediately. The most supercilious lot of people who ever knocked at people's doors! I invited him in.
>
> As soon as he settled down, I produced the full reproduction of what you see below [a 1957 issue of *Awake*]. Pointing to the monograph at the top of the page, I asked, 'Is this yours?' He readily recognised his own. I said, 'It says: "50 000 Errors in the Bible", is it true?' 'What's that!' he exclaimed. I repeated, 'I said that it says there are 50 000 errors in your Bible.' 'Where did you get that?' he asked. (This was published 23 years ago, when he was perhaps a little nipper). I said, 'Leave the fancy talk aside – is this yours?'...He said, 'Can I have a look?' 'Of course,' I said. I handed him the page. He started perusing. They (the Jehovah's Witnesses) are trained. They attend classes five times a week in their 'Kingdom Halls'. Naturally, they are the fittest missionaries among the thousand-and-one-sects-and-denominations of Christendom. They are taught that when cornered, do not commit yourself to anything, do not open your mouths. Wait for the Holy Ghost to inspire you with what to say. I silently kept watching him, while he browsed the page. Suddenly he looked up. He had found it. The 'Holy Ghost' had tickled him. He began, 'The article says that *"most of those errors have been eliminated."* I asked 'If *most* are eliminated, how many remain out of 50 000? 5 000? 500? 50? Even if 50 remain, do you attribute those errors to God?' He was speechless. He excused himself by suggesting that he will come again with some senior member of his Church. That will be the day!

The booklet *Resurrection or Resuscitation?*, which underscores the point that Jesus did not die for the sins of human beings, also has an informal, conversational style. Like many of Deedat's works, it was triggered by an encounter with a Christian minister.

> I was about to leave for the Transvaal (South Africa) on a lecture tour, so I phoned my friend Hafidh Yusuf Dadoo of Standerton, informing him of my impending visit,

as well as to inquire whether he needed anything from Durban. He said that as he was taking up Hebrew, I should try and obtain a Bible in the Hebrew language with a translation in English side by side.

When Deedat went to purchase the Bibles, the supervisor, a Reverend Roberts, asked to meet with him. During the meeting Roberts quoted several verses from the Bible. According to Deedat, Roberts did this because,

> despite my numerous purchases of Bibles in English (various versions), in Zulu, Afrikaans, Urdu, Arabic and other languages, I was not yet *converted*. Perhaps what I really needed was a gentle push, the supervisor must have been told. Hence the recitation of the preceding quotations to me. The implication of this reading was that I had probably not read those beautiful passages; how else was it possible, then, that I had not yet embraced Christianity?

Deedat explains in the rest of the booklet the verses that he quoted from the Bible to show its discrepancies:

> This was more than the Reverend had bargained for. He politely excused himself by saying that as he had to get ready to close his office, he would look forward to meeting me again. This was sheer evasive politeness! With the Bible Society, I won the debate but lost the discount! No more discount for me from the Bible Society. But let my loss be your gain. If you dear reader, can remove a few cobwebs from your thinking on the subject of the Crucifixion, I will be amply rewarded.

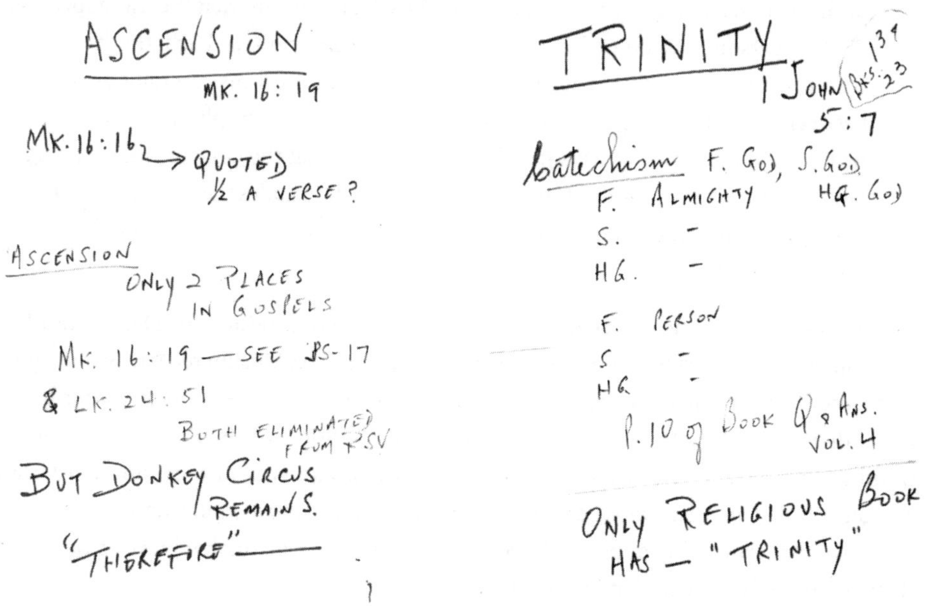

*[Handwritten notes:]*

ASCENSION
MK. 16:19

MK. 16:16 → QUOTED)
½ A VERSE?

ASCENSION
ONLY 2 PLACES IN GOSPELS

MK. 16:19 — SEE PS-17
& LK. 24:51
BOTH ELIMINATED FROM RSV

BUT DONKEY CIRCUS REMAINS.

"THEREFORE" —

TRINITY
1 JOHN 5:7 (¹³⁴) (²³)

Catechism  F. GOD, S. GOD
F. ALMIGHTY   HG. GOD
S. —
HG. —

F. PERSON
S —
HG —

P. 10 of Book Q & Ans.
VOL. 4

ONLY RELIGIOUS BOOK
HAS — "TRINITY"

Deedat kept a file for his notes on each booklet he wrote and each debate he took part in; these notes were made prior to his debate with Jimmy Swaggart.

Deedat's publications were not intended to accrue revenue for the IPCI. The booklets have always been distributed gratis, and have never contained the usual copyright restrictions; on the contrary, his publications included the following statement encouraging people to copy them and pass them on to others:

> Open Order
> We grant you an open licence to reproduce or translate into any language this booklet as well as other publications of ours. You may publish them for sale or for free distribution without any prior permission. We ask for no royalties or 'copyrights'. Wallahi! If we had the means we would have flooded the world with our free literature.

Deedat often referred to Christian missionaries as 'modern-day crusaders' and 'B.A. (born again)' Christianity as 'a new sickness'.[28] Terms such as these, as well as 'Bible-thumpers' and 'hot-gospellers', have been described by Deedat's critics as 'derogatory'.[29] In *Crucifixion or Cruci-fiction?*, for example, he wrote 'the Bible-thumpers have developed a new sickness of glamourising despicability and ignominy. Everyone, male or female, of these cultists, will not fail to relate their peccadilloes, their adulteries and bestialities, their drinkings and druggings. It appears that one must have been part of the dregs of humanity to become a candidate for this 'born again' cult.[30] Philip Lewis described the booklets as

> crude but clever compilations of allegedly damning evidence to prove that the Bible is incoherent, full of mistakes and contains sexually reprehensible material, unworthy of any serious publication. Deedat draws indiscriminately from whatever material is at hand, whether the writings of the Jehovah's Witnesses, the Seventh Day Adventists or the American evangelist Billy Graham...Deedat points out that the Bible speaks in the first person for God or Jesus, as well as in the third person. The latter he equates with history. Deedat then triumphantly declares that Muslims carefully distinguish between these three types – God's speech (the Qur'an), Prophetic discourse (the hadith) and the works of Muslim historians. For Deedat the conclusion is clear: 'the Holy Bible contains a motley type of literature, which includes the sordid and obscene – all under the same cover – with the Christian...forced to concede equal spiritual import to all'.[31]

This synopsis does not do justice to the literature and videos produced by Deedat, nor has it attempted to analyse the theological merits of his ideas. Most Muslim readers would agree with Deedat even while opposing his method. Most Christian readers, on the other hand, would disagree with both Deedat's ideas and methods. Some of their arguments can be found at sites such as 'Answering Islam' and in the arguments of local South African evangelist John Gilchrist, whose encounter with Deedat is described in Chapter 13. It was not only Christians who opposed Deedat, however. Some of his harshest critics were Muslims, and it is to them that we now turn.

# 9

# 'REVILE NOT LEST YE BE REVILED'

Such was his self-confidence that Ahmed Deedat's stock response to critics was to challenge them to a public debate.

We may remind Mr Ahmed Deedat and his colleagues that theirs is an *Islamic Propagation Centre*, that is, to present and propagate Islam, and not a *Christian Destructive Centre*, that is to attack the *Christian faith*.

– *al-Mujaddid*, December 1960

WHILE DEEDAT was making waves as a speaker of national repute, his father Hoosen Deedat once publicly rebuked him at the Durban City Hall in front of thousands of people for debating with Christians who merited respect as ahl al-kitab (people of the book). Deedat, usually deferential to his father, did not heed this particular piece of advice. As far as he was concerned, a polite approach was inappropriate because Islam (like the black population of South Africa) was facing a 'total onslaught'. He regarded it as his duty to challenge Western perceptions of Islam and to awaken Muslims from their slumber. He often pointed out that while Muslims respected Christians, Christians saw Islam as a false religion and Muslims as a people whose beliefs had to be 'corrected'. According to G.H. Agjee, this, together with the combined weight of colonialism, imperialism, apartheid, and the massive resources at the disposal of missionaries, led Deedat to conclude that dialogue would always take place on unequal ground. He was determined instead to confront Christian missionaries on his terms.

Deedat faced opposition from within and without Islam. Other Muslims, who cared equally deeply about da'wah, adopted a more conciliatory approach and opposed Deedat vigorously. At the heart of the dispute between Deedat and his adversaries was the proper method of da'wah. While da'wah is theoretically incumbent upon all members of the umma, the contrasting objectives of individuals and organisations resulted in contestation over exactly what it means and how best to conduct it.

Muslim critics such as Adam Peerbhai, Mohammed Makki, I.M. Bawa, A.S.K. Joommal, and Abdullah Deedat felt that Ahmed Deedat's approach was damaging relations between Muslims and Christians. They also questioned the depth of his knowledge of Islamic and Christian theology. They felt that da'wah should be performed with 'gentleness of speech', especially when it involved public argumentation. As Charles Hirshkind put it, many Muslims felt that da'wah should be 'conducted in a calm, respectful manner, protected from the kind of passions that would vitiate the act and the social benefit that it seeks to realise'.[1] Fervent debates about the issue were mainly played out in Islamic newspapers such as *al-Balaagh*, *Majlis*, and *al-Mujaddid*, community newspapers such as *The Graphic* and *Leader*, and through the distribution of pamphlets and other ephemeral materials.

On 25 April 1960, Deedat addressed an audience of around two thousand people at the Durban City Hall on the topic 'Was Christ Crucified?' Quoting extensively from the Bible, the Qur'an, and medical authorities, he argued in his ninety-minute lecture that his research of Christian texts showed that due to the short period of time that Jesus was on the cross, he did not die during the crucifixion, but merely lost consciousness (swooned), and revived again after he had been taken down from the cross.

While most of the mainly Muslim audience applauded Deedat, Adam Peerbhai, a local teacher, sportsman, and author, challenged him for contradicting the Islamic teachings about the fate of Jesus. Most Muslims believe that Jesus was not nailed to the cross but miraculously ascended to the Heavens and will reappear on earth at some future date to establish universal peace. Many Qur'an exegetes translate the Qur'anic verse 4:157 as 'But they did not slay him, nor did they crucify him…But (another) seemed to them similar so that they confused him with Jesus and killed him.' The verse is interpreted as meaning that someone else was killed in place of Jesus, and that Jesus will return to earth as a follower of Islam with a mission to destroy the Anti-Christ.[2] Peerbhai felt that Deedat was confusing the predominantly Muslim audience by presenting the Christian perspective.[3] Aside from a book on cricket, Peerbhai wrote *Glory of Jesus in the Koran* (1950) and two booklets, *Hadis Text on the Second Coming of Jesus* and *Missing Documents from the Gospel of Barnabas* (1967).

Mohammed Makki, the man behind the monthly periodical *Muslim Digest* and the *Ramadan Annual Muslim Digest*, was one of Deedat's harshest and most consistent critics. Makki was born on 22 January 1909 in India and studied under Shaykh Abdul Aleem Siddiqui at the darul 'ulum in Bareilly. Makki had a sound traditional orthodox Islamic training, and could read and write in English, Persian, Urdu, and Gujarati. He came to South Africa in the mid-1920s with his father Essop Suleman Vadachia. In 1934 he invited his former teacher, Shaykh Siddiqui, to South Africa. Siddiqui conferred the title 'Makki'[4] upon Vadachia and helped Makki to initiate the publishing of *Muslim Digest* and the *Ramadan Annual*, which ran for sixty-five years from 1934, ceasing in 1999 when Makki was ninety years old! *Muslim Digest* had a wide circulation among Muslims in many parts of Africa.

Deedat's critics, Adam Peerbhai (left) and Mohamed Makki (right).

Deedat and Makki remained at odds to the very end. Makki's attitude is summed up in an editorial in an issue of *Muslim Digest* published in 1986:

> From time to time religious fanatics have surfaced; also firebrands determined to foist their own kind of religious philosophy on the masses. But none can surpass Deedat for the animosity he has generated among non-Muslims or the bitter resentment he has caused within Islamic circles and his own Muslim community in this country.[5]

As early as April 1960, Makki had criticised Deedat for misleading his majority Muslim audience with the Christian perspective on Jesus' crucifixion. Makki claimed that after a talk Deedat gave in April of that year, Deedat had admitted to Makki and businessman M.E. Paruk that he was not aware of any hadith (traditions of the Prophet PBUH) relating to the re-advent of Jesus. Deedat wrote to Makki on 12 July 1960 accepting the ascent and descent of Jesus. Makki wondered whether Deedat was sincere since he continued to repeat the Christian perspective. Deedat, for his part, insisted that he was not presenting the

Muslim perspective on the crucifixion but tactically using Christian texts to critique the Christian understanding of the death of Jesus.

Makki wrote in 1986 that Deedat was by his own admission 'no man of letters as far as secular knowledge is concerned' and that his Islamic knowledge had been acquired from 'dubious' sources such as Joseph Perdu. Makki argued that Deedat's lack of grounding in Islamic theology meant that he was easily influenced by Muslims with questionable beliefs, such as Perdu, Muhammad Asad, and Rashid Khalifa, which made his views on Islam 'most dangerous'.[6] In Makki's estimation, Deedat was a 'pretender to the Islamic throne':

> Deedat really represents nobody but himself. He does not represent the Muslims of the world; he does not represent the Muslims of South Africa; he does not represent the Muslims of Natal; he does not represent the Muslims of Durban; he does not represent the Muslims of his own little town of Verulam either where he resides, and in fact the Trustees of the Verulam Mosque have even banned Deedat from making a speech in the only Muslim Mosque in his own home town.[7]

There were other sources of tension between Deedat and Makki. They competed for limited local finances, and Makki was upset that the IPC had 'borrowed' his idea of publishing an Islamic calendar. Deedat's eventual success in procuring overseas funds exacerbated these tensions. According to A.S.K. Joommal, both men were headstrong and neither was willing to concede an inch.

Although the IPC's letterhead quoted the Qur'anic verse 16:125, it also captured Abdullah Deedat's main criticism of his half-brother Ahmed Deedat: 'Invite (all) to the Way of thy Lord with Wisdom and Beautiful Preaching; and reason with them in ways that are Best and Most Gracious.'

Abdullah, who was amongst Deedat's harshest critics, was born in 1935 and was sponsored by the Arabic Study Circle to study at al-Azhar University in Egypt from 1954 to 1956. At al-Azhar, Abdullah came into contact with members of the Muslim Brotherhood (al-Ikhwan) which was trying to address both the fact of Western domination and the demands of Muslim piety, something that resonated with Abdullah, who had been influenced by the Egyptian nationalist movement. Abdullah had to return to South Africa without completing his studies because of the invasion of Egypt by Britain, France, and Israel on 29 October 1956 in response to Nasser's decision to nationalise the Suez Canal. The other great influence on Abdullah was Allamah Muhammad Iqbal, whose writings attempted to reconstruct a path back to the scientific and intellectual striving that Muslims once excelled in.

Abdullah initially joined the Ahmedia School in Durban but was recruited by the Central Islamic Trust in Johannesburg in 1961 and taught there for a decade. In 1960, Abdullah started the newspaper *al-Mujaddid* [The reformer/Renewal/Revival of spirit]. Its message

Ahmed Deedat's half-brother Abdullah was both a supporter and a critic.

was that Islam had become fossilised; instead, it should be active everywhere, in the workplace, at home, and so on, and not confined to the mosque. According to Abdullah, the Qur'an was 'clear as clear can be' and Muslims could refer directly to the Qur'an or to hadith instead of consulting the 'ulama on doctrinal issues. Abdullah's perspective was considered 'radical for its time' and remains controversial.

The relationship between Abdullah and Ahmed Deedat was fraught with tension. Abdullah objected strongly to Deedat's approach to the propagation of Islam. In an *al-Mujaddid* editorial headlined 'Stop This Farce' shortly after Deedat's April 1960 lecture on the crucifixion, he wrote:

> It is a well-known fact that the propagation of Islam is the duty of each and every Muslim…When we go through the pages of the Qur'an we notice that this Holy Book breathes into the Muslims a spirit of tolerance and understanding towards all human beings. Verse 6:108 in the Qur'an states 'Revile not ye those whom they call upon besides God, lest they out of spite revile God in their ignorance. Thus have We made alluring to each people its own doings.' This verse is strongly against anyone criticising or condemning the religion of others. In this short and simple verse we notice a psychological truth, that is when we revile the beliefs or point out flaws in the religion of any person, that person even though he may be a seeker of truth, will in turn shun the truth and even insult the truth…One thing is certain, if Mr Deedat and his colleagues are to entertain any hope of bringing about an understanding between Christians and Muslims, then they must *stop this farce*![8]

Abdullah went on to outline the principles that he had deduced from the life of the Prophet (PBUH) and the Qur'an with regard to da'wah.

Muslims should invite others to Islam 'with wisdom and beautiful preaching; and argue with them in ways that are best and most gracious' (16:125). The Qur'an emphasises that the one doing the calling should 'have patience with what they say, and leave them with noble dignity' (73:10).

Abdullah advocated interfaith dialogue and disagreed with Deedat's premise that 'it was absolutely necessary to break the faith of the Christians' because it implied that 'Islam itself will not attract the people'.[9]

The editor of the Muslim newspaper *al-Balaagh*, A.S.K. Joommal, had a field day when Abdullah joined the IPCI in 1987. Joommal was 'shocked' at Abdullah's move after attacking Deedat

> so vociferously, so zealously, and so volubly over so many years. Take out old issues [of *al-Mujaddid*] and present them afresh to Mr Ahmed Deedat – from brother-to-brother – and refresh his memory – and yours. You used to attack your brother. Now you are tied to his apron-strings.[10]

Abdullah joined the IPCI after making a heartfelt appeal to Deedat on 16 January 1987:

> Though I do a fair share of Islamic work I do find that I have done not enough for my Creator and my Rasul (PBUH)...My knowledge of Islam increases by the day as I do my quota of daily Qur'anic Studies, etc. I do have occasions to speak at university Christian, Jewish, and Political Forums – true, many occasions. But is this enough? I find emptiness in my being. My offer to you is to serve Islam under your leadership. You have been a 'father' to me and by the day I have realised your selflessness, sacrifice and dedication to Islam; then ask myself that I have been formally schooled in Islamic disciplines and yet my track record is dismal by any comparison. I do not ask for any wages or salary...My desire is to serve under your guidance and thereby make my humble contribution to the glory of Islam. My experience, you will agree, is far ranging and Allah is the *best teacher* and I offer you my services in any field you deem fit. I repeat – I do not want a salary, a title, a post, etc. I just want to be a servant. If Allah accepts my efforts and endeavours then that will be reward enough.

Dr G.M. Hoosen, a trustee at the time, recalled that Ahmed Deedat was moved to tears when he discussed the request with trustees on 29 January 1987. They accepted Abdullah's offer and the latter ran the international da'wah programme successfully for some years. Hoosen described his classes as 'brilliant. If he focused on education, he would have left a lasting legacy.' Abdullah denied that he joined the IPCI because of the funds pouring in from the Middle East. He said that 'it pained him to see a family member making a fool of himself as he lurched from controversy to controversy'. He insisted that he had 'a genuine desire to assist. I hoped to take the organisation in a positive direction.' He left the IPCI within a few years, he claims, when he realised that Deedat and his son Yousuf were 'obstinate' and that he could not get them to change course. In his letter dated 27 August

1989, Abudllah wrote that he was resigning from the IPCI because of Deedat's 'unbecoming actions which are being exposed to the public through the relevant ulema bodies'.

Some 'ulama questioned Deedat's credentials as an Islamic scholar, and even his right to engage in religious discussions given his lack of formal training. They were critical of his views on Jesus' crucifixion, his distribution of English-translation Qur'ans, and of the fact that he took non-Muslims, and especially women, on mosque tours. One such critic was Mawlana Ahmad Sadiq (A.S.) Desai of Port Elizabeth. Desai started and edited *The Majlis* newspaper, which he used to publish this critique of Deedat:

> It is essential to state – and stress – that Mr Deedat is not a man of Islamic learning. He is not qualified to speak on matters pertaining to the Shari'ah. What is fard upon Mr Deedat is the acquisition of the basic rules pertaining to Wudu, Ṣalah, Ṣawm, etc. so that he may be in a position to discharge his daily Islamic duties. But, Islamic Law is not his avenue. His confusion is the product of his stark ignorance of the Shari'ah.[11]

'Ulama were also critical of Deedat for distributing the English translation of the Qur'an by Yusuf Ali because they disagreed with several of Ali's interpretations. According to the Port Elizabeth-based Majlisul Ulama, Yusuf Ali's 'commentary contains views which are contradictory to the teachings and opinions of the Prophet (PBUH)'. This included the fact that Yusuf Ali regarded heaven and hell as states of mind; denied the existence of Satan; and accepted interest and credit. Muslims who accepted Yusuf Ali's commentary therefore risked lapsing into 'confusion and doubt', as had happened with Christians.[12]

Deedat was also criticised for distributing Muhammad Asad's translation of the Qur'an. The translation by Asad (formerly Leopold Weiss, and author of *Islam at the Crossroads* and *The Road to Mecca*) was popular among many Muslims because, according to G.H. Agjee, he 'rationalised verses of the Qur'an to meet twentieth century expectations…While some of his interpretations may have been objectionable, most were illuminating, and for this he was an inspiration to thousands.' Zuleikha Mayat of the Women's Cultural Group, Daoud Mall of the Arabic Study Circle, Ebrahim Jadwat of the Muslim Youth Movement, and Salman Nadvi, Professor of Islamic studies at the University of Durban-Westville, were all involved in distributing Asad's translation, while some ulama, including the Islamic Council of South Africa, objected particularly to Asad's view that Jesus died on the cross. Ibrahim Bawa, secretary-general of the Islamic Council, issued a statement on 16 September 1978 that since Asad's view was contrary to those of the majority of Muslims, the Qur'an should 'not be distributed to the general public as it will unjustifiably create doubts and confusion in the minds of ordinary Muslims'.

Dr Daoud Mall of the Arabic Study Circle responded in a statement on 4 October 1978, saying that the Council did not have the right to 'assume the status of a board of censors for the Muslim community. Islam knows no priesthood and no matter how learned a body of ulema, they have no right to prescribe to the Muslim Ummah what it should read and what it should not.' In a second statement on 20 November 1978, Mall pointed out that Mawlana Abdur Rahman Ansari, president of the Jami'atul 'Ulama Natal, had stated in the presence of Mawlana Abdul Haq Omarjee that while the majority of scholars held that Jesus was lifted up to the Heavens alive and will come back to earth, a minority believed that Jesus had died. These scholars included Muhammad Abduh, the Grand Mufti of Egypt, and Mahmud Shalut, former rector of al-Azhar University. Tension between Deedat and Mawlana Desai boiled over when Deedat toured Port Elizabeth in June 1980 at the invitation of the Muslim Youth Movement (MYM). Prior to his arrival posters had been put up at the Malabar Mosque advertising the lecture. Mawlana Desai issued a statement on 1 June 1980 dissociating the mosque from Deedat. In a circular, issued on 6 June 1980, Desai stated that 'Deedat is not qualified in Islamic knowledge…In the interests of their Imān [faith], Muslims are strongly exhorted to abstain from Deedat's lectures and MYM activities.'[13]

Fuad Hendriks with Deedat in Uitenhage, 1980.

Deedat and Fuad Hendriks, director of the MYM; Abdul Aziz Shaik, director of the South African National Zakah Fund; and Yusuf Ahmed, a member of the Muslim Students' Association, were assaulted outside Port Elizabeth's Durban Street Mosque.[14] Deedat then proceeded to move his talk to the nearby town of Uitenhage. At the end of his lecture, an Imam Fuad asked Deedat whether he believed in the physical ascension of Jesus. He responded with an unequivocal 'yes'.[15] Deedat later laid charges of assault against three people, one of whom was found guilty.

The dispute between Deedat and the ulama must be viewed in the context of the broader dispute over the means of acquiring 'ilm (knowledge) in Islam. There is no consensus on what constitutes an Islamic scholar. Technically, an 'alim is one who acquires knowledge by studying tafsir (Qur'anic exegesis), fiqh (jurisprudence), 'ilm al-hadith (Prophetic tradition), and 'ilm al-kalam (theology) at a darul 'ulum (seminary). However, some Muslims emphasise that what matters is the content of the knowledge obtained, not the means, and the consequent recognition by fellow Muslims of the 'authority' thus derived.[16]

Fuad Hendriks of the MYM believes that some ulama disparaged Deedat because he 'exposed their incompetence. They felt insecure when he infringed on their territory and attacked him in the broader struggle for the hearts and minds of ordinary Muslims.'

A.S.K. Joommal, who founded and has edited *al-Balaagh* since 1978, is ambivalent about Deedat. He praises what he regards as Deedat's positive contribution and is critical of his shortcomings. He wrote in 1986 that there was 'a mixed assessment [of Deedat] amongst Muslims'. Joommal acknowledged the work that Deedat has done 'in his chosen field of propagating Islam. The literature published by the IPCI is praiseworthy. In all fairness to Mr Deedat, the good he has done must not be overlooked.' However, this was sometimes 'washed away by his abrasive approach'.[17]

Joommal differed from Deedat's other critics in that the two men enjoyed a close association despite their differences. Joommal read Deedat's manuscripts and would comment on them before publication. Joommal described Deedat as a 'marvellous speaker'. Joommal visited Deedat several times during his final years and reported that he 'retained his intelligence and wisdom to the end'. While acknowledging Deedat's 'greatness', Joommal felt that Deedat and the IPCI went 'off-track with the influx of money. It takes a very strong character not to have been influenced under the circumstances.'

Professor Salman Nadvi was not an outspoken critic but disagreed with Deedat's approach and told him so in private conversations:

> My reasoning was that the Qur'an says that you should not abuse other religions because if you do that, you put their back up and in return they will argue back and abuse your religion. I was not very happy with aggressive debate. I was opposed to his asking the Catholic Pope to have a debate – popes don't have time to do any of those things. Iman comes through your reflection of your practical life. We have got lots of examples of that. This reminds me of a story which Muhammad Asad narrated to me. When he was put in jail in India, there were some Jehovah priests there. Asad was jailed because he had written articles in the German press which were critical of British imperialism. He was the only Muslim there. Asad was from a Jewish family. So from a Christian and Jewish point of view, the Jewish religion is first, then came Christianity, then Islam. The Christian is in the middle. So these priests were saying to him, 'You, a Jew, why did you become Muslim, leaving Christianity in the middle. You should have become Christian.' So Asad said, 'I'm prepared to convert even now to Christianity but I've got some questions. If you answer them I'll be very happy to convert.' So the first day they sat down to discuss Christianity and Asad asked them to explain the Trinity. As they were explaining, Asad was raising objections and posing questions so they said, 'Alright, we'll meet tomorrow to discuss this.' The next day again the same thing happened. Finally, the priests got tired because they couldn't explain the Trinity. So the frustrated priest turned to Asad and said, 'Look, if you become a Christian you will understand what the Trinity is.' Asad replied, 'But that is exactly why I became Muslim.'

Nadvi's point was that not all religious beliefs can be rationally debated or refuted. But Deedat did not accept this view:

> Deedat's reaction was always that 'you people are cowards'. Islam means that you must argue with them and he quoted the Qur'anic verse that said that when you confront Christians, argue with them in the best possible way. So he said that the Qur'an itself said that you must argue with them. But that was a misinterpretation of the Qur'an, which was not saying that when you enter into any conversation you start using bad language. The Qur'an gives the other indications also, that if they are not able to accept then you leave them alone. Whenever we had this discussion he never conceded that he was doing anything wrong. I never doubted his sincerity in what he was doing. I respected him for that and respected his knowledge of Christianity, which I didn't have, nobody had.

Deedat felt 'an obligation to continue' because he believed that Muslims were 'dead on the right road [while] Christians were alive on the wrong road'. He was determined to reverse this. Deedat was not an 'alim in the traditional sense, but there is no questioning that he considered himself a da'i in the sense of defending Islam and summoning others to the faith. His project eventually brought him into conflict with segments of the Muslim community. This did not seem to faze him, as he told journalist Keysar Trad when he was asked what he thought of 'ulama who objected to Muslims debating with Christians:

> Very easy, very easy, this means that they are ignorant of their history, poor people. Our Prophet (PBUH) had a debate with Christians. They [the 'ulama] are ignorant. It is a Sunna of the Prophet, the Christians came from Najran, for three days and three nights, they had their debate in the Masjidun Nabawi. Do they know that? Let them go and check up.[18]

Deedat's response to criticism, according to Mustacq Abdullah, was that he would stop when he was 'not needed…when the lecture halls were empty'.

Despite opposition, Deedat was convinced that he was carrying out God's mandate and refused to yield to pressure. Rafeek Hassen, who got to know Deedat as a teenager and maintained a lifelong association with him, doubts that he will ever meet anyone so wholly committed to defending Islam.

And critics there were aplenty, as we shall see from Deedat's tours of the Cape.

# 10
# CAPE OF STORMS

Passions always ran high at question time during Deedat's Cape Town lectures.

While Deedat created controversy in many parts of the world, his tours of the Cape took place in a context of existing tensions created by the attacks that local Christian missionaries had launched against Islam since the nineteenth century.

*I*SLAM AND CHRISTIANITY have had a presence at the Cape since at least the 1650s. The first official Dutch Refomed Church was based in Cape Town as early as 1694, and as historian Robert Shell has shown, some of the sixty-three thousand slaves imported to South Africa between 1653 and 1808, and many of the two thousand political leaders from South and South-East Asia who were exiled to the Cape by the Dutch East India Company, were Muslims.[1] The colonial authorities felt threatened by Islam and imposed harsh penalties for anyone caught spreading the religion. For example, in 1712 or 1713 a Javanese by the name of Santrij had his tongue cut out before being burnt alive for evangelising. Christian slave owners, on the other hand, did not actively try to convert their slaves in case they would then lose the right to sell slaves who embraced Christianity.[2]

British conquest of the Cape in 1795 was followed by the arrival of the Baptist, Presbyterian, Methodist, and Anglican churches. A mulatto slave-owner, Michiel Vos, founded the South African Missionary Society in Cape Town in 1799; this was the first mission specifically for slaves. In 1812, the government passed a law that slave owners did not have to free slaves who embraced Christianity.

Missionaries found it difficult to convert Muslims to Christianity and formed the Mission to Muhammadans in 1824 to devote themselves to this task, but made little headway. Speaking of Islam, Scotsman John Philip wrote to the directors of the London Missionary Society in 1831 that the 'result of this formidable apparatus' was the 'closing of any door before opened'. Similarly, in 1861, Petrus Borcherds of the Dutch Refomed Church (which in 1824 had established a synod in South Africa independent of Amsterdam) wrote that most freed slaves 'attached themselves…to the Mohammedans, with whom they were previously more or less connected'.[3]

While continuous immigration of Christian Europeans, and reduced conversions to Islam post-1840, meant that Christians far outnumbered Muslims in the Cape by the end of the nineteenth century, concern about Islam remained a feature of Christian discourse in that province well into the twentieth century.[4]

Fear that former slaves might convert to Islam was especially acute following the freeing of slaves in 1838. Anglicans, more than any other denomination, confronted the Islamic 'threat' from at least the middle of the nineteenth century. The Church of England acquired semi-official status at the Cape after the second British occupation in 1806, and it was only after the arrival of Robert Gray as bishop in 1847 that the objective of creating a church independent of the state was vigorously pursued.[5] Gray undertook a five-month, three-thousand-mile-long journey around Southern Africa.[6]

He identified Muslims as among the list of hurdles that faced the church's mission: 'In and about Cape Town was a great number of Mohammedans, in part the descendants of the Malays whom the Dutch had brought from their East Indian Colonies, in part liberated African slaves; and even settlers were found to be lapsing to Islam.'[7]

Gray bought a large estate five miles from the centre of Cape Town, later named Bishopscourt, where he trained men for Holy Orders, built a school, and 'plans were made for missions to the Mohammedans and the heathen'.[8]

The Reverend Thomas Fothergill Lightfoot, when he was in charge of the Mission to Moslems, expressed concern in 1900 that Africans were also embracing Islam. A Stellenbosch theologian, Gustav Bernhard Gerdener, observed in 1915 that African migrant workers to the Rand were coming under the influence of Muslim migrant workers who were 'enthusiastic propagators of their faith' and 'many of the raw natives return to their homes strong under the influence of Islam'.[9]

That the Anglicans, rather than other Christian denominations, took up the challenge to convert Muslims was partly due to geography and demographics. The three largest denominations in the Cape at the beginning of the twentieth century were the Dutch Reformed Church, the Methodists, and the Anglicans. The Dutch Reformed Church existed mostly in the rural areas and Methodists on mission stations. Anglicans had the largest presence in the urban areas. Baptists, Roman Catholics, Presbyterians, Lutherans, and members of the London Missionary Society were much smaller in number.[10]

Until the beginning of the twentieth century the responsibility for propagating Christianity in Cape Town was left to priests whose parishes were surrounded by large Muslim populations. In 1911, Stephen Garabedian was appointed the first director of the Muslim Mission Board under the command of the Diocesan Mission Board. The Muslim Mission Board, which was only disbanded in 1976, campaigned resolutely to prevent conversions to Islam and simultaneously to interest Muslims in Christianity. Garabedian, who held his post until 1922, was particularly concerned about Christian women marrying Muslim men and forsaking Christianity.[11] The Anglicans also published several books and pamphlets on this subject. For example, Anglican parishioner A.W. Blaxall's *An Outpost of Islam* (1927) evaluated previous attempts to convert Muslims to Christianity and suggested that more effective strategies be followed, while Reverend A.R. Hampson's 'The Mission to Moslems in Cape Town' (1934) chronicled his experiences of missionary work in the Cape.[12]

After Garabedian's resignation, the work of the Muslim Mission Board was continued by Anglican women who targeted Muslim women and children through sewing guilds and children's clubs. The Board was given new impetus after the Second World War with the appointment of a Miss J.K. Leslie who was concerned about the 'threat' posed by Islam and disseminated propaganda to dispel the myth that 'Muslims were a very fine set of people', to impress on Christians the seriousness of apostasy, to 'win back' lapsed Christians, and to prepare the converted for baptism. She wanted to publish 'picture books' since, in her view, few converts to Islam were literate and had little knowledge of the Qur'an or Islam. To encourage Christian clergy to study Islam, an annual essay competition was held on comparative religion at the national theological colleges in Grahamstown and Umtata.[13]

In a 1946 sermon (subsequently published in a booklet as *Cape Town: Christian or Moslem?*) a Reverend Roseveare expressed his opinons that Islam was anti-Christian, that Muslims were fatalistic because they did not view God as a Father but as all-powerful, and that Muslims lacked morals except those laid down by 'powerful' members of society. He noted that males dominated females, practised polygamy, and divorced easily. Roseveare urged his congregation to 'proclaim the Truth with all our might to those who have been deceived by false prophets'.[14]

In the early 1950s, Canon R.H. Birt followed this with a pamphlet titled 'Win our Moslems to Christ! A Challenge to our Church People at the Cape', in which he advocated that Christians should live among Muslims to convert them and urged Anglicans to minister aggressively in Malay areas.[15] In 1956, Reverend E.L.B. George told the Anglican Synod of the Diocese of the Cape that Christians were 'lapsing in their hundreds' but that little could be done until the 'whole Church became concerned about the matter'. Muslims made 'great play of the brotherhood of mankind' which the church was struggling to counter.[16] Several other pamphlets were published by the Anglican Church, including the anonymously authored *The Cross or the Crescent* in 1959.

In the 1960s, Reverend George Swartz replaced Miss Leslie as head of the Muslim Mission Board. Swartz, a BA graduate from the University of Witwatersrand, was determined to 'defeat' Islam and went to the Church of England's theological college, St Augustine's College in Canterbury, in June 1960 to study Islam under Canon Kenneth Cragg, a prolific author on Christian–Muslim relations.[17] Around this time Stellenbosch University also established a committee to study Islam. This was timely, according to reporter Jan Burger, because Islam was 'a force not to be underestimated.'[18]

These real and perceived attacks on the Muslim faith were taking place in an increasingly volatile political context. The National Party had come into power in 1948 and was busy implementing racial segregation, which was theologically justified by the Dutch Reformed Church, which came to be the 'official' religion of the National Party. The Dutch Reformed Church viewed black people as racially and intellectually inferior, and in 1953 established a state theology justifying apartheid.[19] Like the Anglicans, the Dutch Reformed Church also published anti-Muslim literature. G.B.A. Gerdener, who had worked among Muslims from 1913 to 1917, published a guide for missionaries entitled *Onder de Slamsen in de Kaapstad: Afval en Strijd*; Dr Samuel Zwemer's *The Moslem Menace in South Africa* (1914) suggested ways to combat the spread of Islam; while the Dutch Reformed Church appointed A.J. Liebenberg to undertake house calls among Muslims.[20] Publications such as *The Cross or the Crescent* (1965); Ben J. Marais' article 'Die Kerk en die Islam in Africa' (1965); and David Newington and Hubert C. Phillips's *The Shape of Power in Africa* (1965) were concerned about the threat posed by Islam, 'the secret weapon of Satan', if Christians did not 'reach the heathen'.[21]

All these activities point to the concern among many Christians about Islam. Meanwhile the alleged opposition between 'good and evil' portrayed by Christians in relation to Christianity and Islam caused outrage among many Muslims in the Cape.

In 1961, the Dutch Reformed Church caused a huge uproar among Muslims when it published a booklet entitled *Confessions of Hadjee Abdullah*. This document alleged, among other things, that the Prophet (PBUH) had ordered murder and plunder; had told his followers to kill non-Muslims; was cursed since all his sons had died; and had made Khadija's father drunk in order to marry her. Vanker described the booklet as a 'wanton and irresponsible attempt to discredit the Muslim faith. We do not want the book banned as this would not serve any useful purpose. What we want the Dutch Reformed Church to do is come forward with Hadjee Abdullah and discuss the book, its contents and charges in the open.'[22] Other Muslims joined Vanker in challenging these publications. Imam Abdullah Haron, then the editor of *Muslim News*, remarked that the booklet 'inflicted the severest wound anyone can have the heart to inflict…No true Muslim will tolerate an insult upon his faith, no matter from what source it comes. And let this not be an empty threat to the powers that be, that a true Muslim fears no other might than the Almighty Allah.'[23] Shaykh Nazeem Muhammad of the Muslim Judicial Council (MJC) called the booklet 'really cheap missionary work to poison innocent people's minds against another faith'. He 'assured them that they would get no dividends'.

This then was the context in which Ahmed Deedat entered the fray. Like Muslims in India a century earlier, the Muslims of the Cape, too, were stirring against perceived Christian provocation. And like Mawlana Kairanawi, whose story had inspired him, Deedat was determined to breach the Christian fortress. In a situation where Christians held the political and intellectual aces, ordinary Muslims who felt that they had been on the defensive for too long welcomed Deedat's no-holds-barred style.

According to Mustacq Abdullah, Deedat had valuable allies in the Cape where many Muslims were looking for the 'tools to fight back'. Salie Mohamed was one such person. 'Salie' was his preferred and known name but Deedat always referred to him as Saleh in person and in correspondence. Salie was the son of Mohamed Esack Dawray who had migrated to the Cape in 1914 and established the Rosmead Supermarket Claremont in 1923. Dawray founded several mosques in Cape Town and served on various Jama'at societies. It was Salie who experienced the full force of Christian missionary work and was determined to resist. According to Mustacq Abdullah:

> Salie Mohamed put Islam first in his life and made sure that he influenced others by just meeting up with them. I must still meet a man that was as conscious of his Maker as Salie Mohamed; everything and I mean everything, his getting up, his eating, his business, his meetings, was planned around his salah. He always said, 'You must not make excuses not to make salah; salah must be the excuse to break what you are busy with.'

Salie was involved in Islamic work before Deedat emerged on the national scene. Together with Shaykh Deen, a graduate of al-Azhar in Egypt and imam of the St Athens Road Mosque in Athlone, he regularly toured South Africa to discuss matters of concern to Muslims.

Deedat was introduced to Salie in Cape Town during the 1950s by Mohammad Zubair Sayyid, whose family founded *Muslim News* in 1960 under the editorship of Imam Abdullah

Haron.²⁴ Sayyid's family's involvement in Islamic work dates back many centuries. He is a descendant of the Uthmani family that established the Mia ni Masjid in the village of Dabhel in Gujarat during the twelfth century. Jalaluddeen Uthmani was a shipping agent, mawlana, missionary, and roving imam who settled in Woodstock in the 1890s. Jalaluddeen's son, Mohammad Zubair Sayyid, was born in India but settled in Cape Town. Sayyid started the Islamic Publications Bureau in 1952 following Aleem Siddiqui's visit to South Africa. Aziz Gool, Abdul Kader Palekar, and Salie Mohamed were all part of the network involved in Islamic publications.

Capetonian Salie Mohamed (left) was one of Ahmed Deedat's most faithful friends and suppporters.

Sayyid met Deedat when the latter was still a furniture salesman with a position that entailed countrywide travel. When Deedat approached Sayyid to publish one of his early works, he agreed on condition that Deedat would undertake a lecture tour of the Cape. Sayyid also called Salie to arrange a meeting with 'a person who would interest his religious work and even enhance it'. At their very first encounter, Salie would later say, he had marked Deedat as 'a jewel I cannot lose'. According to Salie's son, Ebrahim:

> When Shaykh Deedat came to Cape Town, we put posters all over the show, sometimes illegally, but one of the ways that he gained in popularity was the fact that there were these posters and everybody wanted to meet this man and see who he was. Shaykh Deedat gave a talk at one of the mosques that ended quite late. He normally stayed with the Sayyids but when he returned to their residence that night, the place was locked and the person driving him said, 'Well, I know somebody that would still be awake this time of the morning,' referring to my dad. And when they came around to the small store that we had, my dad was busy packing fruit and vegetables and offered him a place to sleep and [thereafter] he slept with us whenever he came to Cape Town.

Mustacq Abdullah, Salie's nephew, remembers that 'we, as children, took advantage of his company. Uncle Deedat would sleep for four hours at night and an hour after 'asr salat and the rest of the day was super charged electricity! If you wanted to see the "real" Deedat, it was before or after a debate; that was when one got the best out of him.'

Salie's support for Deedat is remarkable given that many of his customers were white Christians and there was always the prospect of a backlash. According to Mustacq, he never harboured such thoughts because of his 'absolute faith in God as the provider'. Salie, like Deedat, was alarmed at what he regarded as a Christian attack on Islam and helped to

Eventually none of Cape Town's halls were large enough and debates were held at the Good Hope Centre.

organise Deedat's meetings by arranging venues, printing and distributing pamphlets, and placing adverts in local newspapers.

The youngsters in the family, such as Salie's sons Bashier, Abu-Baker, Adam, Esack, and nephews Mustacq, Kamaaludien, and Jaffer, 'would literally paint the town with posters and pamphlets announcing Deedat's lecture tours'. Deedat and Salie faced many obstacles, including from Muslims. The MJC's opposition to Deedat made it difficult to arrange venues for lectures so Salie would book venues under different names, thus breaking the unofficial 'ban' on Deedat. Mustacq recalled that a Mr Maree, a city-council employee at the time, 'gave endless flak. He sabotaged the sound system of the Good Hope Centre for one meeting and this led to our partnering with Parker's Sound from then on.' Salie was also of great help in Deedat's fundraising efforts as he had the trust of the local business community.

Deedat was never fazed by criticism and continued to lecture in the Cape. In the early years he would travel in his 'beaten-up' old 1950 VW Beetle. IPC minutes dated 6 May 1963 record Mohamed Nazeer Ali questioning why R140 had been spent on repairing the vehicle in the previous five months. Deedat reminded him that 'the car has done 129 000 miles travelling all over the land for the collection of funds. The car has gone too old but owing to lack of funds at present, it is not possible for the Centre to get a new car.' En route from Durban to Cape Town, Deedat would stop at small towns along the way to raise funds, keeping meticulous records of every cent raised and spent.

On tours around South Africa in the 1960s and 1970s, Deedat would stop at small towns along the way to raise funds, keeping meticulous records of every cent raised and spent.

Deedat fondly referred to Salie as 'my Abu Bakr Siddique', in reference to the close bond between the Prophet (PBUH) and Abu Bakr al-Siddiq (RA), his close friend, confidante, and first caliph of Islam. Salie and Deedat travelled together to many parts of the world, including lecture tours to India, England, East Africa, and the Middle East. Mustacq recalled that when he and his parents arrived in Durban on a ship from India in 1958, Deedat picked them up at the harbour and took them to his home in Verulam where they spent a few nights. Deedat called Salie every Friday without fail after the midday jum'a prayer for a 'mini-strategy meeting', during which they discussed their activities. Salie himself mastered issues surrounding comparative religion and held his own in discussions with missionaries. Deedat's lectures and debates were preceded by readings from the Qur'an and many qurra launched their national and international careers through Deedat's meetings. The chairpersons of some of the Cape meetings, George Gibbs and Imam Anwar Baker, had an unenviable task trying to control difficult audiences. Imam Baker was described by Mustacq as 'judicious and unyielding to both Christians and Muslims alike who tried to disrupt and take over the meetings at question time'.

A poster for some of the Cape Town lectures.

During Deedat's tour of the Cape in September 1960 he challenged Reverend Joost de Blank, then the Anglican archbishop of Cape Town, to a debate 'to clear the air' about his booklet, *The Cross or the Crescent*. Deedat issued this challenge before a twenty-thousand-strong crowd at the Green Point sports stadium. Two members of the audience, a Reverend van Rensburgh of the Dutch Refomed Church and Father McBride of the Anglican Church, accepted the challenge on behalf of their churches, agreeing to a debate which was to be hosted by the Orient Club.[25] However, when the Orient Club wrote to the churches before Deedat's 1961 tour to finalise the dates, the Dutch Reformed minister accepted the challenge but the Anglican Church did not reply. Muslims criticised the Anglican Church for its failure to respond. Imam Abdullah Haron, for example, wrote in *Muslim News* that 'hundreds of people' were asking why the Anglican Church was refusing to meet with Muslims: 'I am amazed that the responsible church is keeping itself at bay after throwing mud at a religion and its Prophet who revere Jesus Christ more than the Christian's Bible.' Deedat was also 'disappointed': 'I take my hat off to the Dutch Reformed Church who had no part in the early attack, to come forth and discuss the matter amicably. After all a Symposium is not a place where one expects attacks and counter-attacks.'[26]

Deedat's debate with Dr Dawie Pypers of the Dutch Reformed Church at the Green Point stadium in July 1961 was followed by public lectures on 'What the Bible says about Muhammad', 'Christ in Islam', 'Was Christ Crucified?', and 'Jesus, Man, Myth or God?' The 1961 Cape tour created a huge furore. The Anglican Church condemned Deedat who returned to Durban the day after the lecture and left the MJC to face their wrath. While the MJC criticised Deedat's methods and dissociated itself from him, ordinary Muslims were unanimous in their support for Deedat. They blamed disparaging Anglican remarks for the confrontation. Deedat was a 'ready-made' solution for the working-class Muslims of the Cape Flats, according to Mustacq:

> In the 1960s people were very enthusiastic about the meetings. Not once was the hall empty. It was always full to the brim and large numbers of people even stood outside. Parker's Sound knew that they always had to place extra speakers outside the halls. The people were at fever pitch and the atmosphere was electric. This was the case every time Deedat visited. This was partly why the 'ulama opposed uncle Deedat. They could barely draw an audience, yet this man from Durban would come out of the blue and draw thousands. Even the City Hall was too small for him. We never bussed anybody. They came on their own because they had a need in their lives. Uncle Deedat never condemned the 'ulama. He always said that people who wanted shahadah should go to the 'ulama.

Muhammad Haron contextualised the reaction to Deedat cogently in his study of Christian–Muslim relations in the Cape:

> Before passing any form of severe judgement on Deedat, it should be clarified that Deedat felt that his hard approach vis-à-vis the soft approach had to be adopted since the missionaries showed no respect for the Islamic tradition and its adherents…On the whole, the Muslims gave Deedat a warm reception because they identified with his concerns and held the view that these missionaries had to be dealt with in a harsh manner; and as far as they were concerned Deedat was leading the way and setting the example of how to deal with missionaries when they try to drag the Muslim away from his religion.[27]

Missionaries attended Deedat's talks with well-prepared questions in a coordinated effort to undermine him. However, as Mustacq pointed out, he was unfazed and the 'audience loved it because they knew that the missionaries would get banged'. Part of the reason for the MJC's reaction may have been a reluctance to create barriers between Muslims and fellow black Christians. The MJC publicly declared that apartheid was a heresy and joined with the Muslim Youth Movement in Cape Town, the Claremont Youth Association, the Cape Vigilance Association, and the Young Men's Muslim Association in adopting the Call of Islam's declaration of 7 May 1961 in which they pledged to 'stand firm with our brothers in fighting the evil monster that is about to devour us'.[28]

Heightened opposition to apartheid created countless tragedies. For example, Abdullah Haron, imam of Claremont Mosque, who did extensive work in African townships, did not survive to tell the tale of his encounter with the South African security police following his arrest on 23 May 1969. He died in police custody on 27 September 1969. The official cause of death was a 'fall' from a staircase in prison. The bruises on his body, however, told a different story. His janaza prayer (funeral) was attended by 30 000 people.[29] Imam Haron was chairperson of the MJC at the time of his death, and his death polarised conservative and progressive members within the Council.[30] The MJC consistently distanced itself from Deedat. After Deedat's 1975 tour, its president Shaykh Muhammad told *The Argus* that the MJC disagreed with Deedat's use of the Bible to prove that Islam was correct, and called on Muslims to boycott Deedat's lectures.[31]

Editor of Muslim Views, Imam Abdullah Haron, criticised the Anglican Church for refusing to debate with Muslims. He also spoke out against apartheid for which he was arrested, and he died in police custody in 1969.

Yet, *Muslim News* reported, 'thousands of people attended these lectures, many people could not gain admittance to the halls due to lack of space'. Similarly, many ordinary Muslims interviewed by *Muslim News* took issue with the MJC. Mrs Hadji Karrim, in a letter to the paper, described the MJC's boycott call as 'un-Islamic. I wonder if the MJC signed a secret pact with a Christian priest-class,' she wrote. 'The lectures caused no friction. The Priest and Clergy are afraid because they are spreading false teachings of Christ.' S. Seira, secretary of the Muslim Assembly, admonished the MJC for distributing anti-Deedat pamphlets without discussing the matter with his organisation.[32]

The Assembly, launched in 1967 by Dr Hoosen Kotwal and other Muslim professionals in Cape Town such as Zubair Sayyid, Salie Mohamed, and Rashid Sayed, took umbrage at what they saw as the conservatism of the ulama.[33] M.G. Hendricks, president of the Muslim Students' Association, regarded Deedat's 'academic approach as excellent'. H.G. Allie, pipe-major of the Habibia Siddique Muslim Brigade, told reporters that the people of the townships felt that the MJC had 'failed them once again. I personally learnt much from Deedat's lectures. Deedat was just fantastic. He is simple. The halls are too small for his lectures.'[34] Shaykh Abdulkarrim Toffar of the Institute of Islamic Studies was another who rejected the MJC's views on Deedat:

> Mr Ahmed Deedat is undoubtedly an authority on the Bible and we can virtually state without contradiction that he is the only Muslim in the world that can speak authoritatively on the Bible. In fact, he is more well versed in the Bible than born Christians

and their Clergy. We are invited to call unto Islam by wisdom, wise reasoning and proof, and one of those ways is to prove factually your opponents' weaknesses from their own vital sources. That is how Mr Deedat's lectures were seen – it's lamentably pitiful that the Clergy had to get so emotional. It is therefore wrong to have issued pamphlets from mosques banning people from attending the lectures due to the 'repercussions'. The reason is simple – when the Clergy come with their Bibles, our learned cannot reply and that is embarrassing to their status. Our Clergy should know how these Clergy, especially the Apostolic, swear the Prophet's name in trains and the Grand Parade. They got a good dose of medicine for it in the recent series of lectures which they won't forget soon.[35]

These statements reveal some of the tensions among Muslims in the Cape in which Shaykh Toffar often played a mediating role. Shaykh Toffar (who later became a founding member of Radio 786, established by the Islamic Unity Convention in 1995) was an 'outsider' to 'ulama politics in Cape Town, being one of the earliest graduates from a Jordanian institution – most of Cape Town's 'ulama had either studied on the Indian subcontinent or lacked a formal qualification. According to Farid Sayed, editor of *Muslim News and Views*, Shaykh Toffar was more scholarly in his approach and attempted to raise the intellectual level of Islamic discourse. This did not endear him to other 'ulama, who tended to avoid or shun him. Toffar did not join the MJC, but formed the Institute of Shariah Studies in Salt River in 1972.[36]

Deedat's 1975 tour of the Cape was important for another reason though. Deedat often stated that there were two occasions when he had not been sure how to respond to a question. The first was during the 1975 tour when he was asked by a student at Stellenbosch University: 'What good can come from violence by chopping off the hand for stealing?' As he made his way to the microphone Deedat was not sure how to respond but, as he would say, 'Allah gives gives hidayah!' He asked the questioner whether he was Christian. When the reply was a confident, 'Yes I am', Deedat responded: 'Then you should know better the outcome after suffering. Your Lord Jesus suffered violently on the cross and it redeemed you from sin!' Mythology or not, this story has become part of Deedat folklore. (The second question that left Deedat momentarily unsure of his response is discussed in Chapter 17, 'The Swagger of Deedat'.)

Deedat's next tour of the Cape took place in January 1978. He delivered lectures on 'Christianity, Communism or Islam? Which has the Answer to the Problems in South Africa?' and 'The Qur'an or the Bible? Which is God's Word?'

At the Cape Town City Hall on 20 January 1978, Deedat angered some Christians for allegedly saying that 'if all the people in the world were created by God in the likeness of Mr Vorster [then prime minister of South Africa], it would have been a very ugly world indeed'.[37] According to Mustacq Abdullah, members of his family, including Sayyid and Salie Mohamed were harrassed by the government following the speech.

At the Athlone Civic Centre, addressing the topic 'Qur'an and the Jews', Deedat quoted from the Bible and Qur'an to depict Jews as a shameful race. At the Kensington Civic Centre, speaking on 'Jesus, the Prophet of Islam', he said that the Christian belief of turning the other cheek was impractical. 'Just turn the other cheek and see what happens.' The media interpreted this as advocating violence against the state.[38]

The tour drew angry responses from both Muslims and Christians. The *Cape Herald* captured the resulting furore with its headline 'Storm over visit by Muslim Scholar'.[39] Adam Peerbhai, director of the Islamic Centre of Cape Town, attempted to challenge Deedat but was 'shouted down by Deedat who told the audience that he [Peerbhai] was a Judas'.[40] Following one of Deedat's lectures, five Christian evangelists drove through Bryant Street with a loudspeaker condemning Islam. Eyewitness Solly Levy, a prominent Cape Town figure, told a reporter for the *Cape Herald* that there would have been bloodshed had cool heads not intervened. Levy complained that Deedat was undermining interfaith relations. 'You don't go around attacking another man's religion.'[41] In response to Christian complaints, E. Jakoet of the MJC told the *Cape Herald* that his organisation had 'washed [its] hands of Mr Deedat. We don't agree with his policy. We preach tolerance and we have told him once before that we want nothing to do with him…He was lucky he wasn't beaten up.'[42] A few months later, on 31 March 1978, Peerbhai organised a public lecture where he spoke on 'all the beautiful things' mentioned about Jesus in the Qur'an in an attempt to 'restore the good relationship between Christians and Muslims'.[43]

Deedat regarded the coverage of the tour in the January 1978 issue of Mohammed Makki's *Muslim Digest* as defamatory and sued Makki for R10 000. When the matter was heard in court, Deedat was unable to specify the 'particular words or statements' that he regarded as defamatory and the case was dismissed with costs. According to the court records, Justice H.J.O. van Heerden found that

> The article would convey to the ordinary reader that Mr Deedat was an ardent devotee of the Islamic faith with strong personal views in favour of Islam and with equally strong views against the other religions mentioned by him and that he was one to express his views in no uncertain terms and to seek support for them in the Bible and Qur'an. The reader would, on the other hand, also understand the article to be a critical account of Mr Deedat's choice of subject matter and his manner of handling it. It would convey to him that the writer did not approve of Mr Deedat's approach and methods in propagating Islam and that his disapproval was strongly couched. The reasons for the writer's disapproval that would suggest themselves to the reader

would be that Mr Deedat's handling of the matter was liable to cast a bad reflection on Muslims and was likely to cause a rift between Christians and Muslims...The reader even if he should not share Mr Deedat's views would not likely think anything the less of him. It follows, in my view, that the article was not per se defamatory.[44]

Deedat amended his Particulars of Claim and the matter was heard again in March 1981. Deedat's counsel, Advocate M.P. Freemantle, told Justice John Didcott that Deedat would lead oral evidence on matters not specifically alleged in the revised Particulars of Claim. Didcott declined this request and adjourned the matter to give Deedat an opportunity to specify what was defamatory in the reports. Deedat's counsel requested that the case be adjourned *sine die*, that is, without a retrial date being set. In ordering Deedat to pay costs, Didcott offered salutary advice to both Makki and Deedat:

> It is fairly obvious that this is a longstanding dispute with an acrimonious history to it...I suppose it is even arguable at least to say well, alright, the only thing to do is to fight it out to the death. But this is not just a private dispute. Plaintiff is a preacher and the first defendant is the proprietor of a religious publication. So we have got two members of the Muslim community in Durban having this fight. Both of them have got to take account...Is it going to do the Muslim community, as a community, or the image of Islam, any good to have this kind of conflict? The public, at the end of it, does not really remember or care very much who won and who was right and who was wrong; all they know is that they witnessed an unseemly battle which will be published with fairly lurid headlines, and there will be an obvious attempt to sensationalise it because if anybody merely gives a report of a court case it is very dull. It is going to be embarrassing to the whole Muslim community of Durban; it is going to be damaging to the faith itself, to the image and reputation of the faith amongst outsiders. Leaders of the community have got a special responsibility to set an example to their followers to be sensible and to bring about peaceful solutions to things with a minimal amount of damage.[45]

Deedat settled out of court with costs of R3 500 in August 1982. Makki had the last word in the September/October 1982 issue of *Muslim Digest*. The Prophet (PBUH), he said, tolerated abuse with a great deal of sabr (patience) and Deedat would do likewise if his motives were sincere.[46]

Deedat's public presence in the Cape declined in the 1980s. This was partly due to changing conditions domestically, described in later chapters, and partly to Deedat's gaze shifting outwards as he became an international figure. The Deedat of the early Cape lectures must be seen in the wider context of the intrusive activities of the Anglican Church, white domination in South Africa, and Western hegemony in general. Deedat saw the halting of the Christian missionary onslaught as important in undermining both Christianity and the prevailing racist political order.

# 11

# AS-SALAAM: A BRIDGE TOO FAR

Deedat with his son Yousuf (right) and a friend at As-Salaam. The establishment of this school and seminary was a dream come true and he was deeply involved in it for over fifteen years.

> As-Salaam emerged as a result of a youth's ambition to see an Islamic mission in South Africa. Ahmed Deedat as a youngster had dreams like Dick Whittington to see a mission established in South Africa but, like Whittington, he was a poor man unable to make a move...While he was convinced that the establishment of an Islamic Mission was impossible, he cherished his dreams with faith in God.
>
> – Ismail Meer, *Views and News* 16 August 1965

THE LEGEND of Dick Whittington is a rags-to-riches tale in which Dick, a poor boy from Gloucester, makes his way to London to seek his fortune. With help from a feline friend he marries his master's daughter, becomes prosperous, and is eventually made the Lord Mayor of London. This character in a British pantomime is loosely based on the life of Richard Whittington, who was born in Gloucestershire in the 1350s and died in London in 1423. Like Whittington, journalist Ismail Meer suggests, Deedat, the son of a poor migrant, had little chance of realising one of his burning ambitions, which was to create an Islamic seminary. But like Whittington, Deedat was a visionary, and in his case it was not his wife's wealth but a rich benefactor who helped to make his dream come true.

Deedat had been greatly impressed by Adams College when he was working on the south coast and was keen to open a similar institution for the teaching of Islam. He was convinced that the political situation in South Africa would change in due course and that the African majority would ultimately gain political power. He spent much time trying to persuade his peers in the IPC that the future of Islam in South Africa lay with the country's indigenous population and depended on inviting Africans into the faith. More than this, Deedat emphasised, Muslims by definition could not live in isolation. According to Agjee, Deedat would often tell them that the Qur'an obliged them to invite others to Islam and quoted the following verse: 'Let there arise from among you a band of people inviting to all that is good, enjoining what is right, and forbidding what is wrong: they are the ones to attain felicity' (3: 104).

Deedat envisaged a centre where Muslims of all backgrounds could live, work, and study Islam. He was so convincing that the IPC adopted a resolution on 27 July 1958 to 'work for the establishment of a mission where missionaries may be trained for the furthering of the cause of Islam'. Further, 'we would very much like to see the First Seminary of Islam established before the current year is out'.[1]

It did not take long for the resolution to begin to materialise. Deedat was tying his shoelaces outside the West Street Mosque after the jum'a prayer in late 1958 when Hajji Suleman Kadwa of Umzinto came to speak with him. Impressed that Deedat had successfully carried out three conversions in successive weeks at the mosque, Kadwa complimented Deedat and offered him, 'in a classical example of generosity', seventy-five acres of land on the south coast 'for the purpose of carrying out the objects of the Centre, the propagation of Islam in South Africa'.[2] Deedat accepted the offer immediately. When Kadwa suggested that he first look at the land, Deedat responded, 'What is there to

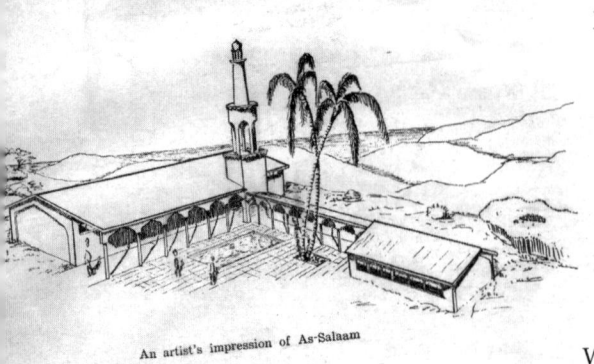

*As-Salaam*
*The Seminary of Islam*
(Braemar — Umzinto — Natal)

An artist's impression of As-Salaam

(An Islamic Propagation Centre Project)

Ahmed Deedat with S.I. Kadwa, the benefactor who donated the land for As-Salaam where the IPC aimed to establish an Islamic seminary.

look at?' He later told a reporter that 'if fifty acres of the land was made up of rocks, I would get twenty-five acres. If twenty-five acres was rocks I would get fifty acres. Natal is not known as the Garden Colony for nothing. It is full of greenery and beauty so even a few acres would be great, I felt, and accepted the offer.'[3] As journalist Ismail Meer pointed out, Kadwa's offer was a godsend 'to a man living all his life in the dreams of an Islamic Mission…and Deedat saw at once the possibility of establishing an Islamic Mission on this vast tract of land'.[4]

Deedat was in for a shock, however. He, Vanker, Agjee, and other members of the IPC had to literally cut down trees to make their way from one end of the property to the other. Deedat was not deterred. As soon as the land was officially handed over on 23 February 1959, he opened a bank account, initially called 'Islamic Propagation Centre No.2', and subsequently changed to 'As-Salaam' to make it a separate entity from the IPC, and set out to raise funds. The As-Salaam Trust Deed was registered on 16 August 1960 with seven trustees: A.H. Deedat, Ahmed S. Kadwa, G.H.A. Kadwa, G.H. Kadwa, Secunder Amod Murchie, A.K. Salejee, and G.H. Vanker.

The name 'As-Salaam' refers to God as 'the source of peace and perfection'. This was in keeping with the Institute's vision that its graduates would impart the teachings of Islam, thereby spreading 'peace, harmony and love'.[5] Half of the estimated building cost of R40 000 had already been collected by June 1959. The foundation stone was laid on 1 November

1959 by Amina King, widow of Reverend Taher King who had embraced Islam during Khwaja Kamaluddin's visit in 1927. The hundred or so guests represented a 'who's who' of Natal's Muslim traders, and included M.I. Paruk, H.A.H. Moosa, Chota Timol, Hassen Raboobee, and Kajee Newadi of Durban; E.M. Vawda, Chota Vawda, Cassim Kathrada, and A.R.E. Maither of Verulam; Essop Kajee of Stanger; and Ebrahim Shaikjee of Newcastle.

Deedat told the gathering that while King's early death had cut short 'his cherished ideals, the example he set has not been in vain for in As-Salaam his spirit will relive'. Amina King was moved to tears as she described her husband's mission and said she was overjoyed that his services in the path of Islam were remembered. Other speakers included Hajji Ebrahim Salejee, Munshi Shaik, the eldest member of the IPC, and Hajji S.I. Kadwa, who recalled an earlier visit to Braemar by Taher King. Kadwa was 'penniless' at the time and had never imagined the day would come when he would be able to donate land for a worthy cause.[6]

The IPC was not the only pioneer in the field of da'wah to Africans. Aside from Taher King and Aleem Siddique, who opened a mosque in Zululand in 1940, around three hundred African Muslims were part of Mawlana Cassim Sema's All African Tablighee jalsa (prizegiving) held at the Waschbank Muslim Institute on 30 October 1960. African converts to Islam, such as Ilyas Mabaso, M. Cwamando, Phineas Moorgazi, Daniel Twala, and Frank Dhlamini, addressed the gathering. Vanker and Salejee also attended.[7] Vanker was impressed by the speakers and wrote to Sema on 1 February 1961 to compliment him for his 'remarkable results'. Vanker noted that the IPC was happy about the 'long overdue' start of missionary activities in Northern Natal and hoped for 'similar institutions throughout the length and breadth of South Africa'. Vanker enquired about Sema's methods of propagation; strategies to 'consolidate them into an Islamic form of life'; and fundraising: 'We learnt that you have in your employ an able publicity man in A.C. Meer. Every pound that is spent in publicity will bring in a tenfold return. We feel that your success is greatly dependent upon your publicity agent who worked so hard for the jalsa.' Sema replied on 9 February 1961:

> We have no extraordinary method of preaching Islam besides those stipulated in the Holy Qur'an (16:25). Our main concern is to first deliver to the 'People of the Book' the 'Great Islamic Truths' [which] are strengthened if argument ensues by supporting verses of the Old and New Testaments. Those who accept these 'Islamic Truths' and enter the Circle of Islamic Fraternity are generally educated in the Islamic form of life. The success of our jalsa was not due to any person in particular; it was due to the joint efforts of everyone young and old, men and women, of our little village [Waschbank]… Alhamdulillah, by the help of Allah well over five hundred Africans have embraced Islam, but I would like to make it very clear that our aim in preaching is merely delivering the Message of Islam to the people of the world, and no more… It is with this duty only that we are charged. Whether we have hundreds of converts or whether we have nil is immaterial.

The success of As-Salaam cannot be assessed in terms of the number of people it led to Islam, or the number of Muslim missionaries it produced. The programme was ambitious, the conditions difficult, and its impact was far reaching, as many of its graduates, who have contributed in various fields of Muslim life in Natal, can attest.

Sulayman Paruk, for example, first went to As-Salaam in 1968 when he was ten years old. Deedat was instrumental in his mother's conversion to Islam, and Paruk's father felt that Deedat would be a good influence on his son. Sulayman recalls that he went to As-Salaam around the time that 'the man landed on the moon. Yousuf [Deedat] was showing us all the pictures about it.' The move came as a shock because, until then, Sulayman had led a comfortable life in Cato Manor where his father owned a business:

As Salaam graduate Sulayman Paruk.

> My life changed because I came from a home where you had everything – electricity, my father had 16mm projectors, and this wealth of movies from London and all that stuff. Coming from a home to a farm where you only have lanterns, no electricity, and everything was done manually, you were milking cows, and ploughing with the ox... was a big change in my lifestyle. At As-Salaam, I had to get into a group of people who were mostly poverty-stricken, basically new converts, orphans. We lived in a hostel where we had about twenty to thirty beds in one huge hall.
>
> Our first Ustad was the late Umar Kantito, a brilliant teacher. I can tell you that my foundation was set by the right person. He was from Kings Rest. After Umar Kantito we had Adam Massaji of Newcastle. He was a very good Arabic teacher of hadiths, Qur'an, Arabic language. He studied in Zanzibar. Then came Hafez Abdul Rahman from Chatsworth who studied in India. English education was provided by a man named Cassim from Stanger. We had Qur'an in the morning and English education in the afternoon and sometimes the other way. When you left the place, you were educated in all fields – history, geometry, maths.
>
> I also did things like carpentry and bricklaying. Shaykh Deedat, myself, Yousuf Deedat, Abdul Vari, Salim Malazi, and a few others came down to Durban at Corobrick and did a bricklaying course. I have a certificate and Shaykh Deedat also has one for bricklaying. And somebody came from Durban to teach us carpentry. Shaykh always thought of our future, that when we leave we would have something to hang onto.
>
> We played sports. Soccer was our favourite, and swimming too because we had so many dams. Shaykh Deedat arranged teachers to come from Durban to teach us swimming. There was a person to teach us karate, 'Karate Mohammed' we called him. We also did judo and weight lifting. We were such good swimmers that the instructor wanted us to enter us in the Natal championship. We had boxing matches every Friday

Top: Many of Natal's most prominent Muslim businessmen attended the laying of the foundation stone at As Salaam in 1959. Centre: Apart from hosting a steady stream of visitors, Hawa Deedat (centre right) was central to the everyday running of the seminary and her kindness is fondly remembered by many students. Bottom: The curriculum was designed to include physical work, practical skills training and an academic component.

night in our hostel. We would move the beds aside, make a ring with the beds and see who the best fighter was.

The normal routine was to get up for fajr. You read your salah and then had chores until about eight o'clock. My responsibility was the swimming pool. I had to clean that and the other guys would feed the animals, milk the cows, attend to a certain garden, cutting grass here and there. Each guy had a chore until breakfast. Breakfast was porridge. After breakfast you went for madrasa or school until zuhr. After that you had a small chore, which means feeding the animals, maybe for half an hour, and then you had lunch. Then it was back to school or madrasa until 'asr. Between 'asr and maghrib you had another chore, depending whatever Shaykh Deedat told you to do. Then it was supper.

Lunch was mostly mealie rice with curry and supper was basically bread with a curry. Shaykh would go to town and buy fresh bread for us everyday. At times we'd have braai, sometimes if we did planting, like mealies, we'd braai mealies. And then we had maas because we had cows…We sold maas – the sour milk – to residents that lived around our land. We used to take out the cream, separate the cream from the maas because fresh milk, you leave it overnight, the next morning all the cream floats to the top and the bottom is the milk. You scoop that with a spoon, put all the cream into one container, and make butter out of it. It was simple. Mrs Deedat taught us how to do it. Out of the butter we made ghee, which Shaykh Deedat sold in Durban. When it came to meat, a lot of people used to donate meat at qurbani and we stored that at Goolam Hoosen's [Kadwa] shop in Braemar.

Eid was a very big occasion. Out of the six years I lived there, I could count exactly twelve cups of tea I had. Bakri Eid and Eid was when we had tea. Otherwise we would only have tea when someone invited us to Umzinto to read the Qur'an. Eid was a very special occasion. We'd all dress up. We had a special pinstripe, black uniform with our burnt orange coat with an Islamic badge – the Qur'an Universal Guidance – on our pockets. The red Moroccan fez was our hat. That was our uniform, with our khaki shirts. Shaykh kept that as our outing uniform and we had special shoes for those occasions because every day you walked barefoot the whole day.

At Eid, with that cup of tea, Mrs Deedat would make some chillibites and something sweet. After fajr we would all fill the jeep to the top, whether we had ten students or thirty, and we drove to Umzinto for Eid namaaz. After namaaz we would rush to the back of the masjid and read, singing 'Ya Allah,' the song of Mr Vanker, and each student had a verse that he had learnt. I was always the guy appointed to read the du'a [prayer]. People would contribute generously – Eidy. My eyes used to light up [laughs]. The money would be shared. Some was given to the Institute and we were given a certain amount of spending. It was quite a bit of money and we used to buy whatever we wanted. Bakri Eid was different, same thing in the morning, but rushing back because we had to make qurbani. Now you have 300 animals to slaughter so for two days we used to slaughter. Every one of us had to slaughter an animal. We used to do so much of it, I'm bloody good. A lot of people came to pick up their animals because they placed the order in Durban at the IPCI's office and some had to be delivered by our van. The majority of the carcasses were given to the students.

Sometimes I would clean Shaykh's office. He had a small pantry where his books were. He had an index concerning the Bible verses. I looked through it and mentally would memorise the verse numbers. I got caught twice by Mrs Deedat. She didn't scold me but she called Shaykh and said, 'What's written in this book?' He explained that it was an index. They were speaking Gujarati because Gujarati was the only language that Shaykh communicated in with his family. I wasn't born Gujarati but I can understand it. She said, 'This boy, everytime I find him with this book.' So he called me and says, 'Why?' I said that I looking was for verses concerning Prophet Muhammad (PBUH) in the Bible. Then he said, 'Okay, I'm going to give you guys lessons.' He bought Bibles for six of us, in Zulu and in English and everyday he initiated classes. He used to give me verses to study in Arabic and English. He also gave me biblical verses and he used to make me learn it in Zulu. Shaykh gave us a biblical education, taught us how to handle the Bible in Zulu and English. His wisdom of handling debates and talking to people I can't forget. He also had this gift teaching us how to do it.

Mrs Deedat worked very hard. She cooked for us, mended our clothes, you know, you had boys that were fighting amongst themselves, playing games and messing around and your clothes got torn. If she was not on the machine, she was cooking. When the children fell sick, Shaykh used to take us to doctor. She used to be there to see to our health. Alhamdulillah she took very good care of us. She was responsible for us, you had a problem, you went to her. We were scared to go to Shaykh and we went to her because she was basically like a mother to us. That's one lady that had the children at heart.

Sulayman Paruk left As-Salaam at the same time as Deedat did. His recollection of life during these years there provides a wonderful insight into Deedat's novel scheme.

While life for students continued, some legal difficulties developed behind the scenes. A dispute arose at Braemar between S.I. Kadwa and Deedat in the very early days when Deedat applied for a trading licence in the name of the As-Salaam Trust to operate a store on the property. Deedat maintained that he wanted to open a 'tuck shop' so that students would not have to walk several miles over hilly terrain to Braemar for their basic necessities. Profits, if any, were to be used for running As-Salaam. G.H. Kadwa lodged an objection with the Umzinto Rural Licensing Board on 30 November 1960, together with a deposition from his father, stating that he intended opening a store on the five acres that he had reserved for himself on the land donated to the As-Salaam Trust.

Since the trust deed prohibited the erection of buildings to raise funds, and specified that disputes were to be referred to a 'Religious Body of Muslims', the matter was referred to J.C. Jackson on 9 December 1960. Deedat testified that he was developing an Islamic mission and intended establishing cotton industries that would also entail trading. This was permitted in Islam, he said, and pointed to the fact that both the Grey Street and West Street mosque trusts owned shops and used rental income for the upkeep of the mosques.

At a meeting of trustees in January 1961, Deedat was elected president, Vanker secretary, and Salejee treasurer of the As-Salaam Trust. As S.I. Kadwa refused to transfer the land until the licensing issue had been resolved, the Trust instituted legal proceedings to compel him to do so. Kadwa argued that the Deed stipulated that the land could be used for missionary activity only and that running a business would distract Deedat from his core mission.

Mohammed Makki then criticised Deedat in the March 1961 issue of *Muslim Digest* where he wrote that Kadwa would not have been so foolish as to donate land to a competitor:

> It is inconceivable that Mr Kadwa would be so foolish as to give away land next door to his business premises to Mr Ahmed Deedat or anyone else who intended to open business premises in competition. This is more than can be expected of any Muslim, no matter how charitable he may be. Muslims do not act quite so foolishly.[8]

Deedat's response was swift. He wrote to Makki and published a pamphlet in which he informed the public that it had taken eighteen months to finalise the Deed. He noted that during this period the number of trustees had been increased from five to seven to include two of S.I. Kadwa's sons; the addition of these trustees had reduced the IPC's representation to 43 per cent even though it did one 100 per cent of the work; and that S.I. Kadwa had taken back five acres after the original donation of land. Deedat disputed Makki's description of the premises as being 'next door' and 'near',

> which suggested that it must be 'a few feet away or in Mr Kadwa's back yard. In fact the terrain is over two miles away over rough, stoney and hilly terrain. No student or inmate of As-Salaam could be expected to traverse those hills and return fit for any other physical duty. I am willing to hand over the whole of the seventy-five acres together with all the additions and improvements the IPC has made to the Jami'atul 'Ulama *without any strings attached.*

After further skirmishes between the lawyers representing both sides, the two parties agreed to arbitration in August 1961 and an official request was put to the Jami'atul 'Ulama of Natal by the end of that year. A few months later, the Jami'at's secretary, Mawlana Cassim Sema, issued the following response:

> Ours is an ecclesiastical organisation concerned mainly with religious matters. We are only prepared to take cognisance of a matter which can be decided on the basis of the

law of Islam…Both parties are known to us and we feel that if they are sincere in wanting to settle their disputes, we are prepared to assist…However, we must be allowed to deal with the questions in a manner completely in our discretion as to what evidence to hear, what issues to decide and how to decide them. The parties must agree beforehand to abide by our decisions.

While the IPC accepted these terms immediately, S.I. Kadwa prevaricated for several months, agreeing to arbitration only in August 1962. In view of the ongoing accusations, innuendos, and rumours flying around, Deedat called a public meeting at the Pine Street Madrasa towards the end of 1962 to discuss 'The Truth About As-Salaam'. He invited Kadwa and Makki to 'debate the facts'. Deedat made a 'special appeal' to Makki to be present because 'in our humble opinion, pamphleteering is doing a disservice to the cause of Islam'. Neither Kadwa nor Makki attended. Kadwa was, in fact, gravely ill around this time and passed away shortly thereafter. After presenting his side of the story, Deedat told the meeting that he would not open the store.

The two parties eventually agreed to arbitration by visiting scholar Mawlana Muhammad Tayyab, principal of the Darul 'Uloom Deoband in India, who visited South Africa in March 1963. In terms of the agreement, dated 5 April 1963, seventy acres were to be transferred to the As-Salaam Trust and five acres were to be reserved for Kadwa. However, due to S.I. Kadwa's death and the long delay in winding up his estate, and the fact that the law with regard to agricultural land prevented the transfer of less than ten acres to an individual, it took over ten years before the transfer was eventually effected. The entire property (seventy-five acres) was transferred to the As-Salaam Trust in July 1976, with a separate lease in perpetuity between the Trust and the S.I. Kadwa family in respect of the five acres. In fact, by the time the transfer took place, Deedat had left the mission, and it had been taken over by the Muslim Youth Movement.

The trading licence was not the only matter that divided the trustees. A second dispute arose over the attempt by the trustees representing the Kadwa family to introduce a clause that individuals paid by the Trust could not be trustees. This would have disqualified both Deedat and Vanker. At the very first meeting, on 14 December 1960, A.S. Kadwa stated that under Clause 8 of the Trust Deed, a trustee could not be employed by the Trust in any capacity. The minutes of the meeting recorded that 'this was hotly debated' when A.S. Kadwa called on Deedat to either resign from his employment or forfeit his position as trustee. Deedat maintained that this interpretation was incorrect because S.I. Kadwa did not intend that a trustee should be prevented from working on the project but that trustees should not receive remuneration for being trustees. A.S. Kadwa rejected Deedat's suggestion that they approach S.I. Kadwa for clarification. He wanted the decision based on interpretation within the 'four walls of the Deed'. A trustee could not be both 'master' and 'servant' at the same time. The meeting terminated without resolving this issue.

At a follow-up meeting on 25 December 1960, Secunder Amod Murchie exclaimed in frustration that he was 'fed up with this bickering. Some unanimity should be shown in the action of the Trustees. We are in charge of an institution to propagate Islam and not to satisfy our personal egos or for personal aggrandisement. The previous meetings have left a very nasty taste.' Vanker too called on 'the Trustees to stop this "womanish" attitude. This is the third meeting going into ruins.' When the representatives of the Kadwas walked out of a meeting on 8 January 1961, the remaining trustees decided that enough was enough and proceeded with elections. Trustees representing the Kadwas boycotted the following meeting on 11 June 1961 because they did not recognise the office-bearers. In terms of the constitution, however, the decisions were valid since a majority had voted (namely, Deedat, Vanker, Murchie, and Salejee), and the Trust then continued to manage As-Salaam without input from the Kadwas. Once the question of the trading licence had been resolved, however, the trustees began to work in harmony.

Deedat did not let divisions in the Trust delay the start of building however. Vanker reported on 30 October 1960 that the prayer room, ablution chamber, minaret, and cottage for the caretaker had been completed. The dam, reservoir, central building, rondavels, and dining hall were built by July 1961. The rondavels were to house married students. Deedat personally collected funds, had the land surveyed, drew up plans, hired personnel, gave out contracts, and even purchased raw materials.

Unfortunately, Deedat faced other problems too. By 1961, As-Salaam's staff included Dr E.M. Gabellah (missionary), D.Y. Abdul Khalick, Yusuf Abdur Rehman (Imam), Ebrahim Khan (caretaker), and S. Vengetasamy (driver). Gabellah, Khalick, and Rehman accused Deedat of being autocratic.[9] Mohammed Makki published a pamphlet on 31 December 1962 titled 'Nemesis overtakes Deedat' in which Gabellah claimed that Deedat had treated him as a criminal; Khalick alleged that Deedat had inflated the number of converts; while Rehman gave a 'graphic description of brutal assault'. Makki also alleged that Deedat called a public meeting on 25 November 1962 but did not allow his detractors, chief among them prominent businessman 'Kosaan' Kajee, Adam Peerbhai, and Zubeida Haffejee, to speak. Deedat was also condemned for not attending S.I. Kadwa's funeral. Soon after this, Zimbabwean-born E.M. Gabellah (who had studied theology at Adams College before accepting Islam at the IPC) left the seminary amidst accusations that his conversion was fake. Gabellah formed the Bureau of Bantu Churches in 1962 and by the 1970s had become involved in Rhodesian (Zimbabwean) politics as a member of the African National Council led by Bishop Abel Muzorewa.

In the face of all this, Deedat insisted that he had nothing to hide, and during his Cape tour in January and February 1963 he used his lectures to clarify his position on As-Salaam. At the Habibiya Madrasah Hall in Athlone on 21 January 1963, for example, a proposal introduced by Salie Mohamed and seconded by Hajji Ahmed Ebrahim, 'condemned Mr Makki's pamphleteering campaign which is bringing Islam and the Muslims into dispute'.[10] The proposal was reported in *Muslim News*, which Makki threatened to sue for libel. Instead

Deedat sued Makki, claiming R10 000 for defamation. In August 1964, judgment was given against Makki for R1 000 with costs.[11]

IPC minutes dated 6 May 1963 reflect that Deedat used his own money to fight these legal battles: 'I am fighting my own battle, assisted by friends and sympathisers to vindicate the integrity and prestige of the Centre'. The minutes go on to note that 'The House wished him every success.' Furthermore, although Deedat had not been able to attend S.I. Kadwa's funeral, the minutes of the first meeting of trustees after his death, held in July 1963, reflect that Deedat, in his capacity as chairman, 'placed on record the expression of sympathy by the Trustees of the Trust to the family of Mr Suleman Ismail Kadwa on his death at Port Shepstone on 9 December 1961'.

Many Muslims, such as journalist Ismail Meer of *News and Views*, were sceptical as to whether the As-Salaam project would materialise:

> I must admit that I was one of those who felt that much Muslim money was spent in a project that would not bring in returns to the community. I must admit that I thought much energy was wasted by young men who vainly tried to achieve the impossible. I must admit that time and again I laid emphasis on the fact that the site chosen for As-Salaam was wholly unsuitable and was out of the way where no one could take advantage of it. Yes, the As-Salaam dream of Messrs Ahmed Deedat and company I was convinced was another piper's dream. The colossal sum of money already spent and the yearly collections for As-Salaam began to worry me.[12]

Dr Mohamed Khan (an IPCI trustee at the time of writing) tells a different side of the story, however. Khan's connection with the IPCI began during informal discussions with G.H. Vanker in the 1960s. Khan often visited Vanker in Madressa Arcade and got to know Deedat too. In 1962, while Khan was on a visit to Durban, he was 'dragged' to As-Salaam by Deedat, and was amazed at the 'fantastic progress. It was a really hard thing to do...to shuttle between Durban and As-Salaam on horrible roads, see to the building programme, go on fundraising drives, and see to the IPC...It is simply amazing what he achieved.'

When Dr Khan established his practice in Port Shepstone, he invited Deedat to deliver lectures at the local mosque and was kept abreast of developments at As-Salaam. According to Dr Khan, it became 'impossible to run the place [As-Salaam], even for him. He had the idea but not the support. He used to get crumbs from the community. What happened subsequently should not detract from Deedat's exceptional achievements at As-Salaam.'

The Trust decided in late 1963 that Deedat could not oversee the building project from Durban and should relocate to As-Salaam. The dilemma was that Deedat, as trustee, could not be paid for his services because trustees were not entitled to remuneration. Senior Counsel H.J. May proposed a solution in February 1964 in terms of which the Trust would make 'donations' to the IPC, which could then reimburse Deedat for his work and for out-of-pocket expenses such as the cost of running his car. Deedat resigned from Beare Brothers and moved to Braemar.

Deedat faced a monumental task. There was no piped water, electricity, roads, or telephone. Monies were hard to come by. For example, while trustees agreed that a telephone line was necessary, the Umzinto Post Office required an advance of three years rental and R79 deposit towards 'trunk calls'. Trustees resolved at their October 1963 meeting that they would do so 'as soon as funds permit', and the issue was only resolved in late 1964. As Ebrahim Jadwat explained:

> Deedat was the builder, the carpenter, the plumber, the one that established a dam and brought the water from the river. He made the roads. So almost all his time went into building the structure. He remained there for over fifteen years but in that time we were starved of funds. The development of As-Salaam was indeed a milestone. It was the idea of one person who was perhaps too far ahead of his time. The community around him was not quite ready to establish such a vast institute.[13]

Ismail Meer also noted the lack of community support:

> The saddest thing is that...there is no active interest in the institution. It is a pity that with the exception of not more than two members of the Jami'atul 'Ulama, not a single other maulvie has sought fit to visit the institution, nor have our Muslim leaders found time to visit the institution. The *Views* appeals to Muslims active in educational, social, and religious work to visit As-Salaam and see for themselves the great possibilities this institution offers. Mr Ahmed Deedat, through sheer hard work and courage has started something that every Muslim must be proud of. Will Muslim leaders in the Republic now take up the challenge, and turn As-Salaam into an institution bringing honour for all times?[14]

The deadlock between the trustees further impeded progress between 1959 and 1963. For example, Ebrahim Essopjee of Klerksdorp had donated R1 500 in 1960 for the electrification of As-Salaam. He wrote to the IPC on 10 April 1962 asking for the money to be returned because of the impasse. Essopjee rejected Vanker's proposal that the monies be held in trust by the Jami'at until the Trust had resolved its differences, and the money was returned to him on 4 May 1962. After the dispute was resolved, the As-Salaam Trust wrote to Essopjee in January 1964 'that by Allah's grace, the Trust will function without a hitch in the future for the glory of Islam'. Essopjee requested proof that the land had been transferred to the Trust. As this was only legally possible in 1976, the funds were lost. These setbacks also meant that it took until 1974 before As-Salaam was connected to the electricity grid; until then, diesel generators were used.

Quite apart from his building and management duties, Deedat also had to establish a syllabus and curriculum to teach new converts about Islam so that they would become 'model Muslims'. This included familiarising students with other faiths and training them to talk 'intelligently about their religion.'[15]

Deedat informed the Trust in October 1963 that the two-year course for students who had passed Standard 6 comprised theoretical and practical teaching of elementary Islam, reading the Qur'an with meaning, the study of comparative religion, public speaking, and preparation for a trade, such as typing, book-keeping, or carpentry. The curriclum had been prepared in conjunction with Professor Hashim of Pakistan.

Ismail Meer of *News and Views* reported in August 1965 that twenty-five African students were being taught to read and memorise the Qur'an and instructed in elementary aspects of Islam. Meer noted that Deedat was assisted by Hafidh G.M. Desai, and that students were using the translation of the Qur'an into Zulu by Rashid King.[16] As-Salaam made a favourable impression on Meer who wrote that 'the story behind this mission is a story of perseverance, pain, courage, determination, and devotion to a cause. It is a story of young men striving to achieve an end and the story of lukewarm interest of the Muslim community.'[17]

Deedat's involvement in the IPC meant that he spent considerable time away from Braemar. During his absences, 'Mama Hawa', as students knew her, ran As-Salaam. Fluent in Zulu, she oversaw the construction of the buildings while bringing up her young family.[18] Ismail Meer paid a special tribute to her: 'This thin frail woman has not only developed love and responsibility for the work but is completely devoted to the cause. She speaks fluent Zulu and is completely in charge of feeding and clothing the students. Her work at As-Salaam begins early in the morning and only ends when the sun sets.'

The mosque built by Deedat at As-Salaam.

Despite Deedat's perseverance, however, As-Salaam was not a success in the short term. Eventually, the burden of running the institute and travelling to the IPC offices in Durban proved too much for Deedat.

Deedat reluctantly conceded to Vanker and Agjee that As-Salaam was 'breaking my back'. His 'escape' came when USA-based Islamic scholar Dr Ahmad Sakr visited Durban as a guest of the Muslim Youth Movement (MYM) in 1973. The MYM, formed in 1970, held its first convention at As-Salaam in 1972, with Professor Fazlur Rahman as guest speaker. Sakr and his wife Zuhar were guests the following year. Sakr suggested that the MYM take over the running of As-Salaam. Dr Sakr explained what transpired:

> I was privileged to visit South Africa four times between the 1970s and 1990s, during the height of apartheid and during non-racial rule. I met Imam Deedat in the Zulu area at As-Salaam where he was teaching Islam and Qur'an to Muslim children. While talking to him, I realised that he was a good Muslim scholar, an excellent public speaker and a very knowledgeable person. He was effective in how to conduct dialogue with non-Muslims. I felt that he had much more to offer to the Ummah and I requested the local Muslims of South Africa to ask him to come down to Durban.

Deedat had also conveyed his frustration to Advocate A.B. Mahomed of the MYM, who recalls:

> I had many private discussions with Ahmed Deedat where he confided in me that he would like to talk to people, large audiences, debates, which he could not do if he was stuck at As-Salaam. On the basis of that discussion, the MYM took over As-Salaam. Discussions took place with the late Goolam Kadwa and his family, and the agreement was concluded that the MYM would substitute for Deedat. That resulted in Deedat coming back to Durban.

The MYM took over As-Salaam on 16 August 1973 on a ninety-nine year lease at a nominal rental of R120 per annum. By the time Deedat left, the property had a guest house, a supervisor's house, the imam's cottage, a two-roomed hut with a separate kitchen, a dormitory, a dining hall with kitchen, a mosque with ablution facilities, a swimming pool, a reservoir, and several dams stocked with fish.

Deedat's exit from As-Salaam provided his opponents with yet another opportunity to attack him. Mohammed Makki published a pamphlet 'Has Deedat Something to Hide?' on 13 December 1973 and covered the issue in greater detail in the December 1973 issue of *Muslim Digest*. He wrote that (unnamed) donors were demanding to know what had happened to their funds now that Deedat had 'abandoned the project'. He called on Deedat to 'clear up the various doubts of the general Muslim public and enlighten them regarding the Trust'. Makki's comments were accompanied by thirty-five questions that ran to six typed pages. They included such things as whether Deedat had published an audited balance sheet of the As-Salaam Trust; how much money had been collected and how it was spent;

staff salaries, including that of Hawa Deedat; the amount spent on propagating Islam; the number of students who had completed courses in missionary work; and how much preaching had been done in African areas. Makki implored Deedat to

> state truthfully whether the Seminary at As-Salaam was worth all the trouble, the energies and money of the Muslim public…And would you deny the charge of having taken the Muslim public for a ride and having failed to fulfil your promises to them when you quit?

Makki's sentiments were shared by Adam Peerbhai, who wrote in *Muslim Digest* that Deedat 'failed at As-Salaam as he got not even one person turned out in eighteen years as a fully fledged Muslim missionary for which As-Salaam was established'.[19]

Instead of replying in writing as requested by Makki, Deedat decided to respond to these charges at the Friday khutba (sermon) at the Grey Street Mosque on 31 May 1974. He called Makki twice to ask him to attend the khutba. Makki did not attend that mosque that day, and the imam, Abu Bakr Khatib, prevented Deedat from delivering the khutba on the instruction of the mosque's trustees.[20]

By 1977, the MYM realised that it too could not manage As-Salaam, and handed it over to an independent committee, which formed the As-Salaam Educational Institute in 1978. The first trustees were Mohamed Khan, Suleman Cotwall, G.M. Hoosen, R.A. Karrim, and Yusuf Patel. Classes restarted in July 1978 with thirteen students under Ameer Yusuf Mahomedy and resident caretaker Isaac Albertyn. Yakoob Dube (1979) and later D. Mdletshe (1980) were employed to oversee secular education. By the mid-1980s, around fifteen pupils were graduating every second year in Islamic studies, and students could pursue secular studies via correspondence. From 1991, students could study up to matric. Deedat's efforts were thus not futile. A decade after his departure, *al-Qalam* paid him the following tribute:

> As-Salaam was an embodiment of Mr Ahmed Deedat's vision and aspiration to train Islamic da'ees. Deedat toiled and built for twelve years the dream which became As-Salaam. But Deedat could not burn the candle on both ends by running As-Salaam and IPC simultaneously and thus decided to hand over the running of As-Salaam to an independent committee…However, his heart is still with As-Salaam, ever committed to its development and success.[21]

After leaving As-Salaam, Deedat returned to Durban and lived just north of the city in Verulam. He resumed his full-time position at the IPC, and, free to pursue his original objectives with even greater vigour, he transformed the IPC into an international organisation, IPCI.

# CREATING CHANGE

Deedat's growing popularity meant that local venues often could not accommodate the crowds that turned up to listen to him speak.

The benefit of these symposia will be tremendous and provoke food for thought in the minds of the Christians, and will help the Muslims to equip themselves in discussing with Christians, and at the same time strengthen the morale of the Muslims. The Christian's lecture will in no way affect the iman of the Muslims, whereas the Muslim's talk will definitely make a lot of Christians to think anew on the teachings of their Church.

– Minutes of an IPC meeting, August 1963

THE IPC was at its most innovative during what one member described as the 'exciting' 1960s and 1970s when it undertook a host of groundbreaking activities in the traditionally conservative Muslim community. According to G.H. Agjee, most of the ideas were coined by Deedat himself. 'He would think of something and as soon as he walked into the office he would say, right, let's do this or that, without taking into account the cost or consequence.' Ebi Lockhat, who was the IPCI's public relations officer, told a reporter in 1991 that Deedat's 'modus operandi in raising funds is to commit himself to a project and thereafter raise the money to pay for it'.[1] This included placing advertisements in local newspapers, conducting mosque tours, writing to newspaper editors in defence of Islam, distributing English-translation Qur'ans and, above all, participating in public lectures and debates.

As an exercise in da'wah, the IPC placed short extracts from the Qur'an under the heading 'The Qur'an Speaks' in major Durban newspapers, including the mainly white-read *Sunday Tribune* and *Daily News* as well as the Zulu newspaper *Ilanga lase Natal*. The hadith (sayings) of the Prophet Muhammad (PBUH) and his companions featured in these newspapers under the heading 'Islamic Thoughts'. These advertisements were later placed in newspapers aimed mainly at the Indian population, such as the *Post* and the *Sunday Times Extra*. The messages, which by the late 1970s reached around 150 000 people weekly, were short and thought provoking. Each advert ended with an invitation to the public to contact the IPC for literature and information about Islam.

The strategy was effective. *Indian Views* reported on 25 March 1959 that 'the response to this feature has been so great and the volume of correspondence from those interested in Islam was so vast that a full-time person is employed to handle the correspondence in English and Zulu'. Vanker told an IPC meeting on 9 May 1963 that he was receiving numerous letters from readers because of the adverts. He felt that even if the series did not result in new converts it helped to clear up 'massive misconceptions' about Islam. For example, Deedat told the meeting, when he was canvassing for adverts for the Islamic calendar he invited the director of a multinational company to visit the 'largest mosque in the Southern Hemisphere, which was at his doorstep. We nearly fell head over heels when he stated that he was happy to visit and "see how we worshipped the phallus."' Deedat felt that it was 'incumbent on us, irrespective of what it cost, to go on inserting "The Qur'an Speaks". The Christians in the Cape are spending thousands of rands to convert the Muslims, but thanks to Allah they have been unsuccessful.'

An Islamic calendar was published annually for almost a decade from the mid-1960s. This popular scheme was G.H. Vanker's brainchild. Featuring a quotation from the Qur'an and hadith for each day of the year, the calendar promoted Islamic education and was an important source of income during the early years.

Deedat (seated right) organised tours of Durban's Jumu'ah Mosque for visitors from all over the world.

The IPC protested at what it perceived to be the denigration of Islam in a range of contexts. For example, when Vanker saw a photograph in the Natal Mercury in 1962 in which a swimsuit at a Paris fashion show was called 'Islam', he brought this to the attention of Imam Muhammad Tufail of the Woking Mosque in London who, in turn, referred the matter to the World Congress of Faiths in Paddington, London. The IPC also wrote to the agency that supplied the photograph. The agency apologised and suggested that the IPC write to the modelling agency, which Vanker did. There is no record of a response being received from the agency.[2]

The IPC also responded to what it considered to be distortions of Islam in mainstream commercial newspapers, magazines, and on national television. On 29 November 1964, during an edition of a popular Sunday evening Springbok Radio quiz show, the contestants (Bob Griffiths, Arthur Bleksley, Eric Rosenthal, and Grant Larden) were asked what was common among a number of world personalities, including the Prophet Muhammed (PBUH), and they answered 'epilepsy'. Vanker wrote to the organiser on 5 December to express his 'shock that members of the team being intellectuals should insult the Holy Prophet of Islam by creating the impression in the minds of half a million listeners that he was suffering from a nervous complaint and sick in the mind. This is completely false and we take strong exception to it.' The letter was accompanied by several IPC publications.

The *Graphic* was taken to task on 2 February 1965 because its Eid supplement contained photographs of Buddhist architecture: 'We want to make it clear to Buddhists that we are not against their faith. We only question the wisdom of choosing articles for publication which are completely irrelevant to Eid or Islam.' In December 1962, the IPC got the Indian

Teacher Training College in Sydenham to install water facilities in toilets to meet the hygienic requirements of Muslim students. The IPC also provided three water vessels to Sastri College in March 1963 for the use of Muslim students.

Bible classes were conducted for Muslims to teach them about comparative religion. These were attended mainly by younger Muslims. As the popularity of these classes increased, they were extended from Durban to Mayville and Verulam. Deedat, Vanker, Agjee, Dr E.M. Gabellah and Dr Derrick Kean (editor) launched the *Criterion* on 19 May 1961.[3] The first issue covered the state of da'wah in South Africa and the role of the IPC, as well as E.M. Gabellah's conversion to Islam, which took place after several discussions with Vanker and Deedat.[4] *Criterion* was published for a few months but fizzled out due to lack of management capacity.

Deedat and Vanker were concerned about inter-religious marriages, and tried to alleviate some of the practical day-to-day issues by conducting the nikah ceremony and providing classes for newly married (mixed-religion) couples. IPC officials visited the homes of Muslims who had married, or intended to marry, a non-Muslim to discuss the implications, and they also published handbills explaining the consequences of inter-religious marriages.

Deedat introduced non-Muslims to Islam through organised tours of the mosque in Grey Street. He believed that many people were unaware of the differences between Hinduism and Islam and wanted to correct this by showing them the difference between temples and mosques. Vanker told an IPC meeting on 9 May 1963 that

> Western people who visited the mosque from all parts of the country and the world were shocked and surprised at the absence of idols, etc. in the mosque. If we can only remove these prejudices from their minds about our faith, we have done our duty, irrespective whether they embrace Islam or not.

Visitors were given a lecture on Islam, as well as a special booklet, *The Muslim at Prayer*, which explained the purpose and method of prayer, and carried references to biblical similarities in prayer and ablution. A guide was trained to conduct tours and explain why Muslims take off their shoes before entering a mosque, the rationale behind ablution, the significance of the Islamic greeting, and so on. The mosque tours proved very successful. The IPC reported in 1982 that around fourteen hundred non-Muslims were visiting the mosque annually. The Durban Town Council included the visit in its tourist guide for the city. According to G.H. Agjee, many visitors said that they would 'never again associate Muslims with idol worshippers'; while others stated that they were glad to have seen Islam 'as it was practiced rather than as it was usually presented in an oriental museum'.

Shabaan Khan conducted many tours of the mosque in the 1970s and early 1980s when he worked for the IPCI. Visitors came as part of what was called the 'Oriental Tour'. Shabaan would hand out literature, take the visitors on a tour of the mosque, and field questions. Tourists, in Shabaan's words, 'were particularly amazed that Islam was so close to Judaism and Christianity'. Although Deedat saw the tours as an excellent 'advert' for Islam, and hence a form of da'wah, and visitors respected the rules and decorum surrounding mosque attendance, some Muslims objected to non-Muslims entering the mosque. Mawlana A.S. Desai, for example, regarded these 'tourist calls' as 'despicable and unIslamic', and said that for him, 'the sanctity of the masjid is rudely rent asunder by the invasion. Masjids are not tourist attractions. The purpose for which masjids have been built is noble and lofty.'[5]

Desai was adamant that Deedat did not have the right to allow women into the mosque. Deedat, however, maintained that there was no prohibition in the Qur'an against women or non-Muslims entering these sacred spaces.[6] Desai's riposte was that Deedat was 'dabbling in matters about which he has no knowledge and possesses no ability and no qualification'.[7] Historically jurists have disagreed about this matter, but most interpretations of Islamic law permit non-Muslims to enter mosques as a sign of openness to the rest of the community and as a means of encouraging non-Muslims to embrace Islam.[8]

---

While Deedat is best known for his debates with Christians, he had a passion for the Qur'an. According to A.S. Ballim, from a very young age Deedat would tell them, 'Wallahi [by God], if I have the means I will distribute Qur'ans free to everybody in the world. I would place one in every hotel where there is a Bible.' S.A. Parak, who owned a fruit and vegetable store in Camperdown, took him up on the offer and provided funds for this purpose. Others followed with contributions, and donations were later received from international donors as well. The IPCI eventually distributed almost half-a-million English translations of the Qur'an by Yusuf Ali free or at a nominal price. In May 1988, for example, one hundred thousand copies of the Qur'an were ordered. Sections of the Qur'an were also translated into Zulu by Omar Moleleki, and a Zulu version of the Qur'an translated by Mawlana Cassim Sema of Newcastle was also distributed.

Deedat implored Muslims to study the Qur'an as he wanted them to understand the text. During an interview in Australia shortly before his stroke, Deedat was asked what advice he had for Muslims: 'Familiarise yourself with your deen, go to the Qur'an, go to the Qur'an, see what Allah is telling you and try to see if you can live by that.'[9] A letter to the IPCI from 'Salim of Clairwood', dated 12 April 1991, is typical of those who heeded Deedat's advice:

> I write this letter to thank you [for] of the many visitors we have had in Ramzaan, your visit stands out. My reading habits recently have been a search. I have been reading Islamic Philosophy, Fiqh, and History. The day you visited me, you mentioned that I should read only the Qur'an because it has everything. Since that day I have

been reading the Qur'an (your copy obviously) before I sleep and after Sehri. I am thoroughly enjoying it and am disappointed at myself for not having done this earlier. Thank you for your kind advice.

Deedat made the Qur'an widely accessible and, by default, brought into question the role of 'ulama as the only authoritative interpreters of the Qur'an. As Francis Robinson put it, the consequence was that 'increasingly from now on any Ahmad or Muhammad could claim to speak for Islam'.[10] When Deedat toured Port Elizabeth in June 1980, Yunus Chohan of the local jami'at claimed that Deedat had told him in private that he (Deedat) would 'take the sins of all those on my head who listen to my lectures and touch, hold, handle, read and study the Qur'an [in an impure state]'. When this was put to Deedat before a public audience in Uitenhage, he insisted that he was referring to the English translation and not the Arabic version of the Qur'an.[11] The Qur'anic injunction 'none shall touch [the Qur'an], but those who are clean' (al-Waqi'a: 78–80) has been interpreted by most scholars as applying to the Arabic text only.[12]

These technicalities did not deter Deedat from distributing the Qur'an. He told Gina Lewis of Radio Freely Speaking during his tour of Switzerland in 1987 that the Qur'an's message would transform anyone who read it with an open mind.

> I have sometimes orthodox Christians coming along. There was one young man who was a Roman Catholic. I said, look, I'd like to present you with this Qur'an. He jerked back as if I was offering some fire [for him] to hold on to. He said no, he can't have that. I said, look, read it man, and see. It took me a long time to persuade him to take the book and after reading it he was a changed man. He didn't expect what he was seeing. Another elderly gentleman, we presented him with a Qur'an, this Holy Book, and after some time I phoned him up, 'How is your progress?' He said, 'No, I haven't read it yet.' Again, another time, he says, 'I haven't had time to go to it yet.' Three or four times I phoned the man, then he says, 'Look man, I've been reading it all along, you know, I can't help agreeing with the book and I'm too old to change now.' This is the problem, 'I'm too old to change,' but he's reading it all along and he can't help agreeing with every principle that is there. If you, without prejudiced minds, open the book, you see what it does to you, it must create a change.[13]

Deedat's struggle to secure funding to distribute Qur'ans freely is taken up in later chapters.

---

Deedat's reputation was earned primarily through his debates and lectures. One of the first lectures was hosted by the Young Men's Muslim Association in 1955. The handbill described the talk on 'Muhammad in the Old and New Testament' as 'a challenge to the narrow prejudice of the centuries'. In what would become Deedat's modus operandi, he explicitly invited Christian scholars and priests to his lecture. An Ismail Mayat of Johannesburg was

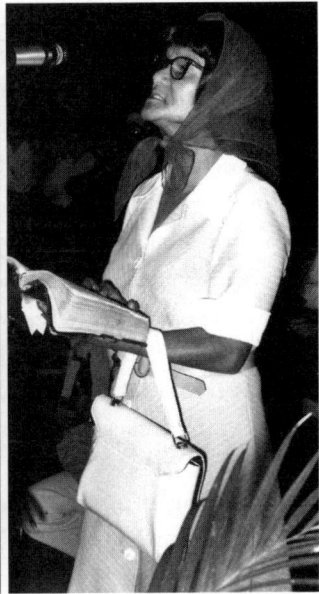

Public debates always included time for questions from audience members.

on holiday in Durban and attended this lecture. He was very impressed and invited Deedat to give a talk at the Johannesburg City Hall on the occasion of the Prophet's (PBUH) birthday. According to Agjee, the success of the lecture gave Deedat great confidence and catapulted him onto the national stage. He delivered around fifteen public lectures between October 1958 and December 1960. Three lectures were held at the City Hall in Durban, three in Verulam, one in Pietermaritzburg, and a lecture in Zulu was held at the Bantu Social Centre in Durban. Lectures were also held in Stanger, Umzinto, at the Kolbe Association to a group of Roman Catholic professional men and women, and at the Anglican St Xavier's Young People's Guild.

Well-attended talks included 'Jesus Christ: Man, Myth or God' (1 September 1957); 'The Truth about Trinity' (6 October 1957); and 'Is Atonement True?' (10 November 1957). This was followed by a talk in English and Zulu on 'Muhammad: A Prophet like Moses' with V.M. Mgadi at the Pine Street Madrasa under the auspices of the Arabic Study Circle and the IPC. Deedat spoke at the Durban City Hall on 17 December 1958 on 'What the Bible Says About Muhammad (PBUH)'. This was followed by 'Muhammad the Natural Successor to Christ' on 15 April 1959. Pamphlets advertising the talks invited 'questioners trained in Christian dogma' to attend with their Bibles as they would be given 'ample opportunities to ask questions'. On 29 March 1959, Deedat spoke on 'Islam's solution to Africa's Problem' at the Islamia Madrasa in Lodge Grove, Overport. There was a succession of debates, symposiums, and public lectures. Deedat also shared a platform with Swami Venktesananda and Reverend P. Holland on the Philosophy of Religion at the South Coast Indian Sports Ground on 19 November 1961.

Deedat and Vanker viewed lectures and debates as opportunities to spread their message. The minutes of the IPC for a committee meeting on 9 May 1963 reflect discussion about an invitation from the Reverend Hamilton of the Church of Christ to two debates against visiting American Professor Cyril Simkins on the subjects, 'Is Jesus God?' in Johannesburg on 11 August 1963, and 'Was Christ Crucified?' in Durban on 19 August 1963. The IPC approved the challenge, according to the minutes of a meeting in August 1963, because Deedat and Vanker saw this opportunity as a godsend.

Deedat's booklet *Muhammad in the Old and New Testament*, which dealt with prophecies in the Bible concerning the advent of Muhammad (PBUH) and the humanity of Jesus, had come to the attention of the Reverend Hamilton of Kimberley who arranged a debate between Deedat and Simkins, professor of philosophy and New Testament exegesis at Johnson Bible College, Tennessee, USA.[14] At an IPC committee meeting on 30 September 1963, Deedat reported that the hall was packed to capacity, with 'people sitting on the floor and aisle. Lots of people were turned away.' The minutes noted that 'Muslims in the audience were overjoyed' with Deedat's performance. A.K. Salejee felt that there should be more debates because youth were 'in love with the West. It is good for youth.' Deedat replied that he was 'ready at any time but nobody else is ready to debate'.

Such debates continued from the 1960s to the 1980s across South Africa. One of the most widely publicised debates took place in August 1981 at Westridge Park Stadium in Durban against USA-based evangelist and author Josh McDowell. They debated the topic 'Was Christ crucified?' According to one observer, 'when you read through Mr Deedat's speech, you realise that he is a very skilful speaker. He knows how to take facts and present them in

Posters advertising Deedat's debates were common all over Durban from the 1960s to the 1980s.

a way that is supportive to his arguments. He makes himself out to be both knowledgeable and correct about the topic, while his opponents are made out to be mistaken and brainwashed.' McDowell himself acknowledged that Deedat's strength was that 'he had a way with words'.

Another of Deedat's more interesting debates was with Gary Miller, a mathematician and theologian, at Westridge Park in 1982. Miller subsequently embraced Islam and adopted the name Abdul-Ahad Omar. Deedat's lifelong friend, Suleman Shaikjee, who attended Deedat's lectures from the earliest days, remembered the following during an interview:

> *Interviewer:* The footsteps of that first night [as a public speaker] can still be heard by those who listen hard enough. Once a shy, young businessman, fresh from Gujarat, Suleman Shaikjee can still remember the exact spot where he sat over half his lifetime ago. For him Deedat is still on the stage, his distinctive arms flying about, his booming voice echoing throughout the auditorium. He can still feel the excitement of the crowd and the tension in the air.
>
> *Shaikjee:* Very long time, over forty years. Ahmed Deedat would talk about the Prophet Mohammed (PBUH), Jesus, Mohammed and Islam, What the Bible say about Christians. He speak very well, simple English, all understanding, even small children used to come, they used to like him, understand him. We all liked him, a few of them just hate him. Some Christian missionaries, they used to hate him.[15]

Deedat's debates had a powerful effect on his mainly Muslim audiences. They moved Islam out of mosques, into the public domain and away from the notion of religion as only being about private worship. In his study of the IPCI, Riaz Jamal observed:

> Deedat communicated his message with extreme simplicity, choosing many common words in his discourses. Most striking is his in-depth knowledge of the Bible; Deedat is able to quote with ease from memory relevant verses without reading from the source itself. For this reason he was given the title 'Al-Shaykh' in the Middle East.[16]

Deedat's public performances were also instrumental in forming certain ideas about Christianity in Muslim minds. If, as many interviewees pointed out, Muslims knew little about Islam, they knew even less about Christianity and gained their knowledge of it from Deedat, who boasted that he knew the Bible 'better than anybody in this country, and authorities on the Bible are like putty in my hands during debates'.[17] Professor Salman Nadvi, for example,

> was impressed with his enthusiasm and knowledge of the Bible. We Muslims don't know as much about Christianity as we should. All that we know is that Christians believe in the Trinity and things like that. He was a hafidh of the Bible and no priest could stand up to him. The Christian priest would carry a Bible to quote and Deedat, as soon as the man started to say some words, [Deedat] would quote the Bible, 'this is what you are talking about'. He had the Bible on his pulse.

Some Muslims regarded the debates as counter-productive. An editorial in *Indian Views*, for example, dated 14 May 1962, stated that while it had 'nothing but praise' for Deedat's efforts, he 'should not deliver his lectures in a form of *challenge* to other religions. The title of his lecture on the question of the Crucifixion Of Jesus Christ was *disgusting*.'

Deedat's lectures did lead to tension. For example, on 19 February 1979, he lectured to an audience of almost 2 000 at the Durban City Hall on 'The Qur'an or the Bible? Which is God's Word?' After the lecture anti-Muslim graffiti was peppered on the walls of the City Hall and Post Office. They included such lines as 'Moslems, Dogs, Devil' and 'See Papers... Iran Murderers'. Ibrahim Bawa, secretary-general of Islamic Council of South Africa, felt that Deedat's lectures

> certainly don't help to build sound human relationships...Islam also does not teach us to criticise other scriptures. Mr Deedat is a very capable man, but by drawing comparisons between the Christian and Islamic faiths he is provoking strong reactions. It is not in our teachings to either debase or condemn other religions.[18]

Deedat was unrepentant. He told a reporter that Hindus and Muslims were 'living in an ocean of Christianity and Christians are constantly knocking at our doors seeking converts. We are like sitting targets. I realise that religion is a highly emotional issue but I give the lectures because it is necessary to educate people on Islam to counter Christianity.' In twenty years of preaching, he said, he had never been pelted on stage or assaulted by opponents because he 'handle[d] the subject delicately...The Christian fanatics have written this [graffiti] because they cannot find answers to the questions I raise.'[19]

Deedat embarked on several international tours during these years. He initially focused on Africa because he believed that it was an 'ideal' target for Islam and quoted historian H.G. Wells in *The Shape of Things to Come* to support his argument: 'Africa is a fair field for all religions but the religion which the African will accept is a religion which best suits his needs. And that religion, everyone who has a right to speak on the subject says, is Islam.'[20] One of his adverts pointed out that 62 per cent of Africa was Muslim but that Southern Africa was the exception. It made the following appeal: 'Help us to Islamize Southern Africa before it is too late.'

Deedat's foray into Africa must be seen in the context of the spread of Pentecostalism on the continent from the 1970s. Pentecostal churches appealed to younger, better educated and more Westernised Africans. Methods of propagation included door-to-door evangelism, meetings in private homes, preaching on trains, buses, street corners, and other places of public concourse, and 'tent crusades'. In this context, many Muslims welcomed Deedat's arrival.[21]

In August 1975, Deedat visited Zambia where he lectured in Lusaka, Ndola, Chipata, Livingstone, and Mazabuka. Mohamed Haniff Badat, who served as MC for Deedat's lectures in Zambia, recalled Deedat's impact:

Brother Shaykh Ahmed Deedat requested me to set up a programme in a remote school in a place called Kafue, outside the capital of Lusaka, about twenty-five kilometres away, one Saturday afternoon. And I said to Ahmedbhai, 'Why do you want to go there? You will get no response. It is a total waste of time and effort.' But he stood his ground and said to me, 'Young man, ye know not what the Lord has in store for you – Do what I request and stand by my side as my custodian.' This is what followed: at two o'clock Mr Deedat, an African principal and myself were present; at two-thirty, two students arrived; at three o'clock the programme begins; the school classroom started echoing with his beautiful voice and to my amazement the classroom started getting full to capacity with students, ladies and children. There was no place left to sit and as always, traditionally, the Africans, quietly, respectfully takes their seat on the floor, with so much humbleness one cannot imagine, their faces reflecting one theme: 'Let's listen to this man who sounds like a God-sent Messenger.' The message was delivered and definitely absorbed. The programme terminated at four-thirty with lots of well wishing. When the crowds and the three of us were ready to leave, Ahmedbhai said to me, 'If only to one out of these persons have I delivered my message, that is all I require. Now do you understand why I brought you here young man?'

We also held a programme at Brother Ayoob Limbada's pleasant residence one evening in Makheni, just outside of Lusaka. The attendance consisted mainly of all the 'ulama Ikraam and madrasah teachers and huffaadh. I cannot forget that evening because I remember leaving my unwell wife in bed and driving as fast as I can towards Makheni in order to officiate and declare the programme officially open for Shaykh Deedat, making Qadar and upholding his respect. Because I was speeding that night in the city of Lusaka, the law in the country at that time was to leave the driver of the speeding vehicle on the roadside and tow the vehicle into a police compound, only to be released the next day. But look how Allah plans. I stood in the rain at the roadside, praying that Ahmedbhai's programme must not be delayed, whatever the consequences, have mercy upon me and destine me there. An unknown car with strangers pulled up and asked me whether I wanted a lift. I did not care who the strangers were and how safe I was going to be. I just sat in the vehicle and directed them to Makheni. Enquiries were made as to why do I want to go to Makheni and especially at night. When I mentioned that I was dressed up in my immaculate black suit to especially conduct a programme, which is due to be held by Shaykh Ahmed Deedat, they said, 'Deedat, the messenger of Allah who preached at the Evelyn Hone College of Education?' I said, 'yes' and they said, 'Brother, we will not only deliver you there safely, but we are not going anywhere either, but to the messenger.' That is the magnetism Brother Deedat possessed. The next day at the police compound I was supposed to appear in the presence of a Police Commissioner for disciplinary hearing and possibly a charge of driving negligently and speeding in the city. When I arrived in the yard of the Compound a prominent police traffic officer said to me, 'approach that office, your key is there, you may drive your vehicle away'.[22]

After visiting Deedat in Verulam in 2003, Badat wrote to the family:

> Shaykh Ahmed Deedat's memory served him well when he acknowledged that I was the MC in all his programmes which [were] so packed with capacity that Shaykh Ahmed even allowed members of the audience to sit on the window sills and all around us on the stage, although at that time I found that experience most frightening, because of the controversial subject matter. None the less, after that evening's lectures, it was gratifying to read in the Zambia *Daily Mail*'s front page 'Allah's Messenger comes to Lusaka'... Over many years I have had the opportunity and blessings of Allah, to travel along with Shaykh Ahmed Deedat, in a quiet and concealed manner, where people only acknowledged me as just another Master of Ceremonies. But I have gained and treasured volumes of knowledge.[23]

In 1978, Deedat drew large crowds during his tours of Zambia, Botswana, Lesotho, Swaziland, and Rhodesia (Zimbabwe). The Muslim Students' Association in University of Dar-es-Salaam invited him to Tanzania in 1981. He participated in a seminar and delivered two public lectures. Deedat's presence in Dar-es-Salaam 'was felt overnight and his name and arguments on the sanctity of the Bible spread like bush fire'.[24] The church hierarchy tried unsuccessfully to get Deedat deported as a 'prohibited immigrant' since South Africans were barred from entering Tanzania while the white minority government was in power. Several Muslim Bible scholars emerged in Tanzania in the wake of Deedat's visit, the most prominent being Ngariba Mussa Fundi and Mohamed Ali Kawemba.[25]

Although Deedat focused increasingly on the Middle East from the 1980s his belief that Africa was a 'fair field' for Islam remained strong. In a lecture titled 'Islam in Africa', given at the Abu Dhabi Chamber of Commerce on 31 May 1992, he asserted that Islam and Africa were 'inseparable' but that Muslims were not doing enough to spread the din (faith) while Christian missionaries were aggressively proselytising across the continent.

Until the mid-1980s Deedat travelled throughout South Africa, covering long distances and visiting remote areas to raise funds for the IPC. During Ramadan, the IPC distributed appeal forms to mosques countrywide. Many individuals and organisations contributed funds on a regular basis. While the IPC made great strides during these years, it was when Deedat was able to focus solely on the IPC that he was able to extend its reach internationally.

# 13

# CONTROVERSIES AND DIVERSIONS

Never shy of controversy or one to back down in a tight corner, Ahmed Deedat fought several court cases against various opponents during his lifetime.

Advance, and never halt, for advancing is perfection.
Advance and do not fear the thorns in the path,
for they draw only corrupt blood.[1]

– Khalil Gibran

DEEDAT THRIVED on 'battles' and was willing to risk defeat rather than compromise. This is apparent in several of the disputes in which he was involved. Even when he was advised by the likes of G.H. Agjee, G.H. Vanker, and Ebi Lockhat to change course, he remained resolute. The stories of his litigation against the evangelist John Gilchrist and his persistent peddling of the theories of Rashid Khalifa are testimony to this.

In late 1974, the Benoni branch of the Young Men's Muslim Association invited attorney John Gilchrist, a Christian evangelist, to participate in a symposium with Deedat on the subject 'Was Christ Crucified?' The seminar was held at Willowmoore Park Stadium in Benoni on 25 February 1975. Gilchrist was a formidable opponent who had published a series of booklets that essentially sought to rebut Deedat. These included: *The Crucifixion of Christ: Fact not Fiction*; *The Textual History of the Qur'an and the Bible*; *Christ in Islam and Christianity*; and *Is Muhammad Foretold in the Bible?*

There was drama towards the end of Deedat's presentation when he accused Gilchrist of anonymously distributing a booklet titled *The Prophets: What was God's Real Message to Them All?* among Muslims. Deedat charged that Gilchrist used the Arabic names of the Prophets, such as Musa for Moses, Dawud for David, and Ibrahim for Abraham, to create the false impression that the booklet was a Muslim publication and hence 'authentic'. Deedat further claimed that Benoni attorney A.E. Lambat had told him that it was illegal to omit an author's name and that Gilchrist could be charged with 'impersonating a Muslim, false representation, deception and chicanery'.

Gilchrist asked Deedat to retract his allegation in the weeks following the seminar. When Deedat refused, Gilchrist sued him for for defamation. After three adjournments, the matter went to court in October 1975. During this delay, Deedat advertised the court record containing Gilchrist's cross-examination in prominent South African newspapers such as the *Natal Mercury*, the *Daily News*, the *Leader*, the *Sunday Tribune*, the (Johannesburg) *Star*, the *Cape Argus*, and *Muslim News*. Deedat's case unravelled, however, when Lambat contradicted Deedat's evidence. The judge described Deedat as an 'aggressive' witness, presumably because he became very personal in his attacks on Gilchrist. At one point Deedat retorted (to Gilchrist): 'You are not hospitable. You cannot show hospitality to black people. I took you to the poshest restaurant in Durban, and when I was in Benoni you didn't even offer me a glass of water.' Under cross-examination, Deedat admitted that Gilchrist had given him a book as a gift.

Magistrate P.J. Fourie delivered judgment on 14 February 1977. He accepted Gilchrist's explanation that he had used the Muslim names of the Prophets because his Muslim acquaintances had told him that they were not familiar with the corresponding Christian names. Fourie considered it 'illogical' to assume that the omission of Gilchrist's name on the publication was intended to make it seem as if it had been written or published by a Muslim.

Page 18     THE MUSLIM DIGEST     February, 1977

Mr. John Gilchrist.

Dr. E.G.M. Gabellah

comparative study of religions and who formerly accepted Islam at the Islamic Propagation Centre so as to join As Salaam in Muslim mission work among Africans. Soon differences arose between Mr. Deedat and Dr. Gabellah, first over methods of preaching and then Dr. Gabellah was accused of not being a Muslim. Disappointed, he left South Africa in 1962 and the same Dr. Gabellah incidentally, is now in Rhodesia and is Vice-President of Bishop Abel Muzorewa's African National Congress. A real loss to Islam.

3. The unhappy incidents that took place wtih convert Abdul Khalick, who claimed of being accused of theft and also told to 'go back to Pastor Rowland's Church'.

4. Controversy and Court Case with Mr. S.I. Kadwa, the donor of the As-Salaam land, which land Mr. Deedat was not able to take transfer of in the name of As-Salaam all those years he was associated with As-Salaam.

5. The controversy with Mr. Ebrahim Khan, the caretaker at As-Salaam, which ended up in Court. Mr. Deedat had to admit defeat in the middle of his cross-examination by Mr. R. Allaway.

6. The Controversy that arose with Rev. Pypers at the Green Point Track, Cape Town, when tens of thousands of booklets were distributed against Islam and the Holy Prophet at Mr. Deedat's meeting. Mr. Deedat politely returned to Durban the next day and the MUSLIM JUDICIAL COUNCIL had to do all the explanations for months on end in the Cape press and through other means. The Muslim Judicial Council had then condemned Mr. Deedat's method of propagating Islam, and was obliged to do so once again over a year ago when Mr. Deedat again gave a series of lectures in the Cape. The Muslim Judicial Council had in fact to issue a pamphlet disassociating itself with Mr. Deedat's lectures in the Cape Peninsula.

7. The recent Court case with Mr. John Gilchrist of Benoni which resulted after the symposium "WAS CHRIST CRUCIFIED?" between Mr. Deedat and Mr. Gilchrist. Judgement in this Court case is pending.

8. Now, the controversy with Mr. Bobby Muthusamy who according to Mr. Deedat was employed by the Islamic Propagation Centre and was fired "because the Centre was dissatisfied with his work". Mr. Muthusamy is now reported as having gone back to Christianity.

The *Muslim Digest* often devoted pages of vociferous criticism to Deedat and his work.

Another controversy centred on the figure of Rashid Khalifa.

Deedat's impulsive nature revealed itself in his obsession with the numerical theories about the Qur'an of Egyptian-born Rashid Khalifa (1935–1990), who held a Ph.D. in biochemistry. The Arizona-based Khalifa's booklet *Miracle of the Qur'an* (published in 1972), which was expanded into a full-length book *Qur'an: The Final Scripture*, hypothesised that an arithmetical pattern based on the number 19 ran through the Qur'an.[2] Khalifa argued that this was physical proof of God's existence as it showed that the Qur'an had to have been written by a superior Being, God, and that it has been perfectly preserved, unlike the Bible. Khalifa's claims included, for example, the fact that the Qur'an had 114 suras (6 x 19); there were 6 346 verses (334 x 19); the Qur'an contained 329,156 letters (17 324 x 19), and so on. Based on the traditional belief that the Prophet Muhammad (PBUH) could not read or write, the embedding of 19 throughout the Qur'an was proof, according to Khalifa, that Allah had dictated it.[3]

Deedat embraced this theory wholeheartedly and published *al-Qur'an: The Ultimate Miracle* in 1979, in which he argued the significance of the number 19 in order to prove that it was the word of God. Deedat was humbled by Khalifa's insights: 'I have in all humility taken the liberty of bringing scientific findings of that great servant of Islam – Dr Rashid Khalifa, PhD – in my own humble way…In places I have used his eloquent words verbatim for lack of better expression.'[4] Deedat published the booklet even after he learnt that other Islamic scholars considered some of Khalifa's claims heretical. Deedat sent a copy to Dr Ahmad Totonji at the World Assembly of Muslim Youth on 1 November 1984 with a message that the 'mathematical miracle…makes bold our claim that even atheists and agnostics have been shaken out of their complacency, leave alone the lukewarm Muslim, on being confronted with this miracle'.

Professor Salman Nadvi had met Khalifa while studying at Chicago University in the late 1960s and early 1970s, and advised Deedat not to get involved in his theory:

> Khalifa was studying in Texas at the time when we were there. He knew me in the sense that he was in the Muslim Students' Association so he sent me that part of the Qur'an which he had translated into English. After reading it I told him that this was not his task, that he should stick with his computer studies. Soon after that he got involved with the number 19. I opposed that but Ahmed Deedat saw the book and took it up. I told him that it was not the right thing to do because you are trying to prove that the Qur'an is a book of God because of numerical calculations. What happens if somebody rebuts the theory so that your whole thesis collapses?…What are you trying to say about the people who accepted the Qur'an as the word of God before Rashid Khalifa? He didn't accept my opinion but after Khalifa started claiming that he was a prophet of God, Deedat removed that book from his publication.

Khalifa's group, the United Submitters International, which considered itself representative of the 'true' Islam, removed two verses from the Qur'an (9:128 and 129) because they broke the word-frequency patterns of multiples of nineteen.[5] He claimed in the March 1985 issue of his monthly publication *Muslim Perspective* that these verses were added by Satan after the Qur'an had been written: 'The computer exposes a historical crime; tampering with the word of God; two false verses unveiled in Qur'an.'[6] Khalifa also claimed that the Prophet Muhammad (PBUH) was the last Prophet but not the last Messenger, and he himself claimed to be the so-called 'Messenger of the Covenant' mentioned in the Qur'an (3:81). Khalifa's work was condemned as kufr (atheist) in the Muslim world. Deedat's critics had a field day once Khalifa was exposed as a fraud. A.S.K. Joommal wrote in *al-Balaagh*:

> From the very beginning, when this Bahai Theory of nineteen was first propounded by Dr Rishad Khalifa, we fought it tooth and nail. Our simple logic was that Allah's word does not need a mathematical buttressing and bolstering. If non-Muslims wish to accept Islam and believe in the Qur'an, then they must do so on the impregnable integrity, awe inspiring beauty and compelling appeal of the Qur'an per se...and not because of some spurious mathematical computation.[7]

Despite mounting suspicion of Khalifa, Deedat waited until April 1987 before he withdrew his booklet. This delay prompted Mohammed Makki to write in *Muslim Digest* that it was 'unforgivable' that Deedat continued to refer to Khalifa 'as "That Great Servant of Islam"!' Makki described Khalifa as Deedat's 'Guru No. 2' (Joseph Perdu had been designated 'Guru No. 1').[8]

Deedat's association with Khalifa had started in 1978, and although it invited criticism from the beginning, it took almost a decade for him to renounce Khalifa. It was only in May 1988 that Deedat denounced Khalifa's 'dastardly false and fictitious claims'.[9] Khalifa died after being stabbed at the Tucson mosque on 31 January 1990.

Deedat seemed to have an obstinate gene that compelled him to stay the course irrespective of the consequences. Caution was certainly not a trait one would easily associate with him. He did not take criticism lightly; he was highly combative and always fought fire with fire.

# 14
# PALESTINE

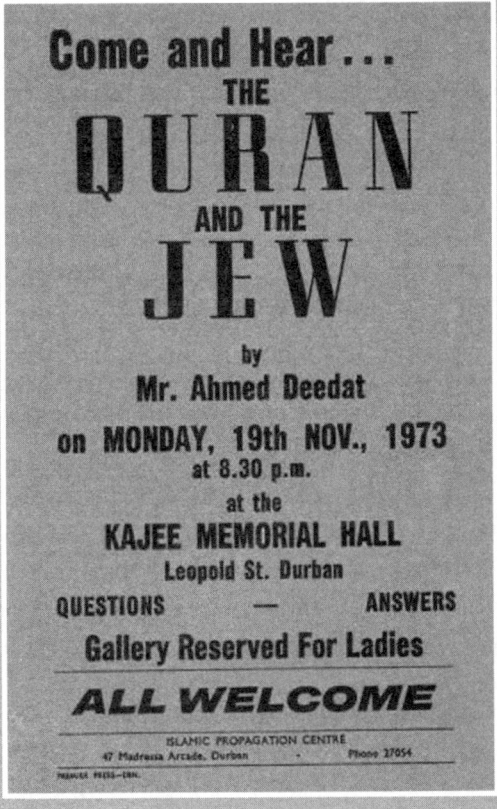

> **Come and Hear...**
> **THE QURAN AND THE JEW**
> by
> Mr. Ahmed Deedat
> on MONDAY, 19th NOV., 1973
> at 8.30 p.m.
> at the
> **KAJEE MEMORIAL HALL**
> Leopold St. Durban
> QUESTIONS — ANSWERS
> **Gallery Reserved For Ladies**
> **ALL WELCOME**
> ISLAMIC PROPAGATION CENTRE
> 47 Madressa Arcade, Durban · Phone 27054

A poster advertising one of Deedat's first lectures on the Palestinian issue.

We support the Palestinians in their fight for recognition and repossession of everything that has been taken away from them by force. I don't think local Muslims and the Muslim world in general should rest until the Palestinians' rights have been restored. The problem facing local Muslims is not whether to help the Palestinians, but how.

– Ahmed Deedat[1]

**I**QBAL JASSAT of the Media Review Network regarded Deedat's 'most profound contribution [to be] the national awareness that he created of the plight and suffering of the Palestinians'.² While Deedat's debates and polemics with Christians were largely motivated by religious factors, his arguments with Jews were inspired mainly by political developments following the creation of the state of Israel in 1948 and the displacement of millions of Palestinians. As Deedat pointed out:

> The Jew has fallen out of the [evangelical] race. He has made the religion a racial religion. You have to be born a Jew to be a Jew. If you fall in love with a Jewish girl and if you want to become a Jew, they will put hurdles in your way and eventually, when you overcome them, they'll convert you willy-nilly but you are still a third-grade Jew. They don't want you. They only want political recognition. If you accept that Palestine belongs to them, that they have a title deed to it; they'll be satisfied with you. Our battle with them is not a racial battle; it is not a religious battle, its politics.³

Deedat's talks on Palestine were usually prefaced by an account of an incident that took place in 1956 while he was employed at Beare Brothers. His Jewish boss, Bernie Beare, was hosting a Jewish couple from Argentina and asked him to recommend an Indian restaurant. Deedat suggested that his wife Hawa would prepare an 'authentic' Indian meal and that Beare bring his guests to their home. He promised Indian music to create the 'atmosphere' that Beare's guests were seeking. And so Beare and the Argentinian couple had supper with the Deedats. Shortly after they had completed their meal they heard the adhan for the night prayer from the nearby mosque. Deedat explained to his guests that this was the 'National Anthem' of Islam. The message of the adhan was that God was One, Muhammad (PBUH) was His Messenger, and that people should stop whatever they were doing and proceed to the mosque. Deedat's guests accepted his offer to observe the prayer in the mosque. He elucidated all aspects of the namaaz, making the connection to Judaism and Moses where possible.

When they returned to Deedat's home, he handed an English translation of the Qur'an to the guests and told them to look up 'Moses' in the index. The guests were taken aback by the many references and remarked, 'Your book speaks in favour of the Jews but you people are against us.' According to Deedat, when he tried to explain that the conflict was over Palestine, Beare replied: 'But Palestine belongs to the Jews. God promised it to us.' Deedat wrote of what he saw as the irony of this statement:

> One of [the Jews that I know] bemoaned the biggest joke in Israel. If you ask any Jew in Israel, 'Who gave you Palestine?' [They have all programmed themselves with the idea of Genesis 17:8], without the slightest hesitation every Jew will reply '*God*!' But over 75 per cent of the Israeli Jews if questioned 'Do you believe in God?' they immediately respond with '*No!*' Yet these atheist and agnostic Jews falsely use God's name for their usurpation of the land of the Palestinians!

Deedat's son, Yousuf, remembers that his father often used this anecdote in his speeches, publications, and DVDs on the Arab–Israeli conflict to make the point that 'Jews had programmed the Western world into believing that Arabs were barbarous in not allowing Jews to live on their own land'.

There was another incident at Beare's that influenced Deedat. He was delivering furniture to Beare's home one day, and while the furniture was being offloaded, Deedat browsed through the books in the library. Sholem Asch's 1951 *Moses* captivated him. Asch was a highly regarded Polish-born novelist and dramatist who wrote about Jewish experiences in eastern European villages. Many Jews, however, turned against Asch when he published three historical novels, *The Nazarene* (1939) based on the life of Jesus, *The Apostle* (1943) based on the life of Paul, and *Mary* (1949). In 1951, Asch published *Moses*. The books catapulted up America's best-seller lists, but his fellow Jews accused Asch of blasphemy.[4]

Finding the first few pages of the book riveting, Deedat asked Michael Beare whether he could borrow the book. Beare replied almost apologetically that it was not in Jewish culture to borrow or lend books. Deedat realised that his request had embarrassed Beare and immediately apologised. Beare's response took Deedat by surprise: 'But Deedat, that does not mean that I cannot give you one as a present.' The book (signed, 'Michael Beare, 13 July 1956. Wishing you luck and prosperity in your future life'), occupied a prominent place in Deedat's study and remains part of the 'Deedat Collection'. Deedat often cited this story to illustrate the generosity of his Jewish employer who won him over through this simple act.[5] Deedat, importantly, embraced Asch's message about the common heritage of Judaism and Christianity, to which he would add Islam.

This did not prevent Deedat from confronting Jews over the Palestinian question, however. When he was invited to the University of Cape Town shortly after the Six Day War of 1967, he spoke on 'The Qur'an and the Jew'. Deedat wrote about this meeting in his booklet, *Arabs and Israel: Conflict or Conciliation* (1989):

> After a very hearty and enthusiastic introduction by the young chairman, I stood up to speak, beginning with the following verse from the Holy Qur'an, spoken in Arabic without giving its corresponding meaning: 'Qala rabbi shrahli sadri wa yassirli amri wahlul 'uqdatam mil lisani yafqahu qawli' (Holy Qur'an 20:25–28). *A hypnotic effect!* I perceived expressions of puzzlement on the young faces. They had all expected me to speak to them in English but this was something different. So I said, 'Mr Chairman and my dear children, the words you have just heard from my lips is a prayer of the Holy Prophet Moses, when the Lord God commanded him to go to Pharaoh and ask him to release The Children of Israel from the Egyptian bondage and slavery…' Addressing the young Jews, I said, 'I have more need for such a prayer than the Holy Prophet Moses. My "tongue" is not my impediment. But in communication, language and psychological barriers are real problems.' English is not my mother tongue. It is

a foreign language to me. Gujarati is my mother tongue…Psychologically the speaker and the audience are at cross-purposes. The topic is an emotional one and highly charged. In the study of psychology we learn that we can make a person to *stop, look and listen!* But we cannot make them accept our *message* or *understand our meaning!*'

Deedat went on to say that Jewish Prophets were Muslim Prophets, that Jews and Muslims were cousins, and that 'guns were not the answer'.

In November 1973, Deedat spoke on 'The Qur'an and the Jew', a topical issue as it came hot on the heels of the October 1973 Yom Kippur War. Deedat evoked Jewish anger when he told the mainly Muslim audience that there would only be peace in the Middle East when Jews converted to Islam; then 'they would automatically become Muslim brothers'. Jews and Muslims, he said, had lived in harmony for a thousand years but the 'trouble started when the persecuted Jews of Europe began setting up their own state' in Palestine. No matter how many times Arabs were defeated, they would never give up, he said, and their eventual victory would mean the end of Israelis. 'For their own safety, the Jews will have to change their label.' Deedat did not foresee a problem since both were 'seeds' of one father: 'Your heroes are our heroes, your prophets are our prophets [and] it will not be difficult for us to accept one another.'[6] Mohammed Makki criticised the talk as 'not conducive to promoting a harmonious relationship between Muslims and Jews in South Africa at a time when emotions had run high over the Middle East conflict'.[7]

By the early 1980s the international community increasingly labelled Palestinian attempts to free themselves from Israeli occupation as the work of 'terrorists'. In June 1982, shortly after Israel had invaded southern Lebanon and attacked PLO and Syrian forces, Deedat angered Jews when he distributed fifty thousand pamphlets stating that Menachem Begin, Israeli prime minister from 1977 to 1983, was a terrorist. The pamphlet pointed out that Begin had been involved in terrorist activities during the 1930s and 1940s, including the bombing of the King David Hotel in Jerusalem on 22 July 1946, which resulted in the deaths of ninety-one people. The British government had offered a reward of $48 000 for Begin's capture because of his terrorist activities.[8] Deedat considered it ironic that Begin was now hailed as a hero in the West, while victims of Jewish aggression were considered terrorists.

In October 1982, the IPC issued a statement that South African Muslims were prepared to take up arms against Israel. Deedat told reporters that if the PLO was 'short of manpower our people will be encouraged to join'. Deedat held Israel responsible for the massacre of Palestinian refugees by right-wing Christians.[9] Deedat was referring to the attacks on the Sabra and Shatila Palestinian refugee camps in September 1982 by Lebanese Christian militia in an area under Israeli army control (the number of Palestinian deaths resulting from that attack has been estimated at between 700 and 3 500). Ariel Sharon, Israeli defence minister at the time, was found by an Israeli investigation to have been personally responsible for the atrocities and was forced to resign, but later became Israel's prime minister.[10]

Deedat published *Arabs and Israel: Conflict or Conciliation?* in 1989. The booklet was based on a debate between Deedat and Dr E. Lottern, who was the consul at the Israeli Embassy in Pretoria during the bombing of Beirut in 1982. Dr G.M. Hoosen recalled that debate. He said that during one of the 'Palestine Weeks' at the University of Natal, Jewish students challenged Muslim students to a debate. They brought Lottern to speak. The Muslim Students' Association was trying to find someone to match him. Never one to dodge a challenge, Deedat agreed to the debate: 'Arabs and Israel: Conflict or Conciliation'.[11] Deedat accepted the title even though it placed him in an awkward position. If he opted for 'conflict', critics would say that Muslims were not interested in peace; if he opted for 'conciliation', they would ask: 'So why are you throwing stones at us.' However, Deedat wanted an opportunity to put across his viewpoint that the Jews had no moral or ethical right to Palestine and did so using Jewish authors. In the estimation of Muslim students in the audience, Deedat won the argument handsomely.

In *Arabs and Israel*, Deedat wrote of the 'rape of Palestinian land by the Jews' and of the 'atrocities and ruthless brutalities against the hapless Palestinians'.[12] Deedat alluded to the difficulty of discussing the conflict because anyone who disagreed with Jews was termed anti-Semitic, a word that Deedat noted had become 'a magic wand' in Jewish hands, one that 'can bring the Christian world to their heels with the mere threat of labelling them as such'. For Deedat American intervention in the 1973 conflict on the side of Israel showed that whenever the Arabs fought Israel, they were in effect fighting America. The booklet contained many graphic photographs. The most controversial was on the cover, which showed a Palestinian mother trying to snatch her child from an Israeli soldier. Deedat urged his readers:

> Before reading on have a second look at the cover of the book – there's nothing contrived about it. A Muslim woman has just retrieved her 'little David' from the clutches of the Israeli soldiers. A Jewish lad, perhaps the grandson of one who escaped the Nazi incinerators in Germany during the Holocaust. His mission in life – with the prophetic words written on his helmet – '*Born to kill!*' The only thing missing is the swastika on his armband. What irony – the persecuted has now become the persecutor!

Deedat launched the booklet with a competition inviting readers to supply a caption for the photograph. In his introduction to the booklet, Deedat explained why he had included the photograph:

> The initial challenge was to get the photo published into the Zionist influenced Christian media, depicting their illegitimate offspring committing atrocities and ruthless brutalities against the hapless Palestinians. To publicise and highlight the plight of the oppressed Palestinian community from the ruthless policies of the survivors, and descendants of Hitler's Holocaust – the Jews of 'Israel', an essay competition was devised. The picture captioned '*Face of fear!*' is asking the entrants to supply an alternative caption and an impression in their own words. Just stare into eyes of the little boy, study the terror filled face of the mother, and the gaping mouths of the fearful, awestruck, young Palestinian girls and you too cannot help but feel some of the fear. The Zionists got wind of our advertising campaign through their agents and sympathisers in the right places and succeeded in gagging a number of newspapers from publishing the fully paid advertisement. The media which did publish the adverts created an unimaginable uproar from the Jews. A hue and cry was heard from the 'Chosen People', labelling us as 'Anti-Zionists!' and 'Anti-Semites!'

There was an outcry among South African Jews. On 20 January 1989, the *Argus* ran with the headline 'Anti-Israel advert angers SA Jews'. The South African Jewish Board of Deputies and the South African Zionist Council issued a statement that the Jewish community had been 'angered and offended' by the advertisement which aimed to arouse 'hostility against the state of Israel'. Deedat called the reaction 'hysterical hypocrisy'. He insisted that he was not anti-Jewish but opposed Israeli policies in the 'occupied territories'.[13] He pointed to the hypocrisy of South African Jews who were at the forefront of the anti-apartheid struggle because of the South African government's policy of 'racial exclusivity' but said nothing of the 'racial exclusivity' of Zionism.

Deedat criticised white-owned newspapers such as the *Sunday Tribune*, the *Daily News*, the *Argus*, the *Citizen*, the *Natal Mercury*, and the *Transvaaler* for 'being afraid of the powerful Zionist lobby' and 'spurning our paid advertisement'. Recalling the controversy over Salman Rushdie's *Satanic Verses*, Deedat labelled his own critics as hypocrites, saying that when the Prophet (PBUH) was

> abused and insulted by Salman Rushdie they boldly claim for freedom of the press and freedom of expression. They are then not afraid of the injured feelings of millions of Muslims…When Zionism pursues its policies of racial exclusivity they remain silent. Nay, they go further. They want others to remain silent. How strange![14]

Deedat's views were eloquently echoed by Jerusalem-born intellectual Edward Saïd, then professor of comparative literature at Columbia University in New York, whose work analyses the relations between the 'strange' (colonised) Islamic world and the 'familiar' (colonising) West.[15] Saïd argued that the concept of the 'Orient', and the generalisations that tend to be associated with it, is a Western invention that serves an important propaganda purpose in depicting people in the East in a negative light so that they can be demonised. Saïd focused on the historical relationship between the accumulation of knowledge and power. He pointed out, for example, that words such as 'objective', 'impartial', 'sensitive', and 'liberal' are often used to describe the Western press which is, in truth, highly politicised, biased and subjective, and serves as an 'invisible screen' that filters information and shapes people's perceptions by determining what they should and should not know. For example, the Western media has played a crucial role in shaping Western opinion on the Palestinian Question in particular, and on Islam and the Muslim world generally. Those in the Muslim world who were willing to toe the American line were regarded as 'good' Muslims while those who refused to follow the script were portrayed negatively.[16]

In his own way, Deedat made the same arguments. On 3 July 1989, for example, Deedat shared a platform with American Congressman Paul Findley, author of *They Dare to Speak Out*, at the Good Hope Centre in Cape Town. The meeting was attended by around 8 000 people. The IPCI distributed Findley's book and ten thousand copies of *Publish It Not* by Christopher Mayhew and Michael Adams, which argued that the USA and Israel, and their respective media industries, were involved in a deliberate cover-up of the truth in Palestine.

Deedat argued that Palestinians were not only in conflict with Israel but also with the USA because of the 'glaring, open American intervention against the Arabs', which he saw as being due to highly influential Jewish lobby groups in America. Deedat said that American president Harry Truman 'inadvertently disclosed the secret of Jewish power in his country' when, within minutes of the Declaration of Independence by Ben Gurion on 14 May 1948, he recognised the state of Israel. When Truman was questioned about his haste given that a hundred million Arabs would be offended, he replied, 'there [are] no Arabs in my constituency!'

Since the USA would not permit large-scale Muslim immigration, Deedat called on Muslims in the USA to convert at least six million Americans to Islam. He believed that expatriate Muslims were not up to the task since the 'Muslim world, as a whole, are an emasculated people. The American "Green Ticket" [Green card] has seen to that! They dare not say or do anything that might militate against their enjoyment of their newfound heaven flowing with milk and honey.' Deedat had faith in African-Americans, however. Centuries of 'slavery and hammering has turned them into one of the most militant Muslim communities in the world'.

Deedat respected individual Jews but felt that he could not remain silent about the political situation in Palestine where Zionism had taken on a decidedly religious bent. As

Armstrong points out, after the Yom Kippur War of 1973, the Kookists (founded by Rabbi Kook), ultranationalists, and other religious Zionists in Israel formed the Gush Emunim (Bloc of the Faithful), a pressure group that rooted itself in Judaism. Zionism made no sense when it was divorced from religion and they rejected its old socialist and nationalist discourse in preference for the language of the Bible.[17] It was Gush Emunim that pushed for the establishment of settlements in occupied territories and helped Menachem Begin's right-wing Likud Party defeat the Labour Party for the first time in 1977.

Likud initiated the systematic building of settlements in the occupied territories. Ariel Sharon, then head of the Israeli Lands Commission, announced that a million Jews would be settled on the West Bank within twenty years. Rabbi Kook preached and wept before crowds of thousands as each new settlement was built. Despite the rhetoric of peace, it was clear to most Palestinians that the Jewish state had no intention of conceding any of the occupied territories. Deedat was aghast that it was the Palestinian reaction to the seizure of their land that was condemned by the world community rather than the land grab itself.

Notwithstanding the distinction that Deedat drew between individual Jews and the political situation in Palestine, he consistently highlighted the suffering of the Palestinians, and many of his critics regarded him as anti-Semitic. This is not a sentiment that most Muslims would share. They would probably regard his statements on Palestine as relatively muted given the extent of Palestinian suffering – the Nakba (catastrophe) from 1948 to the 1967 war; the First Intifada (1988); Israeli invasions of Lebanon; the destruction of Jenin in 2002; the building of the Wall; and the ongoing illegal construction of Jewish settlements on occupied land.

Deedat's outspoken views on the Palestinian question helped to make him a well-known figure in the Muslim world. But it was not by chance that Deedat emerged as a transnational religious figure. His reputation was cultivated over an extended period, and he was assisted by several individuals (mainly members of the World Assembly of Muslim Youth) who linked him to a network of major players in the Muslim world.

# 15
# GOING GLOBAL

Seen here with his family at Durban's airport, Deedat travelled widely on speaking tours from the 1980s.

He was a man with wisdom who accepted advice, and consulted with people whom he trusted and who had experience and expertise in the areas in which he needed help. That was an important quality of his.

– Dr Ahmad Totonji

DEEDAT WAS ALREADY IN HIS SIXTIES when he became a familar face in many parts of the Muslim world. His rise to prominence was facilitated by the fact that several individuals and organisations did important organisational groundwork on his behalf. As important was the ideological vacuum in the Muslim world, which made many people receptive to his message. A largely unrecorded part of this story is the role of the Muslim Youth Movement (MYM). Ismail Kalla, Mahmoud Moosa, Ebrahim Jadwat, and Advocate A.B. Mahomed went around South Africa popularising the idea, and the MYM was born in December 1970.

These younger Muslims felt that divorcing Islam from their everyday lives created a kind of split personality in believers. According to A.B. Mahomed, they saw Islam 'not as a religion but a complete way of life'. He argues that it is only 'because of the way the Western world has penetrated our lives [that] we think Islam is a private affair in the same way that Christians approach religion'.

Ebrahim Jadwat, who became be a key figure in Deedat's story from the 1970s, was born in Durban and, growing up, was influenced by the likes of Farouki Mehtar of Orient High, activist Ismail Meer, who conducted tafsir classes when he was banned for his political activities, G.H. Vanker and Deedat at the IPCI, and Mawlana Ansari of the West Street Mosque. By discussing the works of Egyptian Syed Qutb, the pan-Islamist poet Allamah Iqbal, and Pakistani Abul A'la Mawdudi, Jadwat believes that they 'began to understand Islam better, felt proud of Islam, and practised it with renewed vigour'. The MYM organised several youth camps at As-Salaam in the early 1970s while Deedat was residing there. They invited the likes of Dr Ahmad Sakr, the Pakistani scholar Mawlana Fazlur Rahman Ansari, and German convert Fatima Heeran. For Jadwat, these speakers were

> a source of great inspiration and motivation. They addressed young people and students in a language that made sense to them and brought the Qur'an into context and the life of the Prophet (PBUH) as an example for people in this age and time.

Many MYM members came to have a high regard for Deedat, a fact which may seem anomalous given that he was considerably older than most of them. Yet younger people, according to Fuad Hendricks, were 'fascinated with Deedat's passion to share the faith, fascinated with his ideas, and fascinated with the way he presented them'. Those who felt under siege because of the political subservience of many Muslim countries, apartheid, and the 'very hostile' interpretation of Christianity in South Africa were captivated by Deedat's knowledge of Christianity, his 'valour and heroic approach', and his piety. According to Hendricks, 'only those who were close to Deedat appreciated his deep spirituality, reflected by his closeness to the Qur'an and the life of the Prophet (PBUH)'.

Younger Muslims in particular were looking for a 'hero to confront the perceived "enemy". We could not do so in technology and science, where the West was far superior.

Faith was one area where we could compete,' Hendricks observed. According to Jadwat, young South African Muslims were influenced by several tendencies in the Muslim world in the late 1960s and early 1970s:

> The new international influence comprised of people from four main backgrounds. One was the Arab world: Sudan, Jordan, Syria, Egypt, and Lebanon. These students had gone to America and formed the core of the group. Ahmed Sakr, for example, came to As-Salaam. He revolutionised our thinking and approach. The second grouping was the Jama'at Islami from Indo-Pakistani. For example, Professor Salman Nadvi was in that group of people. The third group was from South-East Asia – Indonesia, Malaysia and so forth. Anwar Ebrahim was one of them and there was an influential Indonesian Mohammed Natzir. The fourth grouping was the emerging African American Muslims with whom we felt a lot of affinity, especially with Malik Shabazz's [also known as Malcolm X] grouping. I visited them in 1971 and we were inspired by their discipline, understanding, clarity and social awareness. You could feel that this dimension was missing in our Islam.

Deedat's 'breakthrough' came when Jadwat arranged for him to address the annual congress of the World Assembly of Muslim Youth (WAMY) in 1977. WAMY had been founded in Riyadh to 'establish a relationship of dialogue, understanding and appreciation between Muslim organisations and western societies'. WAMY's programme included youth and student camps, conferences and workshops, and the publication of books and brochures.[1] Its key members included the likes of Iraqi-born Dr Ahmad Totonji, Lebanese-born Dr Ahmad Sakr, Pakistani-born Khurshid Ahmed, and future deputy prime minister of Malaysia, Anwar Ebrahim.

Jadwat described Ahmad Totonji as Deedat's 'key' to the international stage. Fluent in English, Arabic, Turkish, and Kurdish, Totonji was involved in many Islamic organisations in the USA and UK during the 1960s. He was born in Iraq in 1941 and studied engineering in the UK where he was one of the founding members of the Muslim Student Society of the UK & Eire in 1960, the United Muslim Student Organization of Europe in 1961, and the Federation of Student Islamic Societies in UK and Eire (FOSIS) in 1963. Dr Totonji graduated in 1963 and was awarded a scholarship from Pennsylvania State University in the USA to pursue his Ph.D.

In the USA, Dr Totonji helped to establish the Muslim Students' Association (MSA) of the USA and Canada in 1963 with Dr Ahmad Sakr, who was based in Illinois. Dr Totonji was elected president of the MSA in 1965. In 1969, he was appointed secretary-general of the International Islamic Federation of Students Organizations (IIFSO), whose membership included student organisations from the UK, Ireland, France, Morocco, Sudan, Pakistan, Indonesia, Chad, Nigeria, Kuwait, and Eritrea. IIFSO organised youth camps on five continents.

Dr Totonji then took up a position at Al Fateh University in Tripoli and (together with Libyans Mahmoud Sobhi and Dr Mohammed Sharif of the Call of Islam), convened an international conference of Muslim youth in Tripoli in July 1973. The almost four-hundred-and-fifty delegates included four South Africans: Ebrahim Jadwat, A.B. Mahomed, Ismail Kalla, and Mahmoud Moosa. Although the gathering did not produce anything concrete, it brought together Muslims from diverse backgrounds who were grappling with similar concerns.

The project of forming an international student organisation was originally conceived by the Egyptian scholar and activist Dr Tawfic Al Shawy. Dr Al Shawy discussed the formation of WAMY with 'Islamically active' university professors, including Dr Totonji, who had joined the King Saud University, and convened a conference in Riyadh. The founding conference was held in December 1973. Dr Hamad Al Sulai Feah and the Saudi Minister of Education, Shaykh Hassan Al Sheikh, strongly supported the project. Ebrahim Jadwat and Abdullah Osman were present from South Africa. Dr Abdul Hamid Abu Sulayman was elected secretary-general and Dr Totonji assistant secretary-general.

Ebrahim Jadwat was elected to the Executive of WAMY in 1976, and became its Southern African representative. It was in this capacity that he approached Dr Totonji to give Deedat a platform at the next international conference. The immediate reaction of the WAMY executive was, 'Our focus is on youth. What do we have to do with an old man?' Jadwat was adamant and was supported by Dr Sakr, who had met Deedat at As-Salaam, and by Dr Totonji.

Deedat made the most of this brief opportunity. Speaking on 'The Challenges Facing the Youth', his 'blunt and candid approach took the delegates by storm' according to Jadwat. Jadwat explains what happened when he approached Saudi television requesting that they interview Deedat:

WAMY Executive member Ebrahim Jadwat.

> They laughed at me saying that there are fifty or sixty great scholars from all over the world so why should we interview him. I said, 'Look, give him two minutes of your time.' They humoured me and gave him the opportunity to be on television and, of course, the next day they were there because he was an instant hit with his approach, his dynamism, his personality and the ideas that he presented. So they came back every day for more and that's how he was opened up to the Muslim world.[2]

Fuad Hendricks never doubted that Deedat would be a success. 'Although he was a "non-entity" in international terms at that stage, he charmed delegates. While delegates like Dr Sakr and Dr Totonji were ideologues, Deedat was a salesman. He would take a hundred no's

*Deedat was a hit at the World Assembly of Muslim Youth conference in 1978; this event marked the beginning of his international reputation.*

before a yes came, but he persevered.' Dr Totonji explained his role in providing an international platform for Deedat:

> When I attended the Second Southern African Islamic conference in Botswana I met Shaykh Deedat. I had heard a lot about him from Brother Ebrahim Jadwat, and I was looking forward to meeting him with a plan in my mind: how can we can benefit in da'wahh from such a talented and dedicated brother who can defend Islam and its values with the highest level of debaters in the Christian hierarchy? I was immediately impressed by his dedication, modesty and capability to present Islamic views on many issues and show its advantages. The Muslim youth at the Botswana conference were very happy to meet and get acquainted with this great man.
>
> We invited him the next year to the WAMY conference in Riyadh, and the leaders of Islamic thought and students and youth movements from all over the world met him. They enjoyed his presence and learnt a lot from him. It was at this conference, I believe, that he realised the possibility of visiting different parts of the world in defence of the onslaught against Islam by Christian evangelical missionaries and televangelists. The Muslim youth and students got strength from his eloquence and beautiful presentations and clear arguments. From here the invitations poured in for Shaykh Deedat to visit various countries and address large audiences in each country. Shaykh Ahmed Deedat took up the challenge and applied himself sincerely and there were great results in many corners of the earth.

WAMY members were impressed with Deedat and created opportunities for him to tour internationally. This increased his standing in the Muslim world and later facilitated the procurement of funds. Prominent Saudi businessmen made contributions to the IPCI in the late 1970s. This was Deedat's first exposure to the potential of fundraising in the Middle East. In March 1977, Dr Totonji, Dr Sakr, and Abdul Hamid Sulayman (who later became rector of the International Islamic University of Malaysia) arranged for Deedat to go on a lecture tour of the USA and the East. Deedat himself said that Riyadh 'was a turning point for me, not because it opened up the East, but because it opened up the West'.[3]

Lebanese-born Dr Sakr was a founder member and president of the MSA of the USA and Canada while he was a student in Chicago. He was also a founder member of the World Council of Mosques, which has its headquarters in Makkah, and the first director and representative of the Muslim World League to the United Nations.[4] According to Dr Sakr:

> I stayed in communication with Imam Ahmed Deedat after my visit to As-Salaam. I visited him at his house, and he visited us in our house in America. He spoke at many venues and made a very big impression on local people. Allah (swt) chose him to be an International Public Speaker and spread the Message of Islam through dialogue. He was a gifted communicator and many non-Muslims accepted Islam through him. His technique and approach in delivering the message of Islam has been adopted by many. I consider myself as his student but, more so, I consider him my friend. May Allah bless him and reward him with Paradise.

Deedat's first tour of the USA kicked off at the New Jersey Islamic Center in New York on 5 March 1977. The following day Deedat met Elijah Muhammad's son Wallace D. Muhammad and spoke at Mosque No. 2 in Chicago under the auspices of the World Community of Islam in the West. For the next month, Deedat spoke at twenty-five venues across the USA. From there he visited Singapore, Hong Kong, Mauritius, and Bombay, but failed to get a visa to enter Malaysia, despite the personal intervention of WAMY executive member Anwar Ebrahim. Deedat returned to South Africa on 24 April and prepared a report on his visit for Dr Totonji and Dr Sulayman, noting:

> I gained immense knowledge about our brethren around the globe at places I had touched. As a whole it was a pitiful experience. Finding the Muslims in America and Hong-Kong, in Singapore and in India utterly demoralised [and] suffering all sorts of inferiority complexes. If I may be allowed to say so – the Muslims of South Africa have come out tops from the three hundred years of hammering they have been receiving. We have been transmuted into tempered 'steel'. Many who have seen the Muslim communities of the world, have come to the conclusion that 'the liveliest Muslim community in the World is the South African Muslim Community.' I now

have no doubt about their judgement. This saddens me all the more because we Muslims of this country realise our shortcomings. If we are the 'liveliest' how sorrowful must be the condition of our brethren across the seas? (27 May 1977).

Deedat had little faith in the 'Old World' but saw a glimmer of hope in African-American Muslims.

> One can see the noor [glow] of Islam shine on their faces and one can feel the strength of iman in their hearts...They can well become an example for the 'old' world of Islam. They are needed to infuse new blood into our creaking bodies. They must be galvanised for the service of Islam in America and the rest of the world. They must be pushed into proselytising the Afro-Americans. As a youth I learnt that it takes a diamond to cut a diamond. Our own Zulus here have a saying, 'you need a sharper thorn to take out a thorn'. To give battle to these missionaries, whether in Indonesia or Malaysia, India, Arabia or Africa, the most suitable mujahid is the Bilalian. He has the go and the gumption, the will and the psychology to prevail.

Deedat said he thought Wallace D. Muhammad could organise future debates at Madison Square Garden and the Yankee Stadium in New York 'to shake the whole fabric of Christianity in the mightiest nation on earth, and the ripples will reach the far-flung nations of the world'. Deedat was prepared to offer a course in 'live comparative religion to prepare people for battle with Christianity on an intellectual level based on the Christians' own book of authority – their Bible'. Deedat felt that Arabs had failed to carry out the mission of the Prophet (PBUH) and should instead provide funds to those who were willing to do the work. During his tour of Australia in 1995, he told reporter Keysar Trad,

> You know, I am talking to the Arab, a professor of Arabic in Abu Dhabi. He tells me, 'Deedat, how did you learn to speak Arabic?' I said, 'I don't...I have chosen the wrong job, I am a lorry driver, working for a firm, now I am talking about religion. It is the wrong job that I have taken. This is your job,' I am telling the Arab, 'Allah says, "We have revealed the book in your language."' Whose language? Yours, you Saudi, you Lebanese, you Abu Dahbian, in your language, not in the language of the Hindi nor the Indonesian. What for? To give glad tidings to the God-fearing. So I ask this professor, 'How many mosques do you have in your country?' He says, 'one thousand.' I said, 'Every mosque must have an Imam, who are they talking to?' To give good news to the muttaqi (believer).' Who is the muttaqi? The guy who goes to the masjid, he is giving them the good news. Allah will give you Jannatul Firdaus [the highest place in heaven], He is doing his job. But Allah doesn't stop there. He says: 'and to warn a people, "Ludda."' I am asking, 'You are a professor of Arabic, now tell me, who are people "Ludda"?' If unbelievers are Ludda, show me one out of those thousand masjids who is talking to the Jew. If there are Christians, I want to know, is there one out of those thousand imams out there who is talking to the Christians?

Dr Totonji enhanced Deedat's international profile by distributing his booklets and providing him with influential contacts. In July 1978, Deedat sent fifty copies of *Who Moved the Stone?* to ninety-seven people in various countries whose addresses were provided by Dr Totonji. In return, Dr Totonji provided Deedat with sixty copies of Yusuf Ali's translation of the Qur'an. Deedat wrote to Dr Totonji on 19 September 1977 that he would like to distribute 20 000 copies of the Qur'an and appealed to him to find a sponsor. Dr Totonji wrote a strong recommendation on behalf of Deedat when he applied to the Saudi Government and the Islamic General Secretariat in Jeddah for a grant of US$25 000 to publish and distribute free Qur'ans. Although this application was unsuccessful, Dr Totonji's support for Deedat was significant.

Deedat asked Dr Totonji for permission to attend the WAMY conference in March 1979 and requested his help in arranging for him to address university students in Riyadh, ad-Dahran, Jeddah, Makkah, and Medina. Shortly thereafter, Deedat published *al-Qur'an: The Ultimate Miracle*. He sent copies to Kamal Hilbawi of WAMY on 15 February 1979 for his 'frank comments. I hope you will not forget me for the WAMY conference. If I am invited, I would like to visit Universities in Saudi Arabia on a lecture tour after the conference.' Deedat wrote to Dr Totonji on the same day noting that he was distributing fifteen hundred copies of the booklet worldwide on WAMY's behalf. Deedat asked Dr Totonji to write to the Islamic Solidarity Fund 'in an encouraging manner' on his behalf and arrange a meeting with Adnan Koshogee as 'I am still obsessed with the idea of publishing the 25 000 Holy Qur'ans'. Included with every correspondence were adverts that Deedat had placed in local newspapers as well as pamphlets that the IPCI had distributed.

In July 1979, Dr Totonji, 'deeply concerned about the plight of the Malawian Muslims', asked Deedat to visit that country and present a report on the work of Christian missionaries there. WAMY's increasing confidence in Deedat was also clearly reflected in January 1983 when Deedat was asked to prepare a

> comprehensive study on the activities of Christian missionaries, focusing on their main arguments and how best to counter them. This report would assist Islamic workers and Muslim students in the West [who] could be victims of their endeavours for creating suspicions about Islam. We have also noted with satisfaction your pioneering efforts in this field using your God-given talents to remove the suspicions and silence the Christian preachers.

So keen was WAMY on Deedat's input that they suggested that if he found it difficult 'to spare time for writing the above study, you may kindly speak it out on a cassette tape and we shall get it transcribed here'.

The toppling of Shah Mohammed Reza Pahlavi in Iran in 1979 further enhanced Deedat's international profile. The Iranian Revolution came as a blow to Western powers because it resulted in the collapse of a regime heavily financed and protected by the USA. The revolution gave Muslims the world over new confidence to proclaim Islam as an alternative to capitalism and communism. 'Neither East Nor West, Islam is Best' became the popular slogan of the time. The shah had held power from 1941 to 1979, except for a brief interlude in 1953 when Prime Minister Mohammed Mossadegh nationalised the country's oil fields. A CIA-engineered military coup then restored the shah to the throne. The shah's policies led to opposition from leftist, nationalist, and religious groups, which mobilised under the exiled Ayatollah Khomeini. Khomeini's supporters developed an efficient network of opposition inside Iran through mosque sermons and audio recordings of his speeches. The wave of opposition was so strong that the shah was forced into exile and Khomeini returned to take power on 12 February 1979.

Deedat was invited to, participate in celebrations of the third anniversary of the Iranian revolution.

Deedat supported the ayatollah without reservation. He told a reporter it was common knowledge that

> the Shah had millions in foreign banks. Did he sweat for that money? No. He and his chosen few lived a life of luxury while millions suffered. The Shah ran one of the most oppressive regimes in the history of mankind. The Iranian Revolution has shown the world that Islam is dynamic, alive to the principal problem of the age – the ruthless domination of the weak by the very powerful. Iran's example...has proved that man is yet capable of struggling against heavy odds in order to right the wrongs perpetuated by the forces of oppression and evil.[5]

Deedat was invited to Iran in 1982 to participate in celebrating the third anniversary of the revolution. In his address on 3 March 1982 he said:

> What I find is [that] the whole nation is geared towards Islam. And they are talking about nothing but the Qur'an. I have never had a single experience with an Iranian when the man contradicted me when I'm talking about the Qur'an. Whereas [with] our Arab brethren, again and again, you quote them the Qur'an and they try to contradict you with the Qur'an. They are Arabs, they are supposed to know the Qur'an better than us.

A keen bodybuilder in his youth, Deedat compared South African Muslim men with their Iranian counterparts:

> Unfortunately we Muslims in South Africa are like jellyfish. Our young men do not participate in that kind of activity. Who here does athletics, gymnastics, acrobatics? It's not for us. Who does jogging? Almost every young man you meet in Iran appears to be an athlete. They are doing sports on a world standard and it makes one feel so happy because there they are not projecting Iran. They are not talking about Iran 'we are Iranians, we are Aryans', instead they are talking about Islam, Islam, Islam.

Deedat was impressed with Khomeini whom he described as 'a man like a computerised Qur'an. And the electric effect he had on everybody, his charisma, was amazing.' In the same speech, Deedat pleaded for Sunni–Shi'a unity:

> You know, between the four Sunni Madhaahib, the Hanafi, Hanbali, Maliki and Shafi'i, there are over two hundred differences in Ṣalah alone. But we take it for granted… But when it comes to the Shia you see he is not in the formula that we are taught as a child, so whatever little idiosyncrasies there exist between us and them we can't tolerate it…We Sunnis are ninety per cent of the Muslim world and the ten per cent who are Shiahs want to be brothers with you in faith and the ninety per cent are terrified! They should be the ones terrified.

Advocate A.B. Mahomed, who was part of the South African delegation to Iran, points to an important lesson that Deedat learnt during the visit.

> I carried a video camera and took shots of the revolution, the military parades, and there were nineteen such tapes, even the war front. When we came back the Muslims of South Africa were awaiting a report about this epoch-making event so I summarised this in half an hour at the Kajee Memorial Hall in Leopold Street and that had a great impact with the audience because they had come to listen. Deedat took the cue from there – the power of video presentation made an impression on him – and he told me, 'In future I would like my debates to be videoed.'

A few months after the visit to Iran, Deedat delivered a talk on 'Christ in Islam' at the Durban City Hall on 23 August 1983. The 'success' of the talk was made known to donors and potential donors. For example, on 13 October 1983 a letter was sent to Saleh Bin Abdul Aziz Al Rajhi, the senior member of the clan that owned the Al Rajhi Bank. The letter referred to the fact that the lecture had been attended by 2 000 people and the package included a video of that lecture. Repeating Deedat's own words which feature on the inside covers of all his books, Yusuf Buckas, secretary-general of the IPCI, added:

> Wallahi…if we have the means we would flood the world with our free literature. It is by means of the generous support and assistance from our brethren that we have been able to expand our activities for the cause of Islam. We hope that you continue your assistance for spreading Allah's message to the whole world.

Through such correspondence 'Deedat' became a familiar name in influential circles in the wider Muslim world.

In June 1984, Deedat distributed thousands of pamphlets in English and Arabic challenging the pope, the head of the Roman Catholic Church, to a debate. He also sent a letter to the pope's secretariat requesting a meeting, and addressing the pope as follows: 'whenever you visit a foreign land where Muslims abound, your desire to have dialogue with us is one of the themes in your message. We call on you to meet us in this dialogue at St Peter's in Rome.' Pope John Paul II was the most travelled pope in history. During visits to Muslim countries he called for interfaith dialogue and Deedat wanted to take him up on this. The pope's secretariat replied that the pope was agreeable to a meeting but no further communication was received in reply to the intitial or to subsequent invitations from the IPCI dated 17 September 1984, 29 November 1984, and 27 December 1984.[6]

The IPCI then sent a telegram to the pope on 4 January 1985 stating that his failure to respond was 'creating the sad impression that your wanting to have dialogue with Muslims was a Big Bluff. We are hoping this is not so.' The IPCI issued a pamphlet in January 1985 'His Holiness Plays Hide and Seek with Muslims.' He told a local reporter in April 1985:

> I didn't challenge him to debate. You see, the Pope, he says, we must have a dialogue with Muslims, 'we' meaning the Catholic Church. When he was in Turkey the same pronouncement; when he went to Nigeria the same pronouncement; when he went to Kenya the same pronouncement; when he went to Senegal; the same pronouncement: 'we must have a dialogue with the Muslims.' So I was waiting for some Arabs to go along and have a dialogue with him, or some Pakistani 'alim, but nobody came. I wrote to him. I said 'your holiness you are talking about having a dialogue, I am prepared to have a dialogue with you in the Vatican, you tell me when and I will come along.' It is just a hoax. He is trying to bluff the people by 'dialogue'. Actually he is telling his people, don't convert to Islam. He uses the word 'dialogue'. If he used the word 'convert', then you would start getting a shock when the Christian missionary comes, those Catholic priests with the dog collar, you are going to chase them away. You would say 'You are going to try and convert my child.' But if he says 'dialogue', you cannot say no because the Qur'an says: 'O People of the Book, come, talk to them,' Allah is telling you to go and talk to them, and He is talking about dialogue. You cannot say no.[7]

Deedat interpreted the Vatican's failure to respond as a sign that the pope feared that the church's central doctrines would be 'indefensible' to scriptural evidence and that he would be embarrassed when his followers realised the 'real message as clarified in the Qur'an'.[8]

On Deedat's last tour of Britain in 1995, he focused on John Paul II's just-published *The Threshold of Hope*. In the course of Deedat's lecture, as reported in the *Adviser*, 'the Pope emerges from this treatment as, at best a self-deceived clown, at worst a consummate and skilful deceiver…bent on attacking Islam under the guise of false calls to a dialogue'.[9] According to Philip Lewis:

> Deedat invited the audience to join him in mockery of the papacy. He scolded them because they remained ignorant of Papal trickery: behind the smooth talk of dialogue there was a dangerous attempt to undermine and attack Islam…Deedat uses humour and scurrilous innuendo to make sure his audience sees Christianity, the Pope, the Catholic Church and the Bible as unworthy of respect…This was an opportunity to sneer at what the prevailing culture [still based on Christianity in Muslim eyes] forbids them to do.[10]

Despite some opposition to his methods, Deedat's reputation flourished among Muslims in many parts of the world. The Institute of Islamic Thought in Washington, for example, promoted him as an 'authority' on comparative religion. On 20 July 1984, Hisham Altalib, its financial director, put Q.M. Farooqi in contact with Deedat for his literature, which had been requested by organisations in the Philippines. On 8 October 1984, Altalib informed the IPCI that he had received enquiries about Islam from many countries in Africa and was directing them to the IPCI. 'I am confident that your aggressive approach to da'wah and your dynamism will bring the seekers of truth in Africa to the fold of Islam in flocks.' In April 1985, Dr Totonji asked Deedat to send two sets of his video recordings to Ahmad Lemu of the influential Islamic Foundation in the UK, thus giving Deedat access to a different audience. A visit to Malaysia and several high-profile debates catapulted Deedat onto the international stage, and when he received the King Faisal Award in 1985, it gave him an iconic status among Muslims in many parts of the world.

# 16

# THE KING FAISAL INTERNATIONAL PRIZE

One of his proudest moments, Deedat receives the King Faisal International Prize from Crown Prince Abdullah bin Abdul Aziz al-Saud who has since become King of Saudi Arabia.

We were all proud of the King Faisal Foundation, when their committee consisting of many of the top scholars and Islamic workers all over the world, chose you, Ahmed Deedat, for the most outstanding reward for your service to Islam. The echoes of your lectures and debates will remain for years to come, alive in the minds and hearts of the people who listen to you. Some of these people you have seen, others you have known and millions you will never get to know. They really admire you and are proud of you as the son of Islam.

– Dr Ahmad Totonji

AS A TEENAGER, growing up in As-Salaam, Yousuf Deedat regarded his father as 'a bully who unnecessarily took on other religious groups'. He was so 'embarrassed' that at school he hid his surname from his peers, telling them that he was Yousuf Ahmed. He silently agreed with the sharp criticisms he heard about his father: 'Deedat is too hard with everyone'; 'Deedat causes relationships between religious groups to be strained'. But Yousuf Deedat grew up in a time when children 'knew their place'. So instead of openly speaking out against his father he quietly disapproved, choosing to stay at home, immersed in his comic books rather than attending the City Hall lectures that everyone was talking about. Deedat never questioned his son about his conspicuous absence and remained a protective father. In fact, it was Deedat's gentleness that Yousuf Deedat later began to value.

Yousuf remembers how when learning to memorise the Qur'an, he was a great fan of renowned Egyptian qari Shaykh Abdul Basit, and would often try to imitate him. When Deedat learnt that Shaykh Basit was going to recite the Qur'an at the Grey Street Mosque after the 'isha' prayer one night, he drove Yousuf from As-Salaam to Durban for the performance. The fact that the drive from As-Salaam to the mosque and back was a long and eerie one at night did not deter Deedat. During the recital, an announcement was made that children should move to a designated area upstairs. 'Get up, move, get up,' a man shouted, as he moved through the congregation, pushing children along towards the stairs. But Deedat clung tightly to his son and retorted, 'won't move from here.' At that moment, Yousuf Deedat recalls, his heart filled with a feeling of security. However, he would only 'truly appreciate his [father's] esteemed international reputation' many years later when, in his early thirties, he first accompanied Deedat on an overseas trip.

It was no ordinary trip. The year was 1986: a year when the *Challenger* space shuttle exploded, killing seven astronauts; the Chernobyl accident, the first nuclear disaster, took place in the Soviet Union; Corazon Aquino deposed Ferdinand Marcos and assumed the presidency of the Philippines; Argentina won the soccer World Cup; the Oprah Winfrey show aired for the first time; and Ahmed Deedat was awarded the prestigious King Faisal Foundation International Prize for Service to Islam.

King Faisal, one of the sons of Ibn Sa'ud, the founder of Saudi Arabia, reigned as the kingdom's third monarch from 1964 to 1975. The King Faisal Foundation was established in his memory in 1976 by his sons. Awards have been made annually since 1977 for service to Islam, Islamic studies, and Arabic literature. A prize for medicine was added in 1981 and one for science in 1982. The Service to Islam Award is generally considered the Foundation's most prestigious. The selection committee is secretive and the procedure stringent. It includes pre-selection by peer reviewers and submission by nominees of their work for review by internationally selected referees. In the Foundation's words, the King Faisal International Prize embodies the 'firm belief that through the collective efforts of outstanding individuals, the highest aspirations of mankind are realised'.[1]

The World Assembly of Muslim Youth (WAMY), at the urging of Ebrahim Jadwat and Dr Totonji, nominated Deedat for the award. They had to motivate why he was a worthy candidate. They accepted that he was not an outstanding political thinker, such as Egypt's Syed Qutb or Iran's Ali Shariati, nor was he a renowned Islamic scholar, such as Pakistan's Mawlana Abul A'la Mawdudi or Egypt's Yusuf al-Qaradawi, nor did he directly convert large numbers to Islam, but, according to Jadwat, there was a 'unanimous feeling' within WAMY that Deedat had 'bravely accepted the challenge of Christian missionaries and raised the morale of the youth through his public debates, and deserved the award'.

In winning the prize, Deedat followed in the footsteps of some of the leading lights of the twentieth-century Islamic world, such as Dr Mohammed Natzir; Mawlana Abul Hasan Ali Nadwi, Mawlana Abul A'la Mawdudi, Shaykh Abd al-Aziz Bin Baz; Shaykh Hasanein M. Makhlouf, and Abd Rab al-Rasoul Saiaf. The nomination certainly enhanced Deedat's reputation. In early January of 1986, Dr Totonji, who was still pursuing the 'Qur'an project' on Deedat's behalf, counselled him to write to the King Fahd Holy Qur'an Printing Complex for translations of the Qur'an. The IPCI's secretary-general, Yusuf Buckas, wrote to the Holy Qur'an Printing Complex on 15 January 1986, informing them that the IPCI functioned as a full-time Islamic information bureau in South Africa and distributed copies of the 'Holy Qur'an free of charge to all public libraries, mosques, madrasahs, schools, and universities'. Buckas described Deedat as:

> a well-known international religious lecturer, a scholar and expert in comparative religion, who has travelled many times to all six continents of the world delivering the message of Islam to all and sundry, has been nominated for the coveted/prestigious prize in the Muslim world, the King Faisal Award. This does not come as a surprise to those who know Mr Deedat's dedication to the cause of Islam, having rendered unstinting service for the past forty years in propagating Islam...Deedat is not only an accomplished debater and lecturer but has authored a dozen booklets on comparative religion which have been, and still are, distributed free of charge worldwide. These booklets have been reproduced in Hong Kong, Singapore, UK, and Saudi Arabia. The printing of our literature abroad illustrates the point that it is contemporary and relevant to present-day needs.

WAMY, the Darul Iftah organisation, and Shaykh Abdullah Nassief of Rabitat al-Alam al-Islami were referees for the grant application. The IPCI requested a grant to publish 20 000 Qur'ans 'which will no doubt boost our da'wah activities...May Allah Almighty make us true and sincere soldiers of Islam.' There was no immediate response.

When Deedat was selected as a recipient of the award, the Foundation requested that his sons Yousuf and Ebrahim (but not his wife Hawa) accompany him to the gala awards function. This was Yousuf Deedat's first plane journey and his first visit overseas. The three were flown first class to Saudi Arabia where they were welcomed by a high-profile Saudi delegation and whisked through customs. From there, they were taken to the five-star Al Khozama hotel in Riyadh, where Yousuf Deedat witnessed for the first time his father's impact, not just on dignitaries but on ordinary Muslims. Many Indian and Pakistani expatriates visited Deedat at the hotel, clamouring for attention, hugging him and kissing his forehead and hands.

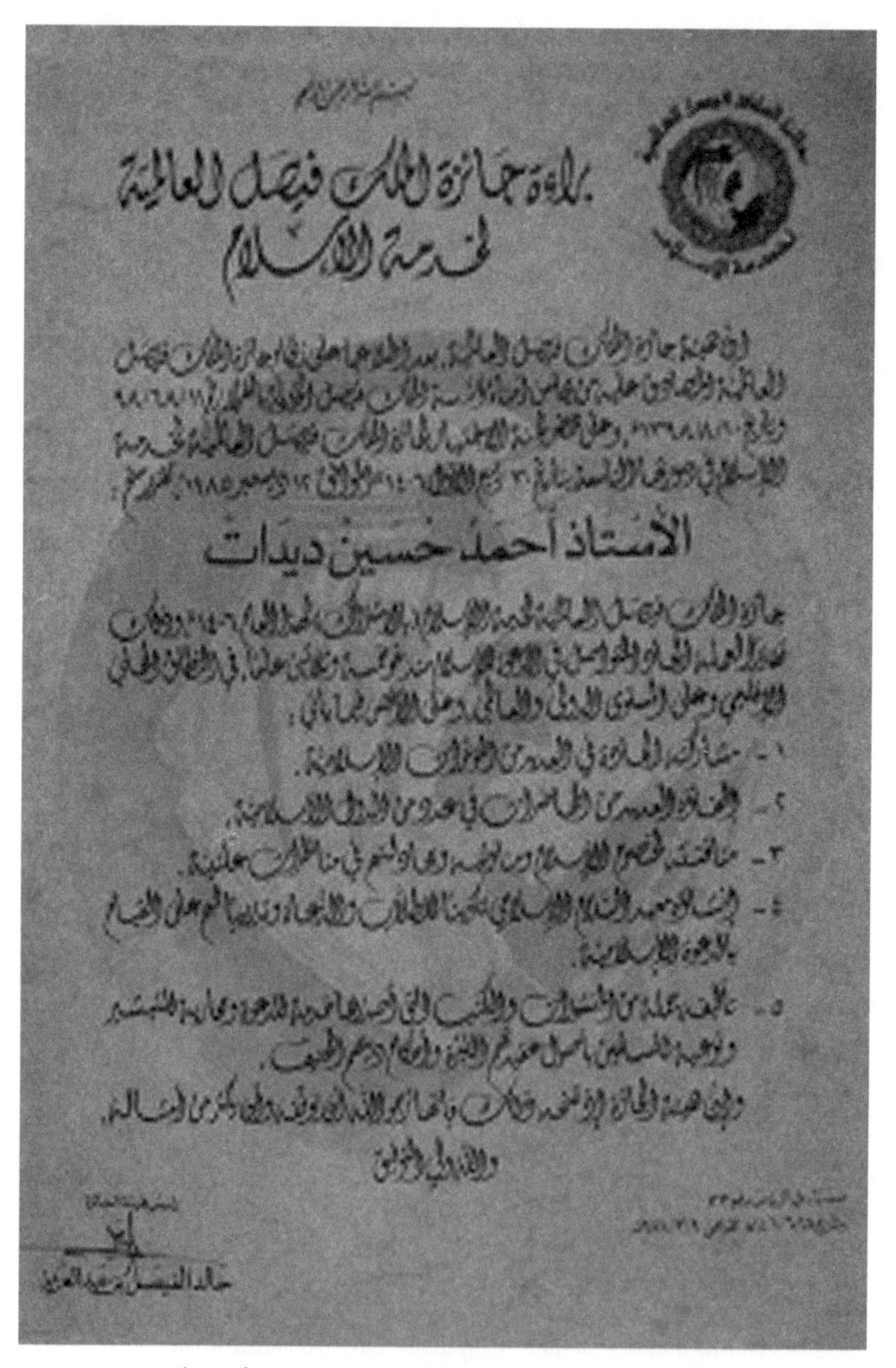

The certificate awarded to Ahmed Deedat with the King Faisal Prize

Yousuf was struck by their deference to the Saudis. They would cluster around Deedat but as soon as an Arab walked in they dispersed. 'Humare izzat badha hogaya aap ka liye' (Because of you our respect has grown in this country), they said to Deedat. It was while contemplating these distinctions between rich and poor, and Arab and non-Arab, Yousuf Deedat recalls, that his father's remarkable achievements first dawned on him.

At the award ceremony on 9 March 1986 Deedat, who refused to comply with the Foundation's rule that all recipients submit a transcript of their speech in advance, expounded the importance of da'wah and the failure of Arabs in this regard. Deedat's award consisted of a certificate (handwritten in calligraphy) which summarised his work, a commemorative gold medal, and a cash endowment. Deedat was the first person from Africa to receive the award. He shared the prize with Dr Roger Garaudy, a French philosopher who had recently embraced Islam. Deedat regarded it as an achievement to be in the same company as this renowned activist.[2]

According to the citation, Deedat's award was for:

> Articulation in Islamic conferences, lectures, argumentation against the opponents of Islam, and debating with them in open meetings, his founding of As-Salaam for training students to take up the task of Islamic propagation, and writing pamphlets and books for the cause of propagation and combating missionary activities in addition to enlightening Muslims on the principles of their illustrious belief and the rules of their religion.

Deedat was commended for taking up the challenge to convince Jews and Christians that they had drifted from the 'true teachings' of the prophets Musa (Moses) and Jesus, which are in harmony with Islam. The letter concluded by 'supplicating that Allah grant him [Deedat] success, and increase the number of men like him'.

South African, Faisal Dawjee, was a student in Riyadh at the time and recalled some aspects of Deedat's trip:

> I was struck by the contrast between Deedat's sons. His eldest son, Ebrahim, also accompanied his father to Riyadh...Ebrahim maintained a low profile, preferring to stay within the confines of the hotel or in his room. Occasionally he ventured out into Riyadh in one of the many limousines placed at the disposal of the Deedats but he stayed away from the endless stream of fawning guests continually making their way to his father's room. While Ebrahim was reserved and, at times, seemingly disinterested in the fanfare surrounding the Faisal Awards, Yousuf was excitable and seemed to be revelling in his father's achievements and the attention being showered on him.

> The ceremony itself was held at the ultra-modern King Faisal Foundation in Riyadh. The mainly by-invitation-only guests, comprising the cream of the most influential glitterati of the kingdom, were joined by an equally impressive galaxy of international guests who were long-time associates of the Saudi royal family. The guests were treated to a spectacular laser show tracing the history of the kingdom from Muhammad ibn

Saʻud to the present Saudi dynasty. Complementing this extravaganza was an equally jaw-dropping feast of Middle Eastern cuisine. The award ceremony itself was surprisingly low key as Deedat was called up and handed his prize.

News of Deedat's award was well received by his supporters in South Africa. *Al-Qalam* paid the following tribute to Deedat:

> The award is well deserved by a man whose whole life was dedicated to the mission to make Allah's message prevail over all other ideologies. He did not expect the award, but when it came he welcomed it as an award in recognition and encouragement of the Islamic da'wah throughout the world.

In Durban, the Arabic Study Circle organised a reception for Deedat on 19 July 1986, where he spoke on 'There is a Siddique in your Life'. The lecture was based on the conversion of Musa, a fellow employee at Simplex Furniture in the 1950s, who was the first person to embrace Islam after receiving Deedat's message.

The King Faisal International Prize was followed by a high-profile debate with Jimmy Swaggart. These two events were crucial in the making of Deedat as a global figure in the Muslim world, and meant that raising funds for his many ambitious projects ceased to be a hurdle.

# 17
# THE SWAGGER OF DEEDAT

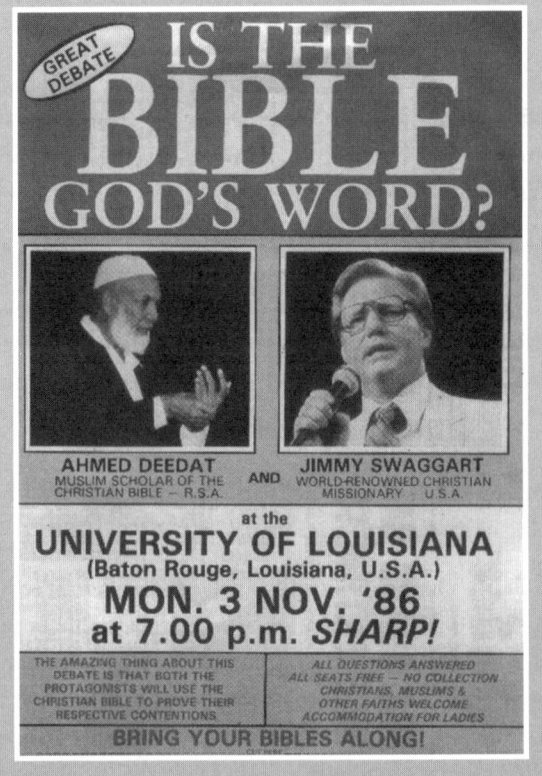

*Several newspapers in the US carried advertisements for the Deedat–Swaggart debate.*

One day I met someone who told me he had a videotape on Deedat versus Swaggart. Dee-who? Swaggart I knew, on TV thumping his Bible. So I watched the tape. And was I in for a nice (make that NICE) surprise. I watched several more of his tapes. Great! Here was a Muslim analysing the Bible and, from my point of view, putting to shame the Christian preachers.

– Abul Kalaam[1]

STORIES JUST LIKE ABUL KALAAM'S (on the previous page) have been told thousands of times by viewers all over the world. Canadian Mahomed Taha, who watched the Deedat–Swaggart debate on video with family and friends, was so taken by it that he he wrote to Deedat in 1991, 'My family and friends watched your video several times and are grateful. To us your lecture is better than a thousand Imams. I am not exaggerating.' Kenneth L. Jenkins, a former minister in the Pentecostal Assemblies of the World from Indiana in the USA, embraced Islam and changed his name to Abdullah Muhammad al-Faruque after viewing the debate:

> As a young boy I was raised with a deep fear of God…Every Sunday we would go to church dressed in all of our finery. After graduating from high school and entering university, I studied the Bible for days and weeks at a time. I acknowledged my call to the ministry at the age of twenty. I began preaching and became well known very quickly. I soon discovered that money, power and position were more important than teaching the truth about the Bible…All of this, coupled with a failure to receive answers to what I thought were valid questions, was enough to make me seek a change. That change came when I accepted a job in Saudi Arabia. I immediately expressed a desire to learn more about this peculiar brand of religion [Islam], but how could I entertain the thought of abandoning a teaching that had followed me since childhood? I was then given a videocassette of a debate between Shaykh Ahmed Deedat and the Reverend Jimmy Swaggart. After seeing the debate I immediately became a Muslim… It was truly a birth from darkness into light.[2]

Like Jenkins (Abdullah), Taha, and Kalaam, many were won over by the debate with Swaggart where Deedat gave free rein to his own swagger. Until the early 1980s, Deedat had largely confined his activities to the Southern African region, with the occasional foray abroad. The halls were packed for Deedat's debates and lectures and the predominantly Muslim crowds were drawn to his confrontational method of argumentation. Those Muslims who regarded Deedat's methods as contrary to the prophetic method were in the minority. The 1980s, in the context of the emergence of transnational televangelists, saw Deedat propelled onto the international stage. It not only won him new fans but was the deciding factor in his endeavours to attract funding from the Middle East.

Jeffrey K. Hadden and Charles E. Swann coined the term 'televangelism'to refer to Christian evangelists who used the medium of television to impart their message to the masses. The main features of the 'modern electric empires of the Pat Robertsons, the Jerry Falwells, the Billy Grahams, and the Jimmy Swaggarts are commercial television, audience support, strong and media-savvy personalities, and a materialistic and consumerist value system'.[3] In the USA, religious programming was considered 'in the public interest' from the time that national radio networks such as NBC and CBS were formed in the 1920s. Evangelical churches, however, were denied airtime and mobilised to form the National Religious Broadcasters (NRB) in 1944 to lobby for airtime. Billy Graham was the first major figure to cut through the liberal church monopoly and acquire paid and free network television time. The selling of radio and television airtime for religious programmes from the 1960s buoyed evangelical broadcasters, and paid-time programming increased from 53 per cent of religious broadcasting in 1959 to 92 per cent by 1977.[4]

The videotape was a key technological innovation. Prior to its invention, film had to be mailed from station to station across the country, which required careful planning and made these programmes both expensive and time-consuming. The videocassette permitted cheap and quick reproduction of programmes that could be aired simultaneously across the country to coincide with significant religious occasions, thus making them relevant and enhancing their audience appeal.[5] The USA enjoyed its longest period of economic growth in the years from 1945 to 1970, and the increasing economic importance of southern states gave fundamentalist Christians the financial muscle to challenge the established churches and secularists.[6] The appeal of televangelism was that it 'seemed to make God who was banished from so much of the public sphere a dramatic and tangible presence…through adeptly packaging and marketing Christianity.'[7]

The most powerful televangelists of the 1980s, such as Billy Graham, Pat Robertson, Jimmy Swaggart, Jerry Falwell, and Jim Bakker raked in around a billion dollars per annum as they turned out 'highly professional products'.[8] Deedat's foray onto the global stage must be viewed in this context. As Larkin points out,

> the massive boom in Christian media brought about by the Pentecostal revival created a model to be aped and a force to be resisted. Deedat's religious practice is constituted by its engagement with Christian forms by both copying them and overtly resisting them and foregrounds the polemical, dialogical nature of the encounter. Deedat's public debates present this polemical encounter in spectacular fashion, and the force of his argument resides precisely in the performative excess of inhabiting a Christian register while at the same time mocking it. It generates a thrill of transgression. It is why audiences find him funny, and why they relish his mastery. Deedat's importance depends upon his inhabiting the physical and discursive spaces of Christianity – its modes of biblical exegesis, forms of public debate, its buildings, pamphlets, video- and audiocassettes – as he is asserting a Muslim presence in the world of Islam's opponents.[9]

Deedat's pre-tour publicity for a visit to England in July 1985 boasted that it would be 'an invasion in reverse. The British ruled over India, Egypt, Malaysia, for over a hundred years. Now for the conquest of Britain by Islam. Not with bombs and guns, but with love, compassion and logic. Let us hope the Anglican bishops will prove more manly than the Pope.'

Deedat's most prominent European debates included:

- 'Was Christ Crucified?' with Floyd E. Clark of the Johnson Bible College at the Royal Albert Hall in London on 7 July 1985;
- 'Crucifixion – Fact or Fiction?' with Robert Douglas;
- 'Was Christ Crucified?' with Bishop General Wakefield;
- 'Is Jesus God?' with Pastor Erik Bock;
- 'Is the Bible the Word of God?' and 'Is Jesus God?' with Stanley Sjoberg in Stockholm in October 1991; and
- 'Is Jesus God?' in London in December 1985 and 'The Qur'an or the Bible: Which is God's Word?' with Dr Anis Shorrosh in Birmingham on 7 August 1988.

IPCI trustee Ebrahim Jadwat remembers the debate with Clark as significant because:

> it was the famous Albert Hall, and it was opportune because it was also the summer and a lot of Muslims from different parts of the world were coming for their holidays to London at that time. And so it was an instant hit. Once that Albert Hall event took place, the floodgates were up. Deedat was raising his flag of Islam in the capitals of the Western world.[10]

Deedat's debates with Anis Shorrosh were also important in that they attracted large audiences. Shorrosh was a Palestinian-born evangelist who had been displaced by Israeli occupation and spent most of his youth as a refugee in Nazareth. After moving to the United States he became a full time preacher and, like Deedat, engaged in inter-religious debates. Shorrosh first came to public attention when he showed up at Q&A sessions during Deedat's 1985 debate with Dr Floyd E. Clark. Deedat and Shorrosh then engaged in two highly contentious debates. In December 1985, six thousand people packed the Royal Albert Hall for their first encounter, 'Is Jesus God?' Another two thousand were turned away. Around ten thousand attended the second debate at the National Exhibition Centre in Birmingham on 7 August 1988 on 'The Qur'an or the Bible: Which is God's word?' The latter event lasted a mammoth four hours.

Deedat's most celebrated encounter, however, was with Jimmy Swaggart, which many Muslims describe as the 'greatest' interfaith debate ever. The debate took place on 3 November 1985. Swaggart, born in Louisiana in 1935, was a Pentecostal preacher and pioneer of tele-vangelism whose lucrative ministry, started in 1974 under the Assemblies of God, was earning an estimated $150 million per year by the 1980s.[11] Swaggart had a weekly television audience of around eight million in the USA where his programme was transmitted to three thousand stations and cable systems, and to a worldwide audience of eighty million in over a hundred and forty countries, including South Africa.[12] One writer describes him as 'the greatest Jesus-promotion salesman in the world'. According to the scholar Karen Armstrong, he 'preached a religion of hatred...He cast off the restraints imposed by the discipline of charity as well as those of reason...[His] religiosity was, in its way, self-destructive and nihilistic.'[13]

Swaggart's animated on-stage sermons in which he 'jabbed the air, kicked up his knees, chuckled and cried', earned him the tag of 'the Elvis Presley of the church'.[14] American journalist Lawrence Wright was one of the thousands who responded 'ecstatically to Swaggart's preaching':

> He would sink deeper and deeper into his subconscious, he would journey past reason and conscious meaning into the slashing emotions and buried fears and unnamed desires that bubble below. His voice would rise and tremble, his grammar would fall away, but still he stumbled toward that cowering raw nerve of longing. He knew where it was. One watched him with both dread and desire, because this is the nerve that is attached to faith. Longing to be loved and saved – it is when he finally touches this nerve that the tears flow and the audience stands with its hands upraised, laughing, wailing, praising the Lord, speaking in unknown languages and quivering with the pain and pleasure of their thrilling public exposure.[15]

Swaggart was a formidable opponent, but the debate provided Deedat with an international stage to exhibit his encyclopaedic knowledge of the Bible and great prowess at argumentation.

Yousuf Deedat was in awe of Swaggart, whom he regarded as a 'genius'. He once bought videos from the Swaggart Ministry in West Street and showed them to his father and warned him never to challenge him. Yousuf was working at Natal Videos when his father came home one day and told him that they would be going to the USA to debate with Swaggart. Deedat ignored the pleas of both Hawa and his son to decline the challenge and asked the Muslim Students' Association (MSA) in the USA, which was to host the debate, to send him Swaggart's books and recordings. The MSA had previously hosted Swaggart's debates with Gary Miller and Jamal Badawi. As soon as he received the books, Deedat worked late into the night, carefully reading and digesting every word and preparing his responses.

In addition to Swaggart's intellectual challenge, Deedat could not match his opponent's financial resources. His solution was a 'practice run' through the Middle East. Deedat left South Africa on 16 October 1986 and visited Karachi, Dubai, and Abu Dhabi. The reception was 'beyond imagination', according to Yousuf. In Dubai, a 'friend', Saleem Sharief, got a contact in the USA to place an advert in USA Today at a cost of US$30 000, and to take care of logistical arrangements such as hotel bookings and transportation. Other businessmen chipped in to cover the entire cost of the tour.

Deedat reached New York on 31 October 1986. He was hosted by two African-American Muslim groups, the supporters of Imam Siraj Wahaj of the al-Taqwa Mosque in Brooklyn, New York, and the Nation of Islam led by Louis Farrakhan. Deedat sent a telegram to Farrakhan on 1 October 1986 which read: 'Debate with Jimmy Swaggart arranged for 3$^{rd}$. Need your unstinted support for resounding victory.' Farrakhan did not let him down. Wearing tuxedos and driving limousines, Farrakhan's men met Deedat's entourage at JFK airport.

Many Muslims helped in different cities. For example, in Lawrence, Kansas, Hamed Ghazali, currently principal of the Islamic School of Greater Kansas City, printed ten thousand copies each of *Is the Bible God's Word?* and *What was the Sign of Jonah?* for distribution during the tour. Deedat addressed meetings across America. Recognising the potential spin-offs, he hired Cyril Ritson and Rob Oakley of Natal Video to record and edit his lectures in Atlanta (2 November), Louisiana (3 and 4 November), Tucson (5 November), Kansas City (6 November), Wichita (7 November), Kansas City (8 November), Los Angeles (9 and 10 November), Okhlahoma (11 November), and Chicago (12 and 13 November). The Swaggart debate was crucial in marketing Deedat internationally. Ebi Lockhat recalled a conversation with Deedat:

> Deedat believed that you don't sell Islam short. He gave me the example of the Jimmy Swaggart debate when I asked him one day, 'How did you become famous?' He said, 'You know, if you had to draw a graph, there was steady growth but after the Swaggart debate my reputation shot up.' So I said, 'What was different because in all your debates the same thread of argument runs through, apart from the fact that Swaggart was a known name in the western world?' He said to me, 'Look, whenever I went on these debates abroad, I always tried to find someone to video my talks,' and tended to rely on local organisers and they invariably, would say, 'I've got an uncle or a friend who will do it,' or, 'I've got a reduced price,' and when he came back, invariably he never got the tapes because it wasn't edited or someone else had it and it belonged to them. He used to have such problems, so for the Swaggart debate he decided that he was not going to cut corners even though he didn't have enough money. He said that he borrowed funds and took across a company called Natal Videos. He used a word which is now archaic but was common in the apartheid world, 'I took two European technicians. These were *my* people. They were working to my schedule because they were getting paid for it. They had a job to do and they were professional. They shot the video and delivered a professional job to me.' That video was dubbed and put on the overseas channels, which opened up many doors. So he again gave proof of not cutting corners but investing in the best technology.

Deedat's crew faced many practical difficulties. One was the difference in voltage. To overcome this, they purchased a car battery for each recording and gave it away after the debate. They also hired an Egyptian crew as backup in case something went amiss with their recording. The Egyptians, however, sensing that they were onto a 'good thing', disappeared after the debate. The sound on the IPCI's recording, according to Yousuf Deedat, was considerably better than the recording of Swaggart's team. There is a story behind this too. There was only one sound jack in the auditorium and Yousuf Deedat managed to grab it ahead of Swaggart's men. Another practical problem was that the format required the speakers to stand at the podium. Deedat, however, wanted a microphone. The hosts said that it would not be possible to obtain one at short notice. Farrakhan's men dashed to a church across the road and brought Deedat a microphone.

***

The Swaggart debate was organised by the MSA of Louisiana State University. The Assembly Hall on the Baton Rouge campus was packed to capacity. There were around eight thousand people, mainly Muslims, from as far afield as San Francisco, Dallas, and Chicago.[16] The atmosphere was 'electric', according to Yousuf Deedat. Imam Siraj Wahaj was master of ceremonies. Swaggart spoke for thirty minutes, Deedat for forty, and Swaggart was given ten minutes for a rebuttal. An hour was allocated for the speakers to field questions from the audience.

Deedat argued that while Muslims believed in the Bible as part of their faith, they did not consider it to be the literal word of God because of contradictions in the text, incorrect translations, and the existence of several versions.[17] Swaggart disputed Deedat's arguments. He said that the Bible contained prophecies and history, and that archaeologists had not been able to disprove a single word of it. He compared Deedat to the Apostle Paul who experienced a dramatic conversion and urged Deedat to accept Jesus as saviour and Lord. Despite the size of the audience, the debate was conducted amicably. Deedat described Swaggart as 'charming; he steals your heart away' and was glad that they were 'big enough to speak to each other'.[18] For his part, Swaggart said that two years previously he had made uncomplimentary remarks about the Qur'an: 'I apologise for that. I have never done it since, and will not do it again.'[19] Swaggart was referring to a 1984 sermon in which he dismissed the Qur'an as 'no more than weird incantations of a frail man'.

There were two occasions when Deedat claimed that he was unsure how to respond to a question. The first was in Stellenbosch, when a student asked what good could come from chopping off the hand for stealing (see Chapter 10, Cape of Storms). The second was in the course of the debate with Swaggart when he was asked whether he was willing to debate with Swaggart in Makkah, and thus reciprocate his invitation to a Christian country (non-Muslims are not allowed to enter Makkah). Deedat was unsure what to say as he made his way to the microphone. The answer, he said later, came from God. Each country, he said, had its own visa requirements. For example, to enter Zambia in the 1970s he had to sign an undertaking that he did not recognise Ian Smith's Rhodesia. America and Canada also had conditions attached to their visa applications. Likewise, Makkah had a condition that you declare your belief that

> there is but one God, not Father, Son and Holy Ghost, not that Jesus is God, [but that] you believe in the one and only God, Allah, which is his name, and that Muhammad is the last and final messenger of God. If Swaggart fulfils that condition he is welcome to visit Makkah.[20]

Deedat's speaking style was described by a local Louisiana newspaper as 'animated, full of hand gestures'.[21] Another report noted that Deedat had offered evangelists Billy Graham, Jerry Falwell, and Pat Robertson $10 000 each to debate with him in Madison Square Garden on a topic of their choice.[22] The IPCI video team went to work immediately after the debate and produced a tape for international distribution. Deedat titled the debate *The Beginning of the End of Jimmy Swaggart* and showed it around the clock at the IPCI building in Durban and distributed it worldwide. According to Larkin:

> The video of this event opens with an image of the headquarters of the Islamic Propagation Centre International before cutting to a U.S. flag fluttering under a superimposed title: 'Deedat's American Tour'. To the accompaniment of trumpets the flag is replaced by successive images of the Statue of Liberty, the Golden Gate Bridge, a mansion in Baton Rouge, and the University of Louisiana. Starting with America at its most symbolic level, the sequence telescopes us from the general context to the particular one of Jimmy Swaggart's home base, Baton Rouge, where the debate takes place. As with his debates in the Royal Albert Hall and in other parts of the United States, Canada, and elsewhere, Deedat physically enters into the terrain of the opposition. When he argues with Swaggart that recent versions of the Bible 'prove' the errancy of the King James Version, he states: 'I didn't print it. The Jews didn't print it. The Hindus didn't print it. You, Christians, you produced this book and you are telling me it is the most up-to-date Bible according to the most ancient manuscripts.' He continues to cite the critique emanating from the Revised Standard Version, pointing out to Swaggart and the audience that 'these are not my words,' that this is not a critique from within the Islamic tradition but one that comes from the discursive and rhetorical world of Christianity itself.[23]

A carefully orchestrated distribution of the tape by the IPCI followed, targeting influential Arabs and potential donors in the Middle East. Deedat toured Abu Dhabi, Bahrain, Qatar, and other Middle Eastern countries to promote the debate. He met the likes of Prince Al-Walid (who appeared on the Forbes List of the world's wealthiest men) and Sultan al-Qasim. The Swaggart debate gave Deedat's international reputation a boost and was pivotal in procuring funds for the IPCI. The videotape reshaped Deedat's mission as he was able to edit his debates and present his message in alluring packages that captivated and fascinated his mainly Muslim audiences.

There were negative consequences for Swaggart. Church members criticised his 'poor' performance. He claimed that the video recording was unfairly doctored. Swaggart had expressed a desire to continue the debate in the Middle East. Deedat sent him a telegram on 20 July 1987 accepting the challenge in Abu Dhabi with United Arab Television agreeing to televise it live to the Middle East. According to Deedat, 'whilst watching our video some influential gentlemen in Abu Dhabi heard your frantic request to appear in Makkah on television as a last resort. They immediately indicated to televise another meeting between the two of us live to all the Middle Eastern countries including Makkah.' Swaggart ignored the telegram from Deedat who sent him a second telegram a few weeks later:

> Your earnest desire during our last meeting in Baton Rouge to appear on TV in Makkah made me impress on the authorities in the UAE to allow your wish to be fulfilled. Now that the way is open for you, why is there no formal reply from you? Were you just jesting or joking? The authorities in the UAE are inundating me with phone calls as they are ready for us. *Please Jimmy, help me out of this and please respond.*

I.B. Lock, director of the Jimmy Swaggart Ministries, replied on 4 February 1988 that Swaggart will 'at no stage take part in any of your proposed debates which prove to have been a set up to disgrace and discredit Rev. Swaggart'. Deedat responded to the Swaggart Ministry on 17 February 1988, saying that Swaggart had claimed in the thirty-fourth minute of the debate that God speaks to him and had given him a message for Deedat. If this was the case, why did God not warn him that Deedat was 'setting him up'? Was it perhaps 'Satan pretending to be God'? He also criticised Swaggart 'for not having the courage of his conviction to go into direct correspondence with me. God and Jesus do not show as much detachment from even the sinners. But Jimmy, he is different.' It was true, Deedat continued, that Swaggart had been 'disgraced and humiliated', but this was due to the paucity of his

> knowledge of the Christian Scriptures and his feeble and irrelevant rantings to prove his point…[His] utter hopelessness was reflected in his ten minute rebuttal when he likened me to 'an ass carrying a load of books'…You are accusing us of being dishonest in a rather vague and ambiguous manner. There are no special instances to prove that we have edited the tapes to give an untrue picture.

At the beginning of the debate Swaggart told the audience that Deedat had commented on his wife's beauty on their way to the hall. He said that he reminded Deedat that, as a Christian, he was allowed to marry only once and therefore had to choose the best.[24] Just over a year later, in February 1988, Swaggart tearfully confessed on his television show that he was guilty of an 'unspecified sin'. He was involved in a sex scandal with a prostitute, Debra Murphree, and the Assemblies of God revoked his ordination. Deedat had the last word, relating the story during a lecture in Abu Dhabi, and adding, 'It seems the best was not good enough for our Jimmy.'[25]

Deedat's high-profile international debates in the USA and UK 'launched' his career as an international preacher. When Deedat toured Switzerland in 1987, he was interviewed on World Radio Geneva's 'Freely Speaking' program by Gina Lewis on 16 March. She asked him about the debate with Swaggart:

*Lewis:* You just came from the United States and you made a tour there and some very interesting things happened to you. Why don't you tell us about that?

*Deedat:* Yes, you see there is a man, I think he's a giant today in the Christian world, a missionary that preaches, Jimmy Swaggart.

*Lewis:* Yes, Jimmy Swaggart is a well-known Bible-believing Christian with a TV ministry as well as another one who is very famous in America.

*Deedat:* He is boasting that he has appeared on two thousand TV stations of the world in a hundred and forty different countries. His daily budget is a million dollars a day.

*Lewis:* That's almost as big as mine for three years.

*Deedat:* A million dollars a day. And somehow, you know, he is in Baton Rouge, Louisiana and there's a university there. The town has grown around the university, Louisiana University. And there are some Muslim students with whom they have been having a little kind of argument and debates with Swaggart and his ministry. So he had a debate with some Muslim once and he had a debate with another Muslim once, and for the third time, they called me over from South Africa to debate with Jimmy Swaggart. And, I think from the Muslim point of view, it went off fantastically well in the debate as well as the questions and answers that followed. I made two separate video tapes of that – the debate with Jimmy Swaggart and the Q & A session lasting for about two hours.

*Lewis:* Was there a winner and a loser, and was it friendly?

*Deedat:* As far as the winning and losing is concerned, we would leave it to the audience.

*Lewis:* Leave it to God probably.

*Deedat:* Leave it to God, yes, He is the ultimate. But the audience will also be able to see for themselves, you know, where truth is weighed heavily, on which side. But our relationship was exceptionally good from the word go. When we finished off, we embraced one another and he invited me home for lunch, you know, that person was something fantastic.

*Lewis:* But what about the rest of the people from the Christian faith?

*Deedat:* There again, you see on the screen that as soon as the debate was finished, the people were shocked. They couldn't even speak to one another. You watched them, you know, usually as soon as the thing is over, you start chatting, cross-chat, this time there was nothing at all…as if they all had seen a ghost. So it proves something. You see, it was something beyond their expectation that a Muslim can come forward and speak about the Bible, quote from the Bible more than the preacher can, because everything Swaggart spoke I proved it from the Book, the Book, the Book, the Book – this is what the Bible says, this is what the Bible says, you know, in other words I was able to use the Holy Bible against the Bible-thumper, the Bible preacher. He's an expert on the subject but he found that he was...

*Lewis:* Okay, didn't somebody refuse to debate with you at all and wouldn't even see you and wouldn't let you have...

*Deedat:* You see he had been praying very, very hard, Billy Graham. He won't touch me, he won't come anywhere near me, Billy Graham. Then we tried Jerry Falwell, then we tried Pat Robinson and each and every one of them seemed to be frightened shy.[26]

Swaggart was key in the making of Deedat as a transnational figure. A.T. Rasool, IPCI trustee in the 1980s, was in no doubt that 'before Swaggart, Deedat tried in the Middle East but made little headway. That debate opened the door.' According to Ebrahim Jadwat, 'I don't think it was planned. The Islamic world was crying out for heroes...Suddenly this guy stands up and he had the stature physically, he had the command of the language, he had the knowledge and when they saw this, the invites started pouring in from all parts of the world.' Journalist Keysar Trad was one of many who were influenced by the Swaggart debate:

I have been a fan of Shaykh Ahmed Deedat ever since I saw his debate with Jimmy Swaggart. I found it captivating because finally we had a Muslim speaker convincingly answering a popular Islam-bashing evangelist. I come from Lebanon, a country where I was forced to study science and mathematics in a foreign language. One of the negatives of this was that it created a false belief that Arabic could not cover scientific knowledge. It ignored the centuries of Arab advance in the scientific fields. So seeing Shaykh Deedat hold his own was not only captivating, but it also led me to want to read more about his work and view his videos, and that I did until I had a copy of everything that I could find of what he had said and written. I even acquired Arabic and English copies of the book which Ahmed Deedat said 'taught him' everything he knew about comparative religion – Mawlana Rahmatullah Kairanawi's *Izhar-ul Haq*.

The spread of Pentecostalism throughout Africa, Latin America, and in some Muslim countries, coupled with negative media coverage of Islam, resulted in many Muslims looking at Deedat's work through the lens of conflict between Muslims and Christians, hence their support for him. The resources that this attracted led to a new image for the IPCI, signified by its smart new headquarters.

Deedat's growing international reputation resulted in the IPC's scope and activities extending beyond those envisaged by its founding members and it became necessary to reorganise the organisation's governing structure. A new trust deed was registered on 29 March 1985, and the organisation was renamed the Islamic Propagation Centre International (IPCI), reflecting Deedat's global reach. Its board of trustees comprised of five members: Ahmed Deedat as president; G.H. Vanker and G.H. Agjee as joint secretaries; M.Y. Buckas as secretary-general; and Yusuf Ally as treasurer.

In Yusuf Buckas, the IPC seemed to have found Deedat's long-term successor. Buckas was a young man in his twenties and a lawyer by profession, having completed his law degrees at the University of Durban-Westville. He had been an IPC volunteer as a teenager. Deedat told a reporter that he was 'very much elated to know that a person like Yusuf Buckas has committed himself to this mission. And it is evident that he is measuring up quite well to the challenges.'[27] Buckas held his first public meeting at the Durban City Hall on 13 December 1983, and subsequently held several public debates, gave lectures, and published various booklets while he was with the IPCI. Yusuf Ally, proprietor of Queens Jewellers in Durban, was an obvious candidate for the position of treasurer because of his family's long association with Deedat, his own admiration for Deedat, and his financial acumen. When the Trust was formed, Deedat asked him to become a trustee. Ally accepted the offer because he regarded it as a 'singular honour' to work with Deedat. The appointment of Dr G.M. Hoosen, son of Deedat's longtime friend A.H. Lutchka and a founding member of the Islamic Medical Association of South Africa (IMA), as trustee on 24 June 1986 and that of A.T. Rasool of the Arabic Study Circle in August 1986 increased the number of trustees to seven.

The addition of new trustees (and, simultaneously, a number of new staff) created tensions within the IPCI. Deedat had long been accustomed to doing things his way and was not comfortable with making space for new members. Eventually Buckas resigned when some staff who worked directly for him were dismissed without the matter being discussed with him. The resignation of Yusuf Buckas on 26 January 1987 and G.H. Vanker's demise on 25 August 1987 left two vacant positions on the Trust. These were then filled by Deedat's son Yousuf and Yusuf Ally's son, Naushad, a young medical doctor. Rasool resigned as trustee on 26 June 1990 and Dr. Hoosen on 10 June 1990, both for personal reasons. These changes, and especially the addition of new personalities with new ideas, impacted both on individual members and on dynamics within the organisation. Despite these tensions, the decade from 1985 was arguably Deedat's 'finest hour' as he undertook numerous lecture and debate tours all over the world and in the process enhanced his standing in the global Muslim world.

## 18

# 'FAISAL LAUREATE'

Ever the consummate performer, Deedat addressing a large crowd in India in 1988.

> The Muslims are weakened and demoralised; negligent and lazy; victims of unproductive stupefaction…This is the moment to cast off laziness, to summon from far and near all those men who have blood in their veins.
>
> – Salahuddin, Twelfth century[1]

'I SAW A REAL LIVING SALAHUDDIN,' a member of the audience exclaimed during one of Deedat's lectures in Mumbai in 1988, recalling the heroics of Salahuddin Ayyubi who bravely defended Muslim lands in the twelfth century when England's Richard the Lionheart was threatening to conquer Syria and Palestine. In two decades of struggle, Salahuddin pushed the Crusaders back from the Holy Lands. Notwithstanding the hyperbole, Deedat was seen by many Muslims as a modern-day crusader who, armed with the 'weapons of the enemy', resisted missionary 'invasions' of Muslim lands – comparisons of Deedat and Salahuddin have been often been drawn in interviews, on internet blogs and in newspaper reports.

Indeed, it can be argued that Deedat helped to cultivate this image as he constantly peddled the message that Muslims were under political siege from the West, and collectively threatened by rampant missionary activities. In an interview with *Arabia: The Islamic World Review*, he complained that 'Christian missionaries are active in almost every Muslim country'.[2] He noted that 'not many Muslim institutions take the Christian evangelical missions seriously', and expressed concern that levels of conversion were consequently bound to increase. In August 1987, Deedat wrote to Dr Totonji, 'Pakistan has become killing fields for Christian missionaries. Leaving for Karachi Fri 4 Sept for 3-week shake up. Insha Allah. Pray for success.' Upon landing in Pakistan, Deedat warned locals that Christian 'crusaders have come to preach in this country from America which is ten thousand miles away. And what are we doing? Nothing.' He related that missionaries were handing out stickers to children in Arabic calligraphy with subliminal Christian messages. An 'angry' Deedat said that he did not mind a 'fair fight' but 'if they deceive you and your children, this is unforgivable.'[3] Interviewed on television in Pakistan in March 1987, he said:

> There's freedom of religion but this is a one-way invasion. You see, from the West there are, I have facts here from *Time* magazine that there are in the world today seventy thousand crusaders. Sixty per cent of them are Americans. There are thirty-five thousand occupied in Africa, they are here in Pakistan, in Bangladesh, in Indonesia. What do they want? They want to convert us.[4]

Christian missions, Deedat continued, placed advertisements on Islamabad radio, which had a programme for Christians in Pushto and distributed magazines such as *Pray, Watchtower, Plain Truth*, and *Awake*. Deedat raised this with General Zia-ul-Haq because ordinary Pakistanis seemed oblivious to the 'danger'. The reporter wanted to know whether Deedat would be visiting Pakistan in future in light of its problems: 'It looks like I will be forced to. I have to do that to force more and more people to think in the right direction. This is vital because the other forces are doing that.'[5]

Deedat blamed ordinary Muslims for the 'sorry plight' of the Muslim world. This included choosing leaders of questionable quality, failing to carry out da'wah, and lacking the commitment of their Christian counterparts.[6]

Deedat felt that Arabs lacked 'the grit and conviction of their ancestors' and should finance Muslim missionary activity:

> Allah has blessed them with abundant wealth and has sent the world to them in the form of migrant workers from almost all parts of the globe. Some of them come in the guise of 'tent makers' [missionaries], as Saint Paul called them. Instead of we Muslims giving them Islam, these migrant workers are beginning to convert us, if not by direct conversion then by subtle influence that their civilisation is superior to ours. We must deploy the petro-dollar wealth to push back the frontiers of western encroachment upon our value-system of Islam. Islamic da'wah should be financed to the hilt.[7]

One of Deedat's favourite anecdotes was that of an American citizen in Riyadh who embraced Islam after meeting him. The (unnamed) American told him that he had been in Riyadh for twenty-five years but nobody 'ever knocked at his door. He had changed seven houses, moving to seven different places and yet nobody came to see him.' Deedat lamented Muslim complacency.[8] He returned to the theme of Muslim lethargy during an interview in Pakistan in March 1987:

> I went to Peshawar, Sialkot, Islamabad, Quetta, Lahore, and I found Christian activities. They are boasting that they have converted more Pakistanis to Christianity since independence than in the previous hundred and fifty years of British rule. In Peshawar there are seventy-two Christian and Zionist units looking after the mujahids, truly, truly, as against them there are only nine Muslim community units, nine against seventy-two, and these are supposed to be our brethren. There are more than fifty Muslim countries in the world. They couldn't send a unit each...This is their [Christian] way to win the hearts of people, show compassion for them. Where are the Muslims?[9]

Deedat understood the importance of publicity. As Charles Hirschkind points out, 'in terms of the norms and practices of a modern consumerist public, publicity has become a condition of all religious practice'.[10] Italian scholar Armando Salvatore emphasised that in the modern age

> actors within the religious field organise their interests, fulfil their functions, acquire cultural capital and social prestige and reinvest them in the culture market according to dynamics that increasingly involve stakes of public definition along with skilled crafting and marketing of religious services and products. This is not a 'free market' but a highly oligopolistic one, as the new religious media star resembles a media

notable who chases after market shares at the same time as having to make a show of personal virtue, of charismatic energy...in order to check the loyalty of adept clients.[11]

Deedat masterfully manipulated the media. He obtained widespread publicity through appeals in Middle Eastern newspapers such as *al-Sharq al-Awsat Arabic Daily*, *Arab News English Daily*, and *al-Muslimun Arabic Daily*. He advertised in South African newspapers, and in the USA, placed adverts in *Time* magazine, and *USA Today*. His visits to the United Kingdom were covered by the mainstream media including *The Guardian* and *The Independent*. The following excerpt from *Saudi Gazette* (14 May 1988) is typical:

> Mr Ahmed Deedat is doing Islamic Da'wah work for the last 30 years. He has been awarded the King Faisal International Award for service to Islam in the year 1986. He is training Muslim students on comparative religion and debates on Islamic topics. He is the President and founder of the IPCI, Durban, South Africa. The main aim of the IPCI is to spread Islam throughout the world. More than 6 000 people have accepted Islam on account of Da'wah activities of Mr Deedat. He is now engaged in a worldwide campaign to gather contributions for his Da'wah.

Yousuf Deedat also understood the importance of advertising, as he told a meeting of trustees on 26 March 1990:

> People are giving us money for advertising in the *USA Today*, in the *Time* magazine, US$68 000 a page. A man has given us $100 000 to be spent in the *Time* magazine. That money of his, he wants to see you spend it in the *Time* magazine, and you show it to him, and he can give you a million dollars. First he wants to build confidence in you. He has lost confidence in the Muslim umma.

Ebi Lockhat underscored the importance of the videotape in Deedat's rise to international prominence.

> Deedat bought into TV media. You saw what he did with the Hinduism tape, the Swaggart tape. He was very mindful of that and we used to produce in our own little way, Deedat on the Gulf War, etc., which we used to post worldwide. This was a very good marketing principle. He would always urge us, 'Let's send everybody a tape about what my views are on the Gulf War, etc.' but we said, 'Those cost R50 to post.' He says, 'Send it. Look at the value. One person out of a posting of five or six hundred likes what I say about the Gulf War, he sent $13 000 and a note "keep up the good work."' Remember, for the Arab, English was a second language and they liked what he produced. When you write, they don't reply but what it did is that it kept Deedat's name alive there because he sent a person three or four tapes throughout the year, so when Deedat did go to an Arab country, when he walked into the person's business, that person already knew him well and was on the backfoot to say, 'Sorry, I didn't reply to you.' So that principle of his was very good, you give, you get, you give, you get. He did not skimp on that. He believed that the medium is the message.

Where Deedat did not travel, his videos did. Videotapes allowed Deedat to forge a parapersonal relationship with audiences across the globe. Every tour, lecture, and debate was followed by the now almost mandatory video (and later DVD) recording, with adverts proclaiming, '*Now see and hear the giant in your own home*'. Blogger Abu Ilyas was probably not too far off the mark when he asked on his website on 15 May 2007:

> How many times do we meet a Muslim who maybe prays two or three times a week but has a complete set of Ahmed Deedat videos which he can dip into whenever he wants to 'feel good' about his religion without having to do any specific religious act?[12]

The IPCI's audio and video departments expanded as the demand for Deedat's recordings grew. The opening of IPCI stores in the Middle East made Deedat's work available to a wider audience: the al-Amanah Centre opened in Abu Dhabi in 1983; a second store was opened in Dubai in 1985; the Abul Qasim Book Store opened in Jeddah in 1986. The IPCI also opened offices in the UK and USA. Journalist Shafa'at Khan described Yousuf Deedat as 'a marketing genius…The IPCI became a business venture under him, modelled on successful televangelists.' Deedat explained that the stores were opened because

> the whole world was crying out for tapes. This was a novel method. For centuries Muslims were told and taught to read namaaz, give zakah, and be good. They were tired of it. In the Western environment there was an onslaught from missionaries; they were under attack. The tapes were doing an important job and there was demand from all over the world.[13]

Deedat embraced technology wholeheartedly. He told a reporter that people remembered 1 per cent by taste, 1 per cent by touch, 3 per cent by smell, 11 per cent by hearing, and 83 per cent by seeing.[14] He targeted the Middle East with a video onslaught because, he said, there were more video machines there than anywhere else in the world.[15] Deedat told a reporter for *al-Burhaan* in July 1989 that 'the success of any organisation depends on the presentation and quality of work it produces. If it fails to adopt the new methods, it begins to lag behind until such time its operational work and systems become extinct.'[16] Deedat's actions were revolutionary for their time. As Ebi Lockhat pointed out:

> For an Islamic organisation, it was an antithesis to what we were normally used to, you know, cut the cost, go to this printer that we know, etc. He could have done that but he always went that extra mile when it came to image and marketing and this is something that he was very good at. He was open to ideas. He understood very quickly that whereas previously he filled fifteen to twenty thousand people at Greenpoint Stadium or the City Hall, people had televisions and he produced videos to make his message accessible at home.

Video crews accompanied Deedat on his tours, meeting professional standards of reproduction with state-of-the-art equipment supplied by leading Saudi company M. Jamil Al-Dahlawi Co. New technologies were crucial in internationalising Muslim participation in Deedat's enterprise. Listening to the recordings on video brought home his 'powerful presence, facial expressions, hand gesturing, and postural shifts'. Deedat's recordings expanded Islamic public interest in comparative religion. He became an instant source of knowledge on a range of issues involving Islam and Christianity, and profoundly shaped many ordinary people's understanding of the authenticity of the Bible, the doctrine of Trinity, and the depiction of Jesus in the Qur'an.

An indication of the IPCI's wide reach is that it published thirty-five thousand copies of *al-Burhaan* each month. To ensure that the publication met the highest standards, Deedat employed journalist Shafa'at Khan who had degrees in journalism and communication, including in video production. As a young man, Shafa'at wrote periodically for the *Post*, the *Daily News*, and *al-Balaagh*, whose editor and proprietor, A.S.K. Joommal, was his great-uncle. Shafa'at began working as a journalist with the *Daily News* in the mid-1980s and applied for the position of editor of *al-Burhaan* in 1989. His interview lasted 'one whole minute', he recalls. Deedat's only concern was whether he could produce an eight-page glossy newsletter within twelve hours. *Al-Burhaan* was a PR tool to market the IPCI. Modesty was not a characteristic of the publication. For example, the July 1989 issue described Deedat as 'the original, the pneumatic, others who try to emulate him are mere copies. His authority and knowledge in the field of comparative religion is legendary.'[17]

Deedat's 'bluntness', and what some regarded as an inflammatory approach, led to altercations in many parts of the world: in the Maldives they censored his advertisements; Singapore banned him from entering the country; France and Nigeria turned him back from their airports; Malaysia placed restrictions on what he could discuss; India refused him a visa; and Australia threatened to deport him. And yet in capitals across the Muslim world, he was feted by royalty and adored by many ordinary Muslims.

From the mid-1980s Deedat met a host of international leaders. He met Malaysian prime minister Mahatir Mohammed and other government officials during his visit in November 1984. He met Pakistani president General Zia-ul-Haq, Prime Minister Muhammad Junejo, and Acting President Goolam Ishaaq in October 1987 when he toured in response to an invitation from Muslim Aid to 'combat' Christian missionaries working among Afghan refugees in Peshawar. He exchanged ideas with General Zia on the role of da'wah and the work of Christian missionaries in Pakistan, and lectured at thirty venues across the country, including Peshawar, Sialkot, Lahore, Islamabad, Rawalpindi, Quetta, and Karachi.[18] Shortly after he received the King Faisal Prize, Deedat was invited to the UAE. Hassan El-Najjar, a correspondent for Al-Jazeera, was in the audience. He recalled the visit in his obituary titled 'Ahmed Deedat: A Relentless Caller to Islam with Wisdom':

> I had the honour of meeting with Shaykh Ahmed Deedat in Ras Al-Khaimah, UAE, in 1985. He gave a lecture in Dubai but an official in Ras Al-Khaimah invited him to visit the city and give another lecture. He came and was celebrated by an unexpectedly (due to the short-notice announcement) large audience. When Ahmed Deedat started his lecture in English, there was no interpreter and the audience was predominantly Arabic-speaking. I introduced myself to the hosts as the teacher of English in the Sai'd Bin Jubair High School in Ras Al-Khaimah. I told them that it would be an honour to translate Ahmed Deedat's lecture. They were very happy and so was Shaykh Ahmed Deedat. It was a great pleasure and turned out to be one of his favourite topics, 'The Crucifixion: Is it Reality or Imagination?'[19]

In March 1987, Deedat toured Geneva, where he spoke at the University of Geneva. This was followed by a visit to UAE to attend the tenth anniversary of the opening of al-Ain University. He also visited Kuwait, Oman, and Qatar. He visited the Maldives, Sri Lanka, and India in December 1987. He was invited to the Maldives by the Islamic Call Society of Libya, which was hosting an international conference there. The president of the Maldives, Mamoon Abdool Khayoom, paid a special tribute to Deedat in his opening address, while his public lecture on 'Missionary Inroads: Maldive Islands' was broadcast on television.[20] In India, Deedat spoke to a packed audience in Mumbai.[21]

The Indian tour also unearthed Zakir Naik. Dr Naik was born in Mumbai in 1965 and qualified as a medical doctor from the University of Mumbai, but it is as a scholar of inter-religious debates and discussions that he is internationally renowned. In February 2009, the *Indian Express* placed Naik third on the list of the 'Top Ten Spiritual Gurus of India' after Baba Ramdev and Sri Sri Ravi Shankar.[22] According to Naik,

> I got inspiration from Shaykh Deedat. Believe me, if it hadn't been for Uncle Deedat, I'd have been in the surgery doing some operations. Uncle Deedat has changed many people like me – I've met several hundred who told me this personally. As far as I am concerned, he has completely changed my full life, every hour of my life, every second.[23]

The young Naik took a risk when he asked Deedat, 'uncle why are you so strong on stage?' The reply surprised Naik: 'My son, there are two ways of fighting the battle, either with holy water or with fire and I have chosen to fight with fire. If you can fight with holy water you are most welcome, but I have chosen the fire.' The response, according to Naik, 'changed my complete outlook of Shaykh Ahmed Deedat. I was a youngster and he could have said, "Shut up." But the way he replied made me realise that he was very humble.' Naik began giving classes in da'wah from 1994. He visited Deedat at his Verulam home in 1988 and again in 1994. On the latter occasion he raised questions which so impressed Deedat that he labelled Naik 'Deedat Plus'. Deedat's endorsement motivated Naik to enter the mission full time, against the wishes of his mother who wanted him to become a heart surgeon:

> She was a fan of Dr Christiaan Barnard and it was her desire that I follow him. When I asked my mother, would you want me to become like Dr Barnard or like Shaykh Ahmed Deedat she said, 'I want you to become both.' But now, I asked her, 'Mummy, do you want me to become Chris Barnard or Shaykh Deedat?' And she said, 'I can sacrifice a thousand Chris Barnards for one Shaykh Deedat.'[24]

Dr Naik has a message for those who felt that Deedat was too aggressive:

> There are people who say that Shaykh Deedat should have shown humility. As far as da'wah is concerned I don't think there is anybody in the world who knows him [Deedat] better than me because I am in his shoes now. He had no option. What he has done for the Muslim umma is immeasurable. Muslims have forgotten that it was a single man taking on the full might of the Christian missionaries. I mean it. All the Muslim 'ulama, what did they do? He inspired thousands of Muslim youngsters. Because of his effort, the Muslims are proud of Islam. Only if you were in his shoes and in the field, you will understand the way he talked. Actually if you were doing da'wah you will never say that he should have done things differently.[25]

For Deedat, 1988 began with a prominent Saudi businessman, Abdul Maksood, holding a banquet on 4 January to recognise Deedat's 'services to Islam'. Deedat addressed around two hundred Saudi businessmen, dignitaries, and Islamic scholars, to whom he asked the following question: 'If the Prophet had our petro-dollars and the printing presses we have at our disposal, would he not have churned out millions upon millions of Qur'ans and Islamic literature to flood the world?'[26] From 13 to 19 June of that year, Deedat toured the UK, lecturing at Cambridge University, Wembley Stadium, and the London Central Mosque near Regent's Park. From 22 to 29 June, he went on a follow-up tour to Mumbai where he

A highlight of Deedat's travels in the Middle East was his July 1988 meeting with Prince Sultan Bin-Salman Abdul Aziz, the first Muslim to visit space.

delivered six lectures. He was introduced to enthusiastic audiences as 'Darling Dynamite', 'Staunch Defender of Islam', 'The Dashing Mujahid of God', and 'A Real Living Omar Mukhtar' (in reference to the Libyan freedom fighter who organised resistance against Italian occupation of Libya for two decades until he was captured and hanged in 1931).

Deedat also presented talks on several television channels in the Middle East, which he visited under the auspices of Rabitat al-Alam al-Islami (the World Muslim League). As Deedat's reputation grew, the crew of a UAE television station visited South Africa to cover his work. Another highlight for Deedat was his July 1988 meeting with Prince Sultan Salman Abdul Aziz, the first Muslim to visit space.[27]

In August 1988, Deedat was back in the UK where twelve thousand people attended his five-hour public debate with Dr Anis Shorrosh at the Birmingham National Exhibition Centre. On 9 November 1988, Deedat, who was now referred to as 'Faisal Laureate', lectured at Jeddah's Industrial Training Centre at the invitation of businessman Tanweer Zaman. The two thousand seats were taken up within minutes of the hall being opened. Closed-circuit television broadcast his speech to adjacent rooms that housed double that number. Deedat spoke to the audience about 'Contemporary Christian Evangelistic Deception'. He focused on 'attempts at deceit by those who claim to be followers of Jesus'.[28]

Early in 1989, Deedat was back at Jeddah's Industrial Training Centre, where several princes attended his talk under the auspices of the Muslim World League and the Forum of Social Studies on the Collusion of Jews and Christians against Muslims in Palestine.[29]

Deedat's visit to Sweden in October 1991, where he debated with Pastor Stanley Sjoberg on the topic 'Is Jesus God?', was his first tour of a Scandinavian country. Prior to his departure Deedat sent an open letter to his Muslim supporters for their 'duas that Allah (SWT) gives me guidance, strength, wisdom, and victory so that the Trust and beauty of Islam prevails'. He debated against Erik Bock of Denmark on the same topic. Deedat toured Malaysia and Indonesia in February and March 1992. In December 1994 he met with the president of the United Arab Emirates, Shaykh Zayed bin Sultan Al-Nahyan, at the presidential guesthouse in Rawdat Al Reef. Deedat described the shaykh to a reporter of *Khaleej Times* as one of 'the most prominent, sincere and faithful' leaders in the Islamic world, and praised him for his commitment to the cause of Muslims everywhere, especially Bosnia-Herzegovina.[30] He visited Canada in July 1994, the UK in 1995, and Australia in April 1996.

This anecdote from Ebi Lockhat shows that Deedat left no stone unturned:

> In 1991, I think it was, I got a call from Ahmed Deedat while he was visiting Saudi Arabia and then the UK. It was part of his modus operandi that, when he undertook a lecture tour, he would go to his well-wishers and tell them about his upcoming tour, etc. It was his way of raising funds by showing his supporters what he was doing. So I got a call from Saudi Arabia and he said to me, 'It's Uncle here and I want you to be my chairman in my talks in London.' I got to London thinking there must have been some special assignment. When we went to the talks I had to introduce Deedat, I had to chair his Q&A session in the same pattern that he lined up here, one question at a time. I asked him after the second or third day, 'Look here, Uncle, you've brought me from South Africa, but what work am I doing here? Firstly, I'm not an orator, that's your job. Secondly, the English born Muslim here has a better command of the English language so why did you want me to come all the way from South Africa to do exactly the same thing that he could do?' He said to me that he had been sabotaged previously. 'What do you mean?' He says, 'Well, in one of my previous trips I came to a meeting. Before I could go to the talk, I had paid for the publicity, etc. from South Africa. This person from the local organising committee stands up and when he introduces me, he goes on to a little speech about why they don't agree with Brother Deedat's method of preaching but since he's a guest they still welcome him.' So he says to me in typical Deedat language, 'the guy gave me a knock-out below the belt before I even started.' He then told me that during the same tour he had another talk that was lined up on a Sunday and he had paid for the venue and this particular hall was full of people and 'what I hadn't known is that the organisers were having their in-fighting between the trustees and I was working with the people who I thought were the organisers, they indeed were, but because they never had this kind of audience before, the guy spent forty-five minutes explaining their plans for the future, etc.'. So he said, 'I thought about it while I was in Saudi Arabia and felt that I'm paying for it, I rather have my own man because he's not going to stab me in the back and that's why that call to you.'

Deedat's travels, like his mission generally, sparked much controversy. In October 1989, for example, he was criticised for meeting with Idi Amin in Jeddah. Deedat was, however, impressed by Amin's knowledge of South African politics, noting that Amin was aware of the sacrifices of Ahmed Timol, Imam Haron, Ahmed Kathrada and Yusuf Cachalia.[31] Deedat undertook a lecture tour of Malaysia and Indonesia in February and March 1992. He delivered twenty-six public lectures and met with government officials in Brunei. He had been invited by the Ummah Resources of Kuala Lumpur, which had to clear the visit with Prime Minister Mahathir who imposed strict conditions:

> He should avoid making comparison with other religions or criticising them when speaking in open public lectures. Any criticism toward other religions will create ill feelings, hostility and problems among their followers. In these open places, it is preferable that the speaker should focus his talk on Islam. He should explain about the goodness and truth of Islam without making reference to the shortcomings and weaknesses of other religions. Where talks are performed in closed doors specifically for Muslims, the speaker can give his explanation by making comparison with other religions.[32]

According to Professor Salman Nadvi, these strict conditions were probably due to the fact that on a previous visit, Deedat warned the Malays that if they did not heed his advice, the '"Chinese will swallow you Malays up like malaai". Malaai means cream in Urdu. So the Chinese didn't like it, the government didn't like it, and they restricted him.'

In 1992, Deedat flew to Nigeria which has a long history of ethnic and religious tension. When he landed in Kano, a predominantly Muslim state in the north, Deedat and his son Yousuf were separated from other passengers and asked to submit their passports to airport authorities who declared him a 'prohibited immigrant'. Deedat had been invited to Nigeria to counter the activities of Jehovah's Witnesses and was shocked at the decision to ban him. He was irked that South African President F.W. de Klerk, 'a representative of the white man who had been oppressing the black man in my country was given a royal welcome in Nigeria with a 21-gun salute, the highest you can give any man'.[33] Nigeria's barring of Deedat happened in the context of ongoing tensions between Muslims who are dominant in the north and Christians who predominate in the south. In October 1991, fighting between Muslim Hausa youths and Christian Igbo traders in Kano had been sparked by the visit of the German Christian evangelist preacher Reverend Reinhard Bonnke. Muslim youth were upset because Babangida's military regime had previously refused both Deedat and Louis Farrakhan permission to visit. Deedat had a large following in Kano where his videos were 'circulated widely in the underground.'[34] In May 1992, around the time that Deedat was to visit, a land dispute in the northern state of Kaduna led to fighting and church burnings, with over two hundred people killed.[35] The authorities feared that the situation would spiral out of control if Deedat was allowed to visit.

In October 1993, Deedat was interrogated at the Charles De Gaulle Airport for three hours and refused entry into France even though he had a valid visa, on the grounds that he constituted 'a public threat'. The IPCI formally protested to the French Consulate in Johannesburg that the incident had caused 'considerable anguish and embarrassment'. Ebi Lockhat, the IPCI Liaison Officer, complained that Deedat's

> dignity and standing in the international community has suffered irreparable harm. As a man of peace he has remained apolitical and never advocated interference in the political affairs of other nations...Your government's action was unjust, indefensible and against the very ideals it fought so hard to preserve: liberty, fraternity and equality.[36]

In 1994, Deedat visited Canada, where he spoke in Vancouver on 8 July and in Toronto on 17 July. In Toronto he was to debate Bishop-General Wakefield on the topic 'Was Christ Crucified?' A pre-tour article in the 1 July 1994 issue of the Toronto-based *India Journal* promised that 'both events would be full of fire and brimstone'. Several hundred supporters welcomed Deedat's entourage. According to the *India Journal* (22 July 1994), the event attracted six thousand people. Outside the venue, representatives of various Muslim and Christian groups handed out literature and pamphlets while 'Deedat Tour-'94' t-shirts were on sale. Reporter Ahsan Khan wrote that 'the entire evening was held in a civilised and respectful manner. From listening to the conversations of people after the debate, it was obvious that people were enthusiastic to learn more.'

Deedat received certificates from prominent (non-Muslim) Canadians such as the mayor of Brampton and the minister of citizenship, as well as several Muslim organisations. He caused controversy, however, when he called Canadian Muslims 'cowards...timid sheep and goats' for failing to wear the traditional topi (headgear) and to proclaim their Islamic heritage; in comparison 'the turbaned Sikhs look like lions, the rest of us look like sheep and goats, afraid to be identified'.[37]

When Deedat toured Australia in April 1996, in what to be his last public appearance, he praised Australia's Lebanese Muslims for inviting him:

> The worst guy in the whole world in sight of the Christian is me, in the eyes of the Jews or Hindus is me, in the eyes of the Muslims, they say this guy is causing trouble. So I come. On Friday, I want to arrange a meeting on Good Friday. Alhamdulillah, the Muslims are strong here, otherwise the Muslims would have spat me out, you know that? They would say Uncle, don't upset them, you know we are having a good time here. These Australian girls, and we have good jobs, and we get the dole here too. It is far better, we are in heaven here compared to Lebanon, please don't disturb the apple cart, Mr Deedat, go back to South Africa.[38]

Venues in Sydney, Melbourne, Brisbane, and Preston were filled to capacity during his lectures, which were covered in the national media. On Good Friday, Deedat spoke in Sydney on 'A Muslim Viewpoint: What Makes a Good Friday Good.' *The Australian* labelled him a 'Bible-basher', and many Australians saw the tour as provocative as Deedat argued that Jesus did not die on Easter Friday. Sydney's Wesley Central Mission head, Dr Gordon Moyes, was 'scandalised' and wondered how Muslims would react if Christian activists targeted the beginning of Ramadan with an evangelistic talkfest. Deedat retorted: 'What do they expect us to talk about during Easter, Mahatma Gandhi?'[39]

An Australian immigration officer, Ian Campbell, threatened Deedat with deportation under a section of the immigration law that prohibited fostering 'discord among any group by a visiting party'. Deedat insisted that he would continue his tour 'until we have got our Muslim point of view across on the death of Christ'.[40] Deedat's 'passionate' Good Friday talk was even mentioned on the official website of the government of New South Wales, which recorded the following reference to him during a debate on racism:

> Of course, other victims of racism are often Australians who are visibly different, especially women who wear Muslim attire. While I condemn such attacks, I also condemn attacks against Christians by Muslims who come to Australia to sow the seed of religious hatred. In this regard I refer to Islamic evangelist Shaykh Ahmed Deedat, a South African who, on Good Friday, spoke about Easter, indulged in Bible-bashing and incited racial hatred. I am all for freedom of speech, but our leaders should show some understanding and, above all, respect for the views and beliefs of others. Australia can do without people like Shaykh Deedat.[41]

Keysar Trad attended Deedat's lectures and had several discussions with him:

> Ahmed Deedat visited at the invitation of IPCI Australia and one of the Sydney groups arranged private meetings to which I was invited. I handed Shaykh Deedat a stack of papers, which represented internet discussions between me and non-Muslims about Islam and other ideologies. The next time that I saw him was in the afternoon of the same day on which I handed those papers to him. I was amazed to hear from him, 'I like the way you use your mind.' When I handed the papers to him I did not know what to expect as my style was completely different. As I reflect on his comments today I know that what he meant was that the style needs to be flexible in order to remove the differing barriers that the other person erects in your face. Each person who crosses your path is different and each person requires an individualised approach even if they may fall into broad categories of particular styles. There were two other meetings with Ahmed Deedat. One was to be trained by him in a gathering. Every person in that training session received their own copy of the red letter Gideon Bible's and we went through a number of passages. Each time Ahmed Deedat highlighted how these particular passages impacted on Christianity. This was probably one of the most informative training sessions that any person is likely to attend. Ahmed Deedat showed many facets of his personality, he showed his depth of knowledge, his sense of humour, his care, not only for fellow Muslims but for humanity at large, and his analytical brilliance in analysing 'religious' discourse.

Deedat's Australian tour was to be his last. A month after his return he suffered the stroke that left him completely paralysed. Deedat's exhausting overseas tours after the Swaggart debate, when he was already in his seventies, may have reinforced his global reputation but they eventually took their toll on his health. According to Ebi Lockhat:

> This was the time where perhaps Deedat needed a strategist with him, [someone who would say] 'Look, you are getting old, you will have a stroke, You can only manage two tours a year. Do this as it is your core business. Who's your successor? What succession planning?' That was all put on the backburner because it was just go, go, go…We get an invite to Malaysia, we go; we get an invite to Australia, we go; we get an invite to Nigeria, we go. We get an invite to the UK, we go. In the end it all got too much even for him.

While Deedat stirred controversy in many parts of the world, there was one particular foreign expedition that received enormous publicity, and that was his visit to the UK and USA to rebut Salman Rushdie's *The Satanic Verses*. This tour was another of those occasions when Deedat veered from his favourite topic – the Bible – and both his supporters and detractors were critical. His detractors felt that he was meddling in issues about which he had no expertise, while his supporters feared that his core mission was suffering as a result of these distractions.

# 19
# RUSH-DIE?

Rushdie is a hypocrite. First, he writes obscenities against everybody and when he finds that life has become difficult for him to live, he appears on TV and puts on the apologising act. He is a hypocrite and has blasphemed holy personalities. He should not be pardoned.

– Ahmed Deedat[1]

*S*ALMAN RUSHDIE'S *THE SATANIC VERSES* created a worldwide storm when it was released in September 1988. The publishers received thousands of letters and phone calls requesting the withdrawal of the novel, the government of India banned the book, with Bangladesh, Sudan, South Africa, Sri Lanka, Kenya, Thailand, Tanzania, Indonesia, Singapore, and Venezuela following suit. Protest marches were held in London, Bradford, Islamabad, Tehran, Bombay, New York, Dhaka, Istanbul, and Khartoum.

The symbolic burning of copies of the book by Muslims in Bradford in January 1989, followed by the fatwa sentencing Rushdie to death issued by Ayatollah Khomeini, caused Western critics to portray Muslims as fanatical 'medieval fundamentalists' who opposed Western 'liberal' and 'democratic' values. This marked the beginning of what has been termed 'religious racism' against Muslims, or Islamophobia as it is more commonly known.[2] According to political theorist Bhiku Parekh, anti-Muslim reaction in Britain began as 'a wholly mindless anger first against all Bradford Muslims, then against all British Muslims, then against all Muslims, and ultimately against Islam itself'.[3]

Many Muslims regarded *The Satanic Verses* as a blasphemous novel by a self-proclaimed atheist. In the book, Rushdie discusses religion through the two main protagonists, Saladin Chamcha and Gibreel Farishta, who represent the opposite poles of good and evil. As the novel develops, Gibreel loses his faith and commits suicide to free himself from his confusion while the 'evil' Saladin becomes increasingly content. Islam is discussed through Gibreel's dreams. As the Pakistani-born London-based writer and cultural critic Ziauddin Sardar and the Welsh Muslim writer and broadcaster Merryl Wyn Davies point out,

> dreams are Rushdie's stratagem for presenting his own ideas…without having to acknowledge the limits of propriety, respect for the sensitivity of others or the complexity of historical records. Most of all, the dream stratagem enables him to play with historical fact, spicing the novel with a grand sufficiency of historical detail to establish his credentials without having to be responsible to accuracy, or honesty, in handling these facts.[4]

While much of the narrative is factually inaccurate, critics such as Sardar and Davies were concerned readers might accept the novel as fact. Rushdie refers to the Prophet Muhammad (PBUH) by the derogatory term Mahound, which is defined by one dictionary as 'a contemptuous name for Mohammed; hence, an evil spirit; a devil'. He also refers to characters as Hadith, Salman the Persian, and the Prophet's (PBUH) wives in abusive language such as 'bunch of riff-raff' and 'goons'. Such language and naming fills the novel and many Muslims took offence at the disrespect shown for figures that they revere. The Prophet's (PBUH) wives are depicted as indecent, while the Prophet (PBUH) is accused of changing revelations.

Egyptian Zaki Badawi, a past editor of *Islamic Quarterly*, equated *The Satanic Verses* to 'a knife being dug into you – or being raped yourself'.[5] Sardar and Davies state that it was as if Rushdie had 'personally assaulted and raped every single believing Muslim man and woman'.⁶ Ali Mazrui, the Kenyan-born pan-Africanist scholar, related an analogy given to him in Islamabad: 'It's as if he has composed a brilliant poem about the private parts of his parents, and then gone to the market place to recite that poem to the applause of strangers.'⁷ For the Oxford-based author Richard Webster such comments 'help to locate the obscenities of *The Satanic Verses* in a human context and to convey…Muslim feelings that in the novel Islam is the victim not simply of criticism and satire but an act of cultural rape'.⁸ According to Timothy Brennan, lecturer in literature at the University of Minnesota, Rushdie, as an 'insider/outsider', used 'the knowledge he has of Islam to hurt Muslims where it hurts most…he exploits what he understands Muslims hold most sensitive'. Rushdie 'knew all the pressure points and went about pressing them'.⁹

Deedat entered the fray by publishing a booklet and undertaking an international lecturing tour. He later said that he became drawn into the affair because of the clumsy Muslim reaction to Rushdie in the UK. Time and distance from the immediate hysteria, he said, allowed him to formulate a cogent response. According to Deedat, no one in Britain seemed capable of articulating the root causes of Muslim anger. Deedat claimed that he saw on television a reporter asking a young Muslim why he was angry and the 'young man was going through hell'. After some deliberation the Muslim replied that Rushdie had used the word 'Bhen-Chud'. Deedat scoffed at this. He said that the fifty million people watching the programme in the West had no idea what this term meant and remained ignorant of the motives for Muslim protest. Shamshad Khan, a British friend of Deedat's, told him that Pakistanis were being taunted in the streets of Yorkshire and that Muslim leaders were afraid to speak out. Deedat decided to take action.

Deedat read *The Satanic Verses* from cover to cover and published a twenty-four-page booklet titled 'How Rushdie Fooled the West' in which he set out to show that Rushdie not only insulted Muslims but also Londoners, the queen, Margaret Thatcher, Hindus, and white women. Deedat was pleased that *The Satanic Verses* had been banned in South Africa. He told reporter Owen Bowcott of *The Guardian* that 'in a country where we form two per cent of the population and have no vote and no voice we were able to perform a miracle and get the book banned'.¹⁰ A year of protest by British Muslims had failed to evoke a similar response from the British government.

Deedat undertook a lecture tour of the Cape from 20 June to 12 July 1989 on the topic 'Should Rush-Die Die? What is the Judeo-Christian Verdict?' He argued his case from the point of view of Christians and Jews so as not to make it a Muslim issue. He also challenged Colin Gardner (from the University of Natal) and Andre Brink (from Rhodes University), who had both argued against the banning of the book, to debate the issue of freedom of speech.¹¹ Both men ignored his challenge.

Rushdie's book sparked anger among many South African Muslims as well. When Rushdie was invited to speak on censorship at the November 1988 *Weekly Mail* Book Week Farid Choonara, director of the African Muslim Agency, Iqbal Jassat, and Imthiaz Jhetham convened a meeting in Lenasia, Johannesburg, to organise protest against the visit. They met with the organisers of the Book Week, Anton Harber and Irwin Manoim, who initially refused to withdraw the invitation. The organisers later changed their minds on the grounds that they could not guarantee Rushdie's safety. 'Loud-mouthed local extremists prevent Rushdie from coming to South Africa', wrote the *Star*'s book editor, James Mitchell, in response, while Booker Prize winner J.M. Coetzee referred to Muslim opponents of the visit as 'terrorists' who had no place in the anti-apartheid struggle because of their opposition to free speech.[12] Deedat questioned why, if these people were so concerned about freedom of speech, they did not speak out when the mainstream media had denied him the opportunity to express his views on the Palestinian question. Deedat toured the UK and USA during October and November 1989. A master publicist, he had extensively advertised the tour even before arriving at Heathrow. He offered to to pay BBC television £50 000 for five minutes of airtime to demonstrate that Rushdie's novel was racist and insulting to the British. The offer was turned down but his visit was covered in local newspapers such as *The Independent*. Deedat argued that *The Satanic Verses* was not an attack on Islam per se but on other denominations as well, and that everyone should join in the criticism of Rushdie. He disagreed with Muslims who were upset that Rushdie had 'sworn at our mothers, our fathers, our spiritual mentors, our Sahabah'. If Muslims cried about themselves, the authorities would say,

> Good luck to you. You are a people who have been a challenge to us for over a thousand years. You conquered Christian lands. And even now when we are down and out, we tell them, 'no drinking, no alcohol, no gambling, no eating pig'. We have been a thorn in their side. Now that one of our own has put a pineapple up our backside, he [the white man] is getting sadistic pleasure. You wail, you march, you complain…he's happy.

Deedat called on Muslims to turn the tables and say, 'Look Saheb, this is what he is saying about you.' Deedat was especially keen that British academics and intellectuals should attend his lectures, as he told *The Independent* newspaper:

> Rushdie has been taking you British for a ride. He had made monkeys of you. He eats your food and you are godfathers to him. Yet he shits in the pot from which he eats. I am asking the Englishman, what are his standards? What does he think of this? I want the giants of literature to come. I want all those people who signed in defence of Rushdie to come and debate with me. I want the British to read the book and see what it says about them. I want your reaction. Then you will understand our feelings.[13]

Deedat hired the Royal Albert Hall and over five thousand people attended the lecture. His original subject was to have been 'How Rushdie fooled the West' but because the British press refused adverts under that title, he changed it to 'A Challenge to the Giants of British Literature'. According to reporter Owen Bowcott, Deedat, 'who appeared to be preaching almost exclusively to the faithful, refused to denounce the death sentence pronounced by

Ayatollah Khomeini. His attack was delivered as a jovial lecture. A show of hands revealed that only one person in the hall had read the book.'[14]

Deedat was convinced that his strategy of showing the book up as racist and insulting to the British would work. He told the audience that while 'some claim the British have grown a thick skin, I say they are sensitive in highly selective areas'. He claimed that the F word appeared fifty-two times in the book, that one character fantasised about having sex with the queen, and that Margaret Thatcher was referred to as a 'bitch'. The Albert Hall lecture was followed by lectures in Bradford (2 October), Manchester (4 October), Leicester (5 October), and Birmingham (8 October). The organising committee in England included members of Young Muslims UK and IPCI Birmingham.

Deedat filled London's Royal Albert Hall when he lectured there on Salman Rushdie's book, *The Satanic Verses*.

Deedat sent a copy of his essay 'Can you Stomach the Best of Rushdie?' with an open letter dated 28 October 1989 to Margaret Thatcher, who was the British prime minister at the time. The three-page letter pointed out that Rushdie referred to her as 'Mrs Torture' and 'Maggie the Bitch' and asked:

> Maybe you can stomach it Ma'am, because you are truly great. But how about the feelings of your son Mark Thatcher? What if he is called 'The son of a bitch'. And how about the feelings of Carol [Thatcher], what if she is called 'The daughter of a bitch'. And what about the British Muslims, how can they tolerate the head of their government being abused and insulted in this way?...Then there is also the question of the Muslim vote. British Muslims are watching and whichever party either bans or promises to ban this book, will, I am sure, get their votes...A solution has to be found, either in the form of extending blasphemy law or the introduction of new laws.

Deedat was criticised by some British Muslims for his approach. Ahmed Andrews of Derby University, writing in *Crescent International*, claimed that the average British citizen did not care about such insults since newspapers such as *The Sun* and the magazines *Punch* and *Private Eye* consistently ridiculed the British; in fact, native Britons 'may even applaud what they perceive as cleverness'.[15] Andrews questioned whether Deedat's loyalty was to 'Islam or to the Queen?...Why is he so vehemently defending the queen, who is head of the Church of England, rather than defending the honour of Islam?' Since Rushdie insulted the Prophet (PBUH) and his wives, how could Deedat 'claim that this is not an Islamic issue?' Andrews was critical that Deedat's booklet, which contained many swear words, was distributed at meetings and circulated by parents 'with little or no knowledge of the English language, to their children'.[16]

There was opposition to Rushdie's book and to Deedat's booklet among some Muslims in South Africa. Abdullah Deedat, for example, told reporters that it

> was the biggest load of squalor and filth yet to be penned by a Muslim. It would appear that my brother wanted to outdo Rushdie as far as vulgarity is concerned. He is supposed to reason with grace. Instead the booklet contains wild swearing against the publishers and everyone who sides with the British author.[17]

On the two-week tour of the USA that took place from 2 to 16 November 1989, Deedat shared the platform with Betty Shabazz X, widow of slain civil-rights campaigner Malcolm X. He said that he was going on the tour to 'give new life to the anti-Rushdie campaign and kindle new protest [against Rushdie]'. On Friday, 3 November Deedat offered the jum'a prayer at the United Nations' offices, gave a talk after the prayer, and lunched with Muslim ambassadors. On 4 November he was guest of honour at the Masjid Fatime, where he handed out certificates to students who had completed a course under Hamza Abdul Malick. The anti-Rushdie programme was conducted under the auspices of the IPCI New York, and took place at Patterson College, New Jersey (5 November); University Center, Los Angeles (7 November); Holiday Inn, Chicago (9 November); and Queens College, New York (11 November). The lectures were well attended but the issue, and Muslims in general, did not generate the degree of negative publicity that was to emerge in the 1990s and intensify during the 'War on Terror'.

On his return from his month-long tour overseas tour, Deedat told *Sunday Tribune* reporter Vasantha Angamuthu that his 'fight with Rushdie is now over. I have tried to right the wrong done to humanity by Salman Rushdie's *Satanic Verses*. I can rest while my booklet spreads the message.'[18]

# 20

# FOR PROPHET OR PROFIT?

Reflecting the architecture of the nearby mosque in its impressive glass façade, the IPCI's new headquarters was intended to be a focus of worldwide attention.

Things changed when they moved to Sayani Centre. Within a few years it was a big organisation, more staff, more structured, more bureaucracy and Mr Deedat became absolutely famous. The family atmosphere was gone. The IPCI became a corporate. My dad felt that we had lost our soul.

– Shabaan Khan

*F*IVE HUNDRED of Durban's wealthiest Indian businessmen crammed into the Isaacs Geshen salesroom in Smith Street in March 1986 to bid for the Sayani Centre. The building, at the corner of Grey and Queen Streets, was up for auction. Owned by the Moosa Hajee Cassim family for almost a century, it was described in the advertising brochure as 'arguably the most prestigious in the Grey Street Complex, the heart of the Indian commercial district'. Auctioneer Trevor Warman's remark 'Gentlemen, I have only one serious question to ask before we begin. Who is looking after the shops in Grey Street while you are all here?' reflected the unprecedented interest in the sale.

Seated among the business executives were Yusuf Ally and A.T. Rasool, who were representing the IPCI. Deedat was in the Middle East collecting the King Faisal Award. It was Ebrahim Jadwat who suggested that the IPCI purchase the building. When the property became available, he explained to Deedat that if he put down a deposit, rental income would cover the repayments. This would allow the IPCI to create a sustainable waqf (endowment) and use the income generated from the rental for future projects. Rasool, experienced in the property market, was given a private valuation of R6 million and Deedat gave them the go-ahead to bid up to this amount. Ironically, one of the IPCI's main opponents in the bidding process was south-coast property developer and businessman G.H. Kadwa, whose father had provided the land on which As-Salaam was built. Ally and Rasool outbid Kadwa and the other businessmen at R4.75 million – the highest price paid for a property in the Grey Street CBD up to that point.

After acquiring the property, Deedat humbly reflected that he was 'reminded of the fact that we started our Centre with a mere R6.50. Today, we are a multi-million-rand organisation. However, we are inspired by the same thoughts with which we began.'[1] He emphasised that the building belonged to the 'worldwide Muslim community' since many Muslims had assisted with its purchase.[2] Deedat also pointed to the metamorphosis in the organisation's fortunes when he told reporters that he and Vanker were earning a pittance when they started the IPC under difficult circumstances: 'I can remember whenever we had to print a handbill we had to have endless meetings to discuss costs and ways and means of raising money.'[3]

In addition to the record price paid for the building, Deedat spent an additional R2.5 million to refurbish it. Renovations began in June 1989 under the supervision of architect Cassim Kadwa. An additional floor and an auditorium were added. The large glass facade on the Queen Street side reflected the Jumu'ah Mosque that stood across the road. The 'brilliant idea of having the minaret of the Jumu'ah Masjid reflecting onto the IPCI building', Deedat told reporters, 'captured my imagination. For the first time in many years I had the feeling that something extraordinary was about to be undertaken.'[4] Deedat hoped that the eight-metre shatterproof gold-tinted glass in the top portion of the building would add to the 'beauty and splendour of the CBD and encourage other property owners to renovate their buildings'. For Deedat, the glass had both an aesthetic and a spiritual function: 'In a world dominated by materialistic inclinations, the first impression is the lasting one.

The building would dominate the surroundings, emitting an aura of power. This is what attracts the modern man. He will be impressed and make the first step towards inquiry.'[5]

Deedat wanted the new IPCI to 'be the focus of world attention'.[6] The design, he added, ensured that 'Islamic identity could be projected and instantly recognised. Muslims have always been world leaders and trendsetters in the field of architecture. Egyptians laid down the basic fundamentals and principles of building techniques and planning. Their pyramids and historical monuments that carry the Muslim signia stand firmly in India, Spain and Turkey.'[7]

The Sayani Centre was initially renamed the Bin Laden Centre after the major donor, the Bin Laden family of Saudi Arabia, who had built a fortune in the construction industry in Saudi Arabia,[8] but the name of Bin Laden was subsequently removed because the family did not wish to attract publicity from its contribution. Following the 9/11 attacks on the World Trade Center in New York, the international media remembered Deedat's link with the family. Bala A. Muhammad, a Nigerian student who was studying at the University of Natal, recalled:

> In the aftermath of 9/11, everyone seemed to remember that old name. A plethora of journalists from all over the world descended on Shaykh Deedat's home, wanting to know [his] relationship with the Bin Laden family and, ostensibly, with Osama. It was speculated in the South African media that Yousuf, the Shaykh's son, was a personal friend of Osama. And so it was that I was visiting Shaykh Deedat when a French television network arrived early in October 2001. The first question was: 'Did Shaykh Deedat know the Bin Laden family?' He answered: 'Yes. I did know the Bin Laden family quite closely. In fact, the most senior Bin Laden, had contributed the largest chunk of money during the building of the IPCI. Therefore, when the building was completed, we felt that we should name it Bin Laden Centre, and we did. The senior Bin Laden humbly declined the honour. So we reluctantly had to remove the family's name.' 'But has Shaykh Deedat personally met Osama bin Laden?' At this question, the Shaykh's eyes shone and he smiled before he answered, using his eyes, interpreted by Yousuf. 'Yes,' Shaykh Deedat said, 'I did meet Osama, a rather shy, respectful young man. One day when I was visiting Shaykh Muhammad bin Laden, his brother Osama was sitting not too far away. He showed interest in what we were discussing, but did not utter a word since his comments were not sought. Such decorum, such respect to elders. It was after our conversation that the senior Bin Laden called Osama closer and introduced him to me as his brother just back from the Afghan jihad. That was the first and last time I met Osama.'[9]

The IPCI's new headquarters were designed to project its 'international' status. The King Faisal Prize and high-profile debates procured large contributions from the Middle East. In July 1987, for example, after visiting Saudi Arabia, Abu Dhabi, and the United Arab Emirates, Deedat proclaimed that the pledges that he had received had put the total repayment of the loan for the purchase of the building 'within reach'. Shaykh Sultan Bin Muhammad al-Kasim of Sharjah, who received Deedat at his palace, was one of the benefactors. Deedat told a reporter in June 1989 that 'the Arabs support me – to put it simply, they have bought me, so I can spend their money in spreading the word of Islam'.[10] He attributed his success to the Swaggart debate. For example, he pointed out, 'a man in Saudi Arabia saw the tape. At the time I had bought our present headquarters and still owed R3 million on the building. I received a phone call from the man who…agreed to pay off the balance of the building. I didn't ask him but he also paid for a property across the road.'[11]

Within a few years of the Swaggart debate, the IPCI had raised millions of rands, much of which was used to purchase properties. The Rajab Centre in Victoria Street, which included the Shiraz Cinema, was purchased for R3.375 million. It was transformed into the 'Ibrahim al-Ibrahim Centre' in honour of its Saudi sponsor. In August 1988 the IPCI acquired a property in Smithers Road, Stanger, for R2.9 million and in October 1988 purchased another commercial property in Sydney Road (Minolta House) for R1.2 million.

Many non-Muslims were concerned by the growth of the IPCI, and sensationalist headlines fuelled local tensions. The *Sunday Tribune*'s caption 'Middle East millions poured into Grey Street' implied an Arab 'invasion' of South Africa aimed at proselytising.[12]

Within a few years of the Swaggart debate, the IPCI had raised millions of rands, much of which was used to purchase properties such as the Shiraz Cinema which was converted into an auditorium and used for lectures and cultural functions.

Ahmed Deedat with Ahmad Totonji, who has been described as Deedat's key to the international stage.

Reporter Nagoor Bissetty warned that 'the thousands of rands collected in rents each month from the Sayani and Rajab buildings are to be used to propagate Islam and spread its message'. Deedat added fuel to the fire when he concurred that rental income would be used for 'propagating Islam'.[13] The conversion of the Shiraz Cinema, for so long a vibrant feature of the Grey Street complex and a meeting place for Indian socialites, into the Abdul Aziz Auditorium, which was to be used for Islamic lectures and cultural functions, seemed to confirm the worst fears of many non-Muslims. Deedat dedicated the auditorium 'to the Ladies of the Muslim Ummah'.[14]

Deedat's publicising his fundraising abilities did not help matters. When he returned from a visit to the Middle East in December 1988, during which he had lunched with King Fahd at his palace and delivered lectures in Riyadh, Jeddah, and Taif to what he termed 'Arabs hungry for knowledge', a local newspaper headline blazed 'Deedat back with bulging purse'. Deedat did not disappoint the reporter when he said that there was 'money in the Middle East. And the Arabs give without counting.'[15]

Between 1985 and 1988, Dr Totonji and the World Assembly of Muslim Youth (WAMY) assisted Deedat's fundraising efforts by introducing him to potential Arab benefactors. such as the Bin Laden family, the Al Rajhi Co., Abdul Ghani Al Ajoo, Shaykh Al Amir, Shaykh

*In his large new office at the IPCI, Deedat received a stream of high-profile personalities from abroad; seen here is a delegation from Saudi Arabia's Islamic Propagation Guidance Centre.*

Mohammed Al Jomaih, Dr Abdul Rehman Al Zamil, and many other donors. He also helped to negotiate a loan from Dr Yamani's Iqraa Charitable Society in Jeddah. Shaykh Abd al-Aziz Bin Baz and Mohammed al-Tuwaijri also assisted Deedat in securing funding. Deedat was highly appreciative and always thanked his benefactors. Thus on 16 February 1988, Deedat, who had adopted the practice of signing off his letters as 'Servant of Islam', thanked Shaykh Bin Baz (who was the head of the council of 'ulama in Saudi Arabia):

> It is indeed a great privilege and honour for our Centre to have an eminent person like your good self influencing prominent men and families to help us financially in order to realise our goals in the field of da'wah which we are humbly committed to. We pray that Allah may grant you long life, health and happiness to serve the Ummah so that it may once again take its rightful place as leaders of mankind.

Through these contacts Deedat met other influential people such as Solaiman D. Angad, Asma Raieq Al-Sayef, and Mahmoud Ahmed (King Faisal Hospital – Fiscal Department); Ishaak Ibrahim Nuamah; Bashir Osman Mahdi (King Khalid University Hospital); Mohammed Akbar Siddiqui (Ministry of Petroleum); Polangi Micunug (AMNCO Co. Ltd.); and Abdullah Rayq Al Musri (Ministry of Commerce), among others.

On 6 April 1988, Dr Totonji complimented Deedat on making 'good headway with our brothers in Saudi Arabia and the response is very encouraging. I am glad that you have already overcome many of the financial problems and Insha Allah you will achieve great success.'

Deedat continued to write, inspired and enabled by the constant flow of funding to produce new work.

On 28 November 1988, Deedat thanked Muhammad Al-Qudwah of Riyadh for

> uniting in the cause through your contribution to illuminate the world with the message and truth of deen-al-Islam. With the help of Almighty Allah and the support of those committed to His will, like your good self, it becomes possible for our Centre to exist and continue with all our efforts and endeavours. To us in the IPCI the name Muhammad Al-Qudwah is synonymous with hospitality, love and generosity.

Deedat did not confine his contact to the Middle East. He worked tirelessly with organisations and individuals in many parts of the world. Thus we also find him thanking Ali Ramadan of the International Institute of Islamic Thought in Virginia in the USA. When Deedat published *Muhammad* (PBUH) *the Greatest* he sent a copy to Ramadan in January 1991 with an accompanying letter, noting that

> the credit for this work belongs to Allah (swt) for guidance and the strength to complete the task, and to yourself. Yes! Your selfless support to the cause not only inspires me, but creates a heightened sense of responsibility which demands that I must continuously produce new works. Anything else means I will be letting you down.

*Al-Qur'an: The Miracle of Miracles* was sent in June 1991 with a note that Ramadan's 'unqualified support over the years serves as a constant reminder and incentive to strive further in the path of Islam. The perfect ideology of Al-Islam is the only ray of light and hope for the entire world. Let us be the torch bearers of this light.' Organisations such as WAMY, in turn, called on Deedat's expertise. In October 1987, WAMY secretary-general Dr Maneh al-Johani sent a copy of the London publication *Impact International* containing an article on anti-Muslim riots in India. 'We hope for your proper action towards this discrimination by the government and majority Hindus against Muslims.'

Dr Tawfik al-Kusayer of WAMY sent Deedat a paper in October 1987 titled 'Introduction to Islam and Muslim Evangelism', which was a 'missionary enhancement' paper prepared for the Malawi office of World Vision International. WAMY requested Deedat's comments on the threat that the article posed to 'less-informed' Muslims in Africa and 'suggestions to counter the threat'. In December 1987, Dr Totonji sent Deedat a letter from a Tanzanian, Omar Juma Msangi, requesting training to counter the 'missionary threat' in that country. Deedat arranged classes in Durban in March 1988, but the students were unable to attend because the Tanzanian government forbade them to do so. A disappointed Msangi replied:

> We wouldn't like to miss this wonderful and rare opportunity. It will be good also in future to consider the political restrictions of some countries concerning South Africa, hence choose a neutral country as a venue. Please send us any material, papers, cassettes, etc. from the programme. May you continue to walk in the shade of Allah's guidance.

Deedat duly obliged by sending a collection of his booklets and cassettes.

The roots of Saudi funding lay in the post-1973 oil boom, the establishment of the Islamic Republic of Iran in 1979, the takeover of the Masjid al-Haram in Makkah during the hajj in November 1979, and the Soviet invasion of Afghanistan in December 1979. In *The Shia Revival*, Vali Nasr makes the point that the Iranian Revolution sent tremors of fear racing through the conservative Arab regimes and instigated the growth of Saudi charities.

In the 1960s, Saudi Arabia had competed with Egypt for leadership of the Islamic world but, as Zaman put it, 'the prestige of al-Azhar University was no match for the oil resources of the Saudis.'[16] Saudi state and private aid has been channelled abroad to finance Islamic centres and mosques worldwide and establish academic chairs at universities. These include the King Fahd Chair in Islamic Shari'ah Studies at Harvard University's College of Law and the King Fahd Chair in Islamic Studies at the School of Oriental and African Studies in London.

Since the 9/11 attack on the World Trade Center in New York, Saudi patronage has come under intense scrutiny for possible links to terror activities. Philip Lewis expressed the view that Saudi Arabia 'was providing economic support to polemicism antithetical to serious engagement between Islam and Christianity'.[17] Such views are an oversimplification, according to Zaman:

There does not seem to be any direct correlation between Saudi patronage and the [Sunni] ulema's activism...We should be wary of any simplistic equation between Sunni militancy and Saudi support. Religio-political activism springs from a variety of causes and to reduce it to any single or overarching cause is to misunderstand its depth.[18]

Deedat was criticised in some South African quarters for allying himself to conservative pro-American Arab regimes. While Deedat emphasised that monies were donated by private businessmen and philanthropists and not Arab governments, critics such as Mohammed Makki and Abdullah Deedat insisted that Arab funding was aimed at rehabilitating their image among Muslims internationally and that Deedat was a willing pawn in their scheme. Abdullah Deedat was adamant that the funds compromised his brother's independence. During the Gulf War that followed the Iraqi invasion of Kuwait in August 1990, the IPCI stood firmly behind Kuwait. For this, Abdullah labelled Deedat

> [a] mercenary whose actions and utterances were motivated by monetary considerations alone. No Muslim in the whole of South Africa has expressed the same sentiments as my brother. He knows that if he speaks out against Saudi Arabia and Kuwait his pipeline will be shut.[19]

Deedat denied the allegation, emphasising repeatedly that he was funded by individual Saudis and not governments, and accusing Abdullah of lacking principles. Deedat argued that when Abdullah had worked for the IPCI he had been pro-Iranian and was critical of Saddam; 'Now what made him change overnight?'[20] Deedat placed advertisements in several publications calling on Saddam to 'withdraw from Kuwait if he wishes to avert a total devastation of Iraq'.[21]

Apart from these ideological battles, some individuals felt disquiet at the effect that petrodollars were having on Deedat and the IPCI. Zuleikha Mayat, who had a long association with Deedat as president of the Women's Cultural Group, recalled an incident where she and Deedat travelled to Dubai separately. While she had to go through lengthy customs procedures and wait for a taxi, a limousine pulled up and whisked him away. 'No customs, no carrying baggage, no formalities,' she noted. It dawned on her at that moment that Deedat did not need his local support base any longer. 'And when you don't need people, they don't need you,' she observed wryly, emphasising that she never had any personal problems with Deedat, who was always polite towards her and the Group.

Saudi oil wealth, some local critics felt, also muted other legitimate voices on Islam because the IPCI, with its financial muscle and media savvy, shaped perceptions of the Islamic viewpoint on a range of issues. Nevertheless, the IPCI's new headquarters was a splendid tribute to Deedat's achievements. For almost a decade Deedat thrived in this role until his ever-demanding schedule of lectures, media appearances, and international travel took their inevitable toll on his health.

# THE BEST OF TIMES, THE WORST OF TIMES: THE 1980s AND 1990s

*Thousands of Deedat's videos were distributed worldwide, but his constant travel and public exposure took a heavy toll in his later years.*

It was the best of times, it was the worst of times; it was the age of wisdom, it was the age of foolishness; it was the season of Light, it was the season of Darkness; it was the spring of hope, it was the winter of despair; we had everything before us, we had nothing before us...

— Charles Dickens, *A Tale of Two Cities*

CHARLES DICKENS' PASSAGE on the previous page provides an apposite description of the IPCI in the period from the mid-1980s to mid-1990s. The organisation experienced rapid growth but the optimism that resulted from the flow of money into its coffers gave way to perpetual conflicts that eventually led to an implosion within the organisation. Essentially, the IPCI had been run by three individuals – Deedat, Vanker, and Khan – for many years. By 1989, it suddenly had forty-six employees, seven trustees, and regularly called on the expertise of lawyers and accountants. The organisation had grown beyond the expectations of its founders yet lacked elementary corporate governance practices. This, together with the entry of new personnel and resulting personality clashes, created a dysfunctional environment. Organisational morale and productivity was deeply affected.

Of the forty-six staff employed at the IPCI in 1989, forty-five had worked there for less than two years. Shabir Basha was one of the 'Young Turks' who joined the IPCI in the 1980s. In his matric year, Basha was writing an English project on religion. He read Deedat's booklet *Who Moved the Stone?* and was so inspired that he visited the IPCI for more information. He met Deedat and chatted with him for almost an hour. Deedat gave him a few books to read and requested that he return within a week for a 'test'. Basha passed his 'test' and Deedat persuaded him to join the IPCI. At the time of writing, over two decades later, Basha was still employed by the IPCI as the office manager. Upon joining the IPCI, Basha, like all new employees, had to complete a Dale Carnegie course in public speaking to sharpen his speaking and presentation skills, and a typing course so that he could respond to the increasing volume of correspondence. Deedat valued professionalism.

Mahomed Khan, the present liason officer, started with the IPCI in 1990. Khan describes himself as a 'normal' teenager with no interest in da'wah who knew little about Deedat when he joined the organisation. He worked closely with Deedat's son Yousuf, handling his correspondence, banking, sorting out his itinerary for overseas tours, arranging visas, and sending thank-you cards, booklets, and DVDs to donors when Yousuf returned from fundraising trips. The likes of Khan and Basha had no connection to the past. Their relationship was mainly with Deedat and his son Yousuf, who employed them, trained them, and moulded them. Two decades on, Khan remains a vital part of the IPCI.

Khan remembers being bowled over by Deedat's 'warmth and generosity', recalling that Deedat would call him beta (son) and points to the similar impact that Deedat had on Zakir Naik, Dawood Ngwane, and Jamaluddin Ahmed. For Khan, the many moving letters that the IPCI receives from people all over the globe whose lives have been transformed as a result of Deedat, as well as the ongoing requests for Deedat's publications and DVDs from far-off places such as Papua New Guinea, Mexico, and Russia, underscore Deedat's magnetic personality and global reach. Khan's advice is as follows: 'Judge Mr Deedat for da'wah, not administration.'

A myriad of responsibilities sprang up with the growth of the IPCI. Ismail Sheik was employed to process foreign income, reconcile petty cash, and prepare wages and salary schedules; Ismail Pochee was hired to manage the nascent computer division; Shabeer Amra saw to the maintenance of buildings; and Fazlur Rehman Khan and Shabir Basha handled international correspondence.

G.H. Agjee, Abdullah Deedat, and Yusuf Ally; staff struggled to keep up with the large volume of mail that the IPCI received during the 1980s.

As Deedat became internationally recognised, the IPCI was receiving correspondence from over a hundred countries, including Romania, Fiji, Yugoslavia, Nigeria, China, Bolivia, Siberia, and Cyprus, which all had minority Muslim populations. A correspondence department was established to respond to mail. By 1990, the IPCI was mailing an average of three hundred letters daily, while at least two hundred requests were received each month for Deedat's literature.

Basha recalls that as long as mail had either 'IPCI' or 'Deedat' on the envelope, there was no need for an address as staff at Durban's Qualbert and West Street post offices knew the intended recipients. IPCI staff visited the post offices three times a day to send and receive mail. A large team received and recorded foreign and local mail, prepared replies, ensured that correspondence was sent without delay, and filed letters and replies. According to Basha, this was an intensive and exhaustive task and they often worked late into the night.

Deedat took public relations seriously and recruited Ebi Lockhat who had a reputation as a wordsmith. Ebi wrote letters as a favour for many local businessmen. In the late 1980s, a friend asked him to write a thank-you letter to the IPCI for donating Qur'ans. Deedat was so impressed with the letter that he asked to meet the writer. At the time Lockhat was a buyer for a large retail store and travelled overseas regularly on buying trips, but he could not resist Deedat's charm, as he explains:

> I go into the office and Ahmed Deedat welcomes me with his customary style. He says, 'Sit down' and I said, 'Ahmed Mota' and he said, 'Call me "Uncle".' He asked me to write a few letters on his behalf and eventually offered me a position full-time, which

I refused, and I said to him that I had my own work but he wouldn't let go..... I can see now why those other big heavyweights caved in against him.

Ebi shared Deedat's office:

> It started as a formal type of relationship but after a few days you become friends because you have your sandwich, you share your food, you share your thoughts, and that became one of the most vibrant times in my life from a knowledge point of view.

Ebi was struck by Deedat's simplicity, loyalty to friends and staff, directness in all pursuits, and 'immense power of concentration. When Ahmed Deedat read a book, he would sit at his desk and you could chat to him and later, when you spoke to him, you realised that he hadn't heard a word because his power to absorb what he was reading was so great.' Deedat's loyalty was another trait that Ebi admired, and he related an anecdote to illustrate this.

> Dr Khalid Mansoor came from America and Deedat asked me to put the programme together. We allowed different organisations to host him. A group of Muslim businessmen had a get-together on the Friday evening with Reserve Bank Governor Chris Stahls. It was a very influential meeting and since Dr Mansoor was a banker lawyer, Ahmed Deedat was invited to take him along. These were the Yale Club members. They had it at an Umhlanga hotel. They had very typical English style drinks, obviously non-alcoholic, where people stood, gathered, chatted and then the time came to start filtering into the hall and the organiser, I don't know if he had a personal gripe against me, suddenly said, 'Sorry, I won't let you in because Yousuf [Deedat] said he's coming with people and I did not make provision for you.' Rather than argue the point, I asked Yousuf Deedat for his keys to go nap in the car. Ahmed Deedat learnt about this before I could go and asked me to sit next to him. The organisers said, 'Ahmed Mota take your place.' He said, 'I'm waiting for Bhai's seat before I can go.' He didn't actually spell it out there but anybody could see the expression was, 'If he doesn't sit, I won't,' and only when the guy came in a bit of a huff and organised me a chair, did Ahmed Deedat sit down at the main table.

Ebi Lockhat, Cassim Deedat, and G.H. Agjee were the proverbial 'spin doctors' who studied the media daily and responded to the issues of the day. In late 1991, *The Leader* newspaper alleged that the IPCI was conducting a letter-writing campaign to defend itself from criticism. The IPCI issued a statement denying the allegations. Ebi Lockhat explained what happened:

> When Deedat took on this mantle of defender of the faith, it was 'all's fair in love and war'. And at that time he would say to the staff, 'Don't be afraid, write to the press, tell the press what you would do.' He said, write and tell them, even if you have to write under noms de plume. I was implicated because we did the letters and someone sent them off from the IPCI faxing machine. But what was very fortunate is that there were real people who authored those letters as opposed to one guy. I think it would

Projecting Islam to passersby. Crowds often gathered on the street outside the IPCI offices to watch Ahmed Deedat on video, while sophisticated recording equipment ensured that video tapes of his talks were distributed worldwide.

have been a real problem if there were letters produced under Ebrahim, Mohammed, Yusuf and they were from one person. So when they asked, 'Who is so and so?' they were there. They asked, 'Were you sending letters?' 'Yes, I did it in my lunch time,' so they had no answer to that. So yes, the staff did write letters but not on a specific instruction. It was a generalised thing…go for it, don't stand back, you know, he had the people quite hyped up.

Deedat embraced the audiovisual revolution locally through the 'Islamic Visions Programme', opening an auditorium in 1987 in West Street, once the heart of white Durban. Several street-level stores at the IPCI Centre in Queen Street were also converted into an eighty-square-metre auditorium in which Deedat's debates and lectures were broadcast. A daʻi (caller to Islam) was available at all times to answer questions. The power of Deedat is reflected in the fact that the hundred-seater auditorium was almost always full, while a large crowd gathered on the pavement to view the debates.

Deedat's debates and lectures, as well as those produced by the World Assembly of Muslim Youth (WAMY), and by prominent Muslims such as Yusuf Islam (formerly pop singer Cat Stevens), were played at the auditoriums. Thus, for example, Deedat wrote to Maneh al-Johani of WAMY in 1988 requesting more literature:

> We have in the history of South Africa opened the first Islamic Telecoms shop where Da'wah is given to passersby. Our Islamic videos and your WAMY series are shown. Reaction wonderful. Are now in position to project Islam to crowds that pass by. Alhamdulillah. Will be grateful if you could send us more of your beautiful series on Islam.

In 1991, the huge Shiraz Cinema in Victoria Street was converted into an auditorium, and Deedat's inaugural lecture drew a full house. This would be Deedat's swansong as far as his local audience was concerned. According to Ebi Lockhat:

> We did a lot of invites for the Abdul Aziz Auditorium's opening. We had built up a database in a very amateurish fashion. In those days we didn't have those word processors so we used to find any names in *al-Qalam* or whatever and keep adding. We sent out invites to all these people to come and celebrate the opening and that night when the auditorium opened, the number of people shaking hands and telling Deedat, 'Mr Deedat you forgot us,' 'How many years since we last came to your talk,' they were telling him these things and he felt good. He was telling me, 'These are our people, our people,' so there was a connection that evening.

That was Deedat's only lecture at the auditorium and although his international appearances contined, it was his last major lecture in his home town. According to Mohamed Khan, Deedat would say, 'We got an auditorium sitting in there, why don't you get a debate going?' But times had changed, Khan pointed out. It was difficult to 'pull a thousand people in just to listen to someone talking'. Further, 'if anybody issued a challenge, he would take it on at the drop of a hat, but there were no challengers locally'. Another problem, according to Ebi Lockhat was that

> people became a bit resentful. In fact the late Essop Timol used to have a good joke: when I said to him, 'Look, I can't get the City Hall, I got Dr Khalid Mansoor coming down.' He said, 'I have to ask you for a security deposit.' I said, 'But Essop Mota you've never asked before.' He says, 'They'll come and break the halls or something like that, because you will go and create controversy.'

Deedat was a master at managing the media and was always willing to use innovative means, such as these billboards, to spread his message.

Other IPCI activities continued and expanded. There were regular mosque tours conducted by IPCI staff – sometimes as many as thirty or forty tours in a three-day period. Visitors included tourists and increasingly schools from all religious backgrounds were bringing pupils for tours. Print runs of the Qur'an and Deedat's popular booklets were often as high as fifty- or a hundred thousand at a time. The production and distribution of *al-Burhaan* and the annual IPCI calendar remained a core activity and required sales staff to undertake extensive local travel.

The 'advertising' of Islam remained innovative. While many Muslim leaders frowned on the medium of television and deemed it haram (forbidden), Deedat broke new ground in May 1989 when he concluded an arrangement with Errol Pretorius, marketing manager at South Africa's independent pay-television channel, M-Net, to place an advertisement promoting the Qur'an during peak-hour viewing of the widely watched soapie *Loving*. The IPCI got Aura Films to produce the advertisement but M-Net subsequently decided that it might lead to criticism from other religious groups[1] and agreed to refund the cost of producing the advertisement. Although the advertisement was never aired, it was another example of Deedat's willingness to explore uncharted territory.

The 'Billboard Project' had a similar objective. Islam was advertised by placing large billboards on conspicuous buildings. Three-by-seven-metre signs that said, 'Welcome to Islam!', 'al-Qur'an – The Last Testament!' or 'Read al-Qur'an!' were placed strategically in Durban's central business disctrict. This prompted local city councillor Arthur Morris, among others, to state that he regarded the 'illuminated sign' offensive to Christians, and argue that if the City Council did not clamp down, 'other religious groups would follow suit, leading to a "Battle of the Billboards"'. In April 1989, Deedat put up R100 000 for Morris to show him a single 'illuminated' sign: 'Tell Mr Morris, he is hallucinating. He fears Islam to such an extent that he sees things which do not even exist.' He also questioned why Morris was not objecting to the advertising of alcohol and cigarettes that were unhealthy for human consumption. A month later, the city council decided that instead of changing the by-laws to prohibit religious advertising, all groups were at liberty to advertise.[2]

At the suggestion of Dr Totonji, a two-month international da'wah programme was organised in 1987 and 1988 under the supervision of Abdullah Deedat. International applicants had to be proficient in English, have completed secondary school, and be able to read the Qur'an in Arabic. Successful applicants were given return airfares, accommodation, and food vouchers for local restaurants. The curriculum included a study of Western and Christian propaganda against Islam, Deedat's lecture programmes, a study of the various versions of the Bible, a comparison of the status of women in the Qur'an and Bible, and other issues pertaining to the differences between various religions. Twenty participants attended the inaugural programme from countries such as the Philippines, Burma, Maldives, Sierra Leone, Somalia, and Palestine. A second programme was held for Africans, in which lectures were presented by Ahmed Deedat, Abdullah Deedat, and Hamza Abdul Malick of the USA. In Deedat's words, the programme aimed to train participants to 'carry the flag of Islam high and be soldiers in the cause'. Newspaper da'wah continued too. For example, during a visit to Saudi Arabia in November 1995, Nelson Mandela was given a copy of *The Choice* by Prince Abdullah Bin Faisal Bin Turki. Deedat placed a photograph of Mandela receiving *The Choice* from the prince in national newspapers with the caption 'President Mandela received his [copy of] *The Choice*. Get Yours Now! Absolutely Free.'[3] When Muslims were persecuted in Bosnia, Deedat placed an advert in the *Leader* with the headline 'The Rape of Bosnia' followed by the Qur'anic verse: 'And let not Unbelievers think that Our [Allah's] Respite to them is good for themselves; We grant them respite that they may grow in their iniquity: But they will have a Shameful punishment [3: 178].' This was followed by an advert for *al-Qur'an: The Miracle of Miracles*.[4]

Deedat gave members of the South African Police Services an 'Open Invitation' to collect their 'Personal Free Copy of this 1920-page constitution, The Holy Qur'an with an English

An example of one of the IPCI's appeals for funds.

Translation. We [IPCI] are bound by our constitution to give you your personalised copy free.'⁵ Rulers and pencils bearing the logo of the IPCI and inviting people to Islam were handed out in their thousands to schoolchildren across the townships.

The IPCI also issued identity cards to individuals who embraced Islam. Each contained a photograph, a statement that the person had embraced Islam, and a note that a mosque or Muslim should be contacted in the event of the person's death. To cater for Zulu-speaking reverts, Omar Moleleki answered Zulu and Sotho correspondence and conducted mosque tours; Adam, based in As-Salaam, lectured in Zulu; while Yusuf Rehmane was a Zulu-speaking daʿi based at the Telecom. He also conducted classes at As-Salaam and assisted Omar Moleleki to translate parts of the Qur'an into Zulu.

The IPCI, it may be argued, was not prepared for its rapid growth. For example, antiquated accounting methods remained in place instead of proper checks and balances in line with the organisation's expansion and new identity. A review of accounting procedures by the Master of the Supreme Court in July 1992 concluded that there was little control over payment received for videos and Qur'ans sold; goods were ordered without proper authorisation; cheques were often signed by one trustee only, which was contrary to the requirement; trustees sometimes failed to cancel invoices after making payment, a practice that resulted in double payment; stock was not stored systematically or insured against theft or fire; and the audit trail was inadequate. Clearly, the IPCI's (lack of) systems left the organisation open to abuse.

Another handicap was the 'internal haemorrhaging' that resulted from a rift between trustees. As Shabir Basha points out, the long-drawn-out legal dispute during the 1990s 'lowered morale among employees and left them confused'. Iqbal Essop said that he felt dejected during this period because 'Muslims were fighting Muslims...funds were utilised for that, while lawyers made money out of us. But we at the lower echelons did our best to keep things going.' Another employee, Abdul Kalic Ally, described the court cases as 'depressing for everyone. The work process was definitely slower. But the demand for our products never stopped.' The tragedy of the 1990s, according to Mohamed Khan, was that 'a lot of our energy was sapped in internal battles. Instead of carrying out the mandate of the IPCI we were busy massaging egos.'

Despite Deedat's international commitments, and the many problems that he and the IPCI faced from the late 1980s, his popularity continued to grow.

# ISLAM AND HINDUISM: SOWING THE SEEDS OF DIVISION

Hundreds of protesters gathered outside the IPCI
building in Durban in the mid-1990s.

Better than the entire world, is our Hindustan,
We are its nightingales, and it our garden abode
If we are in an alien place, the heart remains in the Homeland,
Know us to be only there where our heart is.
Religion does not teach us to bear ill will among ourselves
We are of Hind, our homeland is Hindustan.

– Allamah Iqbal[1]

LIKE IQBAL, whose own views changed from an idealistic secular vision of a composite plural Hindu–Muslim culture into a global Islamic vision, and led him to propose a separate Muslim state in 1930, Deedat eventually made Hinduism the subject of his analysis, and in the process created divisions between Hindus and Muslims in South Africa. This threatened long-standing friendships and had important ramifications for Deedat's support among Muslims in South Africa.

Rafeek Hassen, president of the Islamic Interfaith Research Institute at the time of writing, has been passionate about his faith since his days as a pharmacy student at the University of Durban-Westville in the 1970s where he was a founding member of the Muslim Students' Association. He heard Deedat speak on several occasions and was enthused even though he was uneasy with the stir that Deedat was causing 'in those turbulent struggle days'. Hassen attended Deedat's talks at the City Hall and can be seen on old videos standing in line during the Q&A sessions. Hassen faced many questions about Islam from his (non-Muslim) friends, and often visited Vanker and Deedat at their Madressa Arcade offices for answers. On one occasion Deedat gave him a Qur'an, which remains a prized possession.

After completing his degree, Hassen opened a pharmacy in Durban and remained active in da'wah. At various times he has served as chair of the Inchanga Islamic Centre, the Islamic Da'wah Movement, and the Effingham Islamic Society. He has also been secretary of the KwaMashu Ntzuma Muslim Association and an executive member of the Muslim Youth Movement. His relationship with Deedat remained strong, and Deedat would often visit him after his lecture tours, as his pharmacy was situated on the route to Deedat's home in Verulam. Deedat would present him with videotapes of his tours and ask for comments. Hassen also attended short traning courses conducted by Deedat.

By the 1980s, Hassen felt that he had gained sufficient knowledge of Christianity and was curious to know more about Hinduism because, he explained, Hindus were converting to Christianity at alarming rates and he wanted to know what message Muslims could impart to them. During one of his visits to his home town of Newcastle, he asked his uncle, the late Mawlana Cassim Sema, how he should go about acquiring knowledge of Hinduism. Mawlana Sema told him that Deedat had also studied Hinduism and would be the ideal person to approach. So Hassen approached Deedat, who agreed to give a seminar on Hinduism to a private gathering of Muslim males. Little did Hassen know that his request would see him making the headlines of a local newspaper as the 'Pharmacist in Hindu Row'.[2]

It soon became clear why Deedat had asked for a male-only audience. In addition to questioning various Hindu beliefs, he associated the Hindu symbols Sivalingam and Yoni with male and female reproductive organs, and described Hindu gods as being of an 'unnatural blue colour'.[3]

For some time, nothing came of the lecture, and Hassen was stunned when a video recording of the meeting suddenly appeared in the public domain. There are contradictory accounts of how this occurred. According to Yousuf Deedat, the IPCI catalogued its video collection around this time and the tape was inadvertently included in the inventory and made public. Hassen remembers things differently. He says that during one of the IPCI's legal battles, Yousuf Deedat became upset with a Hindu lawyer and stormed into the lawyer's office shouting: 'Look at this.'

Whatever the case, Hassen suddenly found himself in the public spotlight. A local journalist warned that, as convenor of the presentation, he should condemn Deedat's remarks or risk negative publicity. Hassen dismissed the warning.

There were protests from various quarters when the video became public. Deedat released a press statement calling on Hindus to gather three experts from around the world at the City Hall and, if they refuted anything that he had stated in the recording, he would apologise to Hindus and distribute a video of the debate at his cost. Deedat insisted that the information was bona fide and not a result of 'fanaticism'.[4]

All this meant little to Hassen when the *Sunday Tribune Herald* implicated him with its headline. The Avoca Cultural Society responded by distributing pamphlets in Avoca, Red Hill, Greenwood Park, and Duffs Road calling on Hindus to boycott his pharmacy. Hassen then issued his own pamphlet stating that his involvement was confined to chairing the presentation, that he employed Hindus in his pharmacy by choice, and that he had blood relatives and neighbours who were Hindu and with whom he enjoyed cordial relations. The boycott was largely ineffective as Hassen's loyal Hindu customers continued to support him.

Muslims and non-Muslims alike were critical of the video, however. R.B. Master of the Transvaal Hindu Maha Sabha stated that Deedat had 'done a great disservice to the cause of Islam [by] ridiculing the Hindu mode of worship in most obscene and objectionable language, unbecoming of a person who professes to be a missionary of Islam'.[5] Archie Hirasen of the Saivite Propagation Centre threatened to call for a boycott of Muslim shops if Deedat continued to 'mock, condemn and criticise' Hindus.[6] Ram Maharaj, president of the Hindu Dharma Sabha (National Hindu Development Trust), warned that 'if spiritual saboteurs are hell-bent on casting pebbles at Hinduism, then we will certainly retaliate by hurling boulders'.[7]

The video threatened to affect long-standing goodwill between Hindus and Muslims. Many Muslims expressed criticisms of Deedat. Mohammed Makki devoted all 168 pages of the June 1987 issue of *Muslim Digest* to Deedat in an effort to 'stop him before it is too late'. Makki wrote that 'never before in the history of the Muslims of South Africa and Natal in particular, were relations between Hindus and Muslims so damaged'. The Islamic Council of South Africa stated that such attacks 'merely invite counter attacks, justified or unjustified, adding fuel to fire'.[8] Essop Kajee of the *Daily News* Milk Fund reflected on the repercussions of the video when he wrote to Deedat and G.H. Agjee on 27 August 1987:

> I just do not know where to begin or end. But in my survey of some five thousand Muslim brothers from all walks of life and backgrounds, ninety per cent requested that I tell Mr Deedat to please leave the other madhahib [faiths] alone. I, as part-time rep., service numerous shops, factories, supermarkets, cafes, schools, etc. I, like the late Goolam Vanker, enjoy the respect of all groups of people in this wonderful

Paradise of ours – South Africa. You, Brother Deedat, created such a Happening. All Hell Broke Loose. The small Muslim being hit from all sides. There were talks of boycotts. 'Don't support the Muslim shops; Don't work in the Muslim factories, etc, etc. Panic buttons were pressed on all rounds. Influential people tried to explain to you…But to no avail. You were right and all of the other people were out of step… You, Brother Deedat, have the world at your feet. You have conquered the Arabian world. Your videos are shown in Mecca. You name it and your videos are shown everywhere. You are now an international personality of repute. You have attained the impossible – worldwide recognition. A recent survey of hajjis who had come back, say that your videos are popular in Mecca and also in all other parts of the Islamic world. This achievement is really unique – a Great Honour for the South African Muslims. You, Dear Brother Deedat, have now put us on the world map for which we are grateful. But then let us see what is happening on the home front. So now, my elder Brother, let me tell you of an incident that happened some months back at the Grey Street mosque. Our Emam Ahmed Saeed got out of bed to perform the Fajr Ṣalah and before he could commence the said prayer, on the Emam's musalla was a very huge white cross. It was defaced in a such a way that no amount of cleaning could get the stain off. This matter was hushed up and very few people knew about it. Now in your own words you said the musalleen of the Grey Street mosque are all fanatics. What would have happened if they attacked the innocent Roman Catholic Cathedral in the heat of the moment? Man mellows with age – you should do likewise.

Some of Deedat's close associates felt that releasing the tape was a huge mistake. Agjee believes that Deedat, even with the benefit of hindsight, would have distributed the tape because of his refusal to bow to pressure. In retrospect, Agjee went on, the tape made little sense since few Hindus became Muslims or vice versa, while large numbers of Hindus were embracing Christianity. Jamaluddin was studying at the darul 'ulum in Newcastle when the video was released. He told Deedat that his methodology was wrong.

The IPCI revived Hindu anger yet again when it re-issued the video in August 1989. To add fuel to the fire, a story was published in the IPCI's *al-Burhaan* newsletter claiming that a member of a 'priestly Hindu family' in Mauritius had converted to Islam after viewing the tape:

> Amid the controversy, fate had it that the magic of Ahmed Deedat's message struck a chord in the heart of one Khemraj Chunurum. After viewing this compelling cassette, which had rocked the very core of his being, he threw family relationships in the balance with his decision to convert to Islam. He changed his name to Ashraff Ali and eventually became a stranger in his home; he was consequently disowned.[9]

Meanwhile, in response to the video, a local Hindu grouping issued a thirteen-page pamphlet titled 'Was Kaaba a Hindu Temple? Is Allah a Hindu God?' Prepared by P.N. Oak of Delhi, India, the pamphlet asserted, among other things, that a reference to King Vikramadity in an inscription in the Ka'ba proved that the Arabian peninsula was part of his Indian empire; the Ka'ba houses the Shiva emblem; Muslim pilgrims go around the 'Ka'bah temple' seven times, a practice that proves that the Ka'ba is a pre-Islamic Indian Shiva temple 'where the Hindu practice of circumambulation is still meticulously observed'; the word Allah, the pamphlet alleged, was a Sanskrit word meaning 'mother goddess'. For Mohammed Makki, this 'unwarranted and inaccurate attack on Islam' was a direct result of Deedat's 'attacking other religions...the blame must rest squarely on the shoulders of Mr Ahmed Deedat'.[10]

The serious tensions that had arisen between Hindus and Muslims resulted in the banned Dr R.A.M. Saloojee, then vice-president of the Transvaal Indian Congress and prominent member of the anti-apartheid United Democratic Front, addressing a public gathering at personal risk. Years later he recalled that:

> the tape fractured the long-standing relationship and coexistence between South African Hindus and Muslims. I vividly recollect the anger and schism that followed. At the time I was banned by the apartheid government and commanded not to attend gatherings of any kind. A mass meeting of our Hindu and Tamil neighbours and residents of Lenasia was called at a temple. Rumours abounded of possible boycotts and severance of relationships between Hindus and Muslims. Realising the seriousness of this inter-religious and intercommunal discord, I took the risk of breaching my detention and restriction orders. I addressed the meeting and helped ease tensions. I castigated the mischievous doctrine of troublemaking and apologised for the insult and intolerance of the literature.[11]

Despite the protests, Deedat reignited Hindu anger when an anonymous booklet *Oh Ye Hindu Awake!* was published in July 1995. It contained most of the material in the video. The IPCI denied any link with the publication. Yousuf Deedat claimed that somebody may have seen the video and produced the book. When it emerged that the IPCI had indeed published the booklet, Ram Maharaj, chairman of the United Hindu Front, was extremely agitated. Instead of placating Hindus, Deedat then placed an advert in the local press challenging his critics to a debate and stating that the tape would be distributed until his challenge was accepted.[12]

Deedat's Muslim detractors were not spared. Under the banner 'Trustees With Courage Make a Majority', he invited his Muslim critics to a meeting on 18 November 1995 at the IPCI headquarters to discuss the contents of the video.[13] They ignored the call. Instead, the Islamic Council of South Africa publicly condemned the IPCI for offending the religious sentiments of Hindus. The Council described the video as 'offensive to Hindus and contrary to Islamic norms and values' and encouraged the IPCI to propagate Islam with 'dignity and grace' and to deploy its resources to alleviate poverty, hunger, crime, unemployment, and the 'rapid decline of morals and rampant corruption, which are national priorities'.[14]

Twenty-nine Muslim organisations convened a public meeting to discuss the topic: 'The Qur'anic and Prophetic Method of Propagating Islam'. Guest speakers included Mawlana

> **THE LEADER, 8 DECEMBER 1995**
>
> **PUBLIC MEETING**
>
> A public meeting convened by representatives of the Muslim bodies mentioned below will be held at:
>
> DATE: 11 DECEMBER 1995
> TIME: 7.00 PM
> VENUE: ORIENT HALL, CENTENARY ROAD, DURBAN
>
> SUBJECT: **THE QURANIC AND PROPHETIC METHOD OF PROPAGATING ISLAM**
>
> SPEAKERS:
> (a) Moulana A Razak
> (b) Mr Sajid Makki
> (c) Mr. I. Kathrada
> (d) Moulana Y. Osman
>
> **ALL ARE WELCOME TO ATTEND**
>
> **CONVENORS OF MEETING**
>
> 1. Muslim Charitable Fund
> 2. Islamic Forum
> 3. Anjuman Islam Juma Masjid
> 4. Orient Islamic Educational Trust
> 5. Islamic Dawa Movement of S.A.
> 6. Africa Muslim Agency
> 7. South African National Zakaah Fund
> 8. Muslim Youth Movement of S.A.
> 9. Islamic Relief Agency
> 10. Woman's Cultural Group
> 11. Jamiat-Ul-Ulema Of Natal
> 12. Natal Memon Jamaat
> 13. Islamic Medical Association
> 14. Imama And Dawah Institution (Ladysmith)
> 15. Muslim Darul Yatama
> 16. Muslim Board Of Prison Welfare
> 17. Muslim Gorba Fund
> 18. madressa Anjuman Islam
> 19. Muslim Student Association
> 20. Verulam Islam Dawah College
> 21. Effingham Islamic Society
> 22. Inchanga Islamic Centre
> 23. Merewent Islamic Cultural Group
> 24. Montford Islamic Society
> 25. Newlands West Islamic Society
> 26. Woodview Muslim Society Phoenix
> 27. Musjid-E-Muktar
> 28. Islamic Unity Convention
> 29. South African Dawah Network

THE LEADER, 8 DECEMBER 1995

In the midst of the controversy, many organisations collaborated to call a public meeting on methods of propagating Islam.

Razack of Ladysmith, Sajid Makki of the Grey Street Mosque, community leaders Ismail Kathrada and Mawlana Yunus Osman. Hindu leaders such as Raghbeer Kallideen, Tulsiram Maharaj, Pranilal Lakhani of the Maha Sabha, Ram Maharaj of the United Hindu Front, and politician Amichand Rajbansi were also invited to share the platform in a show of Hindu–Muslim solidarity.

The meeting was chaired by I.C. Meer, an ANC member in the provincial government of KwaZulu-Natal. Ismail Kathrada of the West Street Mosque and Mawlana Makki, imam of the Grey Street mosque were also present. Makki summed up the mood of the meeting when he said that Islam was best propagated by example; if those propagating it 'were crude it would create disturbances. This would be unfortunate as we are living in harmony in a non-Muslim country, I wouldn't like to see the problems of India and Pakistan imported here.'[15] The Indian Consulate rejected Deedat's application for a visa to visit his home village of Tadkeshwar in Gujarat in February 1996. Deedat responded with a full-page newspaper advertisement accusing the Indian government of malice and religious discrimination.[16]

According to Ebi Lockhat, Deedat regarded the reaction of Muslims as treasonous:

> I found that there was hardening of attitudes in certain quarters after the tape. Deedat did not take the criticism easily. When the community tried to do damage control, some said, 'We dissociate ourselves with this remark.' He took that very personally. He took that almost as treason, you know, 'They want to join the Hindus against me' and it was very vociferous. I think that split the community for a while.

One of Deedat's most vocal critics over the Hinduism episode was attorney Saber Ahmed Jazbhay. As a student, Jazbhay found Deedat to be a

> very gregarious kind of guy, very social person who did not turn anybody away. He always made sure that when we were asked questions about Islam we would be able to respond ... We were critical admirers. I believe that the propagation of Islam should be done at a level where dignity is respected. What Ahmed Deedat was doing at that point was

going 'for the guts' of Hinduism and he crossed a barrier, a line as it were, and that's when I started responding with concern that this was unacceptable…The video cassette caused a tremendous rupture, particularly for many of us who lived in 'cosmopolitan' areas with few religious and cultural divides and it was becoming very uncomfortable to explain to people what the tape was all about. There was no diplomacy employed by Deedat but rather a full-frontal attack that insulted even the most rational Muslim.

Jazbhay wrote many letters to the press critical of Deedat. He claims that he did not experience a backlash from Deedat.

This is important to note because Mr Deedat was not a despot or a person of violent means who would hold grudges. I used to tell him, 'Uncle Ahmed, I got a problem with this, it is wrong,' and, of course, I used to be shouted down by people around him and have a label thrown against me but I always stood my ground.

Some Muslims argued at the time that the culpability of the press needed to be probed. A letter to the *Leader* on 8 December 1995, signed 'Moulana', observed:

A public issue equals media interest. Hindus hate the Deedat video. Muslims hate the video. It had no public interest and therefore was a non-issue warranting little or no media interest. It therefore makes you wonder why newspapers [especially the ethnic ones] have been running so long with the story. Here's a suspicion – firstly, the issue is repeatedly churned up to create reader interest, because reader interest equals increased sales, equals increased revenue. Secondly, the IPCI has been responding to the controversy with huge advertisements – which also equals more revenue. While Muslims and Hindus are worried about the issue, the newspapers are laughing all the way to the bank…There is an element of self-interest here and it is disgraceful and is starting to prove to be extremely damaging to the harmonious relationship between the two groups.

Deedat's critics remain convinced that his dabbling with Hinduism was a mistake. Professor Salman Nadvi was not a vocal critic but made his views known to Deedat during their many one-on-one conversations. Professor Nadvi is well placed to reflect on this episode given that he grew up on the Indian subcontinent where Hindu–Muslim tensions periodically gave way to violence. He has also been an observer of Muslim life in Durban over several decades. Nadvi believes that Deedat

should not have got involved with Hinduism because the Indian community here were never at loggerheads with each other but because of that tape he unnecessarily woke up the consciousness of Hindus and got them to organise themselves. He should have kept to Christianity. People could take it even if they did not like his language because Christians were arguing with you and you were arguing back. Islam and Christianity had always had a problem in that in India in the British days, the Christian missionaries started debating with Muslims. They initiated it and Deedat was reacting to that. He got involved with Judaism and especially Palestine, which people appreciated because he was speaking to the 'heart' of the Muslims. We have a saying in Urdu that when you address the bull [saying], 'come and hit me', you are asking for trouble and that is what happened with the tape on Hinduism.

In 1999, after the court case involving the trustees of the IPCI ended, the organisation destroyed all the booklets, video, and audiotapes that were critical of Hinduism.

## 23

# THE COMBAT KIT

A newspaper advertisement for one of Deedat's most widely read booklets.

May Allah put u in paradise Sheikh Ahmed Deedat…I have a lot of friends that hates islam as terrorist way. I have no idea 2fight them back in arguing n debating. But thanks to Allah, coz I've downloaded the combat kit. Allahu akbar…Islam never die…La ilaha illallah.

– Arshad, web post, 2009[1]

DEEDAT PROVOKED THE IRE of Christians from the beginning, but none of his actions created as much furore as his *Combat Kit: Against Bible Thumpers*, which he published in 1992 to train Muslims and Hindus on how to use the Bible as a 'patriot missile' against 'Bible thumpers' such as the 'Jehovah's Witness and other missionaries who harass people in their own homes'. Many Christians felt insulted by Deedat's ridicule and sarcasm. Widespread criticism of the *Combat Kit* can partly be attributed to South Africa's changing political landscape. With the country's first democratic elections looming, however, the historic relationship between Muslims and Christians began to shift.

Deedat's booklet and responses to it must be seen in this wider context. In his study of Christian–Muslim relations in South Africa, Haron writes that from the 1970s Christian missionaries 'were more sophisticated in their approach in that they embarked upon a serious study of Islam and Muslims in South Africa'. The main ideologues were academics such as Jacobus A. Naude of Johannesburg's Rand Afrikaans University (RAU) and Chris Greyling who was based at the University of Western Cape. Both were members of the Dutch Reformed Church (DRC). Naude established the Centre for Islamic Studies in 1979 at RAU, which published the *Journal for Islamic Studies* from 1981. Greyling had been a missionary among Muslims in the Transvaal during the 1950s and 1960s before entering the academic world.[2]

The resurgence of Islam among younger Muslims in South Africa, in the midst of heightened anti-apartheid struggle after the 1976 Soweto Revolt and the Islamic Revolution in Iran in 1979, also prompted the DRC to commission a study on Islam in South Africa. The result of the DRC's investigation was that, at its October 1986 Annual Synod in Cape Town, Islam was branded a 'false religion' and seen as a threat to Christianity 'in South Africa, the African continent and the world at large'.[3] The Synod was concerned that some young Africans and coloured people 'saw Islam as an ideology to enhance the freedom struggle'.[4] Dominee Stoffel Colyn, then chaplain-general of the South African police, stated that

> Muhammad rampaged through the land with a sword to spill the blood of all the children of God into the sand...Ismail, the slave son of the slave woman, Hagar, Abraham's second wife, passed down a generation of Arab terrorists...The Muslims are not your brothers in this country because if they can cut your throat, they will do it.[5]

This view was challenged by progressive Christians and Muslims who had forged relationships in several contexts and took a strong stand against the DRC. For example, Farid Esack of the Call of Islam was a founding member of the South African chapter of the World Council on Religion and Peace in 1984, which he headed with the Reverend Gerrie Lubbe. They spoke out against the apartheid system and worked towards religious pluralism and tolerance. Another important development was the 1985 *Kairos Document*, which challenged the muted response of mainstream churches to the July 1985 State of Emergency during which extremely brutal measures were being used to quell political protest. The *Kairos Document* fell within the tradition of liberation theology and became an instrument of co-operation between Muslims and Christians.[6]

In the political context, Muslims such as Farouk Meer and Ebrahim Rasool participated in the United Democratic Front, which had been formed in 1983 to encourage effective non-racial and non-sectarian opposition to apartheid. As negotiations towards a political solution in South Africa gathered momentum in the late 1980s, many Muslim members of the African National Congress (ANC) participated in or supported talks that led to the historic National Peace Accord of September 1991, and several Muslims served in the country's first non-racial government. In this context, many Muslims felt that it was incongruous for the majority of the country's people to be working towards bridging race and religious divides while the likes of Deedat and some of his Christian counterparts continued to foment division.

It is in this context that the *Combat Kit* must be viewed. In Deedat's words, it was a 'manual to convert the Christian Scud [Bible] into a Patriot Missile'. Deedat called on readers to obtain a copy of the Bible and paste his booklet on the inside cover to function as an index. Readers should select key topics such as 'incest', memorise the definition, and familiarise themselves with the relevant verses in the Bible. When missionaries visited non-Christian homes, they should be asked to define these terms and read the verses. Thereafter they should 'question them as to the moral of the story. There is none! So it's immoral.' Non-Christians were also instructed to mark 'contradictory' passages in yellow and 'pornographic' sections in red. Colour-coded Bibles, Deedat felt, would allow Muslims and Hindus to 'defeat, embarrass and confuse door-to-door evangelists. The Bible would eventually become a family heirloom.'

The booklet was distributed free of charge with copies of the Bible, to which Deedat added a new index that included topics such as 'Types of incest in the Bible', 'Wine', and 'Rape'.

David Foster, a Durban-based Christian who contributed regularly to Answering-islam.org's website, wrote to Deedat on 25 November 1993 to retract the *Combat Kit*. He accused him of 'stooping very low in the way you have ridiculed the Bible. I dare say, if we tried to ridicule your Qur'an… you would be outraged.' Deedat ignored Foster's letter. Foster later recalled that when he met Deedat he asked him why he had ignored the letter. Deedat told him: 'I am like a man riding along in a caravan. A dog barking at the side of the road doesn't really pose a problem to me.'[7] A group of pastors representing a cross-section of the Durban Christian community wrote an 'Open Letter' to Deedat, which was published in the *Daily News* on 13 August 1994:

> We note with sadness that you have been, for many years, promoting your belief primarily by attacking other faiths rather than by positively presenting your own Islamic teachings…In an effort to degrade and discredit the Bible you have resorted to the use of ridicule and vulgar language…We who esteem the Holy Bible find it unacceptable and offensive.[8]

Deedat's publications, as Haron points out, had their parallels among those published by fundamentalist South African Christians such as Deedat's old foe, John Gilchrist, and Gerhard Nehls. Gilchrist formed the Jesus to Muslims organisation and published several booklets, including *The Challenge of Islam in South Africa; Facing the Muslim Challenge: A Handbook of Christian–Muslim Apologetics;* and *The Codification of the Qur'an Text* which sought to challenge Muslim belief in the Qur'an's divine nature.[9] Nehls was based in the Cape where he formed a group called Life Challenge. His publications *Dear Abdullah: Christians Ask Muslims* and *Christians Answer Muslims* sought to counter Muslim assertions that the Bible was corrupt. He also developed a Bible-study course titled *al-Kitab: A Correspondence Course for Muslims* and published *Islam: As it sees Itself, As Others See It, and As It Is* and *The Islamic–Christian Controversy: A Trainer's Textbook*.[10] These publications show that 'combat kits' were being churned out on both sides of the Christian–Muslim divide.

Publicity surrounding Deedat intensified with reports of his involvement in local politics in the lead-up to South Africa's first non-racial election. In May 1993 a local newspaper carried a report that the IPCI was assisting the Inkatha Freedom Party (IFP) to raise money in the Middle East to fund its election campaign.[11] The *Tribune Herald* ran a headline, 'Muslims

Hoping to host an open debate in the early 1990s, the IPCI invited Nelson Mandela, F.W. de Klerk and Mangosotho Buthelezi to speak to Muslims in Durban. Buthelezi was the only one to respond, and shared a platform with Deedat and G.H. Agjee.

back IFP bid for Arab millions'. According to Yousuf Deedat, the IPCI hoped to raise funds from businessmen in the Middle East who opposed what they saw as the socialist policies of the ANC.[12] At the time, the IFP and the ANC were involved in a deadly war for votes in KwaZulu-Natal in which thousands of people were injured or killed. The IPCI's statements were not helpful in this tense situation. A 1994 calendar distributed by the IPCI carried a photograph of Deedat with the IFP leader, Mangosutho Buthelezi, praying in Islamic fashion.

Farhana Ismail, writing in the *Tribune Herald*, added to the hysteria when she reported in April 1995 that the IPCI planned to use Arab funds to finance a television propaganda offensive against Christians and Jews. According to Yousuf Deedat, the IPCI would move

> with full force. Literature and videotapes will be used. We are prepared to challenge the repercussions of our actions. In terms of the new constitution there is now freedom of expression. That means freedom of religious propaganda. It is a war, a religious war – a jihad, if you like.[13]

Paddy Kearney of Diakonia, a Christian organisation dedicated to upliftment of the poor, issued a statement saying that he 'regretted that the IPCI was interested in criticism and attack rather than dialogue'. Meanwhile, Martin Steinberg of the KwaZulu-Natal Council of Jewry told reporters that 'we in the Jewish community are concerned about [Deedat's] sentiments'.[14]

Reporter Alan Dunn suggested that Deedat wanted to provoke Jews and Christians to create the impression that South Africa's Muslims were under threat and thus unlock further funding from Arab countries. Dunn appealed to Deedat to 'carefully reconsider what he was doing'.[15]

Ebi Lockat made a similar point:

> I think that some of the tactics in the later years was like the tactics of the National Party's *swart gevaar* [black danger campaign]. They would create a climate to say, 'we are under siege', so the donors would react. When I first came to work in Durban, I worked in what I called the white side of town. Those whites genuinely believed that they were fighting for their country because they served in the army for two years. They were told the communists are here, they're going to come and slaughter you in your houses, etc. Nobody held a gun to them to go to the army. They were quite happy to go. Of course, journalists would take up any little thing...I think at certain times it was certainly aggravated. I mean, take that Buthelezi thing. It started off when Mandela had been released and I said, 'Why don't we invite the leaders to talks. What have we got to lose?' So we sent a letter to Nelson Mandela who had just been released and it was wishful thinking because the whole world wanted a piece of him. We sent one to F.W. de Klerk and one to Chief Gatsha Buthelezi. We sent them a Qur'an and said, 'Come and talk to the Muslim community, we are concerned with what's going to happen in South Africa.' From Mandela we got a curt letter saying that he acknowledges the invite and thanks us; de Klerk acknowledged and when we persisted he said, 'could you send the presidency a memo of what your concerns are before we can

consider this'; and of course Chief Buthelezi was the least busiest of the ministers so he accepted. Now the minute he took that on we immediately had a lot of flack because Inkatha and the ANC were at war. People wanted to know why we were supporting Buthelezi, and at that particular lecture we had to get Advocate Salim Khan as MC to actually state that we were apolitical, that we had invited ANC leaders, National Party leaders, that this was the first person who had accepted but this did not mean that we supported him. But for other reasons it was sensationalised that we did this and this guy's going to give so much and that guy will give something.

Certainly the antics of the IPCI created profit opportunities for the media. The IPCI's propaganda consisted largely of exaggerated threats but provoked strong local reactions. The sensationalism surrounding the IPCI was out of proportion to its influence among local Muslims but brash headlines added to the hysteria about Muslims and their role in the new South Africa.

The 1990s also ushered in a period of another kind of combat within the structures of the IPCI that severely affected its functioning. The problems began in October 1991 when Yusuf Ally raised questions about the existence of an overseas bank account that had unexpectedly come to light. The matter was discussed at a special meeting of trustees on 26 March 1990. Yousuf Deedat explained that he had opened the account because international sanctions against apartheid had made some some donors wary of sending money to South Africa. Ally expressed concern that this was against the established procedure of receiving cheques in the presence of a fellow trustee and that Yousuf was leaving himself open to accusations of malpractice.

Then, at a Trust meeting on 3 June 1991, the Deedats proposed selling Minolta House to pay for the printing of Qur'ans. This was opposed by Ally and Hoosen, who requested an investigation into the IPCI's finances. Although Deedat's attorney issued a statement on 28 October 1991 denying any irregularities in the handling of the funds, the Master of the Supreme Court announced on 29 October that the IPCI would be audited. Ally and Hoosen then obtained a temporary court order on 9 December 1991 to prevent the sale of Minolta House.[16] Pietermaritzburg attorney Mark Lynn and Durban chartered accountant Verlen Seipp were appointed by the Master of the Supreme Court to oversee the IPCI. However this was successfully opposed by the Deedats. Ebi Lockhat was working for Deedat when the litigation started, and his observations provide an insight into Deedat's frame of mind with regard to the Trust and the IPCI:

> Towards the time that I joined, the rift was already there between the trustees. Ahmed Deedat believed, 'We do the work, we go out and get the donations. Who are these people to question us?' That's where the differences came in. Deedat always said, 'The monies were given to Ahmed Deedat to use as he sees fit. If he says print the Qur'ans,

that's it; if he says sell the building, that's it.' I know it sounds very simplistic but if you really have to take everything else out of it, this was the basic issue: 'Who are you to this IPCI?' 'I'm a trustee,' they thought. 'Well, I brought you in,' he said and from there it just escalated.

Attorney-General Imber issued a statement in August 1993 that no charges would be laid against Deedat,[17] but efforts to remove all the trustees continued when the case resumed in August 1995. While the trustees admitted that there had been a rift between them, they argued that this was not sufficient reason to remove them. Attorneys Geyser and Partners reported to the Master that after the Swaggart debate, funds had been provided to Deedat from the Middle East to propagate Islam. This formed the backbone of the Trust's assets and if Deedat was removed as trustee, he could 'easily' form a new organisation and attract foreign funds. The income of the IPCI, on the other hand, would shrink significantly.[18]

Deedat's stroke, and subsequent paralysis, in 1996 did nothing to bring the dispute to an end. A two-year legal battle between the Master of the High Court and the trustees ended in October 1996 when the Bloemfontein Appellate Division ruled in favour of the Master. Future trustees of the IPCI would be required to lodge substantial deposits for the 'due and faithful performance of their duties'. G.H. Agjee resigned as trustee in response to this ruling. In addition, accounting firm BDO Spencer Stewart was appointed to implement internal controls to ensure proper financial administration.

Deedat, who was bedridden by then, gave power of attorney to his daughter-in-law, Yasmeen, Yousuf Deedat's wife, to act on his behalf. Ally and Hoosen, together with Dr Muhammad Khan of Port Shepstone, who had long been involved with As-Salaam and recently been appointed an IPCI trustee, brought an action in May 1997 to prevent Yasmeen from acting as a trustee because there were no legal grounds for her appointment. Deedat's longtime confidant, Saleh Mohamed, visited Durban in early August 1997 and volunteered to administer the Trust until an amicable long-term solution was found. Another new trustee, Ebrahim Jadwat, officially accepted Saleh's proposal on 29 August 1997. Saleh wrote to Deedat on the same day:

> The Centre, which you built up to be a hive of activity, is rapidly becoming a monument, depicting what we always detested: 'Our Alhambra and Cordoba filled with foreign statues and ornaments for all to amuse themselves with'. I'll try my utmost to bring peace amongst the trustees so that they may always be united for the sake of Islam and Da'wah.

Saleh moved to Durban to administer the Trust but the arrangement was shortlived. In an affidavit dated 22 September 1997, he stated that he found it impossible to reconcile the different parties and returned to Cape Town.

The attempt to prevent Yasmeen Deedat from representing her father-in-law continued in court. Following what he regarded as hostile cross-examination, Yousuf Deedat resigned as trustee on 14 July 1999. Two days later, on 16 July 1999, the Supreme Court of Appeal in

Bloemfontein ruled that Deedat's delegating his decision-making to Yasmeen Deedat constituted 'at least a temporary abdication of his functions in favour of a non-trustee' and that her power of attorney should therefore be declared null and void.[19] In August 1999, the court ruled that Deedat's disabilities made it extremely difficult for him to communicate with other members of the board, and that he should step down as trustee. Instead Deedat was appointed president of the IPCI, a position he held until he passed away in 2005.

# 24

# OTHER PERSUASIONS

*Deedat took great delight in enlightening all who would listen as to the righteousness and value of Islam.*

I could have throttled Deedat a thousand times because he had all the answers. In my realm, as a servant of the Church, I should have known more. I never accepted what he said. I always reread the parts of the Bible he would explicate to find a different meaning. Here I was, being taught by a Muslim, by a man who admitted he had little education. It was hard to stomach.

– Jamaluddin Ahmed

THE PRECEDING CHAPTERS have shown how Ahmed Deedat strode the global stage. It was a remarkable journey from the streets and back alleys of Durban. Along the way he met kings and politicians, and debated with some of the West's leading evangelists. Even more remarkably, he never entirely gave up on everyday proselytising. He engaged with individuals of all persuasions in his home town and, through patient debate combined with his writing, he sought to convince them of the righteousness of the path of Islam. His ability to persuade deeply affected the lives of two learned Catholics, who came from very different backgrounds and were part of Deedat's life at different periods.

Jamaluddin, which translates roughly into 'The beauty of faith', was born Yakub Cunningham in northern England in 1942 to a Roman Catholic father, John, and a Jewish mother, Kathrina. As a child, Yakub attended Yeshiva classes at the local synagogue, but, when he was dropped off there, he would invariably visit the Roman Catholic Church on the opposite side of the road. There was 'something about the church that fascinated me… the kindness of nuns and priests especially'. When Yakub was eleven, his twin brother Raymond died of leukaemia. A few months later, Yakub converted to Roman Catholicism. His father, Sir John Cunningham, was a diplomat in the Foreign Service and served in such India, Egypt, Venezuela, and Zanzibar. Yakub and his siblings would visit their parents during school vacations. A gifted student, Yakub matriculated at fourteen, and although a bright future lay ahead of him in the secular field, he opted 'to work in the vineyard of Christ'.

Yakub applied to join the Dominican Order of Catholic priests, but as a tertiary degree was a prerequisite for their rigorous training, his father suggested that he study law in case the priesthood did not 'agree' with him. He completed a degree at Cambridge University at the age of seventeen but he was below the legal age to be awarded the degree and had to wait a year to graduate. He then enrolled at the Pontifical University of St Thomas Aquinas, which is one of the major pontifical universities in Rome. His six-year training for the priesthood culminated in his ordination in 1969. Shortly thereafter he was sent to South Africa by Pope Paul VI to select a black priest to lead the Roman Catholic Church in South Africa. Yakub interviewed prospective priests and settled on three names, one of whom, Wilfred Napier, eventually became a cardinal and head of the Catholic Church in South Africa.

While studying in Rome, Yakub had made friends with a student who was studying to be a priest at the seminary in Cedara, near Pietermaritzburg.[1] He had informed this friend of his impending arrival in Durban, and was surprised when the friend did not meet him at the airport. He visited Cedara and discovered that the student had left the church. Tracked down to his family home in Essenwood Road, the man refused to see Yakub. Spoken through the window, the conversation went as follows:

'We cannot be friends. I am not a Catholic any longer.'
'What are you? An Anglican? Methodist? What? Tell me.'
'A believer. A Muslim.'
'Good God. A heathen. Why?'
'Ahmed Deedat.'

A distraught Yakub proceeded to visit Archbishop Denis Hurley and asked his host, whom he described as 'a wonderful man', 'Who is Ahmed Deedat?' There was 'a deathly silence. You could literally have heard a pin drop.' The Archbishop instructed him, 'Do not meet this man.' Yakub had no idea who Deedat was, but the archbishop's reaction aroused his curiosity and his enquiries led him to the IPC office in Madressa Arcade. Within minutes he and Deedat 'were at each other's throats'. Meeting Deedat, he recalls, was 'truly devastating. You had to be made of iron to survive him.' Thus began a three-decade 'love–hate' relationship between the two.

Jamaluddin

For example, Deedat once asked him to read the last verse of Luke where Jesus appears in the Upper Room after the 'so-called Crucifixion' and asks his startled followers whether they could offer him anything to eat. They gave him a piece of baked fish. Yakub had read this many times 'without seeing the contradiction'. Deedat's point was that if, as God says, he neither sleeps nor slumbers, why was it necessary to eat? Deedat also made Yakub read Sura Ma'idah (5:75), which states that Jesus 'the son of Mary was no more than an apostle; many were the apostles that passed away before him. His mother was a woman of truth. They had both to eat their [daily] food.'

An increasingly troubled Yakub suggested to Archbishop Hurley that he would learn Arabic and Islam so that he could use this knowledge to convert Muslims to Christianity. Archbishop Hurley agreed but Yakub was slowly losing his faith in Catholicism as he learnt more about Islam 'until, finally, you might say…I got zapped by Allah, hook, line and sinker. I couldn't eat, sleep, stand, think. It was a horrific time.'

In November 1970, Archbishop Hurley received a telegram instructing Yakub to return to Rome within a few days. He accepted Deedat's offer to visit As-Salaam on the day before he was to depart for Rome. Deedat used the opportunity to explicate the Qur'an. They reached As-Salaam as the adhan for the zuhr (midday prayer) was being given, and Deedat asked him whether he had made wudhu (carried out ablutions). 'What for, I am Catholic.' 'Do you love Jesus?' 'Yes.' 'How come you do not make wudhu like Jesus?' Deedat then reminded him that the Bible stated that Jesus fell on his feet and prayed to God. According to Jamaluddin, 'in that sajda [prostration] I began to cry uncontrollably. I knew then that that was how I wanted to pray.'

Deedat, he remembered, 'did not say a word. He dropped me off at the Archbishop's house and went to his home in Verulam which had just been completed. I waited until he reached home and called to ask him how one becomes a Muslim? "Are you interested?" he asked. "No, just curious," I said.' That evening, in the privacy of his room in Archbishop Hurley's home, Yakub offered a prayer without knowing where the qibla (Makkah) was, what to read, or how many rak'as he had to pray: 'I had no idea what I was saying but I loved it.' On Friday morning, dressed in his priestly garb, Yakub visited Deedat and told him that he wanted to be a Muslim. '"Dressed like that," asked Deedat. "Yes," I told him. "Go back to Rome and write to me," he said. This was his style. He never pushed me. I was livid, made salaam, and stormed out.' He met Vanker and explained what had transpired. 'Listen to Deedat,' was Vanker's advice.

Yakub left, but outside he pondered for a while before returning and insisting, 'I want to be a Muslim.' An angry Deedat raised his voice. 'I told you to return to Rome and write to me.' Yakub said, 'Fine, I will do that, but what if I die today? Will I die as a Muslim or Christian?' At this, Deedat's expression changed. 'Come Akhi [brother], let's get you some clothes.' They went to Mawlana Omarjee's retail store across the road, bought some clothes, and Yakub attended his first jum'a prayer. After jum'a, Deedat asked, 'Where are you going?' Yakub replied, 'To Manjra's for lunch.' 'You can't. You are fasting,' said Deedat. 'Do Muslims fast on Friday?' asked Yakub. 'No, but it is Ramadan,' explained Deedat. 'Why didn't you tell me?' joked Yakub, 'I would have waited until next month.' Deedat often took him to Manjra's and treated him to dhal and rice. He remembered once telling Deedat 'If this is the food of Muslims, I hope I become one…And, by Allah, I did.'

Yakub informed Archbishop Hurley of his decision. That weekend, the *Southern Cross*, a local Christian newspaper, warned Catholics to have nothing to do with the 'blasphemer', while his sister, whom he described as 'more Catholic that the Pope', arranged for his excommunication from the Church. 'It is sad…the heavy price reverts have to pay in terms of their family. I lost part of mine.' He did, however, become closer to his parents. His mother and father died while living at his home in Durban, his father 'accepting the shahadah just before his death…I felt unemployed after that.'

Yakub soon changed his name to Jamaluddin, and his story took many twists and turns. He left South Africa after embracing Islam and settled in Vancouver. He entered the legal profession and got married. The story of his marriage is remarkable. For a few weeks he saw a woman on the train and fell in love with her. One day, on a whim, he followed her home and rang the doorbell 'What do you want?' she asked. 'To marry you.' he replied. 'But you don't know me,' she said. 'I have a whole lifetime to do that,' he answered. He met her mother who asked a number of questions and told him that they were Jewish. He replied, 'No problem', and recited the Jewish shema (similar to the kalima). Impressed, the mother and daughter told him to return the following day to sign the pre-nuptial contract. Jamaluddin rushed off to the mosque and asked Imam Abdul Rahman to perform the nikah after jum'a. When the Imam asked for the name of his bride, he replied, 'I don't know. I'll tell you tomorrow.'

He learnt that her name was Peta Lonberg. She held an MBA degree, was a lecturer in business administration, and a national skier. Tragically for Jamaluddin, Peta, his five-year-old daughter Natasha, and his brother-in-law were killed in a car accident. His life turned upside down and, in desperate need of comfort, Jamaluddin sought out his parents whom he had not seen since 1969. They were vacationing in South Africa at the time and he joined them. While here, he took the opportunity to visit Deedat whom he had met only once since his conversion when both of them went for hajj in 1976. Deedat convinced Jamaluddin to join the IPCI. He returned to Canada, dissolved his legal practice, and returned to South Africa.

Jamaluddin's relationship with Deedat remained tempestuous. He worked for the IPCI on several occasions, as Deedat's 'secretary' or doing da'wah-related work. He also worked for an accounting firm. He stopped working professionally in 1997 when he decided to devote his life entirely to Islamic work. He studied at the darul 'ulum in Newcastle under Mawlana Cassim Sema and Mufti A.K. Hoosen, and became imam of the Khagiso Mosque near Azaadville. After four years he handed his duties over to an African imam 'to take the mosque forward' and returned to Durban. Between 2001 and 2006, he was involved with an Aids-awareness foundation that provided care mainly to reverts with Aids; he worked for Yusuf Buckas's Islamic Da'wah College; he was principal of a madrasa for adult reverts at Anjuman School in Leopold Street; and between 2002 and 2004 he ran a school for African children in grades 10 to 12. Jamaluddin retired after his leg had to be amputated in August 2006, but he continued to conduct Islamic classes at a baitul aman (Muslim old-age home) in Durban where he lived until his death in 2008.

Jamaluddin, while full of admiration for Deedat, believed that Deedat lost some of his support towards the end because of his 'agressive approach'. Alhough Jamaluddin had resigned from the IPCI, the two men patched up their differences shortly before Deedat's death. It was 'Allah's rahmah [mercy] that he spent that time bedridden. His brain was still functioning and it gave him time to ask people for forgiveness and vice versa.' Deedat told a mutual friend that he wanted to see Jamaluddin. It was a 'delightful reunion...very moving and sad.' Deedat cried twice, first when he asked 'How are your dear parents?' and Jamaluddin informed him that they had passed on and then when Deedat asked if he had read *The Choice* and Jamaluddin replied, 'Yes. By Allah, it is your finest work.'

---

Dawood Ngwane had to travel a long and arduous journey, and overcome many obstacles, to find what he called 'the light'. While Islam is taken for granted in the lives of most Muslims, Ngwane embraced Islam late in life, and the passion with which he spoke and wrote about Islam reflected the deep impression it made on him. This brief history of Dawood Ngwane – or Uncle Dawood, as he was known – outlines his early struggles and how he came to accept the Qur'anic message.

David Gabriel Ngwane was born on 30 March 1930 in rural Mapumulo in the heart of Zululand. There was an active Roman Catholic mission station in the area and many had become Christians, including David's parents, Joseph and Roseta. David attended St Philomena's Catholic School at the age of eight. When he was eleven, the family moved to Inanda because of his father's ill health. David enrolled at St Michael's Catholic School in Redhill in 1942. He left home at three o'clock each morning and walked for over two hours to catch the train in Phoenix to Redhill Station, where he sold sugar cane to supplement the family income. Although he was tired by the time he started school, he excelled at his studies. When the Catholic mission opened a school in the nearby village of Ottawa in 1944 he transferred there and then walked ninety minutes to and from school each day.

David's mother died of a heart attack in 1946. David, only in Standard 5, was left to take care of his ailing father and his sister, Veronica. He left school and took on menial jobs to support his family, working as a gardener, a 'delivery boy', and as a factory hand.

Through these hard times, David remained a staunch Catholic. He joined the Christ the King mission parish in Congella where he conducted the church choir. In 1954, he married church member Emily Ndlovu. They had four children but eventually separated and David married again in 1964. Three children were born to his second marriage. David joined Lewis Furnishers in 1958 and then British Petroleum in 1974 as a sales representative and he held the latter position until 1985.

David was determined to fulfil his childhood ambition of becoming a lawyer. Despite working long hours and struggling to bring up his large family, he completed matric at the age of thirty-nine in 1969 by correspondence. He then enrolled for an undergraduate law degree at the University of South Africa and graduated in 1978 at the age of forty-eight. He completed his LLB degree in 1985, and, in July 1986, started his own legal practice in Broad

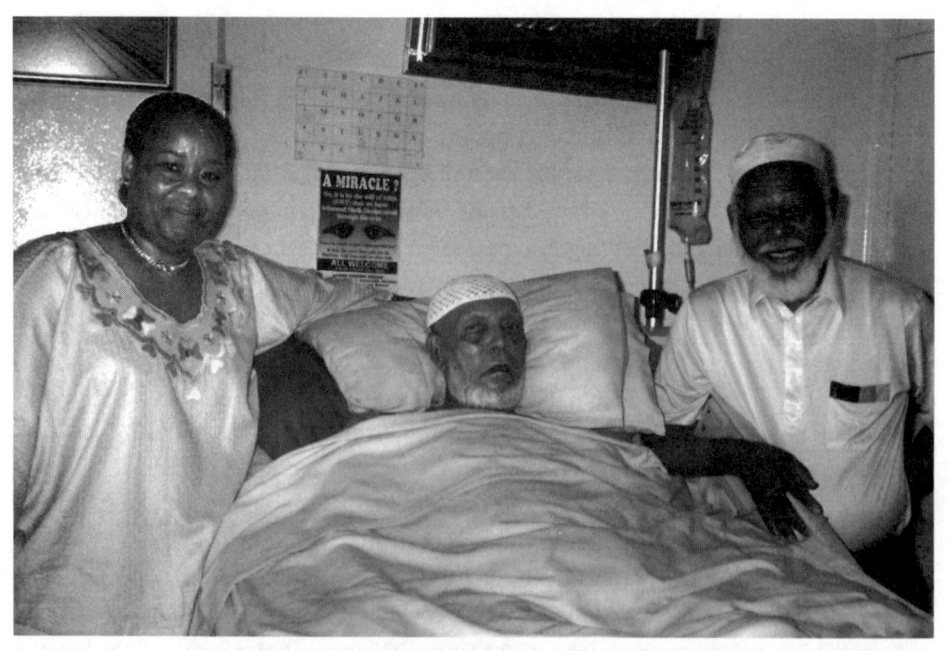

Dawood Ngwane and his daughter Lindiwe Hendricks, who was a minister in the South African government at the time, visiting Deedat at his Verulam home.

Street at the age of fifty-six! Ngwane also continued with his academic studies. He completed an LLM in 1993 and was reading for a Ph.D. when he passed away.

Throughout this time, Ngwane remained active in his Catholic parish as a member of choir and various committees. He was also appointed as a trustee of St Mary's Hospital in Mariannhill. Ngwane underwent a life-changing experience around 1994 when he stumbled upon Deedat's booklet *Crucifixion or Cruci-Fiction?* while preparing for a church meeting. The title grabbed his attention.

> It happened by coincidence because I was looking for a particular book in my son's bedroom when I found this booklet and the title attracted my attention, *Crucifixion or Cruci-Fiction?* I thought, 'What does that mean?' So that day I read the booklet three times. I tell you that I couldn't put the book down during my suppertime. I had the book in my hand when I was eating. I saw this man's name at the end, his address and I thought, let me go and see him. The receptionist telephoned him and said there's a man who insists on seeing you and he said, 'Send him in.' I told him… 'I like what you wrote and it makes sense, it makes a lot of sense. I'm a Christian.' And I asked, 'What do you mean Christ was not crucified?' He said, 'You have the book, you read the book, didn't you find out why I say he wasn't crucified?' I said I didn't believe him. 'If Jesus said, I'm going to die and rise, even though they did not say it, then how can we say it did not happen?' He said, 'You fool, you are a Zulu?' I said, 'Yes, I'm a Zulu.' He said, 'Your forefathers believed in one God and today you believe in three.'[2]

Ngwane is congratulated on his appointment as IPCI president in 2003. From left: Yusuf Ally, Dr Mahomed Khan, Ahmed Saeed Moola, Dawood Ngwane, Tahir Sitoto, Ahmed Shaikh, and Ebrahim Jadwat.

Ngwane's world turned upside down. Deedat's words stuck in his mind even as he carried on with his Christian life but the seeds of doubt had been planted and he found himself constantly in Deedat's office:

> I was confused. The book plunged me into deep questioning and doubting my core beliefs, I kept coming to Deedat to confront him and question him. At first I argued with him. Soon my arguments were less and less convincing. He would answer my questions. I would come through that door thinking today I'm going to get him. He would just laugh at me.

Ngwane visited church elders for clarity. He was a 'big name' in the church and wanted to give the 'elders' an opportunity to convince him that Deedat was wrong. Ngwane met with senior members of the Catholic church in KwaZulu-Natal but they failed to change his mind. He takes up the story:

> 'My Lord, I have a problem.' 'Yes, what's your problem?' he responded. 'I no longer believe that God is a trinity.' He nearly collapsed. He never thought that he was going to hear those words from me, because I was so firmly rooted in the church. In a firm and authoritative voice the father asked, 'What has happened to you?' I handed him Shaykh Deedat's book and asked him to read it and get back to me with his response. Three months passed and there was no response. I informed the Diocese Management Committee what transpired and they were shocked. The committee decided to arrange a meeting with the father to discuss the question. When I met him he had several Bibles with him. He said that I need to understand right from the outset that the *'trinity is not in the bible. It is the teaching of the church.'* I knew then I had to move on.[3]

Aside from this doctrinal dilemma, Ngwane was also attracted by salah, which he found comforting as it gave him 'an opportunity to connect to God in a way that was not possible under Christianity'. Ngwane's decision to embrace Islam was not sudden. He visited his children to inform them of his decision and explain that although he had taught them certain beliefs and practices, he had discovered something new and left it to them to decide whether they wished to follow him or not.

Ngwane officially embraced Islam. He became Dawood Ngwane and married Ayesha though he did not divorce either of his first two wives. Dawood's conversion to Islam did not change his relationship with his extended family. They respected his decision while he respected their choice to remain Christian. An indication of his family's respect for Dawood is that in his lounge was a beautiful calligraphic rendering of a verse from the Qur'an given to him as a gift by one of his daughters who is not Muslim.

Ngwane launched his book, *Ubhaqa: The Instrument of Light*, on 25 October 2002. The book, written in Zulu, was primarily aimed at KwaZulu-Natal's Zulu population. Ngwane regretted that the message of Islam had been kept away from Africans for centuries and was determined to share his experiences. He had made it his mission, he said, to break the

King Goodwill Zwelithini with Dawood Ngwane at the launch of Ngwane's book, *Ubhaqa*.

misconceptions and stereotypes that surround Islam as a Malay and Indian religion and to impress on Africans Islam's universal message. He said at the launch of his book:

> The book is deliberately written in Zulu; for in my contentment with what I had discovered I thought of my people; the Zulu nation. Knowing the misery into which Western civilisation has plunged them; knowing the poverty in which they languish and knowing the depth of ignorance and deception into which they have been subjected; I feel I have a duty to let my people know what I have discovered; expose them to the knowledge and let those who are eager for knowledge drink from the fountain.
>
> Even if I remained a 'Mr Nobody' I would have been satisfied to be an ordinary Muslim; for my becoming a Muslim was not based on anything but my conviction that Islam is the only religion that is able to give one guidance towards happiness in this world and in the hereafter…Islam is the only religion which has the capacity to extricate us from our misery in this country and indeed in the whole world.

The book launch was attended by many young African Muslims as well as politicians and businessmen. King Goodwill Zwelithini was special guest of honour. Addressing the king directly, Ngwane said:

> I spent many years of my life in darkness. In all those years I was happy and satisfied to be where I was for I knew not the light and therefore did not realise that I was in darkness…It is for this reason your Majesty that I have invited you to the launch of the book; because his Majesty is the King of a great nation; a nation that will benefit spiritually, morally, and physically by leaning towards Islam and indeed by embracing Islam as their way of life…I extend my invitation to your Majesty to lead your Nation

into Islam. Let the book that we are launching today be the guiding light to lead the Zulu nation into an informed choice of religion.[4]

Ngwane was optimistic that more Africans would embrace Islam, though he pointed to several hurdles. Firstly, he described the relationship between Indian and African Muslims as 'shallow and superficial', and saw this as a serious problem. Many African Muslims, he pointed out, felt that they were not accepted as part of the Islamic umma. In fact, he told *Youth* magazine that for most of his life he saw Indian Muslims 'go to the mosques and perform worship, but we didn't know much about what they were doing because they kept to themselves. For this reason, Islam was known as a religion of Indians.'[5]

Gender imbalance was a second problem identified by Ngwane; among young African Muslims, more girls tend to accept Islam than boys. The question for Ngwane was who these girls would marry. A third problem is that few townships have mosques or madrasas, which Dawood regarded as essential to establishing a thriving Islamic community. Ngwane stressed that he did not experience these problems personally, and maintained that, even if he had, he would not have changed his beliefs:

> When you discover Islam, you do not have any other choice than to become a Muslim. You feel that you have come to the end of your search, the end of your destiny. I accepted Islam for Islam, not for other Muslims. Let me be honest, I have not had any problems. In fact Baboo Jadwat and Ahmed Saeed Moola have even visited my Family Day. But some African Muslims have had nasty experiences.

Ngwane had one regret. 'Unfortunately, when I embraced Islam it was around the same time that Ahmed Deedat had a stroke and I was never able to share my news with him.' He was sad that he did not have the opportunity to work with Deedat at the IPCI but did visit him at home regularly after his stroke.

His advancing years did not slow Dawood Ngwane down. He became a trustee of the Inchanga Islamic Centre and of IPCI in 1999 and was elected president of the IPCI in 2003. He was elected chairperson of the Africa Muslim League, which was launched on 3 July 2009 at a gala dinner to honour then-KwaZulu-Natal premier, Dr Zweli Mkhize. Dawood Ngwane passed away on 17 September 2009 (28 Ramadan 1430AH) after a short illness.

## 25
# ON GOD'S WAVELENGTH?

Loved by many, reviled by some, Deedat never lost sight of his mission.

Ahmed Deedat was created
the moment missionaries insulted his intelligence.

– Omar Khan[1]

LONG BEFORE Thomas L. Friedman proclaimed that 'the world is flat', and global-justice activists coined the term 'think local, act global', Ahmed Deedat seamlessly integrated the local and the global through his many international tours and the distribution of audio and videotapes.² Deedat rejected the often-parochial religio-cultural practices of many 'ulama in favour of an Islam that shunned national boundaries and attached itself to a worldwide community of Muslims. In seeking to create this globalised Islamic identity, Deedat charted an independent course based largely on destabilising Christian beliefs, and showed that he was willing to interpret Islam and its mission without relying on the traditional interpretations of Islamic scholars. There was both individualism and globalism in his message.

Ahmed Deedat turned the local Muslim world upside down. Internally he challenged the hegemony of the imams and externally he took on Christian missionaries based on his study of the Bible. This not only upset many Christians but also many Muslims who saw him as portraying them in an unfavourable light because of his combative and direct (and at times crass) approach. Globally he challenged some prominent Christian evangelists, most famously taking on Jimmy Swaggart on the latter's home turf in Baton Rouge, Louisiana. In the process, this man of humble beginnings and little formal education became a household name in many parts of the Muslim world.

Deedat left a relatively comfortable job as a salesman to become a missionary for Islam. His journey saw him write booklets and pamphlets, engage Christian evangelists in public debates and deliver lectures to crowds of thousands in cities and towns across North America, Europe, the Middle East, and Australia, feature on television networks worldwide, and produce and distribute his own audio and videotapes. He acquired an international reputation as an 'Islamic scholar' even though he was not one in any traditional sense.

Deedat stood apart from his contemporaries in that he attempted to rigorously analyse the Bible (for Muslim and Christian audiences) rather than expounding the Qur'an to a non-Muslim audience. His mission was important in a context where Muslims have had no central institution that could be said to represent them since the abolition of the Ottoman caliphate after the First World War. Dialogue with Christians tends to take place at local levels and often through individuals such as Deedat who are, on the whole, unable to match the human and material resources at the disposal of Christian missionaries and televangelists.³

Deedat was no saint. His family life, particularly his relationships with his brother Abdullah and his son Ebrahim, was charged with enormous tensions. But this is a familiar tale – many public figures experience great difficulties in their personal lives, with Mohandas K. Gandhi, a fellow Gujarati who walked the same streets as Deedat just a few decades earlier, one eminent example. Difficult family relationships were a feature of Deedat's life but this book does not attempt to engage with Deedat's personal life. Its focus is largely on what he achieved in the public sphere.

Long after his death, Deedat continues to evoke mixed responses. His writings and speeches are available worldwide, on the internet, and even in the embassies of some Muslim countries. While he still inspires many Muslims the world over, as is evident from the numerous websites and blogs where he remains a topic of intense discussion, those who are concerned about the hardening of religious boundaries since 9/11 voice misgivings about his influence on young Muslim activists in the United Kingdom, Pakistan, the Middle East, and elsewhere.

What led to the rise of Deedat and how are we to assess his legacy?

A combination of factors contributed to the making of Deedat. The international context was crucial – namely, the rise of televangelism, the spread of Pentecostalism in Latin America and Africa, and the global hegemony of Western powers. Contrary to the expectations of many intellectuals and politicians, there was a turn away from secularism during the 1970s. In *The Battle for God*, Karen Armstrong writes of a 'fundamentalist assault' that included the rise of televangelists such as Jerry Falwell in the USA, who founded the Moral Majority Party in 1979 and urged Protestants to get involved in politics and challenge legislators pushing a 'secular humanism'. Meanwhile, the Muslim world witnessed the Iranian Revolution (1979), the assassination of Anwar Sadat in Egypt (1981), and occupation of the Grand Mosque in Makkah (1979). In occupied Palestine, after the Yom Kippur War of 1973, the Kookists (founded by Rabbi Kook), ultranationalists, and other religious Zionists formed the Gush Emunim ('Bloc of the faithful'), a pressure group that rejected the old socialist and nationalist discourse of Zionism in preference for the language of the Bible.[4]

Deedat thrived in this dichotomy because he conveyed a 'message' that many Muslims wanted to hear. As Larkin points out, 'the polemical nature of his critique, coming during the emergence of Christian televangelists in the 1970s, promulgated him to enormous fame in the Muslim world. He came to be seen as the Muslim "response" to the massive rise of evangelical Christianity and a media presence to rival Christian preachers.'[5]

Deedat's international popularity must also be located in the context of transnational movements. According to Rony Brauman of Médecins Sans Frontièrs, the period since the 1970s witnessed the emergence of 'sovereignty-free actors', that is, organisations such as Oxfam, Greenpeace, and Amnesty International as well as individuals who positioned themselves on the international stage in ways that previously had been reserved for states:

> This phenomenon also applies to terrorist groups, to religious movements, to businesses, to revolutionary movements. With urbanisation, instantaneous communication, and the democratisation of transport, we are witnessing a revolution in the abilities and aptitudes of the individual. It is within this context that private organisations of all kinds have been multiplying and developing at a rate that would have been unimaginable at any other time. There has also been a rapid development of television.[6]

Support for Deedat was also partly due to Western hegemony and the subservience of many conservative Muslim regimes to Western governments. Deedat was seen as the 'champion' of those waging a battle against Western imperialism, which was interpreted broadly to include the activities of missionaries. As Philip Lewis points out:

The reasons for the popularity of such polemicists and their literature are varied: the trauma colonialism wrought on Muslim peoples whose religious self-understandings as 'best of all communities' led them to suppose that Islam should prevail over all religious and ideological alternatives; the wounded pride of living in a post-colonial world within the continuing hegemony of western culture…the dislocation wrought by migration, exacerbated by racism and Islamophobia…In a world in which history seems to have gone all wrong, some dignity at least can be preserved by the claim to moral and religious superiority.[7]

Deedat's strength was that he cut across the divide between royalty and the 'people', between young and old, between those allied to the West and those involved in Arab nationalism, between those advocating 'interfaith dialogue' and those building Islamic fundamentalisms. In this regard, the growth of Muslim youth movements worldwide from the 1970s, with the World Assembly of Muslim Youth (WAMY) as a co-ordinating body, opened doors for Deedat in many parts of the world.

In South Africa, in addition to the activities of missionaries, white domination in apartheid South Africa provided the impulse for some of Deedat's local support. Black South Africans experienced perpetual humiliation as a result of racial discrimination and, when Deedat debated with Christians, a 'heroic' figure full of 'valour' as Fuad Hendricks described him, his supporters saw him as taking on the 'white' man and were 'exhilarated' when he 'browbeat' his opponents.

The issue of race was no less important internationally. Ebi Lockhat, who went on several overseas tours with Deedat, remembers:

> The debate was always with the Christian, the white Christian. Now in places like Saudi Arabia, I don't know if this has changed but in 1993 they still had an inferiority complex. So for them this person of colour was standing up against white Christianity. He was their hero and they really enjoyed it because he was pummelling somebody

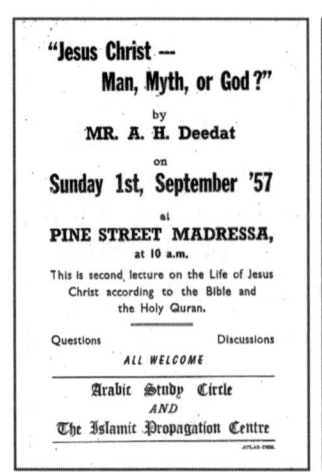

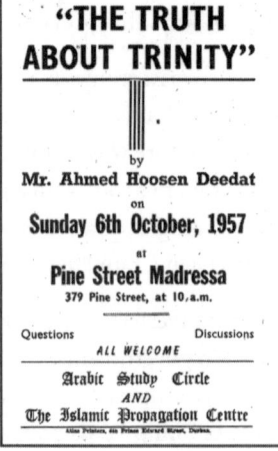

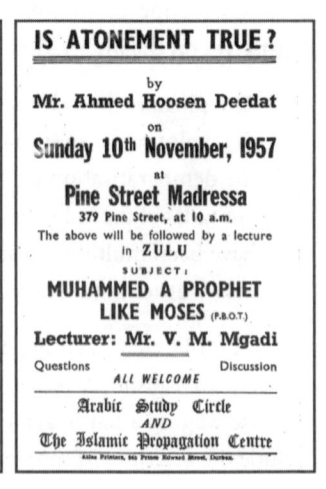

---

**"Jesus Christ — Man, Myth, or God?"**
by
MR. A. H. Deedat
on
**Sunday 1st, September '57**
at
PINE STREET MADRESSA,
at 10 a.m.
This is second lecture on the Life of Jesus Christ according to the Bible and the Holy Quran.

Questions      Discussions
ALL WELCOME

Arabic Study Circle
AND
The Islamic Propagation Centre

---

**"THE TRUTH ABOUT TRINITY"**

by
Mr. Ahmed Hoosen Deedat
on
**Sunday 6th October, 1957**
at
Pine Street Madressa
379 Pine Street, at 10 a.m.

Questions      Discussions
ALL WELCOME

Arabic Study Circle
AND
The Islamic Propagation Centre

---

**IS ATONEMENT TRUE?**
by
Mr. Ahmed Hoosen Deedat
on
**Sunday 10th November, 1957**
at
Pine Street Madressa
379 Pine Street, at 10 a.m.
The above will be followed by a lecture in ZULU
SUBJECT:
MUHAMMED A PROPHET LIKE MOSES (P.B.O.T.)
Lecturer: Mr. V. M. Mgadi

Questions      Discussion
ALL WELCOME

Arabic Study Circle
AND
The Islamic Propagation Centre

and he's from 'our' religion. The Arab world only earned respectability with oil in the 1970s. Prior to that they regarded themselves as inferior although they had nationhood. So I think that part of the explanation for Deedat was that the Arab world was crying out for a hero.

When we went to the UK the halls were filled, even on cold evenings people came out. A large portion was the older generation, the fathers or grandfathers of Asian people living there. They were not born there. And when I spoke to them, 'Mota, why did you come?' He would say simply 'Deedat Mota.' You see, Deedat came to England and he was talking to the white man so he gave them hope. That's why they gravitated towards him. I don't think it's any different to a sports hero, except that you've got religion attached to it, 'That is our man,' they seemed to say.

Attorney Saber Ahmed Jazbhay reinforced this point:

I will say in a complimentary form that his mouth was a weapon of mass destruction in the sense that he destroyed many feelings of inferiority amongst Muslims. He galvanised them, he put them on a pedestal and showed them, 'Hang on, we have the capacity and the power to respond.' His means galvanised the youth. Ahmed Deedat was not a violent man. What he did was to expose the fallacies of the other side, and in doing that he showed people that this is what they are doing to you. He showed Muslims in Nigeria, Kenya, in other countries that this is what your so-called Christian brothers, your so-called white brothers are doing to you.

Cassim Peer, who at the time of writing was acting high commissioner for South Africa in Pakistan, made a similar observation about that country:

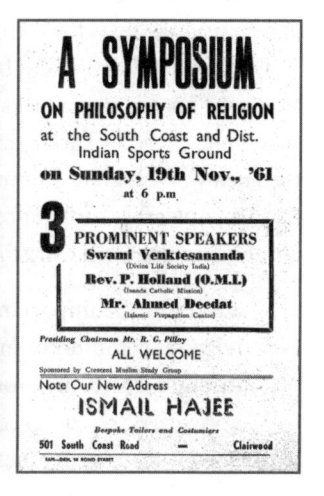

The adoration and respect for Shaykh Deedat remains boundless even so many years after his death. From my interaction it seems that their respect, admiration, and love for him was largely due to the fact that the locals here have not shown any capacity to take on the detractors of Islam in their own cities and towns. In Shaykh Deedat, they found a hero who could take on any challenge to Islam and win against the greatest of their missionaries and televangelists. They feel that he had the guts to say to the world that he carried the true message, and if anyone did not think so, they were welcome to debate him. They always came out second best.

This sentiment was repeated in many of the interviews.

Language was another crucial element in Deedat's emergence as a transnational figure. His use of English set him apart from other powerful figures in the Islamic world during this same period. The work of renowned Muslim thinkers such as Abulhamid Kishk of Cairo was limited to Egypt and the Arab world because he only spoke in Arabic. By using English as the medium for his lectures, Deedat garnered a wider international audience. In the contemporary period, Amr Khaled, an Egyptian accountant who became a fulltime preacher on satellite television (IQRA channel via NILESAT), and whose sermons are distributed over the internet and via audio and videotape, is also handicapped by his vernacular even though he maintains a German website. While operating on a more intellectual level, the importance of language can be seen in Tariq Ramadan's global popularity, which is partly attributable to his command of English, French, and Arabic.[8] Deedat's publications, however, were translated into such languages as Urdu, Russian, Arabic, Bengali, French, Chinese, Japanese, Mayalam, Zulu, Afrikaans, and Dutch, amongst others to ensure that his message was accessible internationally.

Deedat lacked a formal secular or religious education. As Dr Ahmad Sakr pointed out, he 'did not graduate from Oxford, Cambridge, Harvard, Yale, or any high citadel of learning, but from the "University of Muhammad".'[9] Rather than this being a handicap, it may be argued that Deedat's lack of formal education was precisely what enabled him to be so daring. He was not encumbered in the way that many who are formally educated, particularly at more elite institutions, are. More importantly, perhaps, it meant that his works were written in accessible language and built their arguments in a style that appealed to an audience of ordinary people, for many of whom English was a second language. They were able to read the texts for themselves and make their own judgements.

Deedat's confidence and belief in himself and his message meant that he did not need to restrict his counter-attacks against Christian missionaries to the safety of his own space. Instead he chose, as Larkin emphasises, to 'physically and symbolically enter the terrain of the enemy'. He travelled to the heartlands of evangelical Christianity in the USA, the UK, Sweden, Australia, and France, challenging Christian preachers both literally and rhetorically. In engaging with Christianity, Larkin contends, Deedat's project also

> addresses the important role polemic and confrontation plays in the definition of religious community and not just through the mechanism of othering and separation through which the group is defined. It also raises the complicated question of the porosity of religious communities and the tactile and formal ways they learn and borrow from each other even through mutual contest.[10]

[In Deedat's case, his] mimicking of evangelism and secular debate was not confined to rhetorical styles: he also mimicked the infrastructure of missionary evangelism by circulating pamphlets and audio- and videocassettes of public lecture tours and by appearing on television in Muslim countries. By presenting lectures in public spaces such as town halls and staging debates with famous Christian preachers, he also mimicked the rationalist, secular modes of the public sphere. Deedat's distinction lies in his transgression, his inhabiting of Christian rhetorical modes. Speaking as a Muslim in a Christian style, displaying greater biblical erudition than his Christian opponents, and performatively presenting Christianity in both its religious and secular guises, Deedat played with the formal boundaries between religious traditions in order to mock and ridicule his opponents.[11]

There is a politics involved in Deedat's mimicry of evangelicalism and its infrastructure. While he clearly turned the idea of mimicry on its head, mimicry is more than simply an act of rebellion or parody. If, as German dramatist George Büchner wrote in the aftermath of the French Revolution, 'la révolution dévore ses enfants' (revolutions devour their children), then mimicry is not far behind. Witness the use of the internet and audio and video recordings in the propaganda wars of the twenty-first century, and in particular the nefarious uses that certain groups have found for these technologies.

The communications revolution, and particularly video technology, was crucial in reshaping Deedat's mission. He embraced the technological revolution wholeheartedly and sent edited copies of his debates and lectures to potential donors while making them available to a global audience of millions. These enthralling debates and their international circulation were crucial in the emergence of Deedat as a popular figure within the Muslim world. Without this technical means, his influence would probably have been limited. YouTube has since made Deedat's works easily accessible through a dedicated digital space. Just as nineteenth-century nationalists used print capitalism to create unified fields of communication, Deedat built a solid global support base through the distribution of videotapes, booklets, and pamphlets.

Deedat's personal qualities were especially crucial in his popularity. After all, comparable figures, such as Jamal Badawi of Canada, did not achieve the same level of recognition as Deedat. Professor Salman Nadvi remembers him as 'a tall, very impressive person, with an imposing physique…when he walked on the street, you couldn't ignore him and when he stood on the podium he commanded attention'. Fuad Hendricks pointed to the salesman in Deedat: 'He would take a hundred no's before a yes came, but he always persevered. Nothing was a bridge too far.' Mention of Deedat evoked in Dr G.M. Hoosen memories of his self-belief and boldness: 'He always did more than he had money for. He regarded everything as doable.' Deedat was also supremely confident and meant every word when he said that 'authorities on the Bible are like putty in my hands during debates'. However, he did not take anything for granted. He prepared meticulously for every debate and lecture. This included arriving at the venue hours in advance to ensure that everything, from the height of the microphone to the lighting, was in order.

Above all, Deedat was driven by a deep sense of mission. Journalist Keysar Trad met Deedat in 1996, shortly before his stroke:

> I went to his hotel armed with my personal cassette recorder. A number of reverted Muslims were sitting with him in his room, acting as his minders or doorkeepers. It was one of them who ended the interview saying, 'you just got something that no one else got, a full hour's interview'. This interview was most penetrating and informative. Ahmed Deedat, through sharing his thoughts, allowed me to take a stroll inside his pained heart and soul. He was a man troubled by his own Muslim community's historic deficiencies. He had dedicated much of his life to help people of all faiths arrive at the truth, but as we reminisced about Muslim history, all we could see were the grandiose failures at the micro levels of a number of Muslim societies. He said it is not enough to build your mosque and pray there seeking to save yourself and your children. That only fulfils one part of the verse, 'Litubashshira bihil muttaqin' (to give glad tidings to those who are conscious of God). What about the second part of the verse, 'Watundhira bihi qawman ludda' (and warnings to people given to contention), he asked? I reflected, 'Where is our system of friendship, discussion, dialogue and goodwill?'[12]

It is easy to focus on the later Deedat, at the height of his fame and surrounded by the trappings of oil wealth, and to forget the early Deedat and his struggles to establish his mission. The beginnings were humble as Deedat and his wife Hawa, just like G.H. Vanker and his family, struggled to make ends meet. But Deedat's determination and Hawa's fortitude pulled them through.

Rafeek Hassen, in his capacity as president of the Islamic Interfaith Research Institute, travels across Southern Africa on lecturing tours. He was visibly moved during our interview when he tried to imagine how Deedat did the same thing five decades ago in his beaten-up

VW beetle, on gravel roads, often sleeping on the couches or floors of the homes of strangers, sometimes unsure whether he would have enough petrol to get from one town to the next.

Furthermore, Deedat's tastes remained simple and far removed from his public persona which could be extremely confrontational and dogmatic. Ebi Lockhat, who worked alongside Deedat at the IPCI for many years recalls, 'The real Ahmed Deedat that I sat next to for several years was humble. His lunch would be two slices of brown bread with a bit of cucumber...he said that his wife would pack it for him and that hardly ever changed. He drove the same car, certainly from the time I was there he drove a Golf. He claimed to me that he had driven Beetles before that. While I was there, an overseas donor offered to send him a car, and he said no, he was quite happy with the car he had.

Lockhat recalls once saying to him, 'Mr Deedat, you've got a very nice suit.' He said, 'Yes, and I've got five of them.' The tone in which he answered me was almost challenging. So I said, 'No, I don't want to know.' He replied, 'You do want to know. That's why you asked me that question. So let me tell you. I've got five of these. I haven't paid for a single one.' Deedat went on to explain that Mamoo Rajab's uncle was about the same build as he was and one Friday afternoon, after the jum'a prayer, Mamoo Rajab called Deedat and said, 'Listen, we don't want you to take offence [but] my uncle is deceased. He was your build and he had three suits made for him that were hardly used. We would like to offer them to you.' Deedat went on, 'So that was three of those suits, and the other two were done for me by well wishers when I was in New York. There was a tailor who estimated my size because he was so happy that I was coming to talk against Salman Rushdie. So that's how I got five suits but I haven't paid for a single one of them.' That, recalls Lockhat, was typical of Deedat's simplicity, and it seems it was something he never lost.

The IPCI was dynamic in the early period, and it helped to shape the contours of Islam in South Africa. It pioneered organised missionary work, promoted Islam through the media and defended it when necessary. It was the first local Muslim organisation to specifically target non-Muslims. Organisations such as the Tabligh Jama'at focused on Muslim piety, while the Arabic Study Circle and Muslim Youth Movement concentrated on increasing the knowledge of Muslims to make Islam relevant in the modern context and confront Western intellectual hegemony. The IPCI, on the other hand, targeted non-Muslims through newspaper extracts, lectures, videos, debates, the distribution of Qur'ans, and Bible classes.

Dr G.M. Hoosen believes that in assessing Deedat's achievements it is important to factor in his influence on people such as Dr Zakir Naik, the fact that Seventh Day Adventists have stopped knocking on Muslim doors, and the impact that the distribution of English translations of the Qur'an has had on many people's lives. Similarly, G.H. Agjee emphasised that 'the booklets and videos that Deedat published fortified Islam. By putting Christians on the back foot, he created a positive mindset. Before Deedat, Muslims were scared. Now they are confident.'

Zakir Naik is internationally known, but Deedat also inspired countless other less well-known figures. *Arab News* carried an article in August 2009, 'US doctor turns to Da'wah', about Dr Sabeel Ahmed, a Chicago-based radiologist who gave up his medical practice to devote his life to da'wah. Ahmed said that he was 'greatly influenced by Ahmed Deedat and Dr Zakir Naik, my mentors, and have been conducting da'wah work in the United States with great success'. Ahmed is the director of GainPeace, which has chapters in several cities in the USA and Canada. His organisation, according to Dr Ahmed, 'has taken on the responsibility of educating the American public about the teachings of Islam and dispelling whatever misconceptions they have. We have also been building bridges through Islam as the religion of peace, tolerance and coexistence.'[13]

Despite his many achievements, even supporters of Deedat point to his shortcomings and those of the IPCI. The IPCI had led the way in the use of media yet failed to gain access to television channels or start a radio station when the airwaves were democratised in post-apartheid South Africa. Al-Ansaar, Radio Islam, and Channel Islam International filled the breach. The IPCI's legacy in the townships is limited, and it failed to create an Islamic college with the millions of rands at its disposal. Ironically, the IPCI's financial success may well have been its Achilles heel. Its financial base was both an asset and a problem, creating as it did a 'comfort zone' that meant that new members did not have to share Deedat's zeal, energy, and dedication. For Fuad Hendricks the organisation lost 'its identity, its soul' as a result of the petrodollars. G.H. Agjee pointed out that by having its offices in an urban area, the IPCI failed to make inroads in African townships – hence the small number of African Muslims – nor was there any follow-up to provide support for those who embraced Islam. Professor Salman Nadvi stated that during his discussions with Deedat he suggested that 'instead of indulging in debates, why don't you establish a college, a school'. Deedat did not heed this advice and thus failed to leave behind 'a permanent institution that could have met the intellectual challenges of the times long after he was gone'.

The absence of proper organisation meant that the IPCI, for a time, centred on Deedat's personality. The absence of democratic structures, corporate governance checks and balances, and a proper succession system stymied the emergence of new blood and new ideas. The trustees were aware of the difficulty of reconciling the power of the individual with that of the organisation. Shortly after Deedat's death, they issued a mission statement that included the rhetorical reflection:

> Does an organisation with the calibre, charisma, and charm of its founder, Sheikh Ahmed Deedat, have a life span of its own; or one that will outlive its founder? This is a question often posed to us. In many respects Sheikh Ahmed Deedat was the personification of the IPCI, and he did not have a mentoring style to groom a successor. Our answer is simple, not simplistic, that Islam continues after the death of Prophet Muhammad (PBUH) and likewise the IPCI will last many lifetimes longer than its magnetic leader…The IPCI, since Sheikh Deedat fell ill, has been grappling to rebuild an organisation that was essentially moulded around the charisma of an internationally renowned person…Sheikh Ahmed Deedat had the foresight to transform the IPCI, which was a local organisation, into an international and world-class player with a global outlook and outreach…There are encouraging signs that the IPCI which Sheikh Deedat so painstakingly built for close to half a century will outlive its founder and continue his legacy to which he dedicated his entire life.

Entrusted with the task of carrying Deedat's legacy into the future, key IPCI staff in 2012 included (from left) Goolam Rasool Habdar, Hafez Shabir Basha, Ebrahim Mthembu, Iqbal Essop, Abdul Kalic Ally and Mahomed Khan.

The mission statement makes three statements that require comment: Deedat's failure to groom a successor; his charismatic leadership; and the confident prediction that the IPCI would survive his demise.

The criticism that Deedat failed to groom a successor is a legitimate one. There was no one to take over his mantle in terms of continuing his high-profile lectures and debates, introducing new ideas, and being a recognisable figure in the Muslim world. This may have been due to his strong personality, which meant that potential successors such as Buckas and Abdullah Deedat did not survive long in the IPCI. Aside from the personalities involved, the cash injection in the 1980s increased the financial value of the IPCI, and this may have made it more difficult for Deedat to relinquish power. It is also possible that it was hard for him to hand over to anyone else because he thrived on public adulation and so enjoyed the debates. On the other hand, could someone like Deedat have really prepared a successor? Can there be another Mandela, Ali, Gandhi, Billy Graham, people who come along once in a while, who have special personal qualities and are also shaped by particular circumstances? While Deedat had an aura that was unique, there is no excusing the fact that, because of the rupture within the IPCI, the trustees spent the 1990s locked in bitter litigation that not only took up much of their valuable time and human resources but also drained the coffers of the organisation.

The mission statement acknowledges that the IPCI was built around Deedat's charisma, to the extent that he became 'the personification of the IPCI'. Deedat was undoubtedly a leader who fits Max Weber's definition of charisma as

> a certain quality of an individual personality by virtue of which he is set apart from ordinary men and treated as endowed with…exceptional power or qualities. These are such as are not accessible to the ordinary person, but are regarded as…exemplary, and on the basis of them the individual concerned is treated as a leader.[14]

Yet, the charismatic Deedat failed to create a technocratically effective organisation. Ebi Lockhat drew an interesting analogy between two prominent South African retailers, Raymond

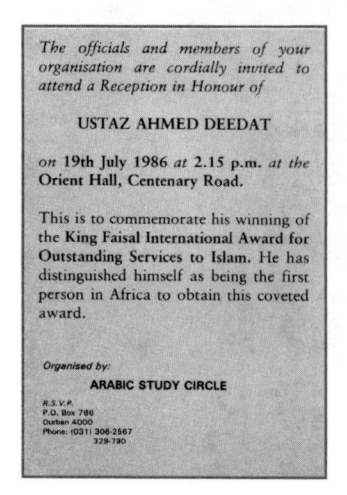

Ackerman and Tony Factor. During the 1970s, Tony Factor and his Downtown Group,

> that guy with the rasping voice who wanted to discount cars, everything...was a personality-based individual. He was big back then but where's Tony Factor's business today? When Raymond Ackerman of Pick 'n Pay goes, he's got 400 stores, he's got a succession plan, he's got a pattern in place.

It remains to be seen whether the IPCI will fufil the claim in its mission statement that the organisation will 'outlive its founder and continue his legacy', even though trustees Ebrahim Jadwat, Haroon Kalla, Yusuf Ally, Akhtar Thokan, Dr Mahomed Khan, Anwar Ballim, and A.S. Moolla have worked hard to steady the ship and repair the IPCI's tarnished image. The once-glamorous IPCI building was in danger of becoming a sad shadow of itself. Ebi Lockhat observed in 2008:

> I don't see much publicity in the paper. And when I go to a Muslim fete I know that if Deedat was around in his heyday you wouldn't have the IPCI with one stand showing his old books. They would be a dominant force. He would have stolen the show. There would be Qur'ans going out, there would be advertisements in the paper, there would have been something different going on, a buzz.

However, since 2008, there has been a noticeable change. The IPCI's records, including photographs, correspondence, and newspaper articles, have been systematically archived. The offices of the IPCI have been refurbished and a museum has been established to highlight Deedat's achievements. It is proving popular with local and overseas visitors. Attorney Yusuf Ismail joined the IPCI as a specialist on inter-religious issues, and has helped to revive its activities. Ismail is operating in a different terrain and his modus operandi is more about engaging members of other faiths than participating in polemical discussions. There has been a resurgence of visits by overseas lecturers, educational classes, and da'wah activities. In this context, the IPCI has brought renowned scholars such as Debra Mubasshir, Yusuf

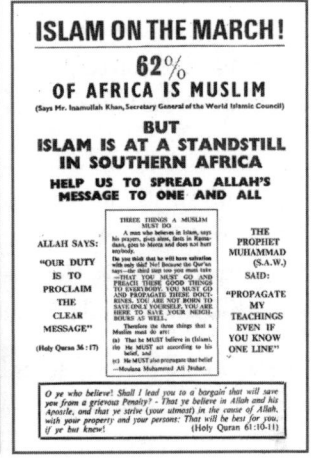

*In 2011, the IPCI was given an Islamic Finance Business Award by FirstRand Bank: a strong endorsement of the organisation's sound financial practices.*

Estes, Akbar Muhammad, Dr Faadil Sooliman, Shabir Ally, and others to South Africa. According to some interviewees, these visits were a reminder of the 'old Deedat days' as they engaged in debates and discussions with Christian scholars in the major centres of the country. The response to their appearances was overwhelming, with capacity crowds of both Muslims and Christians filling all the venues.

Muhammad Haron concludes his in-depth study of the relationship between Muslims and Christians in the four decades from 1960 to 2000 by observing that

> the dynamics of Christian–Muslim relations have radically changed. At the outset, individuals and groups adopted aggressive approaches towards one another in conveying their religious messages with the hope of winning converts to their respective folds. However, attitudes slowly shifted to being less aggressive and more co-operative and tolerant.[15]

Deedat needed the dichotomy between Islam and Christianity in order to attract a following and, for a long time, that dichotomy had existed in South African society as it intersected with identities such as race and class to create communities that were so obviously, and often brutally, separated. That dichotomy was a crucial part of the context for Deedat's support. By the late 1980s, rapid political and economic changes in South Africa resulted in many Muslims becoming more interested in similarities and (possible) connections while downplaying differences and divisions. Deedat increasingly became more popular internationally than within South Africa.

The 1980s and 1990s saw increasing numbers of Muslims adhering more strictly to the tenets of Islam. They were attracted in ever larger numbers to the reformist Tabligh Jama'at movement, the populist Barelwi tradition (with its emphasis on saints and shrines) was more active than ever with mawlids and other activities organised regularly, while a Sufi-oriented Islam (with its focus on dhikr and cleansing of the soul) began sprouting in many parts of the country. Deedat-style religious argumentation was put on the back burner.

Support for Deedat also declined within the Muslim Youth Movement (MYM). As the anti-apartheid struggle intensified in the 1980s, some Muslims became overtly political, with Achmat Cassiem forming Qibla and Farid Esack the Call of Islam. By the 1980s, the old vanguard of the MYM, which included Ebrahim Jadwat, Advocate A.B. Mahomed, Shawkat Thokan, Ismail Kalla, Iqbal Jassat, Dr Rehman Ismail, Fuad Hendricks and younger members such as Mohamed Amra were replaced by a Cape-dominated leadership. The movement under the likes of Rashied Omar, Fatima Noordien, Aslam Fataar, and Rushdie Edries moved from the Islamism of Abul A'la Mawdudi and Syed Qutb and formulated a vision around the ideas of Fazlur Rahman, Fathi Osman, Parvez Mansoor, and others critical of the anti-intellectual emphasis of the Muslim Brothers and Jamaate Islami. The MYM's new objectives, for example, replaced the establishment of an Islamic value system with a 'just social order'; advocated speaking to 'the people' rather than the umma; and instead of seeking to 'convert all people of this part of Africa' to Islam, the movement sought to 'form links with Islamic and other movements with similar aims and objectives'. In the context of heightened anti-apartheid activism and interfaith co-operation it was considered impolitic to engage with other religions in a combative way. The MYM also distanced itself ideologically from WAMY because of that organisation's support for the Saudi state.[16] These changes eroded Deedat's support base.

Assessing Deedat's legacy is difficult because he was a highly contentious figure. Views about him – quite understandably, given the polemic nature of his mission – vary widely. Deedat's detractors view him as a destroyer of interfaith dialogue and blame him for exacerbating religious divisions, while his defenders see him as protecting Muslims from the bigotry and anti-Muslim activities of Christian missionaries. Inside South Africa, he faced opposition from both Muslims and non-Muslims who felt that his message and style were inflaming religious tensions. He crossed swords with many. Mohammed Makki summed up the position of South African detractors when he described Deedat as a 'pretender to the Islamic throne who contributed more to diminishing the happiness that has prevailed in South African religious circles than any other religious fanatic in the Republic's history'.[17]

Deedat's critics were concerned that his views on Christianity and Hindusim would be seen as representative of Muslims generally and that this would threaten religious harmony in a society already riven by racial divisions. Deedat was unapologetic when he was accused of fuelling Christian–Muslim tensions:

> The Christians are complaining about this Mr Deedat. They are thinking of him like Halley's Comet, which comes and goes away. Deedat is the only guy now who is upsetting the hornet's nest. So they ask, why doesn't he keep to Islam? They question why I should talk about Christianity… Well, one third of the Qur'an is addressed to the Jews and Christians. [This] one third has not been used for a thousand years. Christianity is a missionary religion and Islam is a missionary religion. As such, we are supposed to do what he is doing.[18]

In Deedat's defence, Larkin argues, the fact that his career 'was addressed to repudiating Christian evangelism, explains his use of savage humour, invective, and the tactical nature of his practice'.[19] Deedat's polemicist style may be seen as undermining interfaith dialogue but, on the other hand, it can also be represented as countering evangelical missionising, which is not exactly dialogical. As Keysar Trad pointed out:

> The style of Shaykh Deedat was unapologetically confronting. It was debate and not dialogue. However, he was addressing people who were also confrontational and in some of the videos I have seen, some of his opponents were also deceptive in misrepresenting Arabic words from the Qur'an to their English speaking audiences.

Deedat's methods and strategies did not endear him to all, but then he did not seek to achieve popularity. In the face of formidable opposition he implored Muslims not to ignore the Bible because it was the book of Christians or riven with contradictions, but to read it against the grain and use it as a 'weapon' against Christians. He wrote in *Is the Bible God's Word?* 'Show them the holes in the "holiness" which they have not yet seen.'

Philip Lewis believes that Deedat's influence remains insidious because his 'anti-Christian-polemical tradition…continue[s] to shape and colour Muslim attitudes and militate against any honest encounter with Christianity'.[20] Lewis suggests that this hinders serious interfaith dialogue. One response to Lewis is that the category of 'interfaith' is taken as given, yet the very notion derives from the unique conditions of the West, and particularly from the subjugation of religion in Western societies since the Enlightenment. Interfaith dialogue seems to be an attempt to show, or appear to show, tolerance of other religions without abandoning the principles of Western civilisation. The celebration of interfaith dialogue, which means accepting other belief systems, quite apart from being seen as a means of promoting harmony, suits religious leaders of all denominations as they can then protect their own 'territory'. It may also be argued that he was working outside the paradigm set up by interfaith dialogue. While his critics accuse Deedat of destroying interfaith dialogue, it appears that he bypassed more than destroyed it.

Deedat challenged other religions in free and open debate, but also took on members of his own faith. His scathing critique of emptied out, individualist, spiritual Islam, his critique of the excessive focus on beards when more pressing matters were at hand, his description of those who relied on saints as 'weak', his insistence on taking non-Muslims to the mosque and distributing English translations of the Qur'an in the face of fierce condemnation from some 'ulama, all point to a strong-minded individual who refused to be constrained.

Despite what his critics may suggest, and despite his many shortcomings, Deedat was no founder of 'fundamentalist' Islam avant-la-lettre, or even of extremist or militant Islam. He made it clear, over and over again, that he used words and not bombs. He condemned violence, telling a reporter for *Riyadh Daily* in 1992, for example, that 'you can't preach Islam with a laser gun, because the Holy Qur'an says, "There is no compulsion in religion." So you arm your intellect. Once you do that you are able to organise yourself. Then you are able to reach out and talk about Islam.'[21]

Deedat was prepared to debate with anyone. His language was often coarse, his responses often uncouth, but by going into the open, face to face with those who, he felt, were attempting to denigrate Islam, he opened himself up to defeat and ridicule. But such was his confidence and belief that he was even prepared to go into the 'enemy's' lair, armed not with a rucksack full of explosives but knowledge of his opponent's seminal texts. It was often the ultimate weapon. As one commentator put it, Deedat's 'shield would be his extensive knowledge of the Bible and Qur'an and his sword was his frank, piercing style of delivery'.[22]

The analogy with boxing frequently came up in interviews. For example, Yakoob Mehtar, who attended Deedat's talks from the 1940s reflected:

> We heard them not so much for the benefit we would have got out of his talks – not so much for that, or not so much to learn. We were young people in our early 20s, and he was, I wouldn't say hitting back at the Christians, but he was debating and putting our points across to them. And he was like, like when you go to a boxing match and you got your hero hitting the opposite side. That was more it, than anything else, not so much to learn.[23]

In boxing, as in debate, there are rules. To play is about respecting these rules: to shake the hand of your opponent afterwards, not to bask in victory but to seek new and more challenging opponents, not only to fight to defend your own corner but to pursue your opponent to his (and nowadays her) corner. As Nelson Mandela put it in his autobiography, 'boxing is egalitarian. In the ring, rank, age, colour and wealth are irrelevant. When you are circling your opponent, probing his strengths and weaknesses, you are not thinking about his colour or social status.'[24] This was the essence of Deedat's approach, to get his opponents into the ring, one-on-one, with all their power, their racism, and their distortions of Islam, which would either be left behind or exposed. But he always ended with a handshake. As Sweden's Stanley Sjoberg would remark, 'Mr Ahmed Deedat challenged me and he did it clearly, openly, without hesitating to come as a guest to Sweden. He even insulted me with a smile on his face.'[25]

Many of Deedat's critics fail to take into account the post-9/11 context, including the multi-faceted 'crusade' by Christian and Jewish neo-conservatives on Islam, and international political tensions arising from then US president George W. Bush's 'War on Terror', and invasions of Iraq and Afghanistan. Manichaean narratives of good and bad, or a 'clash of civilisations', which was central to President Bush's agenda, created the kind of dichotomy that bred tension. The notion of a gap between 'Muslim' and 'Western/Christian' societies and peoples may be too bland and generalising to be of any analytical use, but it can, and has been, put to political misuse.

Many young Muslims who become politicised may be reacting to personal experiences of racist violence in European countries, ongoing institutional racism, or seeing their parents exploited as low-paid workers. The example of Tariq Ramadan, regarded by most Muslims as 'moderate', who was denied a visa to enter the United States to take up a position at the University of Notre Dame in 2008 and who was dismissed by a European university in August 2009 for appearing on Press TV, an English-language, UK-based, Iranian-sponsored television channel, shows that the terrain on which discussion and debate can take place has changed and new challenges have arisen. Also crucial is the way the internet is being used for counter discourses. The absence of charismatic leaders who command widespread support and prevalence of dispersed communication seems to be more of a problem than Deedat's alleged influence.

Ahmed Deedat was unquestionably one of the most publicly visible Muslim religious figures in South Africa in the second half of the twentieth century. There is no doubt that this self-taught man of broad smiles, waving arms, steely stamina, piles of books, a mind of dogmatic certitude, and ready answers had a profound impact on many in the Muslim world, as well as Christians who were forced to re-examine their texts and their understanding of the Bible. Notwithstanding the controversies that occurred in his public and private life, Deedat always gave the impression that he was at peace with himself and his God as far as his mission was concerned. Anyone whe knew Ahmed Deedat knows that, no matter what, he would have the last word, so it is appropriate to allow him to speak for himself through this extract from an exchange with radio presenter Gina Lewis that took place during his tour of Switzerland.[26]

> *Lewis*: For the first and only time that I was in Israel, I was in the dining room and didn't know anything about the holy days, customs and so on. I was finishing my supper and this beautiful sound went around the room. I can't describe to you how strongly I felt the presence of the spirit there. And that's what I felt when I first saw you, that same spirit, because you have a radiant face, you know, you do. You don't have all those worry lines and those lines of anguish that people that don't know God have, and so I feel that in you is that unity which Christ called the spirit. Did Muhammad have a word for it? What is that?
>
> *Deedat*: I think that it is to be in tune with God. See, if you are trying to fulfil the plan of God, His Word, automatically, I think that this spirit permeates in the person… The Qur'an says that the truth comes from God alone, so do not be of those who doubt. There is only one truth and that truth is from God. Whatever God says, is the truth. Once you are in tune with that, you vibrate on God's wavelength, you don't become gods but you are on the same vibration as His vibration.

## ACKNOWLEDGEMENTS

This book has been in the making for far too long. There were times when it seemed that it might never reach completion, and I owe a special debt of gratitude to the many people who assisted me in different ways. This project unquestionably owes its birth to Ebrahim Jadwat, who was involved in Ahmed Deedat's life in various capacities over an extended period and was determined that his life and influence be recorded.

Anwar Ballim and Haroon Kalla, both trustees of the IPCI, and Shabir Basha, also of the IPCI, embraced the project wholeheartedly and deserve special thanks for assisting in various ways. Mahomed Khan, the IPCI Liaison Officer, must be singled out for taking a personal interest in this project and going beyond the call of duty in his assistance; he helped to track down written sources, provided contact numbers and email addresses, and conducted an extensive search for photographs. In this regard, I would like to thank all members of Deedat's family, as well as his friends and colleagues, who scoured their family photograph collections for us, and so generously allowed us to reproduce selected images here. I would also like to thank professional photographer, Omar Badsha, for granting us permission to use one of his photographs on p. 138.

Interviews are always the most enjoyable aspect of research, and the sacrifices of those who gave of their time for interviews, or responded to telephone and email queries, sharing information about their long associations with Deedat, are much appreciated. Most (including Ahmed Deedat's detractors) responded without hesitation, and their perspectives have made for a more rounded study in the absence of comprehensive written records. The long list of interviewees is included at the end of the book, and my heartfelt thanks go to all of them.

Fatima Asmal assisted with research and editing in the early period, and Sana Ebrahim with proofreading. The skills of freelance production manager Mary Ralphs, designer Jenny Young, and proofreader Mary Starkey were crucial in preparing the text for print. I would like to thank the many individuals from whom I have learnt a great deal over the years, both through generous conversations with them, or through reading their work, about the history of Muslims in South Africa and about the study of Islam and Muslim communities in general: Ismail Manjra, Faisal Dawjee, Salman Nadvi, Zuleikha Mayat, Preben Klaarsholm, Ebrahim Moosa, Karin Willemse, Shamil Jeppie, Abdul Kader Tayob, Naeem Jeenah, Thomas Blom Hansen, Vinay Lal, and Ashwin Desai, amongst others. Finally, I would like to thank my family (Taskeen, Naseem, Yasmeen, and Razia) who have been a source of great strength over many years.

# NOTES

## 1 INTRODUCTION: THE ARGUMENTATIVE MUSLIM

1. Goth, 'Champion of Interfaith Dialogue'.
2. Interview, Pakistan Television, 1987. http://www.youtube.com/watch?v=ulhDA_MnpP8.
3. Interview with Faiza S. Ambah of *Arab News*, al-*Burhaan*, December 1989.
4. Mills, *Sociological Imagination*, 9.
5. See Black, *The History of Islamic Political Thought* and Connell, *Southern Theory* for an overview of the ideas of these theorists.
6. In Zebiri, 'Muslim Perceptions of Christianity', 190.
7. Interview with a Pakistani journalist, published in a*l-Burhaan*, December 1987.
8. 'Freedom of Joburg for Mandela', 26 July 2004. http://www.southafrica.info/mandela/mandela-joburg.htm.
9. Interview with Faiza S. Ambah of *Arab News*, al-*Burhaan*, December 1989.
10. Interview with Faiza S. Ambah of *Arab News*, al-*Burhaan*, December 1989.
11. Saïd, cited in Hirschkind, *Ethical Soundscape*, 213.
12. Fanon, *The Wretched of the Earth*; quote sourced from http://www.culture-of-peace.info/books/history/conquest.html.
13. Ashcroft et al., *Post-Colonial Studies*, 42.
14. *Al-Qalam*, March 1986.
15. Interview on Pakistani television, 1987. http://www.youtube.com/watch?v=ulhDA_MnpP8.
16. Originally published in *Nida'ul Islam*, May–June 1996. http://www.islam.org.au.
17. In *The Gift of the Nile*, Martin Bernal has written extensively about the Greek mathematicians' debts to the Egyptians.
18. Chatterjee, *Nationalist Thought and the Colonial World*, 65–67.
19. *Riyadh Daily*, 14 June 1993.
20. Interview with a Pakistani journalist, published in a*l-Burhaan*, December 1987.
21. Zebiri, 'Muslim Perceptions of Christianity', 180.
22. Siddiqui, *Christian–Muslim Dialogue*, xiii–xv.
23. Interview on Pakistani television, 1987. http://www.youtube.com/watch?v=ulhDA_MnpP8.
24. DVD, *Our 20th Century Muslim Daa'ee-iyah: Sheikh Ahmed Deedat*. IPCI.
25. *Lenasia Times*, August 1999.
26. Goth, 'Champion of Interfaith Dialogue'.
27. Channel Islam International, 24 January 2003.
28. Kanet Malcolm, cited in Gevisser, *The Dream Deferred*, xxiv.
29. Hirschkind, *Ethical Soundscape*, 209.
30. Patrick French, *The World Is What It Is: The Authorized Biography of VS Naipaul*, xvii.
31. From Thinkexist.com.

## 2 THE INDELIBLE THUMBPRINT

1. Introduction to the DVD, *Farrakhan visits Deedat*. Available from IPCI.
2. *Daily News*, 10 May 1996.
3. *Arab News*, 19 May 1996.
4. *Daily News*, 17 May 1996.
5. *Leader*, 25 October 1996.
6. *Riyadh Daily*, 14 October 1996.
7. *Leader*, 28 October 1994.
8. *Riyadh Daily*, 7 November 1996.
9. *Riyadh Daily*, 7 November 1996.
10. *Saudi Gazette*, 18 July 1998.
11. Muhammad, 'Greetings from Shaikh Ahmed Deedat'.
12. *Islamic Voice*, April 2004.
13. Said, 'Muslim Bible Scholars of Tanzania'.
14. Muhammad, Greetings from Shaikh Ahmed Deedat'..
15. Speech on the DVD *Farrakhan visits Deedat*.
16. Interview, Yousuf Deedat, *Channel Islam International*, 24 January 2003.

17 Zakhir Naik, 'How Deedat made me a Da'ee'. www.youtube.com/view_play_list?p=96CFD8EA6DD1770F.
18 Doolarkhan, quoted in Asmal, 'Deedat', 6–9.
19 Muhammad, 'Greetings from Shaikh Ahmed Deedat'.
20 Interview, Yousuf Deedat, *Channel Islam International*, 24 January 2003.
21 Asmal, 'Deedat'.
22 Asmal, 'Deedat'.
23 Asmal, 'Deedat'.
24 http://www.answering–islam.org/Responses/Deedat/downfall.htm.
25 *Natal Mercury*, 9 August 2005; *Daily News*, 8 August 2005.
26 *Natal Mercury*, 9 August 2005.
27 Email from CIS International to IPCI, 13 August 2005.

## 3 FROM ADAMS MISSION TO AHMED'S MISSION

1 Quoted in Powell, *Muslims and Missionaries*, 170.
2 Etherington, 'Kingdoms of this World and the Next', 89–106.
3 Singh, 'Adams College', 2–4.
4 *Daily Reveille*, 4 November 1986.
5 Interview with *Women's Own*, Pakistan, re published in *Al-Burhaan*, December 1987.
6 Quoted in Powell, *Muslims and Missionaries*, 270.
7 Interview with Kuwaiti television journalist, mid-1980s.
8 Powell, *Muslims and Missionaries*, 1.
9 Bennett, 'Christianity and Islam'.
10 Cairo 1899 and 1903.
11 Ibn Taymiyya's work, al-*Jawab al-Sahih li-Man Baddala Din al-Masah (The correct answer to the one who changed the religion of the Messiah)*, was translated by. T.F. Michel and published as *A Muslim Theologian's Response to Christianity*, in 1984.
12 Saïd, *Orientalism*, 1–28.
13 Powell, *Muslims and Missionaries*, 189.
14 Bennett, 'Christianity and Islam'.
15 Powell, *Muslims and Missionaries*, 1–2.
16 Interview with *Women's Own*, Pakistan, re published in *Al-Burhaan*, December 1987.
17 Powell, *Muslims and Missionaries*, 1.
18 Interview with *Women's Own*, Pakistan, re published in *Al-Burhaan*, December 1987.
19 Powell, *Muslims and Missionaries*, 138.
20 Powell, *Muslims and Missionaries*, 132–157.
21 Powell, *Muslims and Missionaries*, 158–162.
22 Powell, *Muslims and Missionaries*, 170–180.
23 Powell, *Muslims and Missionaries*, 210–225.
24 Powell, *Muslims and Missionaries*, 230–231.
25 The verse reads as follows: 'For there are three that bear record in heaven, the Father, the Word, and the Holy Ghost: and these three are one.' This passage, testimony to the Heavenly Trinity, is called the *Johannine Comma* and is not found in the majority of Greek manuscripts. See http://av1611.com/kjbp/faq/holland_1jo5_7.html.
26 Powell, *Muslims and Missionaries*, 226–262.
27 Accessed at Interfaith Department, Islamic Cultural Centre and London Central Mosque, http://www.islams_green.org/islams_green/2007/05/dialogue_works_.html.
28 See Kutbi, foreword to Izhar-ul-Haq.
29 *Post*, 14–17 March 1990.
30 Interview with Deedat, al-*Burhaan*, December 1987.
31 *Post*, 14–17 March 1990.

## 4 THE BEGGAR'S PREDICTION

1 Hawa Deedat, interviewed by Fatima Asmal.
2 Ahmed Deedat, interview, 1993. Available on DVD.
3 Ahmed Deedat, interview, 1993. Available on DVD.

4   Hawa Deedat, interviewed by Fatima Asmal.
5   Ahmed Deedat, interview, 1993. Available on DVD.
6   Ahmed Deedat, interview, 1993. Available on DVD.
7   Ahmed Deedat, interview, 1993. Available on DVD.
8   See Jeppie, *Language, Identity, Modernity*.
9   Mall's son Daoud was one of the first Indians to matriculate at Sastri College and subsequently studied at the University of Sheffield in England and became a doctor. When he returned to Durban in the early 1950s, Dr Daoud Mall founded the Arabic Study Circle.
10  Asmal, 'Deedat'.
11  *The Post*, 2–5 February 1994.

## 5  PAKKA MUSALMAN

1   Hawa and Mohamed Deedat on DVD, *Our 20th Century Muslim Daa'ee-iyah: Sheikh Ahmed Deedat*.
2   Interview with *Women's Own*, Pakistan, 1987, republished in a*l-Burhaan*, December 1987.
3   Interview with *Women's Own*, Pakistan, 1987, republished in a*l-Burhaan*, December 1987.
4   http://www.youtube.com/watch?v=ulhDA_MnpP8.
5   http://www.youtube.com/watch?v=ulhDA_MnpP8.
6   The poem is published in Abramson and Kilpatrick *Religious Perspectives in Modern Muslim and Jewish Literatures*, 31.

## 6  DISCOVERING DA'WA

1   Interview with a Pakistani journalist, published in a*l-Burhaan*, December 1987.
2   *Graphic*, 19 December 1952.
3   *Graphic*, 19 December 1952.
4   Asmal later served in South Africa's first non-racial government as a member of the African National Congress (ANC).
5   For more on the Arabic Study Circle, see Jeppie, *Language Identity Modernity*.
6   For more on the Women's Cultural Group see Vahed and Waetjen, *Gender, Modernity and Indian Delights*.
7   Interview with *Women's Own*, Pakistan, republished in *Al-Burhaan*, December 1987.
8   *Indian Views*, 6 November 1975.
9   See *Muslim Digest*, June/July 1988, 10 and 11, 32, 38 and *Indian Views*, 30 October to 31 December 1957 for correspondence for and against Perdu.
10  The verse reads as follows: 'I will raise them up a Prophet from among their brethren, like unto thee, and will put my words in his mouth; and he shall speak unto them all that I shall command him. And it shall come to pass, that whosoever will not hearken unto my words which he shall speak in my name, I will require it of him.'
11  This is a non-governmental organisation founded in Makkah in 1962 by representatives from twenty-two countries to assist Muslims worldwide.
12  David O' Reilly, 'Preaching the "good news" door to door to door', *Philadelphia Enquirer*, 4 August 2000. http://www.rickross.com/reference/jw/jw45.html. See also http://www.carm.org/religious-movements/jehovahs-witnesses/jehovahs-witnesses-history.
13  Chetty, 'Badsha Peer', 11.

## 7  THE ISLAMIC PROPAGATION CENTRE AND ITS FOUNDERS

1   Interview on Pakistan TV, 1987. http://www.youtube.com/watch?v=ulhDA_MnpP8.
2   Interview on Pakistan TV, 1987. http://www.youtube.com/watch?v=ulhDA_MnpP8.
3   http://www.youtube.com/watch?v=ulhDA_MnpP8.
4   Hawa Deedat, interviewed by Fatima Asmal.
5   Personal correspondence from G.H. Agjee, 23 May 2007. Faxed from Canada.
6   *Arafat* 1.1, September 1946.
7   Interview on DVD, *Our 20th Century Muslim Daa'ee-iyah: Sheikh Ahmed Deedat*.
8   Newsletter from the 14th Centennial Qur'anic Anniversary Council, 1.3 (1968), 3.
9   Newsletter from the 14th Centennial Qur'anic Anniversary Council, 1.3 (1968), 3.
10  *Indian News and Views*, 15 August 1968.

## 8 IS THE BIBLE GOD'S WORD?

1. http://www.jamaat.net/stone/TheStone.html.
2. Interview with *Women Now*, Pakistan, republished in *al-Burhaan*, December 1987.
3. Kalaam, 'The Man Who Took on Christendom', 28.
4. Kalaam, 'The Man Who Took on Christendom', 28.
5. Lewis, 'Depictions of "Christianity"', 212.
6. Westerlund, 'Ahmed Deedat's Theology of Religion'. Deedat's written words reached millions across the globe.
7. Larkin, 'Ahmed Deedat and the Form of Islamic Evangelism'.
8. Armstrong, *The Bible*, 4–5.
9. Kung, *Islam*, 534–535.
10. Armstrong, *The Bible*.
11. Armstrong, *The Bible*, 4–5.
12. Armstrong, *The Bible*, 188.
13. See 'The Centenary of the Modernist Crisis', *The Religion Report*, Australian Broadcasting Company, 2 January 2008. http://www.abc.net.au/rn/religionreport/stories/2008/2123135.htm#transcript.
14. Armstrong, *The Bible*.
15. Armstrong, *The Bible*, 193, see also pp. 183–221 for a discussion of this issue.
16. Kung, *Islam*, 518.
17. This section is based on Westerlund. 'Ahmed Deedat's Theology of Religion', 268–270.
18. http://www.jamaat.net/stone/TheStone.html.
19. Bird, 'A Defender of Islam'.
20. For example, the Q document or Q (from the German *Quelle*, 'source') is a postulated lost textual source for the Gospels of Matthew and Luke. The recognition by nineteenth-century New Testament scholars that Matthew and Luke probably worked independently of one another and used the Gospel of Mark as a source, and that they share much material that is not derived from Mark's Gospel, led to suggestions that there may be a *second* common source, known as the Q document. Also called the Q Gospel, the Sayings Gospel Q, the Synoptic Sayings Source, the Q Manuscript, and, in the nineteenth century, the Logia, this hypothetical lost text is believed to have contained a collection of Jesus' sayings. See http://en.wikipedia.org/wiki/Q_document.
21. Kung, *Islam*, 520.
22. Accessed at http://vodpod.com/watch/55964-freely-speaking-deedat-3-of-5.
23. Westerlund, 'Ahmed Deedat's Theology of Religion'.
24. Deuteronomy 18:18: 'I will raise them up a Prophet from among their brethren, like unto thee, and will put my words in his mouth; and he shall speak unto them all that I shall command him. And it shall come to pass, that whosoever will not hearken unto my words which he shall speak in my name, I will require it of him.'
25. See http://www.politicalquotes.org/Quotedisplay.aspx?DocID=45782.
26. *Argus* 14 May 1985.
27. Westerlund, 'Ahmed Deedat's Theology of Religion', 275.
28. Westerlund, 'Ahmed Deedat's Theology of Religion', 275.
29. Westerlund, 'Ahmed Deedat's Theology of Religion', 275.
30. http://www.jamaat.net/crux/Crux1-5.html.
31. Lewis, 'Depictions of "Christianity"', 212.

## 9 'REVILE NOT LEST YE BE REVILED'

1. Hirshkind, *Ethical Soundscape*, 132.
2. Kung, *Islam*.
3. *Al-Mujaddid*, May 1960.
4. The Qur'an is organised according to verses revealed in Makkah or Medina. The part revealed in Makka carries the title 'Makki' and the remainder is called 'Madani'.
5. *Muslim Digest*, July–October 1986, 4.
6. *Muslim Digest*, July–October 1986, 54–55.
7. *Muslim Digest*, July–October 1986, 140.
8. *Al-Mujaddid*, July–August 1960.
9. *Al-Mujaddid*, December 1960.
10. *Al-Balaagh*, 8 September 1988.
11. *Majlis*, 4.6.

12 *Post*, 25 August 1976.
13 *Muslim Digest*, September–December 1980: 27.
14 *Tribune Herald*, 8 June 1980.
15 *Muslim Digest*, September–December 1980, 27–30.
16 Powell, *Muslims and Missionaries*, 62.
17 Article/letter undated (c. 1986). In Dr G.M. Hoosen Collection.
18 Trad, 'An Interview with Shaykh Ahmed Deedat'.

## 10 CAPE OF STORMS

1 Shell, 'Between Christ and Mohammed'.
2 Shell, 'Between Christ and Mohammed'.
3 Shell, 'Between Christ and Mohammed', 275–276.
4 Shell, 'Between Christ and Mohammed'.
5 Davenport, 'Settlement, Conquest, and Theological Controversy'.
6 Hermitage Day, *Robert Gray*, 16 October 2008.
7 Hermitage Day, *Robert Gray*, 16 October 2008.
8 Pratt, 'The Anglican Church's Mission,' ii.
9 Shell, 'Between Christ and Mohammed', 276.
10 The membership of Cape Colony churches in 1898 was as follows: Baptist 6 777; Roman Catholic 17 508; Lutheran 44 111; Lutheran Missionary Society 41 409; Presbyterian 30 679; Anglican 89 650; Methodist 203 067; Dutch Reformed 225 517. See Davenport, 'Settlement, Conquest, and Theological Controversy', 55.
11 Pratt, 'The Anglican Church's Mission'.
12 Hamson, 'The Mission to Moslems', 271–277.
13 Pratt, 'The Anglican Church's Mission'.
14 Pratt, 'The Anglican Church's Mission', 199.
15 Pratt, 'The Anglican Church's Mission'. Note that the designation 'Malay' was used in the racially divided South Africa to refer to 'coloureds' (another contentious term) of the Muslim faith.
16 *Daily News*, 5 December 1956.
17 His publications include *The Call of the Minaret* (1956); *Counsels in Contemporary Islam* (1965); *The Event of the Qur'an* (1971); *Palestine: The Prize and Price of Zion* (1997); *Muhammad in the Qur'an* (2002); *The Qur'an and the West* (2006).
18 *The Star*, 5 August 1960.
19 Haron, 'Dynamics of Christian–Muslim Relations', 2004.
20 Haron, 'Dynamics of Christian–Muslim Relations', 2004.
21 Haron, 'Dynamics of Christian–Muslim Relations', 2004.
22 *Daily News*, 9 September 1961.
23 Haron, 'Imam Abdullah Haron'.
24 The first edition of *Muslim News* was published on 16 December 1960, and it closed down in 1986. The newspaper was firm in its opposition to apartheid for most of its existence, and faced state harassment. Some editions were banned, while many of those associated with the newspaper, such as Imam Abdullah Haron, Raslud Sayed, Gulzar Khan, and Abdul Qayyum Sayed, were victimised in one way or another.
25 *Muslim News*, 21 July 1961.
26 *Muslim News*, 4 August 1961.
27 Haron, 'Dynamics of Christian–Muslim Relations', 2004.
28 Muslim Judicial Council, represented by Imam Gassan Solomon, 'Testimony before the Truth and Reconciliation Commission', East London, 18 November 1999, from http://web.uct.ac.za/depts/ricsa/commiss/trc/mjctest.htm.
29 'Imam Abdullah Haron. The Martyr of Justice,' http://www.islamonline.net/english/Muslim_Affairs/Africa/PoliticsEconomy/2006/06/01.sht.
30 MJC testimony before the TRC, 18 November 1999.
31 *Argus*, 26 June 1975.
32 *Argus*, 26 June 1975.
33 Interview, Farid Sayed, 12 October 2008.
34 *Argus*, 26 June 1975.
35 *Muslim News*, 4 July 1975.
36 Interview, Farid Sayed, 12 October 2008.

37 *Cape Herald*, 11 February 1978.
38 *Muslim Digest*, January 1978, 15–17; Haron, 'Dynamics of Christian–Muslim Relations', 2004.
39 *Cape Herald*, 11 February 1978.
40 *Cape Herald*, 18 February 1978.
41 *Cape Herald*, 11 February 1978.
42 *Cape Herald*, 4 March 1978.
43 *Muslim Digest*, March 1978, 38–39.
44 TBD, RSC 5A/3107, I16/79.
45 TBD, RSC 5A/3107, I16/79.
46 *Muslim Digest*, September/October 1982, 40.

## 11 AS-SALAAM: A BRIDGE TOO FAR

1 Interview, G.H. Agjee.
2 *Indian Views*, 25 March 1959.
3 *Indian Views*, 25 March 1959.
4 *News and Views*, 16 August 1965.
5 Secretary's Report, 30 October 1960.
6 'As-Salam: The Seminary of Islam,' IPCI Fundraising Brochure, 1960.
7 *Indian Views*, 16 November 1960.
8 *Muslim Digest*, March 1961: 18.
9 *Graphic*, 12 December 1962.
10 *Muslim News*, 3 (4), 8 February 1963.
11 TBD, RSC 5A/703, I411A/64.
12 *News and Views*, 16 August 1965.
13 Interview on DVD, *Our 20th Century Muslim Daa'ee-iyah: Sheikh Ahmed Deedat*.
14 *News and Views*, 16 August 1965.
15 *Indian Views*, 25 March 1959.
16 *News and Views*, 16 August 1965.
17 *News and Views*, 16 August 1965.
18 Interview, Ebrahim Jadwat.
19 *Muslim Digest*, March 1977.
20 *Natal Mercury*, 1 June 1974.
21 *Al-Qalam*, March 1986.

## 12 CREATING CHANGE

1 *Al-Qalam*, December 1991.
2 Jamal, 'Islamic Propagation Centre', 60.
3 *The Criterion*'s name derives from Sura 25 of the Qur'an, which begins 'Blessed is He who sent down the criterion to His servant, that it may be an admonition to all creatures.'
4 *The Criterion*, May 1961.
5 *Majlis*, 1980, no. 9.
6 *Graphic*, 5 August 1980.
7 *Majlis*, 1980, no. 9.
8 http://en.wikipedia.org/wiki/Mosque#_note-mawardi112.
9 Trad, 'An Interview with Sheikh Ahmed Deedat'.
10 Quoted in Zaman, *Ulama in Contemporary Islam*, 55.
11 *Muslim Digest* September–December 1980: 32–33.
12 http://www.islamonline.net/servlet/Satellite?cid=1119503544332&pagename=IslamOnline-English-Ask_Scholar%2FFatwaE%2FFatwaEAskTheScholar.
13 http://vodpod.com/watch/55964-freely-speaking-deedat-3-of-5.
14 *Leader*, 9 August 1963.
15 Interview on DVD, *Our 20th Century Muslim Daa'ee-iyah: Sheikh Ahmed Deedat*.
16 Jamal, 'Islamic Propagation Centre', 110.
17 *Sunday Tribune*, 25 February 1979.
18 In *Muslim Digest*, July–Oct. 1963, 114.

19 *Post*, 21 February 1979.
20 *Sunday Tribune*, 25 February 1979.
21 See http://www.islamictorrents.net/details.php?id=11479.
22 Anderson, 2001.
23 M.H. Badat to Yousuf Deedat, 31 October 2003.
24 M.H. Badat to Yousuf Deedat, 31 October 2003.
25 M.H. Badat to Ahmed and Yousuf Deedat, 1 September 2003, after viewing the video *Story of Ahmed Deedat*.
26 Said, 'Muslim Bible Scholars of Tanzania'.
27 Said, 'Muslim Bible Scholars of Tanzania'.

## 13 CONTROVERSIES AND DIVERSIONS

1 See http://famouspoetsandpoems.com.
2 Khalifa, *Quran: The Final Scripture*.
3 Gardner, 'The numerology of Dr. Rashid Khalifa,'.
4 *Al-Balaagh*, August/September 1986.
5 The verses are 'Now hath come unto you an Apostle from amongst yourselves: it grieves him that ye should perish: ardently anxious is he over you: to the Believers is he most kind and merciful (9:128), and 'But if they turn away, Say: "God sufficeth me: there is no god but He: On Him is my trust, He the Lord of the Throne (of Glory) Supreme!"' (9:129).
6 *Muslim Perspective*, April 1985.
7 *Al-Balaagh*, August/September 1986.
8 *Muslim Digest*, July–October 1986: 54.
9 *Al-Balaagh*, August 1988.

## 14 PALESTINE

1 *Cape Herald*, 20 October 1982.
2 *Lenasia Times*, August 1999.
3 Interview on Pakistan television, 1987. http://www.youtube.com/watch?v=ulhDA_MnpP8.
4 'A Gateway to Jewish Literature, Culture and Ideas'. http://www.nextbook.org/cultural/feature.html?id=117.
5 Anecdote related by Yousuf Deedat, interview, 5 February 2007.
6 *Daily News*, 20 November 1973.
7 *Muslim Digest*, December 1973.
8 *Al-Qalam*, 6 October 1982.
9 *Cape Herald*, 20 October 1982.
10 See http://en.wikipedia.org/wiki/Sabra_and_Shatila_massacre.
11 See *Arabs and Israel: Conflict or Conciliation?* http://www.ipci.co.za/e-books/.
12 Deedat, *Arabs and Israel*, 2,4.
13 *Cape Times*, 20 January 1989.
14 Quoted in *Lenasia Times*, August 1999.
15 Saïd's books include *Orientalism* (1978), *The Question of Palestine* (1979), *Covering Islam: How the Media and the Experts Determine How we See the Rest of the World* (1982), and *Culture and Imperialism* (1993).
16 http://en.wikipedia.org/wiki/Covering_Islam. Accessed on 30 June 2009.
17 See Armstrong, *Battle For God*, 280–288.

## 15 GOING GLOBAL

1 See http://www.WAMY.co.uk/.
2 Interview on DVD, *Our 20th Century Muslim Daa'ee-iyah: Sheikh Ahmed Deedat*.
3 Interview on DVD, *Our 20th Century Muslim Daa'ee-iyah: Sheikh Ahmed Deedat*.
4 See http://www.ahmadsakr.com/bio.html.
5 *Sunday Tribune*, 25 February 1979.
6 *Leader*, 22 April 1985.
7 *Leader*, 22 April 1985.
8 *Al-Qalam*, March 1986.
9 Lewis, 'Depictions of "Christianity"', 213.
10 Lewis, 'Depictions of "Christianity"', 185.

## 16 THE KING FAISAL INTERNATIONAL PRIZE

1. http://www.kff.com/english/homepage/Index.html.
2. Garaudy, who was imprisoned in Algeria during the Second World War, was a French Communist who had tried to reconcile Marxism with Roman Catholicism in the 1970s before becoming a Muslim in 1982. His subsequent writings focused on Zionism, and, in 1998, he was found guilty of 'Holocaust denial' in France for his 1995 book *Mythes fondateurs de la politique israélienne* (see http://en.wikipedia.org/wiki/Roger_Garaudy, and http://www.onlineislamicstore.com/audio-lectures-speeches-single-tapes-ahmed-deedat.html).

## 17 THE SWAGGER OF DEEDAT

1. *The Message*, December 1993, 28.
2. Jenkins, 'Story of embracing Islam'.
3. See Bebbington, *Evangelicalism in Modern Britain*, 4–8; Hadden and Swann, *Prime Time Preachers*, 4–12; Frankl, *Televangelism*, 23–61; Schultze, *Televangelism and American Culture*, 248. All of the above are quoted in James and Shoesmith, 'The Anointing of the Airwaves'.
4. Hadden and Shupe, 'Televangelism in America'.
5. Hadden and Shupe, 'Televangelism in America'.
6. In Armstrong, *Battle for God*, 274.
7. Armstrong, *Battle for God*, 275.
8. Armstrong, *Battle for God*, 275.
9. Larkin, 'Ahmed Deedat', 114.
10. Interview on DVD, *Our 20th Century Muslim Daa'ee-iyah: Sheikh Ahmed Deedat*.
11. http://en.wikipedia.org/wiki/Jimmy_Swaggart.
12. http://www.amazon.co.uk.swaggart.
13. Armstrong, *Battle for God*, 358.
14. Goth, 'Champion of Interfaith Dialogue'.
15. Armstrong, *Battle for God*, 359.
16. *Daily Reveille*, 4 November 1986.
17. *Morning Advocate*, 4 November 1986.
18. *Daily Reveille*, 4 November 1986.
19. *Daily Reveille*, 4 November 1986.
20. Swaggart's question and Deedat's response are available on Youtube at http://www.youtube.com/watch?v=IwxjheEkSbc&feature=related.
21. *Morning Advocate*, 4 November 1986.
22. *Daily Reveille*, 4 November 1986.
23. Larkin, 'Ahmed Deedat', 115.
24. *Morning Advocate*, 4 November 1986.
25. Goth, 'Champion of Interfaith Dialogue'.
26. Accessed at http://vodpod.com/watch/55964-freely-speaking-deedat-4-of-5.
27. *Al-Qalam*, March 1986, 2. Yusuf Buckas was approached for an interview but he declined saying that he regarded this as a closed chapter in his life.

## 18 'FAISAL LAUREATE'

1. http://www.myiwc.com/forums/showthread.php?t=3559.
2. *Arabia. The Islamic World Review*, March 1986, 4.
3. Interview with *Women's Own* Pakistan; republished in *al-Burhaan*, December 1987.
4. Accessed at http://www.youtube.com/watch?v=ulhDA_MnpP8.
5. Interview with *Women's Own*, Pakistan; republished in a*l-Burhaan*, December 1987.
6. Trad, 'An Interview with Sheikh Ahmed Deedat'.
7. *Al-Qalam*, March 1986.
8. *Muslim World*, 20 April 1994.
9. Accessed at http://www.youtube.com/watch?v=ulhDA_MnpP8.
10. Hirschkind, *Ethical Soundscape*, 137.
11. Salvatore, cited in Hirschkind, *Ethical Soundscape*, 138.

12 See 'Islam's Green', http://www.islamsgreen.org/islams_green/2007/05/dialogue_works_.html.
13 *Al-Qalam,* March 1986.
14 *Al-Qalam,* March 1986.
15 *Al-Qalam,* March 1986.
16 *Al-Burhaan,* July 1989, 8.
17 *Al-Burhaan,* July 1989.
18 *Al-Burhaan,* December1987.
19 Hassan El-Najjar, 'Ahmed Deedat: A Relentless Caller to Islam With Wisdom', *Al-Jazeera,* 14 August 2005. http://www.aljazeerah.info/Opinion%20editorials/2005%20Opinion%20Editorials/August/14o/Ahmed%20Deedat%20A%20Relentless%20Caller%20to%20Islam%20With%20Wisdom%20By%20Hassan%20ElNajjar.htm.
20 *Al-Burhaan,* December 1987.
21 *Al-Burhaan,* December 1987.
22 22 February 2009 issue. Quoted at http://en.wikipedia.org/wiki/Zakir_Naik.
23 Zakhir Naik, 'How Deedat made me a Da'ee'. Accessed at www.youtube.com/view_play_list?p= 96CFD8EA6DD1770F.
24 Zakhir Naik, 'How Deedat made me a Da'ee'. www.youtube.com/view_play_list?p=96CFD8EA6DD1770F.
25 Zakhir Naik, 'How Deedat made me a Da'ee'. www.youtube.com/view_play_list?p=96CFD8EA6DD1770F.
26 *Al-Burhaan,* March, 1988.
27 *Al-Burhaan,* January 1988.
28 *Al-Burhaan,* December 1988.
29 *Al-Burhaan,* June 1989.
30 *Khaleej Times,* 9 December 1994.
31 *Leader,* 3 November 1989.
32 *Post,* 12–15 February 1992.
33 *Arab News,* 21 June 1992.
34 Maier, *This House Has Fallen,* 160–166.
35 *Time,* 1 June 1992.
36 *Leader,* 19 November 1993.
37 *Leader,* 29 July 1994.
38 Trad, 'An Interview With Sheikh Ahmed Deedat'.
39 *Leader,* 12 April 1996.
40 *Leader,* 12 April 1996.
41 30 May 1996. http://www.parliament.nsw.gov.au/prod/parlment/hansart.nsf/V3Key/LC19960530031.

## 19 RUSH-DIE?

1 *Riyadh Daily,* 14 June 1993.
2 http://victorian.fortunecity.com/coldwater/439/rushdie.htm.
3 Parekh, 'The Rushdie Affair', 76.
4 Sardar and Davies, *Distorted Imagination,* 157–158.
5 Badawi, 'Sacrilege Versus Civility', 135.
6 Sardar and Davies, *Distorted Imagination,* 165.
7 Mazrui, 'Novelist's Freedom vs Worshipper's Dignity', 210.
8 Webster, *Brief History of Blasphemy,* 95–96.
9 Brennan, *Salman Rushdie and the Third World,* 144.
10 *Guardian,* 2 October 1989.
11 *The Leader,* 14 April 1989.
12 See Suraya Dadoo, 'The Satanic Verses: 20 Years On', *Media Monitors Network,* 1 October 2008, http://usa.mediamonitors.net/Headlines/The-Satanic-Verses-20-years-on.
13 *Independent,* 30 September 1989.
14 *Guardian,* 2 October 1989.
15 *Crescent International,* 1–15 February 1990.
16 *Crescent International,* 1–15 February 1990.
17 *Sunday Tribune,* 12 November 1989.
18 *Sunday Tribune,* 19 November 1989.

## 20 FOR PROPHET OR PROFIT?

1. *Post*, 15–18 July 1987.
2. *Daily News*, 21 March 1986.
3. *Al-Qalam*, March 1986.
4. *Leader*, 30 June 1989.
5. *Leader*, 30 June 1989.
6. *Tribune Herald*, 6 November 1988.
7. *Leader*, 30 June 1989.
8. *Sunday Tribune Herald*, 6 November 1988.
9. Muhammad, 'Greetings from Shaikh Ahmad Deedat', 2002.
10. *Sunday Times Extra*, 25 June 1989.
11. *Sunday Times Extra*, 25 June 1989.
12. *Sunday Tribune*, 3 April 1988.
13. *Sunday Tribune*, 3 April 1988.
14. *Al-Burhaan*, August 1988.
15. *Leader*, 9 December 1988.
16. Zaman, *Ulama in Contemporary Islam*, 174.
17. Lewis, 'Depictions of "Christianity"', 214.
18. Zaman, *Ulama in Contemporary Islam*, 175.
19. *Tribune Herald*, 20 January 1991.
20. *Tribune Herald*, 20 January 1991.
21. *Tribune Herald*, 20 January 1991.

## 21 THE BEST OF TIMES, THE WORST OF TIMES: THE 1980s AND 1990s

1. *Post*, 26–29 July 1989.
2. *Al-Burhaan*, June 1989.
3. *Star*, 23 January 1995.
4. *Leader*, 13 January 1995.
5. *Natal Bobby*, December 1994.

## 22 ISLAM AND HINDUISM: SOWING THE SEEDS OF DIVISION

1. 'Saare Jahan Se Achcha' (1904).
2. *Sunday Tribune Herald*, 11 May 1986.
3. *Sunday Tribune Herald*, 13 April 1986.
4. *Post*, 16 April 1996.
5. *Lenasia Times*, May 1986.
6. *Leader*, 18 March 1988.
7. *Sunday Tribune Herald*, 13 March 1986.
8. *Sunday Tribune*, 30 April 1986.
9. *Al-Burhaan*, 1.6 (July 1989): 6.
10. Reproduced in *Muslim Digest*, July–October 1986, 23–24.
11. *Sunday Times Extra*, 21 January 2007.
12. *Leader*, 3 November 1995.
13. *Natal Mercury*, 17 November 1995.
14. *Leader*, 8 December 1995.
15. *Post*, 13–16 December 1995.
16. *Post*, 14–17 February 1996.

## 23 THE COMBAT KIT

1. http://www.islamicteachings.org/forum/islamic-ebooks/combat-kit-by-sheikh-ahmed-deedat-t731.html.
2. Haron, 'From Exclusivism to Pluralism'.
3. *Al-Balaagh*, February/March 1987.
4. *Al-Balaagh*, February / March 1987.

5  *Al-Balaagh*, February / March 1987. See also Prozesky 1991.
6  See Walshe, 'Christianity and the Anti-Apartheid Struggle'.
7  http://www.answering-islam.org/Responses/Deedat/downfall.htm.
8  *Natal on Saturday*, 13 August 1994.
9  Haron, 'From Exclusivism to Pluralism', 446–450. The author is indebted to the work of Muhammad Haron on Christian–Muslim relations in South Africa. See Haron 2004, 2006, 2007.
10  Haron, 'From Exclusivism to Pluralism,' 446–450.
11  *Leader*, 28 May 1993.
12  *Tribune Herald*, 23 May 1993.
13  *Tribune Herald*, 2 April 1995.
14  *Tribune Herald*, 2 April 1995.
15  *Natal on Saturday*, 22 April 1995.
16  *Post*, 11–14 December 1991.
17  *Leader*, 6 August 1993.
18  *Daily News*, 28 August 1995.
19  *Independent on Saturday*, 17 July 1999.

## 24 OTHER PERSUASIONS

1  Jamaluddin did not name this student during our interview as he had not obtained his consent to do so.
2  Interview on DVD, *Our 20th Century Muslim Daa'ee-iyah: Sheikh Ahmed Deedat.*.
3  http://www.way-to-allah.com/en/journey/dawood.html.
4  *Sunday Tribune*, 27 October 2002.
5  *Youth*, April 1994, 25.

## 25 ON GOD'S WAVELENGTH?

1  Khan, 'Evangelical Islam'.
2  See Friedman 'The World is Flat'.
3  Siddiqui, *Christian–Muslim Dialogue*, xiii–xv.
4  See Armstrong, *Battle For God*, 278–316.
5  Larkin, 'Ahmed Deedat,' 101–102.
6  Brauman, 'From Philanthropy to Humanitarianism', 406.
7  Lewis, 'Depictions of Christianity,' 214.
8  The author would like to thank Dr Franz Kogelmann of the University of Bayreuth, for this point.
9  *The Message*, December 1993, 28.
10  Larkin, 'Ahmed Deedat', 117.
11  Larkin, 'Ahmed Deedat', 101–102.
12  Email correspondence from Keysar Trad, 19 July 2009.
13  Article emailed by Dr Ahmad Totonji, 16 August 2009.
14  Weber, *Theory of Social and Economic Organisation*, 358.
15  Haron, 'Dynamics of Christian–Muslim Relations', 2004.
16  See Tayob, *Islamic Resurgence*, 170–183.
17  *Muslim Digest*, July/October, 36/37, 4.
18  Interview in Pakistan, republished in *al-Burhaan*, December 1987.
19  Larkin, 'Ahmed Deedat', 117.
20  Lewis, 'Depictions of "Christianity"', 209.
21  *Riyadh Daily*, 14 June 1992.
22  Commentator on the DVD, *Our 20th Century Muslim Daa'ee-iyah: Sheikh Ahmed Deedat*.
23  Interview on DVD, *Our 20th Century Muslim Daa'ee-iyah: Sheikh Ahmed Deedat*.
24  'Freedom of Joburg for Mandela', 26 July 2004. http://www.southafrica.info/mandela/mandela-joburg.htm.
25  Interview on DVD, *Our 20th Century Muslim Daa'ee-iyah: Sheikh Ahmed Deedat*.
26  'Freely Speaking' Radio74, 16 March 1987. http://vodpod.com/watch/55964-freely-speaking-deedat-3-of-5.

# SOURCES

## INTERVIEWS AND EMAIL CORRESPONDENCE

Abdullah, Mustacq Ahmed. 9 January 2002. Nephew of Saleh Mohamed, Ahmed Deedat's friend in Cape Town. Also email correspondence on 26 November 2007; 28 November 2007; 4 December 2007.

Agjee, G.H. 14 November 2001. Goolam Hoosen Agjee was Ahmed Deedat's nephew, and a founder member and secretary-general of the IPCI.

Ahmed, Jamaluddin. 14 November 2007. Ordained as a Catholic priest but embraced Islam around 1969 after meeting Ahmed Deedat.

Ally, Yusuf. 22 November 2007. Businessman and trustee of the IPCI from the mid-1980s.

Ballim, A.S. 26 November 2007. Member of the Arabic Study Circle and friend to Ahmed Deedat.

Basha, Shabir. 28 November 2007. Joined the IPCI in 1986.

Bawa, Ibrahim. 20 January 1999. Advocate. Was president of the Islamic Council of South Africa in the 1970s and 1980s.

Butler, Goolam Nabie. 4 January 2002. Worked with Ahmed Deedat during the 1940s and 1950s.

Deedat, Abdullah. April 1994. Ahmed Deedat's half-brother.

Deedat, Hawa. 2006. Wife of Ahmed Deedat. Interviewed by Fatima Asmal.

Deedat, Yousuf. 5 February 2007. Ahmed Deedat's son. Accompanied by Fatima Asmal for the interview.

Hassen, Rafeek. 28 November 2007. Pharmacist; close to Ahmed Deedat since his days as a university student; worked for the IPCI from 2002 to 2007; president of the Islamic Interfaith Research Institute at the time of interview.

Hendricks, Fuad. 25 October 2006, Member of the Muslim Youth Movement.

Hoosen, G.M. 24 November 2007. Son of Ahmed Deedat's friend Ahmed Lutchka and trustee of the IPCI from 1985 to 1991.

Jadwat, Ebrahim (Baboo). 13 October 2008 and ongoing informal discussions. Involved with Ahmed Deedat since the 1970s and a trustee of the IPCI from the late 1990s.

Jazbhay, Saber Ahmed. 11 August 2009. Attorney, observer of local Islamic affairs, and 'critical admirer' of Deedat.

Joommal, A.S.K. 10 December 2007. Editor of *al-Balaagh*.

Kalaam, Abdul. 'The Man Who Took on Christendom,' The Message, December 1993, 28.

Kalic, Ally Abdul. 27 November 2007. IPCI employee since 1989.

Khan, Dr Muhammad, 28 November 2007. Medical doctor, IPCI Trustee, and a pillar of the As-Salaam Educational Institute; he is also a member of the Islamic Medical Association.

Khan, Mahomed. 29 November 2007. IPCI employee since 1990; held position of Liaison Officer at time of interview.

Khan, Shabaan. 25 November 2007. Son of Mahomed Khan who served the IPC/IPCI for over four decades.

Khan, Shafa'at. 22 February 2007. Journalist and editor of *al-Burhaan*, the IPCI newsletter, during the late 1980s to early 1990s. Accompanied by Fatima Asmal for the interview.

Lockhat, Ebi. 15 March 2008. Worked for the IPCI in the late 1980s and early 1990s.

Mahomed, A.B. 12 December 2008. Advocate and founding member of the Muslim Youth Movement.

Mohamed, Ebrahim. 9 January 2002. Son of Saleh Mohamed, Ahmed Deedat's friend in Cape Town. Also email correspondence at various times.

Mayat, Zuleikha. 5 November 2007. President, Women's Cultural Group.

Mehtar, Yakoob. 4 January 2002. Family friend of Ahmed Deedat.

Murchie, Ahmed-Sadeck. 29 November 2007 and 6 December 2007. Son of Secunder Ahmed/Amod Murchie, prominent in the Kamal Study Group and As-Salaam Trust. Telephonic interviews.

Nadvi, Salman. 10 August 2009. Professor of Islamic studies at the University of Durban-Westville from 1974, now retired.

Ngwane, Dawood. 19 June 2004. Embraced Islam after reading Deedat's works. Became a trustee and later president of the IPCI.

Osman, Yusuf. 28 November 2007. Email correspondence. Dr Osman knew G.H.E. Vanker as a student in the 1970s.

Paruk, Suleman. 13 September 2009. Student at As-Salaam from 1968 to 1973.

Peer, Cassim. 14 September 2009. Former South African consul-general in Riyadh, Saudi Arabia and high commissioner of South Africa in Islamabad, Pakistan at the time of interview.

Randeree, G.M. 25 April 2000. Long-time observer of Muslim affairs.

Rasool, Ahmed Tahir (A.T.). 20 November 2007. Secretary of the Arabic Study Circle and IPCI trustee during the 1980s.

Sakr, Ahmad. 13 August 2009. President of the Foundation For Islamic Knowledge. Email correspondence.

Salejee, A.K. 28 November 2007. Founder-member of IPC and member of As-Salaam Trust. Telephonic interview.

Sayed, Farid. 12 October 2008. Editor of *Muslim News and Views*. Telephonic interview.

Suliman, Ashraf. 13 September 2009. South African ambassador to Kuwait. Email correspondence.

Totonji, Ahmad. Scholar, and founding member of various Islamic youth organisations in the USA and the Middle East, helped establish Deedat's reputation internationally. July and August 2009. Email correspondence.

Trad, Keysar. July 2009. Australian-Lebanese journalist and community leader. Various dates. Email correspondence.

Vanker, Ahmed Farouk. 20 November 2007. Son of G.H. Vanker.

Vanker, Khadija. 20 November 2007. Widow of G.H. Vanker.


## BOOKS, ARTICLES, AND DISSERTATIONS

Abramson, Glenda and Hilary Kilpatrick. *Religious Perspectives in Modern Muslim and Jewish Literatures*. Oxford: Routledge, 2006.

Anderson, Allan. *African Reformation: African Initiated Christianity in the 20th Century*. Trenton, NJ: Africa World Press, 2001.

Anderson, Allan. 'Evangelism and the Growth of Pentecostalism in Africa'. n.d. http://artsweb.bham.ac.uk/aanderson/Publications/evangelism.htm.

Anderson, Benedict. *Imagined Communities: Reflections on the Origin and Spread of Nationalism*, revised edition. London: Verso, 2006.

Armstrong, Karen. *The Battle for God: Fundamentalism in Judaism, Christianity and Islam*. London: Harper Collins, 2000.

Armstrong, Karen. *The Bible: The Biography*. London: Atlantic Books, 2007.

Ashcroft, Bill, Gareth Griffiths, and Helen Tiffin. *Post-Colonial Studies: The Key Concepts*. London: Routledge, 2002.

Asmal, Fatima. 'Deedat: The Mission Continues'. *An Nisaa: Straight Path*, August–October 2003: 6–9.

Badawi, Zakawi. 'Sacrilege versus Civility', in M. M. Ahsan and A. R. Kidwai (eds) *Sacrilege Versus Civility*. Leicester: The Islamic Foundation, 1991.

Barber, James. *South Africa in the Twentieth Century: A Political History*. London: Wiley-Blackwell, 1999.

Barnwell, P.J. and A. Touissaint. *A Short History of Mauritius*. London: Longman, 1949.

Bauman, Zygmunt. *Liquid Modernity*. Cambridge: Polity Press, 2000.

Bebbington, David. *Evangelicalism in Modern Britain: A History from the 1730's to the 1980's*. London: Unwin Hyman, 1989.

Benjamin, Walter. *Illuminations* (ed. Hannah Arendt, trans. Harry Zohn). New York: Schocken Books, 1969.

Bennett, Clinton. 'Christianity and Islam: A Survey of Relations Historical and Theological', 2002. http://www.geocities.com/clintonbennett/relative_dialogue.html.

Bernal, Martin. *The Gift of the Nile: Hellenizing Egypt from Aeschylus to Alexander*. Berkeley and Los Angeles: University of California Press, 2001.

Bhana, S. and J. Brain. *Setting Down Roots: Indian Migrants in South Africa 1860–1911*. Johannesburg: Witwatersrand University Press, 1990.

Bird, C. 'A Defender of Islam', *The Commission*, Feb–March 1993: 60–63.

Birt, R.H. 'Win our Moslems to Christ! A Challenge to our Church People at the Cape, c. 1950/51'. Pamphlet. Cape Town.

Black, Antony. *The History of Islamic Political Thought: From the Prophet to the Present*. London: Routledge, 2001.

Brauman, R. 'From Philanthropy to Humanitarianism: Remarks and an Interview', *The South Atlantic Quarterly* 103 (2/3): 397–418, 2004.

Brennan, T. *Salman Rushdie and the Third World*. Basingstoke: Macmillan, 1995.

Burton, Antoinette (ed.). *Archive Stories: Facts, Fictions, and the Writing of History*. Durham, NC: Duke University Press, 2005.

Chattejee, Partha. *Nationalist Thought and the Colonial World: A Derivative Discourse*. Minneapolis: University of Minnesota Press, 1993.

Chattejee, Partha. *The Nation and its Fragments: Colonial and Postcolonial Histories*. Princeton: Princeton University Press, 1993.

Chetty, L. 'Badsha Peer: A Local Muslim Saint', Honours thesis, University of Durban-Westville, 1986.

Cimino, Richard. 'New Boundaries: Evangelicals and Islam after 9/11', 2005. http://www.religionwatch.com/doc/2005-Cimino-Evangelicals-Islam.pdf.

Connell, Raewyn. *Southern Theory: The Global Dynamics of Knowledge in Social Science*. Cambridge: Polity Press, 2007.

Dangor, Suleman. 'The Expression of Islam in South Africa', *al-Ilm*, 18/19: 2–19, 1998/1999.

Dangor, Suleman. 'Towards Understanding Islam', *al-Ilm*, 15: 71–82, 1995.

Davenport, Rodney. 'Settlement, Conquest, and Theological Controversy: The Churches of Nineteenth-century European Immigrants', in R Elphick and T. R. H. Davenport (eds) *Christianity in South Africa: A Political, Social & Cultural History*. Cape Town: David Philip, 1997.

D'Oyly, George and Richard Mant. *Notes, Practical and Explanatory to the Holy Bible* (Vols 1 & 2). London, 1840.

Duff-Gordon, Lucy. *Letters from the Cape by Lady Duff Gordon*. London: Oxford University Press, 1927.

Du Plessis, I.D. *The Cape Malays*. Cape Town: Maskew Miller, 1947.

Esack, Farid. 'Muslims Engaging the Other and the Humanum'. n.d. http://uk.geocities.com/faridesack/femuslimsengage.html.

Esack, Farid. 'To Whom Shall we Give Access to our Water Holes?' n.d. http://www.crosscurrents.org/Esack.htm.

Etherington, N. 'Kingdoms of this World and the Next: Christian Beginnings Among the Zulu and the Swazi', in R. Elphick and T. R. H. Davenport (eds), *Christianity in South Africa: A Political, Social & Cultural History*. Cape Town: David Philip, 1997.

Fanon, Frantz. *The Wretched of the Earth*. London: Grove Press, 2004. (First published 1961)

Foster, George. *A Voyage Round the World*. London: B. White, 1777.

Frankl, Razelle. *Televangelism: The Marketing of Popular Religion*. Carbondale, IL: Southern Illinois University, 1978.

French, Patrick, *The World Is What It Is: The Authorized Biography of V. S. Naipaul*. London: Picador, 2008.

Friedman. Thomas L. *The World is Flat: A Brief History of the Twenty-First Century*. New York: Farrar, Straus & Giroux, 2005.

Gardner, Martin. 'The Numerology of Dr Rashad Khalifa', *Skeptical Inquirer*, Sept–Oct, 1997. http://findarticles.com/p/articles/mi_m2843/is_n5_v21/ai_20121071/pg_1.

Gevisser, Mark. *Thabo Mbeki: The Dream Deferred*. Johannesburg: Jonathan Ball, 2007.

Goth, Bashir. 'Champion of Interfaith Dialogue', *Khaleej Times*, 18 August 2005. http://www.onlineopinion.com.au/view.asp?article=3778

Guan Teh, Henry Hock. 'Legal Apologetics: Principles of the Law of Evidence as Applied in the Quest for Religious Truth', *An International Journal in the Classic Reformation and Evangelical Tradition* 5 (1) 2005. http://www.phc.edu/gj_4_thelawofevidence.php.

Guy, J. The Heretic: *A Study of the Life of John William Colenso, 1814–1883*. Johannesburg: Ravan Press, 1985.

Hadden, Jeffrey K. and Charles E. Swann. *Prime Time Preachers: The Rising Power of Televangelism*. Reading: Addison-Wesley, 1981.

Hadden, Jeffrey K. and Anson Shupe. 'Televangelism in America'. *Social Compass: International Review of Sociology of Religion*. 34 (1): 61–75, 1987. http://etext.lib.virginia.edu/modeng/modeng#.browse.html.

Hamson, A.R. 'The Mission to Moslems in Cape Town', *The Moslem World*. 24 (3): 271–277, 1934. Reprinted in M. Haron (2004 and 2006).

Hansen, Thomas Blom. *The Saffron Wave: Democracy and Hindu Nationalism in Modern India*. Princeton: Princeton University Press, 1999.

Haron, M. 'Christian–Muslim Relations in South Africa (c. 1986–2004): Charting Out a Pluralist Path'. *Islam and Christian–Muslim Relations*. 18 (2): 257–273, 2007.

Haron, M. 'The Dynamics of Christian–Muslim Relations in South Africa (c. 1960–2000)'. Paper presented at the Conference on Christian-Muslim Relations In Sub-Saharan Africa, University of Birmingham, 19–23 April 2004.

Haron, M. 'The Dynamics of Christian–Muslims Relations in South Africa (c. 1960–2000): From Exclusivism to Pluralism', *The Muslim World* 96 (July): 423–468, 2006.

Haron, M. *Imam Abdullah Haron: Life, Ideas and Impact*. Master's dissertation, University of Cape Town, 1986.

Hermitage Day, E. *Robert Gray: First Bishop of Cape Town*. London: SPCK, 1932. http://anglicanhistory.org/africa/day_gray.html.

Hirschkind, Charles. *The Ethical Soundscape: Cassette Sermons and Islamic Counterpublics*. New York: Columbia University Press, 2006.

Huntington, Samuel P. 'The Clash of Civilizations?', *Foreign Affairs* 72 (3): 22–49, 1993.

Ibn Taymiyya. 'al-Jawab al-sahih li-man baddala din al-masah' [The correct answer to the one who changed the religion of the Messiah]. Twelfth century. Trans. T.F. Michel in *A Muslim Theologian's Response to Christianity*. Delmar, NY: Caravan Books, 1984.

Jamal, R.C. *The IPC*. Master's dissertation, University of Durban-Westville, 1991.

Jamal, R.C. 'A Study of the West Street Mosque in Durban'. Honours thesis, University of Durban-Westville, 1987.

James, Jonathan D. and Brian P. Shoesmith, 'The Anointing of the Airwaves: Charismatic Televangelism's Impact on the Church and Community in Urban India', *Journal of Religion and Popular Culture* 18, 2008. http://www.usask.ca/relst/jrpc/art18-annointingairwaves-print.html.

Jenkins, Kenneth L. 'After Seeing Deedat-Swaggart Debate, Mr Kenneth L. Jenkins, a US Former Minister, Became Muslim'. http://www.islamweb.net/ehajj/index.php?page=article&id=48580.

Jeppie, Shamil. *Language, Identity, Modernity. The Arabic Study Circle of Durban*. Cape Town: HSRC Press, 2007.

Kairanawi, Rahmatullah M. *Izhar-ul-Haq: Truth Revealed* (English translation). Madina al-Munawwara, 1989.

Kepel, Gilles. *Muslim Extremism in Egypt: The Prophet and Pharaoh*. California: University of California Press, 1986. (Original French edition published by Editions Le Decouverte, 1984.)

Khalifa, Rashid. *Quran: The Final Scripture*. Tucson: Universal Unity, 1981.

Khan, Omar. 'Evangelical Islam and Some Thoughts on Modern Da'wah', 17 January 2008. http://someideas.wordpress.com/2008/01/17/evangelical-islam-some-thoughts-on-modern-dawah/.

Kollisch, M. *The Mussulman Population at the Cape of Good Hope*. Constantinople: Levant Herald Press, 1867.

Kung, Hans. *Islam: Past, Present and Future* (trans. John Bowden). Oxford: Oneworld, 2007.

Kutbi, Syed Hassan Mohammed. Foreword to the English translation of *Izhar-ul-Haq*, 1989.

Larkin, Brian. 'Ahmed Deedat and the Form of Islamic Evangelism', *Social Text* 26 (3 96): 101–121, 2008.

Lewis, Philip. 'Depictions of "Christianity" within British Islamic Institutions', in Lloyd V. Ridgeon (ed.), *Islamic Interpretations of Christianity*. London: Palgrave, 2001.

Maier, Karl. *This House Has Fallen: Nigeria in Crisis*. London: Penguin, 2000.

Mayat, Zuleikha. *Muslims of Gujarat*. Durban: Women's Cultural Group, 2008.

Mazrui, Ali. 'Novelist's Freedom vs Worshipper's Dignity', in M.M. Ahsan and A.R. Kidwai (eds), *Sacrilege Versus Civility*. Leicester: The Islamic Foundation, 1991. http://victorian.fortunecity.com/coldwater/439/rushdie.htm.

Memmi, Albert. *The Colonizer and the Colonized*. Boston: Beacon Press, 1965.

Mills, C. Wright. *The Sociological Imagination*. 1959. http://www.aare.edu.au/92pap/funnr92261.txt.

Muhammad, Bala, A. 'Greetings from Shaikh Ahmad Deedat', *Weekly Trust* 29 March 2002. http://www.gamji.com/article1000/NEWS1263.htm. Accessed on 20 December 2006.

Nasr, Vali. *The Shia Revival. How Conflicts Within Islam will Shape the Future*. London: W.W. Norton, 2006.

Osmani, F. 'Ahmed Deedat', *Islamic World Review* 10. March 1986.

Parekh, Bhikhu. 'The Rushdie Affair and the British Press', in Dan Cohn-Sherbok (ed.), *The Salman Rushdie Controversy in Interreligious Perspective*. Lampeter: Edwin Mullen Press, 1990.

Powell, Avril A. *Muslims and Missionaries in Pre-Mutiny India*. London: Curzon Press, 1993.

Pratt, Derek Alfred. 'The Anglican Church's Mission to the Mission in Cape Town', Master's thesis, Rhodes University, 1998.

Prozesky, Martin. 'The Challenge of Other Religions for Christianity in South Africa', *Journal of Theology for Southern Africa* 74: 36–49, 1991.

Ridgeon, Lloyd V. *Islamic Interpretations of Christianity*. London: Palgrave, 2001.

Roseveare, Rev. 'Cape Town: Christian or Moslem'. A sermon preached at the quarterly service of the Diocesan Mission to the Muslims, Cape Town, 1946.

Ruthven, M. *Fundamentalism: The Search for Meaning*. Cape Town: Oxford University Press, 2004.

Ruthven, M. 'Introduction', in Lloyd V. Ridgeon (ed.), *Islamic Interpretations of Christianity*. London: Palgrave, 2001.

Saïd, Edward. *Culture and Imperialism*. New York: Vintage, 1994.

Saïd, Edward. *Orientalism*. London: Longman, 1978.

Said, Mohamed. 'Muslim Bible Scholars of Tanzania: The Legacy of Sheikh Ahmed Deedat, 1918–2006'. Paper presented at the International Symposium on Islamic Civilisation, Research Centre for Islamic History, Art and Culture, University of Johannesburg, 1–3 September 2006.

Salvatore, Armando. 'Staging Virtue: The Disembodiment of Self-Correctness and the Making of Islam as Public Norm', In *Yearbook of the Sociology of Islam, Bielefeld*. New Brunswick, NJ: Transaction, 2006.

Sardar, Ziauddin and Merryl Wyn Davies. *Distorted Imagination: Lessons from the Rushdie Affair*. London: Grey Seal, 1999.

Schultze, Quentin. *Televangelism and American Culture*. Grand Rapids, MI: Baker, 1989.

Sen, Amartya. *The Argumentative Indian: Writings on Indian History, Culture and Identity*. London: Allen Lane, 2005.

Sharlet, Jeff. 'Jesus killed Mohammed: The Crusade for a Christian Military', *Harper's Magazine*, May 2009. http://www.harpers.org/archive/2009/05/0082488.

Shell, Robert C.H. 'Between Christ and Mohammed: Conversion, Slavery, and Gender in the Urban Western Cape', In R Elphick and T.R.H. Davenport (eds), *Christianity in South Africa: A Political, Social & Cultural History*. Cape Town: David Philip, 1997.

Siddiqui, Ataullah. *Christian–Muslim Dialogue in the Twentieth Century*. London: Macmillan, 2000.

Singh, C. Adams College: The Rise and fall of a Great Institution. Honours thesis, University of Durban-Westville, South Africa, 1987.

Smith, Christian. *American Evangelicalism: Embattled and Thriving*. Chicago: University of Chicago Press, 1998.

Szulc, Ted. *Pope John Paul II. The Biography*. London: Scribner, 1995.

Tayob, Abdulkader. *Islamic Resurgence in South Africa*. Cape Town: University of Cape Town Press, 1998.

Thomas, David. 'The Past and the Future in Christian–Muslim Relations', *Islam and Christian–Muslim Relations* 18 (1): 33–42, 2007.

Trad, Keysar. 'An Interview With Sheikh Ahmed Deedat', *Nida'ul Islam* 13, May–June 1996. http://groups.yahoo.com/group/islamic_ways/message/6186.

Vahed, Goolam and Thembisa Waetjen. *Gender, Modernity and Indian Delights: The Women's Cultural Group of Durban, 1954–2010*. Cape Town: HSRC Press, 2010.

Walshe, Peter. 'Christianity and the Anti-apartheid Struggle: The Prophetic Voice within Divided Churches', In R Elphick and T.R.H. Davenport (eds), *Christianity in South Africa: A Political, Social & Cultural History*. Cape Town: David Philip, 1997.

Waterson, Roxana. *Southeast Asian Lives: Personal Narratives and Historical Experience*. Athens, OH: Ohio University Press, 2007.

Weber, M. *The Theory of Social and Economic Organisation*. New York: Oxford University Press, 1947.

Webster, R. *A Brief History of Blasphemy: Liberalism, Censorship and 'The Satanic Verses'*. Southwold: Orweld Press, 1990.

Westerlund, David. 'Ahmed Deedat's Theology of Religion: Apologetics through Polemics', *Journal of Religion in Africa* 33 (3): 263–278, 2003.

Zaman, Muhammad Qasim. *The Ulama in Contemporary Islam*. Princeton: Princeton University Press, 2007.

Zebiri, Kate. 'Muslim Perceptions of Christianity and the West', in Lloyd V. Ridgeon (ed.), *Islamic Interpretations of Christianity*. London: Palgrave, 2001.

Žižek, Slavok. 'Berlusconi in Tehran', *London Review of Books*, 16 July 2009. http://versouk.wordpress.com/2009/07/16/slavoj-zizek-on-badiou-and-berlusconi-in-tehran-in-lrb/.

## ABOUT THE AUTHOR

Goolam Vahed is associate professor in the Department of Historical Studies at the University of KwaZulu-Natal. He has co-authored and co-edited several books on the history of Islam, Indians, and sport in South Africa, including *Blacks in Whites: A Century of Sporting Struggles in KwaZulu-Natal*; *The Making of a Social Reformer: Mahatma Gandhi in South Africa, 1893–1914*; *Inside Indian Indenture: A South African Story, 1860–1914*; and *Gender Modernity and Indian Delights: The Women's Cultural Group of Durban*.